MW01487982

All Scripture quotations are taken from the Holy Bible, King James Version.

Library of Congress Cataloging-in-Publication Data is available upon request.

ISBN: 978-1-4276-4846-4

Design and printing: Cenveo-Trafton, Amarillo, TX

Printed in the United States of America

Some names have been revised or changed for the purpose of protection of the private life of the person.

ACKNOWLEDGEMENTS

DIAN WHISENAND----------- *EDITING*
GERALD GRAY----------------- *EDITING*
JACKIE BOLDEN -------------- *EDITING*
SHARON ALEXANDER ------ *EDITING*

Thank you Dian, Gerald, Jackie and Sharon for all the hours you spent in helping to accomplish the completion of this manuscript.

CONTENTS

F_{much}ORGIVEN
L_{much}OVES

INTRODUCTION

In writing the events of my life, I have tried to capture how unspoken love, without embracing, without words of love, or the touch of love shown by parents and siblings, can create and develop many wrongs and misunderstandings as a child becomes an adult. I lived feeling alone and rejected. At the young age of thirteen, I became the whore in our family.

I married for the first time at the age of seventeen to a young man in our little town of Ralls, Texas. I married to get away from my family and out of our town. I wanted to run from all the rejection. I had no idea what love was.

After marriage, Kitti and her first husband became my friends. To this day, Kitti is still my best friend and now I have two best friends (lifetime friends) the other being Linda Curbo. Both of these women never forsook me, never judged me, nor did they ever turn their hearts from me. Much credit is given to these two women who in the hand of God carried me through many of life's storms.

The ending of my story is giving all glory to our Savior, Jesus Christ for bringing to pass His promises to me early during my growth of faith, never ceasing throughout my life to work His calling on my life. I did it His way, making many mistakes during the journey.

The material blessings are many. Yet the greatest joy of my life is to accomplish the destiny God had written in His BOOK OF LIFE long before I was born.

I have seen the dark side of the street life and lived a lot of it. I have seen failure as a mother. I have seen adultery as a wife. I have been in the company of people who destroy others.

I have experienced life as taught by Jesus Christ. Larry, my husband of ten years and I are walking in our destiny. We are Certified Volunteer Chaplain's Assistants at the Clements Unit in Amarillo, Texas. Up to three thousand seven hundred men are housed in this high security prison.

I have relived much pain in writing my story. My husband has shared many tears with me as he read every chapter. It is our prayer to help even one person dying in the mire of sin to willingly accept Jesus Christ into their life. (20 But the wicked are like the troubled sea, when it cannot rest, whose waters cast up mire and dirt. 21 There is no peace, saith my God, to the wicked. Isaiah 57:20,21) Larry has never thrown my past up to me, nor has he, even once turned his back on me. This story is dedicated to Kitti Lambert, Linda Curbo and Larry Martin, these three people who have loved me through it all.

A special dedication, love and thanks to Dwayne, B.J., Stoney and Timmi Elizabeth who loved me beyond all they suffered because of my decisions and actions.

Revelation 12:11

And they overcame him by the blood of the Lamb, and by the word of their testimony; and they loved not their lives unto the death.

This scripture is the foundation for the title of this AUTOBIOGRAHPY

Luke 7:

41 **There was a certain creditor which had two debtors: the one owed five hundred pence, and the other fifty.**

42 **And when they had nothing to pay, he frankly forgave them both. Tell me therefore, which of them will love him most?**

43 Simon answered and said, I suppose that *he,* to whom he forgave most. And he said unto him,**Thou hast rightly judged.**

44 And he turned to the woman, and said unto Simon, **Seest thou this woman? I entered into thine house, thou gavest me no water for my feet: but she hath washed my feet with tears, and wiped *them* with the hairs of her head.**

45 **Thou gavest me no kiss: but this woman since the time I came in hath not ceased to kiss my feet.**

46 **My head with oil thou didst not anoint: but this woman hath anointed my feet with ointment.**

47 ***Wherefore I say unto thee, Her sins, which are many, are forgiven; for she loved much:*** but to whom little is forgiven, the same loveth little.

48 And he said unto her, **Thy sins are forgiven.**

49 And they that sat at meat with him began to say within themselves, Who is this that forgiveth sins also?

50 And he said to the woman, **Thy faith hath saved thee; go in peace.**

A TRUE STORY ABOUT A LITTLE GIRL NAMED
MARY ANN MOSES

BORN AND RAISED IN
RALLS, TEXAS: CROSBY COUNTY

Chapter 1:
NEVER SAY NO

∿

I dressed early. Today is the day I've chosen to take my own life. It's December of 1978 and Christmas is just a few days away. I walked into each room, recognizing the things on the walls and on the beds of our children. Howard's two oldest sons and my youngest daughter lived with us. Howard, the man I was living with, was a truck driver. He was gone on a run to Oklahoma. His sons were with their mother and my daughter was staying with her grandmother. I was alone. I felt no fear. Looking at the things on the walls, the furniture, and the house in general, I saw nothing I wanted. Nothing was of any value to me. Going to the closet, I pulled out a bag that contained a half-pound of marijuana laced with angel dust (PCP; a hallucinogen generic drug). I went out to my car, turning for a few moments to look at the house. I never wanted to have to go into that house again. I got into my car and rolled a joint. I inhaled three or four puffs, turned on the ignition and slowly drove away.

I had been planning this day for some time. We lived in a rented farm house just outside of Lubbock, Texas. Loop 289 wrapped around the city. I had spent many hours, on a daily basis, driving around the loop. I would smoke a joint, (without PCP) and get into my car and drive the full circle around the city trying to decide which overpass I would drive off of. Suicide was my constant meditation. This day was not the first time I had tried to kill myself. This would be my third attempt.

During my marriage to my fourth husband, Kevin, I had attempted suicide on two separate occasions. My first attempt was after I realized that he was an alcoholic. I was extremely naive I didn't know people couldn't always stop drinking just because they wanted to. When my husband drank, he would get violent. The fear I would experience during his rages and the physical abuse I suffered were taking their toll on me. I was so depressed that the only out I thought I had to obtain peace was through death. The more I thought about the everlasting bliss of sleep, the thought of death became more and more inviting. Kevin and I, at the time, had no children between us, but I had three children from two previous marriages. My oldest two children were brother and sister. I had given custody of them to their father when we divorced. Along with his mother and stepfather, he was raising our two children. I had custody of my third son. He was living with me, but was visiting with his dad at the time of my suicide attempt.

The nightlife of clubs, alcohol, drugs and sex, along with theft and every other sin, with the exception of murder, was just about all I knew. Prostitution had also become a way of survival. After divorcing my first husband, while in my twenties, two nightclub owners were paying for my sexual services. One paid my rent the other paid me cash. I learned to drink, even though I didn't like the taste of alcohol. The results of alcohol put me into an existence of feeling no pain, no heartache. In the clubs I learned about pills that would put me to sleep or keep me up. Drinking, drugs and pills had become a way of life for me. I drank when we went out dancing or visited friends, but this was usually the extent of my drinking. I preferred marijuana and pills.

Kevin drank all the time and was violent. Our friends often had to keep him from hurting me when he was drunk. But there were also times when they closed their eyes to what they knew, was happening. I had a lot of hair pulled out of my head on many occasions. I never seemed to know what Kevin was mad about, but he always directed his anger at me. As time passed, the violence grew. I became desperate.

One night after he had passed out and I knew from his breathing he was in a drunken stupor, I slipped out of bed and went to the garage. I picked up a garden hose, and a towel, I quietly raised the garage door and tossed the items outside within easy reach. I then backed my car, a Chevy Super Sport, navy blue and gold, outside the garage and closed the garage door.

It was dark on our street, since there were no streetlights that came on after dark. I was alone. I put the hose into the tail pipe and stuffed a rag around it. Then I put the other end of the hose into a small window on the passenger side of the car and stuffed another rag from the trunk around it, forcing all fumes into the car. I lay down in the front seat and began inhaling the fumes with deep breaths. The only sound coming from the night was the almost silent hum of the car engine.

My thoughts, as I lay motionless, were of the many years of inner hidden pain I had experienced. I forced myself to remember my childhood, and the years of loneliness and rejection suppressed within me. The bitter hate that I had hidden for a very long time was quenched in the closed area of my heart. Remembering gave me even more of a reason to stop living. I simply wanted to go to sleep and not wake up.

Eternity passed as I continued to inhale the deadly fumes. But they were not having an effect on me. At one point, I had to go to the bathroom. I went to the back of the house and took care of the problem. I then quickly returned to my car, trying not to breathe the fresh air as I was having a problem going to sleep. Getting back into my car, I lay back down and again began to breathe the fumes. Why couldn't I go to sleep? How long did it take to kill myself? What was I doing wrong? I had thought it might take thirty minutes to an hour, but I had been in my car a very long time.

In fact, daylight was beginning to start a new day. I could see faint outlines of trees through the car window. I thought that living another day was not going to happen for me. I continued to lie still. Just as I seemed to drift off, I heard a car door slam. Startled, I sat up and saw lights on in the houses on both sides of the street. A man who lived several houses down was getting into his pickup. I panicked. What if he saw the hose in my tailpipe and window?

I quickly jumped out of the car, jerked the hose out of the tail pipe and window and drove back into the garage. I turned the ignition off and sat there in bewilderment. Tears of failure slowly fell from my eyes. I wanted to scream. I wanted to cry out, releasing all the pain, yet only a few drops of tears expressed the pent-up emotions I could not seem to release. I sat motionless, trying to get up the nerve to get out of the car and go into the house.

There was no other choice, I didn't have any money and there was no place for me to run to. Although some people knew of the abuse by seeing it, I had not confided in anyone. There was no option. I had to go back into the house. Once inside, I looked at the clock. It was 7 am. I couldn't believe I had spent somewhere around seven hours trying to kill myself. However ridiculous they were, my first thoughts were Chevrolet's didn't work! I would have to borrow a Ford to get the job done the next time.

Time passed and my marriage grew more and more painful and abusive. I began to think about adultery. Getting a man's attention was my fix. Therefore I reverted to my former lifestyle. I lay in the arms of one of Kevin's long term friends. I'd show him, all the pain he caused me I returned to him, even though he never knew it. I also had an affair with a man that lasted well over a year. The man gave me what I needed most, he was kind to me and he made me feel secure. My lover was also married, he needed sex, and I needed what I thought was love.

Kevin carried a 44 Magnum gun in the back of his Levis all the time. Once when we were in a car with three other people he pulled his gun from his jeans and shot a hole in the roof of the car. To protect me, the man sitting beside me grabbed me and pulled me into his arms. He was a large Spanish man and had known Kevin all his life. My husband was drunk and he dared anyone to take his gun as he pointing it in the direction of each man. When he pointed it in the direction of me and the man holding me, I felt the grip of the man's arm as he gently pulled me protecting me with his body. No one tried to take the gun. The owner of the car said nothing, but I could clearly see the side of his face. The anger showed from the tense glare as his eyes squinted and his jaw tightened. He hadn't had the car very long. If he had also had a gun I'm not sure he wouldn't have shot Kevin himself. The tension was high, although everyone had been drinking, no one else was drunk. I had taken a couple of pills that helped me to be in, an out of reality state. Kevin was carefully coaxed to put the gun away and we were driven back to our car. Knowing I must restrain my disgust, I sat quietly as we drove home showing no signs of my true feelings on my face or my actions. Kevin laughed and said the same things over and over all the way back from Aspermont, Texas to Rotan, where we lived. He was driving fast and all over the highway. I didn't care if he wrecked the car and both of us were killed. I saw Kevin through eyes of nothing but disgust and hate.

Several months later Kevin and I drove to Lubbock, Texas. A friend was having a party in his home. It was approximately a two-hour drive from Rotan. When we arrived at the party the alcohol, pot and other drugs flowed. It was late and the party was going to last more than just a night. Kevin pulled the magnum out of his jeans and shot the gun, the bullet going through the wall into another room where I was leaning against the wall, holding myself up from the drugs I had taken. The bullet flew through the wall just missing me only an inch or so. The music was very loud yet the blaring sound of the gun drew everyone's attention. I heard the bullet when it cleared the wall. In my dope consumed mind, I looked at the hole in the wall wondering if Kevin was aiming at me and missed or just too drunk to know I was there. After this, only the thought of death lived within me. Suicide was always in my thoughts. The gun was taken away from him, as he laughed the whole time. Shortly afterward, a friend drove me back to our rented house in Rotan. I can't remember any conversation we may have had. He stopped in front of our house and I got out of the car. I didn't ask him to come in because I wanted to be alone. My mind was made up long before we reached Rotan. I had what I needed to bring my thoughts of suicide into reality.

After watching my friend drive away, I went into the house, directly to the bedroom, and got a bottle of capsules I had hidden in the closet. Just two put a person into slow motion, zombie state. I walked into the kitchen and filled a glass with water. I opened the bottle and poured the capsules into my hand. I had close to eighty capsules. I took the first handful feeling them as the water pushed them down into my stomach. I took the next handful the same way and the next until all capsules were taken. I walked into the living room and wrote a note to my mother-in-law. I gave her the phone number of my third husband, the father of my third child. As with my first attempt of suicide, in my car, my son was visiting his dad. I asked her to call my ex-husband and tell him to come as soon as possible for my son's possessions and to keep him and raise him, I would not interfere. I then picked up a small picture of Kevin, who was still in Lubbock, as far as I knew, and went to our bedroom to lie down. I felt no regret as I longed for death. The pills had already begun to dissolve. Since I had not eaten, it didn't take long for the comfort of drowsiness to begin. A peaceful sleep was near and life for me would be over. I looked at the picture of my husband I was holding in my hand. Why had I picked it up? I felt nothing, but growing hate for him. Falling asleep, my heart was filled with despair.

Barely able to open my eyes, I realized I was being carried over someone's shoulder. My mother-in-law was in town, she with her friends came by our house to visit. I had not bothered to lock the door. They found me asleep. The note I had written was next to me. Sleep came once again, but in my subconscious I heard voices. "Hurry, hurry!" People were rushing, rushing all around me. Once again, I slightly opened my eyes. I was in a wheel chair. Don't wake me, please don't wake me, I thought. Sleep overcame me again. "Swallow, swallow, you're in the hospital, don't be afraid, swallow, swallow." I heard someone saying. Again, sleep came! I was in the blackness of sleep. I longed to stay in the peace of blackness.

Nearly two days went by. It was sometime in the late afternoon of the second day when I awoke. Where am I? How did I get here? Please, please don't let me be alive, I thought. Then realizing I was in a hospital, a flood of depression filled me. I didn't want to be alive. I lay there alone for some time. Tears of unbelief fell from my eyes. I had left the peace of black sleep to return to the pain of life once again. I was extremely weak and very dizzy. Slowly getting out of the bed, shoulders sloped, unable to hold myself up, I walked to the nurse's station. It was almost directly across from the room I was in. Two nurses looked up at me and one came close. "How do you feel, are you going to be okay?" Great sympathy showed in her voice and her eyes. I looked at her intently. No! I was not going to be okay, I'm alive, how in the hell am I alive, I thought. I asked if I could use the phone. I called the man who had driven me home from the party. He told me the party was still going on. My husband was still there, I felt relieved. I didn't tell Boss that I had tried to kill myself. I simply said, "Goodbye." After hanging the phone up, the two nurses said nothing else to me. They were trying to be discreet in looking at me. I felt no shame, only pain and depression that I had not succeeded. Walking down the corridor into the waiting room, which was empty, I sat down. For the first time I realized it was Christmas. A large tree was richly decorated and stood in the center of the room. I sat looking at the lights going on and off. No tears fell. I was very tired. My thoughts returned to the time I had tried to kill myself by breathing fumes from my car. I didn't understand why I couldn't kill myself. How could I be alive after taking so many capsules? It should have taken no more than maybe ten minutes or less to have killed me.

In my mind I tried to understand how I failed again, in dying, in sleeping forever. It had been very late when I arrived back home from the party in Lubbock. Had I left a light on when I laid down after taking the capsules? Had it been someone else who had come into the house? My mother-in-law would not be visiting at this time of the night. Had she come early the next morning? I was sure a man had carried me over his shoulder. I was also sure I had heard my mother-in-law talking. In my slow motion mind there was no reason to me as to why I was not dead.

The nurse came into the waiting room. I had no knowledge of how much time had passed. She helped me walk back to my room. She stood beside me as I fell back into the wonderful black sleep I so longed for.

My relationships with men began when I was just barely thirteen. My two older sisters and I were allowed to go to dances held at the American Legion Hall every Saturday night. A lot of students from our small town, along with students from the surrounding area schools, gathered there. The dances were chaperoned by adults.

My parents were strict in telling us that we could not leave the dance. They would go visit friends while we were at the dance. This particular Saturday night a senior was paying a lot of attention to me and I was extremely flattered. He never asked me to dance, yet he watched me. I had a natural talent for dancing and I knew he was watching me. I loved it.

He came up to me and asked me if I'd like to ride around with him. "Yes!" was my excited reply. My mother's continuous warnings not to leave the dance meant nothing to me at that moment. A senior wanted to be with me, just me! He drove his car to the side of the auditorium and I quickly got into the front seat. We drove away from the lights of town. There were really very few words spoken. He drove slowly down a dark dirt road. He stopped the car and turned out the lights. He turned slightly and asked, "Are you a virgin?" Am I a virgin? What is a virgin? I thought. I didn't have the slightest idea what he was talking about. I simply smiled at him never answering his question. He held me close to him and kissed me. I responded and enjoyed it. I felt special, because I usually was so very lonely. There was no force, no anger, no shoving. I yielded to everything he did. I wanted to please him. "Does it hurt? Does it hurt when I push?" he asked. "Yes, kinda," I replied. "You're a virgin," he said. He quickly pulled away from me. I thought every senior did this and I had done something wrong. Being a virgin was not a good thing. The drive back into town was a lot quicker than when we had left the dance. Getting out of his car, I went back into the dance. If anyone missed me, I didn't detect it.

My parents came to pick my two sisters and me up from the dance. I sat quietly in the back seat as we drove the ten miles to our home. I knew Mother would be furious with me for leaving the dance. I also knew that I had done something you didn't tell your mother. I was very sad because I felt I had failed at whatever a senior wanted. I thought it had something to do with a virgin. I had to find out what a virgin was.

Dressing for school the following Monday morning, I felt different, not really knowing why. Getting off the school bus, I came face to face with a boy in my class. He smiled at me with a look that

I disliked. "Did you have fun Saturday night?" he asked. My mind was racing, how did he know? He wasn't even at the dance. Did he know? Who told him? Why is he asking me like that? The look and the way he asked made me feel dirty. Fear, pure fear, filled my heart. Who else knows? Would my parents find out?

Both the boys and the girls in my school said many ugly things to me that Monday morning. I could easily tell, by the looks and whispers of the girls, that they all knew. I was not popular in school, but my sisters were. My sisters were accepted and had lots of friends. I didn't understand why I didn't have friends. I just didn't. I didn't understand why what I had done was wrong. Why were the boys looking at me differently? Why were they saying things to me that I didn't understand? From that day forward, I was an outcast in my small hometown. I was a shame and disgrace to my parents and sisters. School was a lonely nightmare. Some of my teachers, classmates and even people working in the drug store, cafe and department store, let me know what a disgrace I was. One woman told me that I should leave home because of all the pain I had brought on my parents. I sat looking into her cold, hard, angry face not letting her know that her words broke my heart. I didn't let her see my pain. I held my tears until I was alone. Then I allowed myself to curse her and hate her. Alone, walking back to school I became the little girl that fought back. My strength in hate was much more powerful than the little girl that had learned to control her feelings, letting no one know that I could shut them out, not even hearing them. I had no idea what love was.

I began to see boys, any boy that wanted to be with me. I learned to cover my actions. My mother would lean over me, her face close to mine and scold me with such anger. It never stopped. My sisters told her everything that was said about me in school. Daily I watched as her face turned to ice when she looked at me. One day when we were about to leave the house to catch the bus, my older sister turned as we were going out the door. "You whore, I hate you. I wish you were dead, you're nothing but a whore," she screamed at me. I didn't know what a whore was, but the yelling at me made me mad enough to attack her. We went through the kitchen and ended up in my parent's bedroom. She was two years older than I, but I was stronger. My mother did nothing to stop us. My sister kept screaming, "Whore, whore, you're a whore!" She stopped trying to hit me when I shoved her against a wall and shoved my fist in her belly. My middle sister was standing in the doorway watching. She looked at me with pure hate. "I hate you, you're a whore," she said. She didn't try to attack me. My oldest sister regained her strength. I said nothing but they both knew if we fought, I would win. They both walked out of the house to catch the school bus. I was so sick and hurt inside that I couldn't go to school. My mother never entered the room while this was happening. She had gone into the living room and sat down. I went into the living room to ask her if I could stay home. Before I could ask her, she said, "They are right to feel the way they do. You have shamed us all," she said. I had long before this day learned to shut out her words. I learned how to look at her and my dad and show no emotions. She once told me that she wouldn't make anyone marry me. I had no idea what she was talking about. Why was she saying this to me? I had no intentions of trying to make anyone marry me. Why would I?

I spent this day at home. It seemed no matter where I went to try and get alone, my mom would show up. She spent the day telling me over and over the same things. By the time my sisters got home from school I was numb with hate. I had accomplished closing my ears and heart to anything and everything. I simply looked into Mom's face and responded with nothing. My sisters didn't say a word to me, they avoided me. I was able to hide away from everyone by staying in the barns until I had to go to bed. My dad said nothing to me. This was the last day I spent at home from school. I never missed school again until at the age of seventeen, I quit school to marry my first husband.

At the age of sixteen I still had no idea where babies came from. I still didn't know what the word virgin meant. I knew a whore was someone everyone hated. I knew sex was wrong, but I didn't know why. I learned to cover my feelings with stubborn, very quiet rebellion. I knew what to do when I was supposed to but no one knew me.

My parents were well respected. My grandfather had purchased land and prospered. My dad was the youngest of seven boys and one girl. I didn't know until many years had passed that he had a drinking problem and committed adultery on his trips out of town. My mother was sixteen and my dad twenty when they married. My oldest sister was born at the end of the first year of their marriage. The following year my middle sister was born and the following year I was born. My dad wanted a boy, as I grew, very early in life I became that boy. I was taught irrigation and it was my responsibility to feed and help tend the animals. To have been raised on a farm you would think I saw animals having sex, but I don't remember it if I did. I would have to hold the animals and watch as my dad cut them or de-wormed them. My sister's sometimes had to help, but not like I did. I never knew why or what dad was doing to the animals. I learned to block out their cries, but I hated having to hurt them.

My first real love was for a goat my dad bought. I spent all the time I could with him. His name was Goatee. He would carry me to the pasture to gather the cows for milking. I never stopped letting him know how much I loved him. I believed he understood what I would say to him. He would answer me with his cry for attention. I would lie beside him and talk to him for hours. I held him around the neck, always letting him know I was there. He was the only friend I had. He would come running to me as soon as I got home from school. During the summer, when I wasn't working, my time was with Goatee. Through him, I learned the feeling of love. Because hail had destroyed our cotton crop, my dad sold everything he could. One day a man came and my dad made me lead Goatee into the trailer. I watched until all the dust was gone from the pickup and trailer as it drove slowly away from our house. I heard the cry of my goat as he cried out to me. I didn't know why the man was taking the only thing I had to love, my friend. I didn't understand that he would never return. The pain was more than I could bear. A strong personality was birthed.

I remember another day a year or so later, when I came home unexpectedly. My dad was killing all the animals he didn't want.

her when I killed her dad. I had no one to take her to, no one to call to come and get her. I probably held the gun to his head about ten to fifteen minutes. It was heavy but I didn't remove it from beside his ear. I simply didn't know what to do with our daughter. It was at this time that I decided to divorce him instead of killing him. It was just a matter of weeks until I filed for a divorce. Elizabeth was staying with me. By now I had a lover, Howard. Divorce was easy.

For the first time in my life I was in love. I had never shed a tear when I separated or divorced from any of my four husbands. I had committed adultery through all of my marriages. I had married three good men that loved me. Only one husband of the four was an alcoholic and abusive.

My need for love was never satisfied. Even with a husband and children I had a void, a hurting inside that never stopped. I didn't understand exactly why at the time but clubs seemed to be the only joy I could find. The attention I received, the games I played to get the man I wanted, something within, a need that drew me. I kept returning to the clubs, the music, the men and the thrills. Howard was the only man during all my life to this point that I gave my heart too.

Today, I was on my way to trying to end my life for the third time. It hadn't taken long for Howard to do to me what he had done to his wife and other women before me. We had been living together for a period of about two years or so. I drove slowly away from our rented country house, just outside of Lubbock, Texas. I had no desire to look back. I had made sure that everything was in order. I had cleaned the house and made the bed before leaving. Even in death I wanted everything in place.

I turned onto the farm-to-market highway. There was no traffic. I drove very slowly. The effects of the pot and PCP put me into the state I needed to kill myself. It didn't take long for me to realize that my hands were not on the steering wheel. I looked down into my lap. My hands were clasped lying gently in my lap. I looked up at the steering wheel. I knew angels were driving my car. I could not see them clearly, but I could see their form. There were two of them. One was on the left side of the steering wheel and the other on the right. They were huge, yet I saw them looking into my eyes. I looked back down at my hands resting comfortably in my lap. I must be on a real high, I thought. I had smoked a joint laced with angel dust. This must be the effect of it.

I then heard a voice. I knew the voice even though I had never heard it before. It was not audible, yet I heard it clearly. *"Mary Ann, it's time. I'm taking you to the top of My mountain in My name's sake. You will teach the word of the Lord, thy God. Be honest,"* God said. I was in a wonderful cloud of peace. I had never felt this kind of love, but somehow I knew what I was feeling was love. It was pure, sweet, gentle, comforting, peaceful and real. I could see the cloud. I could even smell the wonderful aroma of a fresh breeze. I had no fear. I was in total peace. There was no hurting within me. I watched as the cloud gently began to go through my windshield. I watched as it went higher and higher into the heavens. The heavens were a beautiful blue. Just before the cloud became a part of the many beautiful white clouds high in the sky, it turned. Like a person who turns and waves a final goodbye, it turned and dipped just a little. Somehow I saw a smile and I knew it was God.

Tears began streaming down my face. I laid my head back as laughter came rolling out of me. I had never experienced such joy. Within just a moment something totally unexpected happened. I was straight! The pot that I had smoked was drained out of me. It was as if I had never taken any form of drugs. I felt clean. I had never experienced such total peace and joy. I felt like a virgin, way back when I was a little girl and didn't know of the evil in the world, before my youth was destroyed, when I felt safe and loved with my animals. This is how I felt. Clean, my body was clean. I was clean and pure.

Without realizing it, I put my hands back on the steering wheel and was once again driving my car. All thoughts of suicide were gone. I wanted more of God and I wanted to be with Him. I didn't know what to do or where to go. I had never heard of such a thing happening. I was thrilled. God Himself had come to me in the form of a cloud. He called my name and spoke to me. Angels had driven my car. I had no drugs in my system. I must have really been on a high, I thought, "How can this be? Did I really hear God?" Yes, within myself I knew I had.

Right then from this little farm-to-market highway I drove to my parent's house. They still lived in our little hometown of Ralls. I shared my experience with them, but I was greatly disappointed at their response. Leaving their house, pain was once again birthed within me. I drove to my oldest sister's house. She responded much the same as my parents had, when I shared my experience with her. I then went to a friend's apartment. She praised God with me. She knew God. I didn't. She didn't tell me what to do or where to go. She simply thanked God for me. I ended up fasting for three days and nights. If heaven is anything like what I experienced with God, I wanted to go there. Just show me where the ladder is.

It was late on the third day and I hadn't gone back home. I was told that Howard was looking for me everywhere. Finally, I drove back to the house I hoped never to see again. When Howard came in, he listened as I told him all that had happened. He wanted no part of God. He brushed my experience off as if it were nothing. He even got mad at me for having it, as if I caused it to happen. He didn't care to talk about God, but up until now, neither had I.

Somewhere within two weeks after God had spoken to me, I was washing dishes at my kitchen sink. I was extremely depressed. Life was going on as before and I felt empty inside. Looking out of my kitchen window, over the sink, I saw the same kind of big white clouds that I had seen the day God spoke to me. I began to cry silently. Had it really happened? Did God come to me in the form of a cloud? Was any of this possible? I fell to my knees and with my fist I began to pound the floor. "If you're real, if you're really real, come into my life. Help me! God, if you're real, please help me," I cried out. I stayed in a crawl position for a few minutes. I suppose I was waiting for something to happen. It didn't.

When cleaning out a closet, I pulled out a very old Bible. Some preacher had given it to me some years back. I don't think I had ever gotten past the first two pages. I had always been afraid of the Bible. I thought if I dropped it or damaged it in any way, God would be very angry with me. I lay down on the bed and opened the Bible and began to read. Much to my amazement I understood what I was reading. I read every day for hours. I was hungry for the word of God. This Book took me to Him. There was a tremendous pounding in my heart. I realized God was letting me know He was with me. I would search the scriptures as to what to do. It was as though I saw my own sin. For the first time in my life, I saw myself. I loved Howard, the man I was living with, yet God said, "Turn from your wicked ways." This meant no more cop out on drugs, paying for everything instead of stealing, no more lying. I was to love everybody. I hated my family. I hated the whole town I was raised in. I couldn't find anything about myself, or the way I lived, that God approved of.

I had no doubt that God loved me. This love had nothing to do with sex. I also realized that I was chosen, for what I didn't know, but I knew I was a chosen disciple of God! I wasn't anything like the Bible said I was supposed to be. I had to begin somewhere. While seeking Him for answers, He revealed to me what to do. I had to get out of the fornication lifestyle I had become accustomed to.

In my mind it would be impossible to leave the man I loved, even though life was such a living hell. He hurt me with all his actions. I didn't understand why I loved him so much. I just did. I learned to live one day at a time. It was more like one minute at a time. By now I was back to smoking pot with Howard. I didn't try to discuss God with him because it angered him. I was still the person I had been just a short time back, only now I wanted to change. I didn't know how, but I was willing to learn.

Two days before Christmas, Howard was going to make a run into Oklahoma. He would be gone overnight. He kissed me goodbye and walked out of the door. I went to the Justice of the Peace and put him under a peace bond. I went home and couldn't even cry. With help from my kids and a couple of friends, we packed and moved Elizabeth and I into a rented house in about seven hours. My new boss, who owned a used car dealership, let me use one of his cars and I hid mine. He allowed me to go to work late and leave work early. All these arrangements were made to keep me from being found. I didn't want to think of Howard walking into the empty house. I hurt so badly I had no conception of how much he might hurt. He thought he owned me. I smoked pot since I thought I had to have it to exist. God had asked a lot of me and I rebelled because of the hurt. I cried and I begged God to save Howard. Living without the only man I had ever hurt for and loved, seemed impossible.

Peace would come only when I got still and gave all my attention to God. He showed Himself to me daily. I could feel Him within me and I knew I had to have His presence to live. The pain I felt was indescribable. God would give me peace just enough to keep me fighting. I longed for Him. I fought to obtain the joy I had experienced when God had first spoken to me. A little less than two weeks after I moved out, I took the bag of marijuana I had kept. Going into the bathroom, I flushed it down the commode. "I don't need this anymore," I said. "Please, please heal my heart. Kill my love for Howard and take the hurt away," I prayed.

Howard was looking for me everywhere. I fought every minute to cling to God. The pain I felt inside was even pulling my shoulders down. All the shame and hurt I had felt ever since I could remember didn't come close to the pain I was going through now. I felt like I was in a nightmare and I wanted to wake up. One afternoon after getting home from work, I knelt beside my bed. "God are You real? Did You really talk to me? Have you asked too much of me? I hurt for the man I love. I can't help it." I opened my Bible, which was lying on the edge of my bed. With my eyes closed, I put my finger to the top of the page. I slowly began moving it downward. Then I stopped. "God if You are real, if You talked to me, prove it to me," I prayed. "I will never, never, as long as I live ask You to prove Yourself to me again." I then opened my eyes and read, "Then he said, 'The God of our fathers has chosen you that you should know His will see the Just One hear the voice of His mouth. For you will be His witness to all men of what you have seen and heard. And now why are you waiting? Arise and be baptized wash away your sins, calling on the name of the Lord'." (Acts 22:14,15)

My prayer had been answered, "I'll never ask you again, Lord. You have blessed me. You have chosen me. From this day forward, my covenant with You is no matter where You take me, or what task You ask of me, I will.....**NEVER SAY NO.**"

Exodus 13:21
And the LORD went before them by day <u>in a pillar of a cloud</u>, to lead them the way; and by night in a pillar of fire, to give them light; to go by day and night:

Psalm 99:7
He spake unto them in the cloudy pillar: (thunder cloud) they kept his testimonies, and the ordinance that he gave them.

John 10:27
My sheep hear my voice I know them they follow me:

Romans 10:20
But Isaiah is very bold, and saith, I was found of them that <u>sought me not</u>; I was made <u>manifest</u> unto them that asked not after me.

1Corinthians 6:20
For ye are bought with a price: therefore glorify God in your body in your spirit, which are God's.

Mary, second or third grade

Mary, eleven or twelve

Mary, age 16

Jerry was shot soon after
this picture

Mary, age 27, married to Kevin

Age: 13

NEVER SAY NO

My life was total misery, loneliness, heartache and confusion.
I spent my days riding around, a purpose to live, seeking a reason.
There was nothing left for me to do.
All, I had experienced, all, I knew!
There was much torment, drinking, nor drugs could no longer cure.
When I realized around me, a CLOUD had formed.
I heard a voice, I did not hear.
God, had come to me, I felt no fear.
As He spoke and I received His message to me in my mind,
His voice was sweet, gentle and kind.
***"Mary Ann, it is now time, I call you unto Me, to the top
of My mountain shall you climb!"***
As God ascended went back from whence He came.
I was full of joy, laughter as there had never been.
I knew God had come I had been surrounded by Him!
I turned to the Bible and read His word.
And found in amazement, what I read I understood.
I kept His commandments one by one.
And then I gave Him in return,
I gave Him me and all that I had, my all, I did give.
My covenant to Him, to prove my faith love, Him what He asked,
I would be willing and.....**NEVER SAY NO!**

Chapter 2:
NO MORE

My daughter Elizabeth and I were still hiding out, trying to keep Howard from finding us. I had been in and out of jobs now since November, 1978. While Howard and I were living together on the farm, I worked for a retail company. My language was uneducated street talk. My actions were honky tonk, tight wranglers and boots. Howard was a street biker and a truck driver. A new manager was hired for the company, a Christian man. He overheard me call a client a *turd* on the phone and it didn't take him long to get rid of me. I wasn't fired because of poor work performance. I was fired because of the person I was. I then worked about two weeks for an accountant and was fired because I didn't know what I was doing. I had met Frank, a used car dealer who owned the business. Frank hired me to keep books, run errands and other tasks. Howard didn't know that I was looking for work when he was gone on the truck.

For about three months I listened to Frank, a white man in his sixties, talk about his heartaches day in and day out. He would stand at the front door of the small office building and look out the window, most of the day, every day. He would cry real tears and tell me about his relationship with a young woman, who was a prostitute on the other side of town. She would break up with him and he would beg her back into his life. He gave her one of his best cars. She used the things he could give her to keep him attached to her. He drank often and cussed with almost every breath. Jesus' name was always used. He was also unethical with the people who bought his cars.

On the other side of the coin, he was married and went to church, and he and his wife gave tithes there regularly. They lived on the right side of town, in an acceptable home. Some of their friends were pretty well to do, big houses, big cars.

I was a baby Christian at this time and just born again (Jesus answered and said unto him, Verily, verily, I say unto thee, Except a man be born again, he cannot see the kingdom of God. John 3:3). Frank professed to be a Christian. I was confused by Frank's hypocrisy, and I had no idea of where to go from here. I knew very little about the Bible. I thought Jesus had taken the time during His busy days on this earth to write it. Then when He went to heaven, He left it with someone who made copies. The word *scrolls* was not a part of my language. I had no idea what a scroll was.

The King James Version was the only Bible that I would read, because it was the Bible I found in my closet when I first began to read about Jesus. The Bible in the prayer room that I went to was also the King James Version. I didn't trust anything else, by anyone else.

I was faithful in going to church, and I read the Bible daily. Most of the time when being at home, all I did was watch Christian programs on TV and read my Bible. I could understand sentences but the overall understanding, even of a chapter in the Bible, was foreign territory for me. I talked to Jesus in my thoughts, on my knees, in the tub, driving in my car, anywhere and everywhere. The more I learned, the more I felt His Spirit, and it made me hunger for more and more of Jesus Christ.

I had obeyed Jesus and moved out of a shacked-up, drug life style, to follow Him. One day I even shared my testimony with Frank, of how God had come to me in the form of a cloud, and a short time later, Jesus had saved me.

After a while, hearing Frank talk about his heartaches over the divorce of his son and his mistress and his wife and his business and his life as a whole became too much. He wanted to die and at times I wanted to help him achieve his death, but I hadn't been too good at it myself. I kept fighting the total disgust I had for him. I was a Christian and I was supposed to forgive him for things I knew were wrong. I was supposed to love Frank. I was torn between my real feeling for him and the feelings I was supposed to have for him.

Sometimes I wondered if God didn't get sick of hearing all his bull too. Frank had read to me, somewhere in the Bible, that once you were baptized, professed that Jesus died and then was raised from the dead, you were saved no matter what you did from that day forward. His words were, "Once saved, always saved." I was having a real problem with this. I didn't understand how a man could be saved and live as he was living.

In an illegal money-making scheme, Frank was involved with truck drivers who stole the cargo and sold it to him. He in turn would resell it for a nice profit. He also had three women who would steal name brand clothing from department stores. They had learned how to detach the security sensor disk attached to the clothing. As with the truck cargo, they would bring the stolen clothing to Frank, and he would sell it.

I had never seen such beautiful clothing. I thought only the rich wore these things. I had not yet learned how to overcome temptations, and so I got caught up in the lure of the finery. I asked for, and got a black leather suit, which was part of the stolen property. I tried it on, took it off and took it home. My conscience got the best of me. The garment hung in my closet a few weeks and then I threw it away.

I think Frank had used buying it for me from one of the women to entice me into the thrill of fast money. He said I could have half the money of whatever I sold. I knew a lot of club owners. I took the merchandise to a few clubs. Then I took them back to Frank. I couldn't do it. I was totally broke, but I didn't have peace, I could not sell the stuff, I didn't even try.

At this point I was really beginning to question just what a Christian was! Frank would cry all week wondering why God was so cruel to him.

One day when I went to work, I had had enough. When he began his usual complaining, which was as soon as I got there, I picked up my purse and calculator and walked out of the little building. I didn't say a word to Frank. I put his keys back into his car and went to the back of the building where my car was hidden and got into it and drove off the lot. I had no money, and I sure knew how it felt to be jobless. Yet, there was an overwhelming feeling of release and an abundance of peace as I drove away from Frank and all the *stuff*.

It was now the end of the third month since I had moved from the farm. Howard had convinced a mutual friend, Kitti, to come to me and talk me into seeing him. My insides lit up knowing he was waiting for me. I followed Kitti back to her apartment and flew into the arms of Howard. It was shortly afterward, that I let Howard move back in with me. He was living with me again for less than two weeks, when he went back to being himself. It didn't take long for him to begin leaving early in the morning and coming in late at night, if he came in at all.

I had gotten to the point where I didn't care if he was there or not. I didn't care if he never came back. The hurt of loving him was turning into pure disgust. I didn't even like him, yet I didn't understand the hold he had on me. I knew my being with Howard wasn't of God. I was having one heck of a time trying to walk out again. I didn't want to have sex with him, yet I did.

Finally one day I packed Howard's things and had them in the living room next to the door when he came in. "You have to leave, I will not go through this with you anymore." I was calm, but very determined. He again convinced me of his love for me. He stopped staying out all night for another short period of time.

There was another problem that had begun to worry me. I was discovering that I had personality issues that I didn't understand, yet I felt like something was wrong.

I knew from my childhood that when the pain was more than I could bear, somehow I learned to turn *me* off. I had no idea at the time what it was called or that such a thing could happen, but I would go from one personality into another. I was torn between a past of hidden, embedded hate and problems to now being a Christian that had to change into yet another person. My understanding was that I had to stop sinning and change my way of dressing, talking and my actions, and of course, I couldn't have sex and I couldn't steal. I didn't want to do these things anymore, but I didn't know a lot of anything else.

My friend, Kitti, was the first to bring this problem to my attention. She told me one day, "I hate it when you turn into little Miss Aster!" I felt shocked. This was really the first time I realized that someone else saw my problem. I was split, three people in one body. I watched people and learned how to be what I needed to be to have what I needed or wanted to have. I learned to dress professionally when looking for a job. I learned to watch the way I spoke and leave out all the street talk. Then I learned a little about self control. I could be my old self, but only in the places that accepted the old me. In church I had to be the new me.

During the time Howard and I, with his two sons and my youngest daughter, were living together on the farm one of his sons got into trouble and we had to go to the police department. Howard's son took a psychological test requested by the officer. After talking to Howard and me, the officer asked if I would take the same test. I agreed and answered the questions. We then left.

About a week later, I called the officer and when I asked him the results of the test. He became quiet. "Something is wrong, isn't it?" I asked. He replied, "I'm not allowed to discuss it with you, but if you can go to someone else, you might want to." I hung the phone up and never shared this conversation with anyone.

These personalities or unhealthy predominate person I seemed to turn into when needing to escape began during my childhood. They grew as I grew. It had nothing, I thought at the time, to do with Howard. But I felt that they were separating me from Jesus. I wanted Him back. I started praying, asking God to heal me and to make me one person, the person He wanted me to be. I prayed He would destroy the other personalities, the old me and heal me. Here I was living daily in sin, when Christ had told me not to, yet asking Jesus to help me to become a whole, healed person!

I got a job working for a company that assembled metal buildings. Howard, Elizabeth and I moved from the house we were living in into a little house. Howard's two sons didn't move back in with us from the farm house we had lived in together. They were with us at times, but didn't live with us.

Within days of my first day at working for the company, I was asked to lie. Some of the employees, the boss men were making money on the side, on company time, vehicles and materials. I would have to pull invoices which would reveal their theft. They would pay for materials quietly, having benefited from the company discounts, and clearing a nice profit.

The men I worked for were in a class with whom I had never associated with in public. I had been among them at times, at parties, clubs and sometimes in a motel room or back seat of a car. We never knew one another's names. I was the type of woman, or so they thought, they wanted when they weren't with their families or in church. These activities had taken place before I met Howard. I had not been to bed with another man from the first night Howard became a part of my life.

I had made two of the worst mistakes I could have made, under the influence of drugs. I wish I could blame my actions on the drugs, but it was not the drugs that convinced me to do it. Drugs only covered any conscience I may have had. It is so easy to be in bondage to sin, when it is a daily way of living. Because of the hurt, and shame it would bring to others to reveal these two ugly acts, I choose to simply say, when you have no morals, and no ethics, it takes more and more sin to fulfill the need for self satisfaction and gratification. To this day, I am still confronted with the aftermath of one of these sins. I know I have been forgiven by Christ. Yet for some sins, self-forgiveness hasn't yet taken place. The memory lingers on. I relive the shame as the years pass on. Howard knew nothing about one of these sins, but the other one, he was a part of. Unless Howard has shared with someone else, this sin is only known on this earth by him and me.

I had not, until working at the metal building business, had the displeasure of working with men whose finances put them in with the in-crowd, the acceptable, because of money and material things, not because of good integrity. Let me tell you it was *hell*! I was way out of my class. I liked the farmer, who had little, the rancher, who worked hard, the Mr. Fix It person, the low life, as they were called. Any person who had little money was considered low life.

One day in particular, a very nice man and his wife came into the office to do business, and while there, they were given the red carpet treatment. When they were gone, it was the opposite. People in the office called them dumb, country, really down grade hicks.

The mockery made of them was sickening to me. People made ugly jokes about them throughout the day.

Despite my fear at having to learn yet another business, I started out doing very well in the job. I understood the books and was very good at inventory. I knew how to dress and I knew how to talk. I had gotten the job under the secret title of "Little Miss Aster." The men joked and laughed with me, even flirting at times. I wasn't married and they didn't know about Howard. It seemed as if God gave me wisdom and the ability to get the job but once I had the job, my mind became full of turmoil. I kept making mistakes, getting worse instead of better. I could figure out a mistake or problem and get it fixed but my mind was not thinking properly. It took unnecessary hours to redo and correct mistakes.

At the same time, Howard was digging deeper and deeper into drugs, and I wasn't. We still lived together and God was letting me know that He didn't approve. I thought getting him out of my life again was impossible. Even with all the sickening days and nights I had been through, I still loved him. I had worked for this metal building company a little over a month. Howard had shown up at my job several times but waited for me outside the building. He looked like he always did when he was on his motorcycle, drugged up. I was told, without any hesitation what everyone at work thought of him. I would never talk against Howard, nor did I try to explain him to anyone. He didn't come into the building, but I knew I wouldn't have gotten the job if they had seen Howard before they hired me.

One day Howard decided to check things out. He pulled up in front of the building in an eighteen wheeler. He crawled out of the cab and came in to meet my boss. I would have loved to have seen the look on my boss's face when he saw Howard get out of that truck. Howard wasn't the kind of person my boss associated with, and he hadn't seen it in me, until now.

My personal problems were also weighing me down. The different predominate personalities, particularly my very strong personality, were at their worst, greater than all the pain caused by Howard. I was becoming a walking ball of hate. People could see it in my face, my actions and my attitude. I was in and out of love with Howard. Yet, I was never really out. I prayed countless hours for God to heal me. I thought the more I was able to conquer sin, the stronger I would become to be able to be one person, killing the personality I rejected. Jesus Christ was my only hope. I believed He could heal me.

One day, a week or so later, while being at work when everyone besides me was out to lunch, I went into the kitchen for a cup of coffee. I started back down the hallway toward my desk. I prayed with all that was within me. "God, please heal me, take this hate from me, make me whole and complete in You, make me one person, cleanse me," I prayed.

In my next step, and through this one prayer, I walked out of something I don't really know how to describe. I could see black smoke come off of me or out of my body. I didn't know which, but the black smoke was real and it left me. Peace, wonderful peace consumed me. I clearly watched the black smoke go through the ceiling, much like something burning in a barrel, with the black smoke rolling out. I knew it was not a vision. I could have touched it if I had wanted to. In an instant I felt free, whole and complete. I had walked out of the other personalities. I knew it was over. Whatever it was, it was gone! I knew God had heard my cry and had made me whole. Something else happened. I knew I was going to leave Howard.

Once again my strongest desires were to please God. I knew I had a long way to go. I didn't realize it until now, but somehow Howard had once again become the lord of me and my life. I had gone back to only living for him, and he was destroying me. I put my mind into action and started seeking God for help as how to leave Howard again! Leaving him was not going to be easy. I knew he wouldn't just let go of me and move out. This would be the second time that I would have to put a peace bond on him. This time I was not moving out, but he was. The peace I felt gave me the strength to do what I knew I had to do.

Shortly after my inner healing, I was called into my boss's office. I didn't have to wait until I got off work to file a restraining order against Howard. My boss paid me and immediately fired me.

Relieved in a sense, I left my job and went directly downtown and filed a peace bond on Howard. At that moment, I felt torment leave me and peace take its place. I had very little money, my rent was coming up and all the bills were due.

With the exception of Jesus Christ, Howard had consumed my thoughts. Praying as I drove home, after putting a peace bond on Howard, I felt dead inside. No tears fell, but instead a gnawing worry took the place of the peace I had experienced only a short time earlier.

Howard drove into the driveway right behind me. I was somewhat amazed at the timing. I should have still been at work. I told him I had just been fired. He asked me to go with him on his vacation. He was going to Wichita Falls, his old stomping grounds. We had partied there ourselves many times. He told me he was leaving right then. It struck my mind that had I not been fired, he would have gone without saying a word to me. He had all he needed ready to go. His motorcycle, which I had paid for, was on a trailer. He had his clothes, his drugs and his check. He had long ago quit paying the bills. They were left up to me to pay. He offered me no money, and I didn't ask him for any. He began to beg me to go with him. I think he really wanted me with him simply because he really begged me. I refused, using the stress of just being fired. I watched him go out the back door. I sat down in the living room. I listened as I heard his vehicle start, looking out the window I watched until he was out of sight. For an instant I wanted to run after him and go with him, but I refused myself, and my need for him.

I got into my car, a very old, torn up vehicle and drove to a church. My previous husband, Kevin had given me a good car that had been repossessed. He bought it at a good price. It was in very good condition when he brought it home to me.

Howard had an old van but he liked driving my car for his own ego. I let him take it any time he wanted. At times I drove his druggie-looking van so he could use my car. I didn't know he wouldn't take care of my car. But I found this out when it caught on fire while I was driving it. He had either put just enough oil in it to keep the red light from coming on, or he had disconnected the wire. He bought me an old clunker with my rent money, cash that he had stolen from me. It was not long after I had the old clunker that I got in it to go to work early one morning. It was raining, not too much at first. I was on 50th Street in Lubbock, Texas, going east, on a major street. The traffic was heavy. The rain picked up and was turning into a flash flood. I turned on the windshield wipers, but they didn't work. I was terrified. I was in the middle lane with fast-moving traffic all around, all of us trying to get to our jobs.

The windshield wipers still didn't move as I frantically pulled and pushed on the knob. The rain was falling so swiftly that it was impossible to see even the cars passing on both sides of me. I had no idea how close I was to the light. I knew cars were in front and in back of me. Fear, real fear, panic took over. I cried out, "Help me Jesus. Help me. I'm going to have a wreck!" In that one plea, Jesus Christ cleared my windshield. There was not a drop of rain on it. It was still raining fiercely, but no water touched my windshield. I drove to work in amazement. I didn't know Jesus Christ was so close. I thought He was in heaven, a very long way off. I had never heard of such a thing, but of course until now, I had not spent a lot of time hearing about Jesus Christ.

Another miracle had taken place on an extremely hot summer day, Howard and I were together in this car. Howard was complaining about the intense heat, which was making it a miserable day. We had both our windows rolled down. I reached up and for the first time since I had the car, I decided to turn the air conditioner on. Delicious cold air flowed from the vents. It was wonderful. I began to roll up my window. Howard rolled up his window also. He kept looking at me with this strange look of disbelief. I had no idea what was wrong with him. We reached our destination, and Howard parked the car and just looked at me. He had not spoken a word since turning on the air conditioner. Neither had I. "This car doesn't have an air conditioner. It was taken out before I bought the car," he said. I looked at him and replied, "Jesus can do anything."

We got out of the car and he opened the hood and showed me that there was no air conditioner. This was another miracle I didn't know Jesus did, but I had no doubt that He either blew cold air into the car or He somehow made the car blow cold air from somewhere. It was amazement, to the both of us. For this day only, we drove in the comfort of an air conditioned very old and beat up car.

In this same car where Jesus had shown me two miracles, I drove to the church and went into the prayer room I had used so many, many times in secret. Jesus Christ had made use of the car to show me His love and His power. I didn't know much about the Bible. I didn't know where to go for what I needed. Once again I was looking for Jesus Christ, but a blessing was waiting for me. The Bible was already opened to the book of Psalms. As I read, I was amazed to find I was reading about myself. To me it was a miracle that someone had written all the things that I felt. My crying out to God, my needs, hurts, strengths, everything was written down for me to read. God knew I was coming, so He turned to those pages so He could talk to me through His word. I cried in that little prayer room for hours. Then I would read a while, I would pray a while and finally would just sit silently for a while. I stayed in that little room the rest of the day, past evening. It was after dark when I left.

Elizabeth was visiting with her grandmother. I had not had to worry about her for a few days, but I was going home to an empty house. I was glad Howard was gone on his week's vacation. At least I could rest.

By the time I got home I realized something marvelous had happened to me. I wasn't worried, I wasn't hurting. I had no money for rent, I hadn't been paid a full check, I had paid the court for the peace bond, I had no job to go to in the morning, but I was swimming in peace. I did not have a care in the world. God had lifted the yoke off of me and I once again had hope. (Take my yoke upon you, and learn of me; for I am meek and lowly in heart: and ye shall find rest unto your souls. Matthew 11:29). I did have a little gas money, a few groceries and a lot of peace. I was at ease and I felt rich, very rich. That evening, I watched television. Then I did my usual things of cleaning house and going to my room and spending more time with God, on my knees. Then I climbed into bed and fell into a wonderful restful sleep.

I woke up feeling the same way and the restful peace lasted all week. Not once did Howard call and not once did I care. I knew he was coming back, but I didn't want him to. I had called the police to let them know he would be out of town for a week. The restraining order on him was to be served by the police as soon as he got back into town. God had taken the hurt and love for Howard from me, for a season (a short period of time).

When I drove home from church, a week later, there Howard was, standing outside. He looked worse than I had ever seen him. I didn't know where he had spent his time or the people he had been with, but from his looks, it was right in the middle of hell. I drove right on by. He didn't see me.

I called the police to let them know that Howard was back in town. I had moved some of my things into Kitti's apartment while waiting for Howard to be served with the peace bond papers. I was parking my car in another area of her apartment building parking area. I had been staying with Kitti a couple of days.

On the third day after his return to Lubbock, Howard had parked his motorcycle close to Kitti's apartment, waiting for us. He knew I was staying with Kitti, probably through her children. When we saw him, we drove on by. He saw us and tried to follow us on his motorcycle. We drove, breaking the speed limit, about two blocks and turned zigzagging through the blocks until we knew we had lost him. We then drove to a pay phone and I called the police. I even, in compassion, told them how Howard couldn't stand to be in small closed places.

After waiting for a short period of time, Kitti and I drove back to her apartment. I wanted to try and get my car. When we parked her car, we saw Howard standing by his motorcycle. At the same time a police car drove up and then another. The two officers got out of their cars and approached Howard. From the first call to the police after seeing Howard in front of the house it had taken three days for the police to catch up with him. They told him he was under arrest. He turned and looked at me in total disbelief. Then it happened. When our eyes made contact, all the love I had for Howard flooded back. My insides cried out and my heart broke into ten million pieces. God then spoke to me, *"Let him go."* I obeyed. I could have stopped his arrest. I could have followed and gotten him out of jail. Instead I went back home and cried and prayed for him during the night.

At times I felt as though I knew some of Howard's thoughts. I felt his pain. I also felt his hate. I started to get out of the bed, dress and drive to the jail, just to be close to him. When I was almost sitting up in my bed, ready to get up, again I heard the voice of God, *"Let him go."* I lay back down. Any fairytale thoughts I may have had about a wonderful, Christian man in my life left me.

I didn't want anyone but Howard and God had said *"No."* The pain I felt inside was extremely real. God hadn't healed me of my love for Howard. He had only released the pain for a season. I was able to obey Him because of His peace. I could not have put Howard in jail loving him and hurting for him without the peace of God. The three days I had waited for Howard to be served the peace bond had been days of inner peace. I even thought that God had healed me of my love for Howard.

But God had not snapped His fingers and miraculously healed me. He simply rebuked Satan on my behalf for a short time. The pain lay quiet for a few short days. Then the pain returned, after I had obeyed God. I now had a relationship, a personal relationship with Christ. I had a made up mind that I would not live in fear, sin, and pain.....**NO MORE**.

John 5:14
Afterward Jesus findeth him in the temple and said unto him, *Behold, thou art made whole: sin no more, lest a worse thing come unto thee.*

John 15:4
Abide in me and I in you. As the branch cannot bear fruit of itself, except it abide in the vine; no more can ye, except ye abide in me.

Mary, age 34
Howard & I had been living together three or four months.

NO MORE

For you, no more tears will I cry.
I no longer want to be the woman by your side.
God has blessed me, and healed me within.
He has lifted me up, and away from you and your sin.
I no longer dream of the things that could have been.
I no longer hurt, I no longer care, I no longer love you first
of all men!
The weight is gone, the burden, the sleepless nights,
The crushing pain felt inside.
Leave me, leave me, leave me this day.
And to another in time I will say,
I once knew a man, he taught me life,
He taught me love, he taught me joy, he taught me to laugh.
Don't be like him, don't love me this way.
Don't love me, then so easily throw me away.
Love me with a pure love that is true.
Let me know, I'm not a fool.
Love me, love, my darling as I love you.
Tell me, persuade me that you'll make me cry.....**NO MORE!**

Hebrews 10:17
And their sins and iniquities will I remember **<u>no more</u>**.

Chapter 3:
THE BATTLE IS WON

~

I lay in bed for hours until I forced myself to get up. It had been a long night. The hours went by in slow motion. I had prayed all night for Howard. He was in jail, for the second time, because of me.

Going into the bathroom, my strength gone, I stood looking at myself in the mirror. It was hard for me to recognize myself. I had aged, really aged. The lines of sorrow were obvious. The heaviness of the night overshadowed the pain of the last few months.

I knelt right there, beside the commode. I called out the name of the only one I knew who could help me. "Father, oh Father, help me. I feel so lost and so very alone. I hurt." My prayers, as in the night for Howard, did not change. I didn't ask Jesus to hold and protect Howard during his ordeal. I prayed that Jesus would break him, to save Him.

Putting Howard into a locked jail cell was more than just putting him in jail. Howard was terrified of being confined in closed, small places. In having him arrested and jailed, I had nailed him to a wall and forced him to go through his own living hell. I had seen Howard break out in a sweat when he was confined in small areas. There were times that I had to get him out of such places. We could even be in a club and if it got too crowded, the fear and flushed signs on his face let me know to get him out. I protected him in every area I could.

When I had talked to the police, telling them where Howard was, I had warned them of his fear of confined places. I had even called the downtown station and told an officer of Howard's claustrophobia. This didn't give me much satisfaction. I knew Howard would suffer in a way deeper than I or anyone else could imagine, unless they suffered from the same phobia.

I applied my makeup as well as possible to hide the dead face I saw in the mirror. I used eye drops to cure my red puffy eyes. I was numb. "Help me Jesus, help me" was my cry.

I wanted to sit on the couch and allow my head to fall as my body fell with the pain, but this was not possible. Elizabeth would be coming home soon and I had to go to work. I had gotten a job with a wholesale carpet company a couple of days before Howard returned from his vacation.

How in the world do people go through this to stay with Jesus? I thought. I dragged the cross of overcoming with every step. No wonder people don't give themselves to Jesus, was my thoughts. Living in sin is so much easier. It is a life of scattered joy, which always turned into sorrow. Yet, even now, feeling such pain, I still chose Jesus. It was Jesus only who gave me peace.

On the first day on the job, the office bathroom had become my prayer closet.

I would often get up from my desk and go there for another private moment with Jesus. There were two ways to leave my office and go into other parts of the building. I often took turns in going to the bathroom through one of these two doors, in order to keep anyone from knowing just how much time I was spending in the bathroom. No one knew, no, not anyone, how much time I was spending in the bathroom. I didn't allow the pain in my heart to show on my face and I controlled my actions, revealing no signs of my secret life.

After the first hour had passed at work, I probably had spent at least half of the time in my prayer closet. I went back for help to Jesus again and again. I couldn't think, and I had to do my work over and over, trying to get it right, fighting back tears and smiling, feeling as though my face would crack. I tried so hard and had succeeded in keeping my feelings to myself.

I worked in the same office with the warehouse manager, who was away from his desk a lot of the day, every day. His absence made it easier for me to go to my prayer room. Once again, I cried to God, "Help me, help me! Send an angel to help me. I can't do this work."

At this very moment, an overwhelming sense of *everything is okay* flowed over me. I got up, went back to my desk and worked with such speed and accuracy that it amazed me. My heart of pain was quiet and I realized that indeed an angel guided me through the work. I think this may have been the first time that I realized Christ and angels took full control of me in order for me to be able to flow with such ability and achievement.

At noon, the office secretary and I drove to a meeting in another part of town. When we left the building, my thoughts turned back to Howard and the fact that he was in jail. To confide in someone was not my way. I had told her very little about me and nothing about Howard.

While driving back to our company after the meeting, something came over me. This is the only way I know how to describe it. I didn't hear a word of Janet's conversation. I sat very still, wondering what was going on. *"He's free,"* I heard the voice of God say. I sat there a few moments wondering if I heard what I thought I heard. *"He's free,"* I heard once again. A burden inside me lifted.

Returning to my prayer room as soon as we came back to the office, I got down on my knees. "Thank you Father, thank you," I prayed. As had been in the morning, when I returned to my desk, my job was a delight. I still had an angel helping me.

It was about 30 minutes before it was time to leave after a day's work, when my phone rang. A police officer who had my phone number wanted my permission for Howard to get his things from my house. He would have a police escort. "Yes," I replied, "he can get his things." I drove home quickly with the intention of not having to see or talk to anyone, especially Howard.

I drove to the house and told my niece, who lived with me, to let Howard in. Just as I was walking to my car, the police drove up. Howard was in his van, a friend of his was with him. They were just behind the police.

I felt a moment of total fear. Should I run for my car, and drive away, or should I go back into the house? I looked back toward the officers, who were getting out of their car. Then my eyes swiftly looked into the eyes of Howard.

I wanted to fall to the ground with the weight of pain that quickly returned. I had wanted to see Howard. I could have called my niece and told her to let Howard get his things, but I didn't. I had to see him. Kitti had also driven up, and now my niece and Kitti were standing outside also. Both of them were crying. I held back my tears, it was a fight not to just give in, but I refused to. I turned and walked back into my house. Once again I was numb, simply numb. One of the police officers knocked on the door and said, "Howard wants to get his things, is it all right with you?" "Yes, tell him to come in." I said. I went into my bedroom, the bedroom we had shared and began to put Howard's things inside a bag. I took the things into the living room and met Howard face to face. The look not on his face, but in his eyes touched my heart. I began to cry inside. I had to hold myself from running into his arms. He had also aged. It was obvious, to me, Howard was hurting deeply. The night had been a night of horror for him. There was no hate in his eyes or his expression. His look was one of disbelief. How could I have done such a thing to him? He took the bag and walked out the door. The police officer in the room with me asked, "Do you mind me asking you why you are doing this?" I replied, "I have found God. I can no longer live in a lifestyle of drugs, sex and all the rest of it." His expression was one of kindness. He said, "I can tell that you love that man." "Yes, I do," was my reply. He smiled at me and shook his head. Howard came back in and got the rest of his things. I stood beside the officer. Howard looked back at me before walking out the door. I looked at the officer and said, "May I talk to him just a moment, alone?" "You're not supposed to. Just remember that you asked for it." He walked out the door and Howard came to me. We were almost touching. I could tell he was fighting holding me as I was him. "Why, why, Mary Ann, why did you do it?" He asked. "I had to Howard. You would not leave and I can't live in drugs and sin anymore. Howard, I love God with all my heart. I have to do whatever He asks. This doesn't mean that I don't love you, because I do. I've always loved you. I suppose I always will. God talks to me, "Howard. He is alive! Can't you understand? God called me by my name. I can't live in sin anymore. I have to obey God." I answered.

"I'll call you over at Kitti's in about an hour, will you be there?" He asked. "Yes." I replied. He leaned down and kissed me very gently. "I love you, I don't understand." Howard said. "Oh Howard, I'm sorry, I'm so very sorry for hurting you." I said. I reached up and touched his face. He put his arms around me and held me for just a moment. We walked out the front door. His friend had left in his van with what little belongings he had. His motorcycle, which one of the police officers had driven to my house after he was arrested, sat beside the house. Howard got on it. He turned and looked at me with a smile. I smiled back. There was no need for more words. I watched my heart leave with him on that motorcycle.

The police officers got into their car and also left. Kitti and my niece were still standing outside and both of them were still crying. No one understood. I didn't feel like explaining. I didn't even try. I followed Kitti back to her apartment in my car. Kitti hurt for the both of us. She was not only my friend. She was Howard's friend also. She didn't want to take sides.

The phone rang, I knew who it was. I went upstairs to talk with Howard. He was loaded. He had smoked pot when he came for his things. I knew it, and he knew I knew it. From the sounds in the background, he wasn't going to let it wear off. For some reason, his being stoned didn't bother me. I knew Howard well enough to know that drugs separated him from reality. Smoke another joint and be happy! I was in love with the hidden man inside of Howard. This person was capable of making me feel special, pretty, loved, sexy, intelligent, and all the rest of the good feelings I had not ever really felt before from my family or any of my husbands. In the beginning we had spent hours talking and laughing together. We loved dancing and smoking marijuana together. Before I accepted Christ, we were a team, with no real concern for anyone but ourselves.

Howard made me feel like a queen, his queen. He protected me, he fought for me, he was strong, and he was very jealous. Once when I stayed in the women's bathroom too long at a club, he came in, opened the stall and there I sat. It was late and I had fallen asleep with my head leaning against the stall. He never let me get too far from him. If another man showed too much attention to me,

Howard would get into a fight with him. He wasn't afraid of anyone. He was strong and I liked watching him fight. He liked to watch me also.

Another couple, before my salvation, had gone with us to a club. We drank and danced for about two hours. Barb and I went into the restroom which was pretty full. Two other women came in who were close friends with the owner. They wanted to get in front of us. Our answer was no! They went to the owner and she came into the bathroom. We told her the same but she didn't challenge us.

They didn't force themselves in front of us, but Barb and I absorbed their words with hate. We left the bathroom, went back to our table and shortly afterward decided to go to another bar. When we walked toward the back door, the two women were sitting at a table next to the aisle. I reached over and took the jolly green giant's mother's drink and tipped it over, spilling it into her lap. Barb followed my actions and did the same with the other woman. The fight was on. This woman was big. Not fat, big. The top of my head came just below her breast. I grabbed her by her blouse and began to turn into a circle with her. I knew I had to get her down and I was the one who had to be on top. I then put all my weight on her and took her to the floor. We lithely flew out the back door, and I was on top. I ran my fingers in her hair and began to pound her head on the concrete. Barb had hit the other woman with her fist, she hit the wall and it knocked her out. I saw the blood began to fly with each pounding. I didn't stop hitting her with my fist in the face and with my other hand holding her hair. I kept pounding her head on the cement walk. The more the blood flew, gave me assurance and pride in winning. The more the blood, the more I beat on her. I suppose I would have killed her if it had not been for Howard.

Howard got a hold of the back belt loop of my Wranglers and lifted me off her. He was laughing. He was proud of me. I had made him look good. We left and both women were taken to the hospital. I woke the next day with my knees hurting and the skin for the most part was not there. I had bruises all over me and my hands were swollen so much that I could hardly close them. "Not bad, not bad at all." were the words of approval I heard from Howard.

The following week, Kevin my ex-husband called me and asked me to meet him in a bar and I did. He told me that one of the women had three sons and they were looking for Barb and me. I was surprised that Kevin didn't want me beat up or killed. We had not parted on good terms. When I got back to my apartment Howard was waiting. He was not happy that he didn't know where I was. I lied to him, but I did tell him about the three boys looking for me. For a couple of months he wouldn't let me go anywhere without him but to work and back.

This is the way we lived. The fun we had in the beginning of our relationship had turned into a lot of pain, that is for me. I knew he was with other women, but I closed my eyes to it for a little while. I just knew I could make him love me enough to stop. He did for short times, on and off.

Hearing the laughter in the background when I answered the phone made me hurt. He was in a club. "Hi Howard," I said. "Hello Babe," he answered. We talked for a long time. It's impossible to get through the drugs. He asked me the same questions over and over. He was looking for something that he could accept as a good reason to have put another peace bond on him. No matter what I said, I couldn't get him to understand. I didn't have to tell him I loved him over and over, he knew I did. He was accepted in his freakish world. He was somebody. He could not fit in with society. Neither could I.

Driving home from Kitti's apartment, I felt numb. I couldn't even cry. Jesus was carrying me. I knew the pain would return, but for now, because of His love for me, Jesus bore my pain. I read the Bible until it was very late. I couldn't sleep. I needed to read more about Jesus, I was in Matthew. I had been up all night the night before while Howard was in jail. The following morning I had gone to work, and now after work, Howard had come to get his things. It's two o'clock in the morning of the second night and I can't sleep.

I heard a soft knock at my bedroom door. I knew who it was. I had not heard Howard's motorcycle. Nor his car, but I knew he was at my door. I got out of bed, put on my house coat and opened the back door. It's something to me that I had lived with this man, yet I knew it was wrong for me not to have a house coat on to cover myself. Howard stood there, very nervous. "You won't call the police, will you? Tell me you won't call the police." Howard asked. "No Howard, I won't call the police." I said. I was so glad to see him.

I opened the screen and Howard entered my bedroom. He looked awful. He was broken. "Something is wrong with me. I feel lost. I'm afraid. I need you. I don't know what to do. I don't know what's' wrong, please help me." Howard said. He was talking ninety miles an hour and crying out with all that was in him. "I know what's wrong with you Howard, you don't know Jesus. Do you want to?" I asked. "I don't know how. I don't know what to do." He answered. "I do Howard, but I can't ask Jesus to forgive you, you will have to ask Him yourself." I said. "I don't know how, I can't pray, I don't know what to say." He said. "I'll pray with you, but you must talk to God yourself. Tell Him what is in your heart. Talk to Him like you talk to me. Tell Him you're afraid. Ask Him to forgive you for the things you know are wrong. Ask Him to help you. He hears you. God sees you right now and He loves you. He is waiting for you to call His name."

Together we knelt beside the bed we had shared for almost two and a half years. "Father, in the name of Jesus Christ, I ask you to hear Howard. Let him know You and Your power and Your love. Let him know that You hear the cry that comes from his heart." I asked Jesus. Turning to Howard, I again told him I could not ask for forgiveness for his sins. "You must ask Him yourself. Just talk to Him." Howard then began to talk to Jesus. "I don't know why I do the things I do. I don't know why I hurt the people I love," were the first words Howard spoke. He talked to Jesus for some time. I sat quietly beside him. I was praying within myself all the time he was praying. Yet, I heard every word he said. This is the first time I had ever heard Howard talk to Jesus. He was really talking to Him. There was no pretense, no games, no deals, and no lies. Howard was pouring his heart out to God. He asked for forgiveness for all his sins. He named them one by one. He actually admitted all he could think of. This prayer was for real. Howard's ending words were, "I guess that's all I have to say. Make me the man You want me to be."

By now, tears of pure joy slowly dropped from my face. Howard and I held each other without words for a few moments. I wanted to make sure Howard was saved! I asked him to follow me in a simple prayer, which he did. "Father, forgive me for all my sins and fill me with Your Spirit. I believe Jesus Christ is your son that He died and then was raised. Cleanse me and make me whole in you." Then I said, "Father show him who's King! Fill him with joy such as he's never known." Howard began to laugh. Another miracle took place.

Howard was no longer stoned. I didn't know what he had smoked or was taking, but I knew he handled pain by getting away from it. God had given Howard the same purity He had given me the day I was going to kill myself. Howard, for the first time in years, had no drugs in his system. Together we laughed and talked as we had never done. Howard was on a new high, one that he had never experienced before. He was on a Jesus Christ high. He was ready to get on a street corner with a tambourine and shout alleluia. I was ready to stand beside him.

We talked the rest of the night. I believed that Jesus had drawn him to me, and gave me the heart to receive him. When I drove for three days after God came to me in the form of a cloud, I had looked for someone to help me. I had no idea of what to do. I didn't know to ask Jesus for salvation and forgiveness. No one told me. I didn't know about God, Jesus Christ and the Holy Spirit.

Howard left. I dressed for work and went to work. There had been no sexual contact between us. I was so happy. Howard was happy. I believed.....**THE BATTLE IS WON.**

Luke 15:7
I say unto you, that likewise joy shall be in heaven over one sinner that repenteth, more than over ninety and nine just persons, which need no repentance.

THE BATTLE IS WON

Is it wisdom or is it stupidity!
What in the world is happening to me?
When I first fell in love, I was in love with a man living in sin.
Now my love belongs to You, but where have You gone, where have You been?
Are You there, are You somewhere, are You still my Friend?
Have You tried my reins, are You searching my inner being?
FATHER, FATHER, does Satan have control of me again?
I have depression, I'm full of oppression.
I want to scream, I want to die, then there's a moment of hesitation.
Oh God, my Father, King of all Kings.
The wisdom, the knowledge, the testing of all things.
The gifts of the promise, the Spirit You gave me within.
I'm sinking, I'm sinking, GOD, I'm sinking in sand!
As my flesh is covered, there is on my arm put a band.
Satan has claimed me.....No! No!, I'll not work for him again.
Then, I felt the power of Your words,
I remember the verses to me You've told.
"GREATER IS HE THAT IS WITHIN ME,
THAN HE THAT IS IN THE WORLD."
Then from the depth of my soul, I scream a mighty, mighty ROAR!
NO! NO! Satan, you shall not conquer, control, for on the cross my sins were bore.
Through my ears I hear, through my eyes I see.
I have power, I have strength, I shall move a mountain in the name of the KING!
Leave me, through God, I command.
Leave me Satan, as in all HIS glory I stand.
I shall witness to my neighbor and my friends.
I shall prove your ways, I shall carry the burdens of those my kin.
I shall conquer, I shall in the midst of my angels confirm,
GOD IS THE KING, AND THROUGH HIM.....**THE BATTLE HAS ALREADY BEEN WON.**

Chapter 4:
HELP ME

Driving to work soon after Howard left my home, I was bubbling over with pure joy. Howard had prayed, asking for forgiveness. Staying up all night talking with him and sharing his joy, had brought jubilation I had not experienced before. He was my first convert. God had actually used me.

I was on cloud number nine hundred and ninety-nine. I laughed at everything, even if it wasn't funny. I skipped through the day. My work was effortless. Goodness, God surely does reward us with His joy, and the desire to live and be used by Him when we are trying, at least trying, to follow His direction.

Salvation for others had become my first desire. I wanted to win souls to Jesus. I realized my testimony, even in its premature state, was of value to others. Howard had come to me because he had seen a change in me. It was hard for me to know just when he saw the change and wasn't just hearing it. To me the pain of casting off sin was more obvious. I didn't tell Howard of all the pain I felt. I told Him of the love of Jesus. His peace overpowered the pain.

The next day after he had accepted Christ, Howard called me after I got home from work. When I answered the phone, Howard said, "Don't go into a lot of details. Just tell me what to do. I feel like the whole world is caving in on me!" I knew how he felt. I could remember those cloudy days in the very beginning when I was trying to find Jesus.

"Howard, Satan has come to claim you back," I told him. "He has never tormented you before. Why should he? You were his! You have served Satan all your life. He is causing your pain. He will not give you up easily. You have been winning souls to his hell. Now that you have given yourself to Jesus Christ, Satan is putting out a real battle to win you back. You must refuse him. Tell him, using the full name of Jesus Christ to leave you alone. It's called rebuke. Refuse to accept Satan back into your heart. Jesus has filled you with His Spirit. You will have to follow the direction of Jesus Christ. Don't give up, talk to Jesus. You are being tested. Read the Bible and learn about Jesus. Don't give into what you know is wrong. Keep your mind full of what Jesus gave you last night. He gave you Himself."

Up until then, Howard had said nothing. "Okay, I'll be over in a little while," he said. I had no idea where he lived. It was some place across town. We never talked about it. I didn't allow myself to think of what he was or was not doing. I only saw him when he came to me. I didn't know where he was working. It's amazing that I really didn't care about these things. I knew women were in his life, but that was something I wouldn't face. Howard would come to me to keep some kind of control over me. He also came whenever he hurt. When he came, I would feed him Jesus.

I knew some of what Howard had to go through. I also knew I could not go through it for him, although I think I would have, if it had been possible. I began to pray for Howard.

It was about seven or eight o'clock that evening when I heard the knock on my door. Howard had completed his truck run and come over, parking his car away from the house. He was afraid a police officer would see it and arrest him again, since he was still under a peace bond.

I didn't really understand why Howard had come over. At this point in my life, I had no dreams of the two of us getting back together. Yet, I could not turn away from him. Even after he had accepted Christ, my thoughts were not of us. My thoughts were mainly of Howard's salvation.

The reality of hell was something I knew with no doubt did exist. Satan and demons are real. I prayed that Howard would be strong enough to overcome the temptations of Satan. I read the Bible, worked and went to church. That was just about all I did. I knew there was no running away from Jesus. I ran to Him with everything, even those things I didn't have a clue about, such as how did a person lose salvation. I did realize that a person could go to hell. This was something that Jesus revealed to me before I had any understanding of anything.

The car dealer I had worked for showed me in Scripture where it clearly says we are saved. Yet, I knew there was more. I searched for this truth daily. If Jesus says we will not enter into heaven if we are practicing sin. I think He means it. I knew living with Howard was wrong. Yet I went back into this sin, with my knowing better, and had I died, I didn't believe Jesus would take me into His kingdom. I had let Howard move back in with me once. I was not going to let it happen again. I had a real fear of spending eternity in what I had read hell was like. (Revelation)

Despite all my misgivings, I was glad to see Howard standing on my back porch that night. In fact, I wanted to fly into his arms, I loved him so much. But looking into his eyes, I realized he had failed – he was on drugs again. The joy of the day was gone in an instant, and that old familiar pain took its place once again.

I was torn by an inner conflict, and being a baby Christian, I did not quite know how to handle the situation. I knew I couldn't allow myself to hold Howard, nor would I allow him to hold me I knew if I went into his arms, the pain would leave for a brief period of time. I knew I needed the fix that only Howard could give me. But at the same time, I refused to accept Satan's short period of false joy, disguised in the need I had, just to be held. It would have been so easy to simply take Howard to my bed and let him hold me. I had not been close to Howard in the past few months, since he had moved out, but my need for him was real. However, it was not sex I needed. It was Howard's giving of himself to me. Somehow I felt this act would make me feel that Howard really loved me.

I didn't know what drugs Howard had taken, but I could see he was feeling no pain. We sat in my living room talking. He began to fuss at me for having a peace bond on him which he didn't like me having any control over him. Then he became hateful. His words were mean and sharp. I didn't really try to talk to him. I just did more listening.

After Howard thought he had persuaded me to drop the bond, the drugs began to wear off and he seemed more like his old self, the one I had fallen in love with. Now he was trying to reason with me. Yet I knew I had to draw the line and let him know that I would not let him come and go as he pleased. When his strategy turned from demand to kind pleading, my response was "No!" I firmly told him. "I will not drop the bond. I won't let you control me. This is Elizabeth's and my home. You will not scare her or me. You will not tell me what I can and cannot do."

I wasn't afraid of Howard, I had lived with a physically abusive husband, and I was not going to let any man have that kind of control over me again. The control Howard had on me during the time we lived together made me feel safe and loved instead of inhumane. I had told Howard at the beginning of our relationship that no man was ever going to hit me again. Hitting me, pulling my hair out, putting a gun in my mouth or against my temple was the meaning of abusive. Howard had overpowered me with his strength, but it had been my fault since I was laughing with another man in a club. In the beginning we had so much fun together that his control was accepted as love. He didn't have to make me do anything. I did what he wanted because I loved him.

I refused to face the fact that he might hit me. With God he would change, wouldn't he?

Howard's tactics immediately began to change. He promised me if I took the bond off, we would marry and our problems would be over. Here he was, sitting in my home telling me through the drugs he had taken, that the problem was me, not him.

But he was also saying the things I wanted to hear. When Howard was sweet, he could be really, really sweet. He had an agreeable and courteous personality, and always had a way of making people like him and women wanting him. As a biker, drug dealer, he had male friends, but he ran with women.

His persuasive tone was getting to me. I simply wouldn't let myself accept the truth about Howard. I loved his words, yet I hated his actions. As a result, Howard and I argued most of the night. He finally left. I got a little sleep, dressed and went to work the following morning. Sometime during the night, Jesus told me, *"No,"* about Howard, and I heard Him.

Then followed endless days of seeing Howard coming and going to and from my house.

I continued to try and tell him about the stronghold Satan had on him, but he no longer was very interested in Satan or Jesus Christ. He was only interested in conquering me. I had not prayed asking God to keep Howard from me. His visits, at times drug-free, fed my loneliness. It was hard for me to understand how a person accepts Jesus Christ, feels His love and His Spirit and then turns and leaves Him. At that time, I simply didn't know enough about Jesus and His ways to put this puzzle together. When Howard was drugged up, I put up with him. When he was sober, and told me of his love, it helped my need to feel as though I wasn't rejected.

Why didn't I simply call the police and stop him from coming? To this day, I don't know. Why did I keep answering the door? I don't know. I just did. But I knew I couldn't put him in jail again.

Once I even nailed my windows shut when I realized he was getting into the house through one of my back windows. I had put two nails into each window. It wasn't long before I realized he had removed the nails and simply was putting them back, after he was finished going through my things.

I suppose he was looking for evidence that there was not another man in my life. Or at least this was part of it.

It wasn't until I actually went out on a date with a man from my church that I returned home, and my date and I both instinctively knew Howard had been there. My date didn't stay long. I knew he wanted no part of Howard. Sure enough, as he drove off, Howard burst through my door. He rushed to me and slapped me to my knees. Miraculously, I felt no pain. Instead, the force of his hand felt like a feather that simply brushed across my face. I fell to the floor in slow motion. There was absolutely no pain. He left quickly, I guess he thought I would call the police, I should have, but I didn't.

A new realization was birthed in me. Now, without doubt, I knew Howard would physically hurt me if he was drunk or drugged up enough, if he allowed his jealously to control him. He had never been faithful to anyone, but he demanded faithfulness from the women in his life.

"Father, please keep Howard away from me. Protect me," I cried. "Why do You let him come?" I thought because I was faithful in reading the Bible and going to church that God would simply shut a door, put up some kind of barrier and keep him from being able to reach me. I was wrong. Christ had kept me from feeling any pain, yet He for some reason let him barrel through my door.

I wanted God to keep Howard from my home, but I didn't want God to turn from him, so I prayed for Howard. I also prayed for any person involved with him, male or female. I prayed every night for him, regardless of how I felt.

The in-the-middle-of-the-night phone calls didn't stop. Howard began coming over daily at various times. He might come for three days in a row and then it would be several days and I wouldn't hear anything from him. I was worn completely out from all the stress of dealing with Howard.

At the same time, I was trying to figure out if God was bringing Howard to my door, or if Satan was. I thought maybe God was letting go of me. Does everyone have to go through these things? I asked. Was it this way for everyone who wanted to follow Jesus? Was sorrow never ending? Would I have to spend the rest of my life in such an up and down state?

I was high on Jesus one moment, dead and hurting for Howard the next moment. I was walking this walk with no personal friends with the exception of Kitti and a strong Christian woman, Grace, whom I had nicknamed Mother Superior.

In addition to my personal problems, I was also living in what I considered poverty. I wondered if, as a Christian, I had to lose everything I had. It had taken me years to attain what little material possessions I did have. It didn't seem like anyone else in the whole world could possibly understand what I was going through. No one talked about such things. Was I right in seeing Howard, or was I wrong? Why wasn't Howard going to church? Why didn't God talk to Howard like He did to me? Does God really reject someone

He has forgiven? I was so torn between the love of Jesus and the possibility of hell, because of sin.

Alone one day, I knelt in my living room. "God, I'm scared. Where are You?" Even though I had threatened Howard a few times that I would put him back in jail, God knew I wouldn't, and I knew I wouldn't but Howard was not sure.

I'm ready to let go of Howard, again, I thought. My prayers were aimed at a complete letting go. I knew I needed help from Jesus to do this. I could no longer merely try. I had to do what I knew would cause even greater pain for both Howard and me. I had to completely reject Howard, his visits, and his phone calls. Then in the midst of my intercession, I heard a pickup roar into my drive way. I knew it was Howard. I had endured days of crying over him, never knowing what was coming next. I looked awful. My hair was a tangled mess. My face was drawn and puffy. My eyes were swollen from days of crying. "Please God, please don't let him in, please stop him," was the cry from my heart. I didn't feel like I could go through all of it again tonight. But the banging on the door was not going to stop.

Howard began calling out my name. I knew he was not going to leave. I went to the door and before I had time to think, I threw my right hand into the air toward heaven and said, "I rebuke you in the name of Jesus Christ!" Then I slammed the door in his face. The knocking turned to banging. "Mary Ann, what did you say? What did you say?" he cried out. He was yelling now. I decided to try it again. I opened the door and raised my hand again toward God. "I rebuke you in the name of Jesus Christ!" I screamed. Howard looked at me like I had gone completely nuts. He was drugged up and I was taking him on a trip he didn't like. He was trying to dodge my arm flying up. He looked like a yo-yo, up and down, then side to side. He had never seen me like this. He didn't have a chance to say anything. I was freaking him out. I again slammed the door in his face. Then I went to my bedroom and cried out. "Why don't You make him leave me alone? Have You turned away from me? Help me! Oh God, help me. I can't stand any more. Help me!" I cried out in desperate need for the help of God. I guess Howard could hear me screaming to God and he didn't want any part of me.

I then heard the pickup door slam and Howard's vehicle roaring away from the house. Suddenly strength came over me that I had never known. I pranced up and down my bedroom floor, telling God all about it. I quoted scriptures. I began proclaiming to God that He indeed had it all together. His word was true. I confessed to Him I was sorry for not believing Him. I poured out my love for Him.

It was wonderful. I knew He had not left me. I didn't understand much of anything else, but I knew Howard had left. I danced up and down the floor for more than three hours talking to God with all that was in me. I preached a sermon right there in my bedroom. Tears of joy had taken the place of tears of sorrow. My faith was renewed. The Spirit of God within me had come alive. I preached, quoting scriptures that I didn't even know yet. I don't remember a lot of what I said, because I was in the Spirit. God was teaching me. He was giving me His strength, His wisdom and His love. I finally got into my bed and fell into a deep sleep of peace, the first I had had in many a night.

Howard called the following day. "Are you going to turn me into a frog, or something?" he asked, and he was not kidding. He knew I had power in Jesus Christ. He didn't know just how much power I had. He had been a part of, or he had seen what God would do if I asked Him. He had seen some miracles. God had healed his back a few months before. I had simply prayed for healing and he was healed.

For the first time in our relationship, Howard was truly intimidated. He was really scared that I had asked Jesus to turn him into a frog. I'm sure I was quite a sight for him to have watched the night before. The drugs he had taken probably convinced him that at any moment he would begin hopping around.

To this day I wished I had told him to watch his skin convincing him that it would begin to turn green at any time. Knowing him as I did, it would have been great to put such fear in him. But, I didn't do that. I tried to explain to him that I was calling out to God to keep him away from me. I assured him that he wasn't going to turn into a frog. I hung up the phone after our brief conversation and laughed until my sides hurt. I relived in my mind the previous night and pictured Howard trying to dodge the spell he thought I was putting on him. He looked like a bouncing ball and I must have looked like the wicked witch of frog land.

Once again, as always, God had come to my rescue. He held me, gave me strength and gave me a time of rest in Him. He put me under the comfort of His wings when I cried out.....**HELP ME!**

Psalms 33:20
Our soul waiteth for the LORD: he is our help and our shield.

Psalms 121:2
My help cometh from the LORD, which made heaven and earth.

Psalms 36:7
How excellent is thy lovingkindness, O God! therefore the children of men put their trust under the shadow of thy wings.

HELP ME!

I find no peace.....
There is no joy.....
Why do You not turn, when You hear my voice?
I cry, I hurt, I'm broken down.
Why do You look upon me, with the face of a frown?
What have I done, help me, help me, please........Help Me!
The burden is too heavy, I have fallen..... can't you see?
Where are You, there is no purpose!
I'm sinking far below, far below life's surface.
HELP ME, HELP ME, please take my hand.
Let me know You love me once again.
I'm afraid, I'm afraid, I'm afraid.
I'm being buried in the pits of a cave.
I scream, I scream, I scream!
Why is it hell instead of You I'm seeing?
I did not quit, my all I'm still willing to give.
Rescue me, rescue me, come for me with your mighty
ship.....**HELP ME!**

Chapter 5:
EAGLE

Despite my previous victories concerning Howard, I continued to remain in turmoil about this man who had been the cause of so much love – and so much pain. I hadn't seen him in two weeks. This was the longest length of time that Howard and I had not seen each other since we had first met. During this time I spent many an hour in prayer, but relief still hadn't come.

Howard had not called, inside I was fighting to let him go. Seeing him that day two weeks earlier had only made me have to climb this particular mountain over and over again. I knew I didn't want to see him and I had no intention of us getting back together. But I wanted God to heal my love and need for him.

I had tried everything. I knew I was supposed to pray for Howard, forgive him and love and pray for whomever, the girl he was living with also. I had put up a good fight to do just these things.

So I lay in bed wondering why I just simply didn't die. I wasn't praying for death. I had no suicidal intentions. Yet the pain was overwhelming.

It had been months since I had begun this journey with Jesus Christ. I hungered for a lasting peace, at least more than a few hours or even a day, maybe even a week. Instead, my peace came in seconds, minutes, an hour a day or one night. I was fighting for spiritual survival, fighting to get to know Jesus. It was my love for Him that kept me in this game of overcoming. (Wherefore seeing we also are compassed about with so great a cloud of witnesses, let us lay aside every weight, and the sin which doth so easily beset us, and let *us* run with patience the race that is set before us. Hebrews 12:1)

When I met Howard, he had been married about 13 years and had three young sons. It was a natural lifestyle for him to commit adultery. Howard had no longtime girlfriends, just bed partners he had met in clubs along his route to deliver merchandise he was hauling to various towns and cities.

At the time of our meeting, adultery had been a lifestyle for me as well. I considered myself responsible for taking Howard away from his family. I believed his wife must have loved him with all her heart because she knew of his adultery, yet kept trying to keep her family together.

Two of Howard's three sons were around me a lot. Even during the times I tried to keep Howard from me, he would bring his two sons to my home, knowing that I would accept them. In fact, I loved them.

It was during this time as I was studying the Bible that I came to realize and have the understanding that Jesus wants families to stay together. I began to pray for Howard to go back to his wife and sons.

Elizabeth and I went into the church building on Sunday morning and sat in our usual area. Something had come over me and I knew God was going to use me this day. Looking around, I saw many faces of the people who were regulars, faithful, there every Sunday and Wednesday services. I was excited, about what I had no clue. I was sure something was about to take place and I was going to be a part of it.

Gently, at first, the Holy Spirit began pounding around my heart. By now I was able to recognize when He was manifesting Himself to me. I didn't hear much of the music. I was asking Jesus what He wanted. I was praying. The pounding began to increase until I could even hear my heart beating. My whole chest was ablaze with His quickening. Announcements were being made when I stood up, not knowing what to do I began to walk to the front of the church. I trusted Jesus to lead me into whatever He was requiring of me. The pastor continued his announcements. I slowly walked to the front of the church. I had almost reached the platform. The assistant pastor knew me because I had gone to this pastor and talked with him about Howard's wife attending this church with her three boys. I felt drawn to this church but I was very concerned about causing any continued pain for Howard's wife. The pastor had told me to follow God's direction, if God told me to go to this church, then go, and I did. I had been honest and told him everything from my childhood to the present. He told me I needed to follow the direction of the Holy Spirit. He could not make the decision for me. He completely understood about the situation. As I approached the area where he was sitting, he got out of his seat and came to me off the platform. He smiled when I stopped in front of him. By now the announcements had been made and all eyes, about 2,000 were on me. Fear gripped me. Tears slowly fell from my eyes.

It was silent. All I could hear were the words being prayed over me. I looked into the eyes of the pastor and said, "I took a man from his family. I know his wife goes to this church. I don't want to cause her any more harm. May I apologize to her and her sons?" "Yes, follow me," the pastor replied. He then went to the pulpit and announced to the congregation that he believed a woman had come forward obeying the unction of the Holy Spirit. He stepped back, covering me with his approval.

*Still shaking to the point that I thought I might faint, I stepped behind the microphone and managed, "There is a woman that belongs to this church that I want to ask for her forgiveness for all the pain I have caused her and her family. I didn't know Christ as my savior when I began to be with her husband. I pray that she and her children can forgive me." Peace came over me. I told the congregation that I had taken this man from their home and had lived with him over two years. I had asked for forgiveness from Ann, his wife first then his three boys. Then I continued and asked forgiveness from the congregation. I had obeyed Jesus, this meant everything to me.

There was pin-dropping silence. I saw no hate in the eyes of the people as I spoke, yet somehow I knew that many in the congregation should be standing with me asking for forgiveness. I then turned and looked at the pastor. He returned a smile of approval. I walked back to my seat. My legs felt like they would stop working at any moment, and I would fall smack on my face. Reaching where I had sat, Elizabeth had patiently waited for me. I sat down in a daze wondering what in the world had I just done. The church was more than just quiet. It was in shock, disbelief, not knowing how to accept what had just happened. I sat looking only to the front of the church, just above the people's heads. Elizabeth sat quietly beside me.

The Holy Spirit continued to quicken me throughout the whole service. I had obeyed. I sat with eyes glued on the preacher. I sat there like nothing had happened, while my insides were screaming, run!

By the time the service was over, I was fighting back tears. I would not let anyone see me cry. I made myself act normal, whatever normal is. One young man, with his wife following, came to me after the service was over. I stood still, our eyes locked. He had a wonderful smile on his face. I knew that it was important to him to speak with me. He and his wife had the look of Jesus on their faces. He stood in front of me and encouraged me to continue on. I don't remember the exact words he said to me, but I do remember that I gained strength, and determination to press on in Christ because of his encouragement. His wife stood behind him and a little to his right, just enough for me to see her smile, and her approval of her husband leaning down and hugged me in such a gentle way. I accepted his hug and I so appreciated her approval. This young couple had what I wanted, what I was fighting for. They were the pure examples of Jesus Christ. Her husband stepped back and all I could do was smile and say, "Thank you, thank you." In my heart I also thanked Jesus for sending someone to me who truly understands His love.

Walking to my car, I saw looks, but they were the looks of judgment. Jealousy and hate are the ones that stood out to me. I made myself walk with poise. I held my head high, smiling to the people I knew, that is the very few that did not turn from me. Their faces and actions showed that it was a strain to acknowledge knowing me. Unfortunately, there were many who turned from me, and only a very few who would even speak.

Driving home, I experienced all the pain of all my life. It was as though everything that had been hidden came to life, all in one big ball in my heart. It was hard to breathe. The pain was so intense. I knew I had obeyed God. I knew that He had used me. He didn't explain to me what He did through me. My only comfort was that

I obeyed without question. Elizabeth sat close to me on our way home putting her little hand on my arm.

I longed for Howard. I wanted to get word to him to come to me. I knew he was more than likely out of town on a truck. When he called only, and didn't come over, it was usually because he was out of town. He would keep tabs on me by calling when he was gone. I suppose to feed his need to have some control over me. I would not allow myself the comfort of Howard. I desperately wanted Jesus to take total control of my heart. I chose to be alone, pray, and hurt in privacy. I did try to keep Elizabeth from knowing the pain I felt. She was playing with her little friend who lived a few houses down the block.

Going to church to the evening service was something I made myself do. I knew if I didn't go it would be so easy to stop going at all. Letting people keep me from going to church was not going to happen. If no one would speak to me, I was still going to church. Once I arrived, it was the same as it had been after the morning service. People avoided me. I had expected the worst, and it was the worst. Not one person that I knew made me feel welcome. Keeping the tears from my eyes and the pain in my heart from showing on my face was a shear challenge. The preacher who had prayed with me and stood by me at the pulpit during the early service was now standing at the entry doors of the church, greeting people. "I see you're back." were his words to me. He smiled at me as if we had a deep secret. It was a smile of "everything is okay." I was somewhat comforted by this. I don't think anyone who knew me was expecting me to return. I asked him, "Do you understand what I did?" He replied, "Yes, good is going to come out of your obedience." I accepted this reply, even though at the time I didn't have any idea of what he meant. Sitting down in our usual place, I prayed silently. Determined to act normal, at least I looked normal. When the pews were nearly full, I turned to see how full the church was. A woman saw me looking at her husband. I wasn't really looking at him. I was looking in their direction. The woman grabbed her husband's arm. Our eyes locked as she challenged me to leave her husband alone. Pure hate, darts of hate flew to me from her glare. Disgust went through me. I would not allow myself to walk up to her and say, "Lady, I don't want your husband, and if you have to grab him to keep him, you don't have him anyway!" Simply turning back toward the front, I fought again to hold back the tears. Some of the people I had met at the prayer meeting I had been faithful in attending and where I had given my testimony let me know without doubt that I was not wanted. Again, I was cast out.

I was to learn later that a lot of good did come from my obedience to Jesus Christ. Marriages had been mended, relationships of adultery stopped. I'm sure God forgave all those whose hearts were pure. Many repented. One woman who lived double lives, one for Christ on Sunday morning, and the other for Satan on Saturday night told her secrets to a pastor. He in turn told me, not her name, but her testimony. Some people I didn't know came to me to share with me what I had done for them or some member of their family or a friend in being honest and asking for forgiveness in the act of adultery. I never rebelled or fussed with Christ over the pain I had to suffer during these times. It seemed that a whole church rejected me, but of course not all did. Being a baby in Christ, I had not known to do just what I did in obeying His word. Later, I discovered this. My pain was released. It turned into an honor for me to have obeyed. When I allowed Him to control my pain and to continue this growing process and not allowing myself to turn to Howard instead of Jesus, He rewarded me with peace and healing. Out of more than five thousand people attending this church faithfully, I was the one He chose to do a work in His people. I took it, to my understanding that Jesus had chosen me because He knew I would obey.

So this is what it's like to really repent and be sorrowful for the pain I had caused to another woman, I thought. I not only wanted to give up her husband, as they were not divorced yet, I wanted him to go back to his children and his wife. I thought by doing so that they would have lived happily ever after.

After my public apology at church, it had been two weeks since I had seen or talked to Howard. My inner pain was like a volcano. Apologizing to his wife, in front of many people, was to me still trying to release Howard and do it God's way. But no matter how intense the pain, I refused to find him. I had given up, to the best of my ability, lying, adultery, stealing, gossip, or any other sin that I recognized as being a sin.

Some people got really angry at me because of Howard. They thought I was to blame for the problems since I had turned into a JESUS freak! Even my parents told me to just go with the flow. "Don't get tangled up being a Christian," they said.

But this was not my nature. I had to be the best at whatever I did. I fought to win any way it took. I had lived under the power for Satan for years. Now I lived for Jesus. It was a whole new ballgame for me, and I didn't even know the language! I was still rebellious, because at times I wore my tight wranglers and leathers to church. I had to prove that it was not the clothes on my back, but it was the intent of my heart to follow Jesus that was important.

The volcano rumbling inside of me was about to erupt, breaking my heart into so many pieces that I was sure it could not be put together again. Smoke was bellowing out, but only I knew it. I was anticipating the pain to overpower me. Rejection was my number one enemy. It's amazing how I couldn't get my mind off the people who rejected me, and replace the thoughts with the people who had blessed me.

It was early morning. I had not slept well. I had prayed, read the Bible and prayed and prayed and prayed! I wasn't losing faith. I simply didn't know what else to do. I prayed in my Holy Spirit language until I was prayed out. There was nothing left to say.

I had given up, put out, forsaken, cast out, and walked away from everything and everybody that might have drawn me back into the grip of sin. I refused to find relief in clubs with other men or do anything that I knew was wrong in the eyes of God, even though I knew I could find relief in drugs or drinking. I chose to suffer. This was not some great sacrifice. I simply desired Jesus Christ above all.

At that time, my financial situation was bleak. I was very close to losing some of my furniture. I had paid more than $2,000 for it, owed seven hundred on it and was close to six months behind on payments. One of the store's representatives came by once in a while to see if I could pay on the furniture. He knew I had very little money and simply had no money for furniture payments.

After four marriages, I had carried around things to set up my home to make it full of happiness. So far it hadn't worked. Howard had talked me into getting a loan on my rings. I had paid more than $5,000 for them through the years. The loan was for $2,000 which Howard took, and I lost all my rings.

However, now I paid tithes every week, although I was making minimum wages. I knew God would take care of Elizabeth and me if I trusted Him. I had paid tithes from the very beginning of my salvation. Somehow early in my relationship and reading my Bible, I learned it was not the money, but the trust Jesus sought in me.

One night, Elizabeth, then eight, heard my crying. She came into my bedroom and climbed into bed with me. She tried to comfort me."It's all right, Mother. I love you," she whispered. It was at this point that I began to realize that she understood more than I had given her credit for. Some man had always had my attention first, for as long as I could remember. I put my arms around her and drew her close to me. Holding my little girl and feeling her wonderful love, I wanted to comfort her.

I had been faithful in taking my daughter to church. She had developed a relationship with Jesus Christ. Her little arms and love helped me many times through these days of pain. My little girl was at times what I should have been for her. I didn't realize that she was suffering. I didn't realize her need for me, not to mother me, but for me to be her mother. I had never been a mother. I didn't know how to be one. I thought because of her young age that she didn't really know what was going on. I was wrong, she was as lonely as I was, I just didn't know it at the time.

The next morning, she dressed for school and I dressed for work. I tried to keep my hurt about Howard from her as much as possible. But she knew I loved Howard, as much as a little girl can understand, she knew my heart.

I carried my ever-present Bible to work with me. Two weeks of not seeing or hearing from Howard was such a stress, yet I would not allow myself to call out for him. All the way to work, I was trying to kill the tears that kept flowing from my eyes. I hated crying all the time, yet it was the only way I had of releasing some of the pain. I went straight into my private prayer room at my job, the bathroom. Once in the bathroom, I asked Jesus Christ to help me stop crying, to help me do my work, to comfort me. No one had seen me enter the building and I really didn't want anyone to know how I was feeling.

After leaving my prayer room, I went to my desk and asked Jesus for an angel to help me. I wanted to be honorable on my job and to be accurate in my work. This was very important to me. I would last working at my desk about ten to fifteen minutes, and then I would go back into the bathroom and cry out to Jesus with all my heart. It was finally lunchtime. I could be alone. I went into the conference room, opened my Bible and began to read. Other employees routinely left me alone while I was in this room. They knew I was reading my Bible, but they didn't know why I spent so much time reading it.

I had read about eagles in several verses, something about being on eagles' wings. Then tears came. I had no control over them. I prayed, leaning back in the chair. I started thinking about an eagle. In my mind, there was no reality and no noise. I had shut out the world.

"Come to me, my eagle, in the name of Jesus I command!" I heard myself say. Immediately, I was in a vision. I was standing on beautiful grass looking toward the heavens. The day was much like the day God had spoken to me in the form of a cloud. It was a beautiful blue day, with large white clouds. An eagle came forth from the heavens. It grew in size as it flew, moving its wings very gracefully.

Feelings of peace and joy immediately killed the pain in me. I waited patiently, never moving my eyes from the eagle. His wingspread was as wide as the heavens, such power, such grace, such beauty. I was totally immersed in the vision.

The eagle soared, coming closer and closer to me. His feet touched the ground, close to where I was standing. He was big, bigger than anything I had ever seen, but at the same time, he was so gentle. He came to a stop and looked at me. I was completely contented. Two angels then came forth. Each took me by my arms and lifted me upon the back of this magnificent eagle. The angels put me down where the wing is connected to the body, where it doesn't quite close.

The eagle again spread his wings and turned his head and looked at me on his back. I had never seen an eagle up close, but I saw every feather, every feature. He was grand and proud. His look was unexplainable. I knew it was God Himself. He turned his head toward the sky, and in a mighty thrust we were in the air and up into the heavens. He turned his head several times just to check on me and it was as if I knew His thoughts. Then He said, *"ALL IS WELL."* I could hear the angels singing. They stayed with us until the vision was gone. I opened my eyes. During this time, I received a peace that would never leave me and would see me through the heartaches still yet to come.

The volcano that was ready to erupt in my heart was no longer there. For the rest of the day I had so much joy. I was laughing at everything and had everyone laughing with me. It was a little before closing when I went to get the company's mail. I was so full of peace and my mind still so filled with the vision that I accidentally ran a couple of red lights. I remembered very little of driving to the post office and driving back to my job.

This peace is still with me even to this day, that same peace has seen me through many lonely hours, many hurts, many trials, and many tests. This peace is the faith I stand on. God came to me in the form of a.....**EAGLE**!

*Luke 23:34
Then said Jesus, Father, forgive them; *for they know not what they do*. And they parted his raiment, and cast lots.

Isaiah 40:31
But they that wait upon the LORD shall renew their strength; they shall mount up with wings as eagles; they shall run, and not be weary; and they shall walk, and not faint.

This drawing with me sitting on the back of an Eagle with the two angels captures the vision I experienced.

Eagle drawn by;   Frank Kubala
Angels drawn by;   Billy Elmore
                           William P. Clements, Jr. Unit

EAGLE!

As I sat at my desk, from which I worked.
I was full of sorrow, misery and inner hurt!
I did my job as best I could.
Yet somehow my pain, no one understood.
There had been many days, yes months,
That I had suffered; joy for me had not yet come.
It seemed this day I could stand no more.
Yet a release for me, I could find no door!
I thought for a moment, a moment of YOU.
I knew there was PEACE, but somehow I could not get through!
I was bound in such hurting sorrow.
Oh GOD, don't let there be another tomorrow!
When finally, there was a chance I could be alone.
I cried out and asked to come before YOU on YOUR throne.
I asked that YOU, in the name of JESUS,
Would send to me, please send to me an.....EAGLE!
As I closed my eyes and sat back in my chair,
Suddenly I realized, Oh! FATHER, an EAGLE.....was there!
And as I climbed upon its back,
There were angels to protect me where I sat.
And as we went up into the clouds,
Oh FATHER, I realized by You, I was..... held.
I will never forget that beautiful day,
When PEACE for me was to FOREVER STAY!
And when the EAGLE TURNED AND LOOKED AT ME,
I knew that YOU, in me, would FOREVER BE!
What a vision of YOU, in the form of an.....**EAGLE!**

Chapter 6:
I DO FORGIVE

~

I don't know how much time had passed, but it seemed like 555 years. I got up at 15 till 6 most every morning, turned the television to the PTL Club, and then made coffee and watched Jim Baker and his guests while putting my makeup on.

My routines were the same: get my daughter up for school, get dressed while watching some Christian program, take my daughter to school, go to work for eight and a half hours, return home, feed my daughter, take a bath and read my Bible until about nine o'clock. Then I would spend my quiet time with the Lord in prayer and go to bed. This was my daily routine, every morning during the week.

On Sundays I watched Jimmy Swaggart, and then went to church every Sunday morning and evening. I also went to church every Wednesday night, whether it was snowing, raining or sunny. I went to prayer meetings at different homes once, twice and sometimes three times a week.

But I was getting sick of it all! There had to be something more to life than God, God, God, and more God! I was bound in Christianity and I was also fed up with Christianity. I didn't even know myself anymore. All I did was go to work, go to church, go to prayer meetings and go to bed, alone. Glimpses of my old life kept intruding. I felt like getting stoned and just lying back with no cares, no hurts, no problems and no Howard!

After work one evening, I knew full well what I was going to do. I took my daughter to a woman who lived just a few houses down from mine, to babysit for me. I went back home and bathed and dressed in my tight wranglers, boots and long earrings. I was going to find Mary Ann. I had lost myself somewhere during the transition from the old me to the new me. I thought I knew just where to find myself!

After leaving Elizabeth with our friends, I walked down the block in the other direction to another house, just another block away from my home. I went up to the door and knocked. The door opened. A man whom I knew stood there, looking at me wordlessly for a few moments. His hair was well past his shoulders, his beard scraggly, and his black tee shirt and baggy pants were both dirty. He looked like a drug dealer, which he was.

The man wasn't sure of how to take me standing at his door. He looked me up and down, saying nothing. I, in contrast, was very neat, clean and western to the bone. He knew me through Howard. I was the Jesus Christ freak. I knew he was hesitant about asking me to come in, because he and his friends were bagging marijuana, known as pot.

A second man emerged from the kitchen and didn't hesitate in saying, "She's okay." His friend then opened the door, and I went into the kitchen, where a third man sat, whom I knew very well.

The men greeted me with big hugs. It felt so good to be around people I really liked. It was hard for me to understand why I was more comfortable with these men rather than so many Christians in church? I could be myself with these men. I didn't have to prove anything to anyone.

Some time back when I was a part of their lives, I remembered cooking for Howard and two of these men. We ate a pork pot roast, literally stuffed with marijuana seeds, stems and the very best pot money could buy.

It had been really funny to watch Howard and his friends devour the roast. The more they ate, the hungrier they got. It was like watching three pigs eating. They ate so fast that they didn't even look up to talk. They ate until they were stuffed with their bellies hanging over their jeans. We all laughed till our sides hurt. They left with enough food stored up in their bellies for the winter.

Now sitting at the kitchen table with three of the same men, I could not get my mind off Howard. He had introduced me to these men. One had been his friend for several years. I felt accepted from the start by all of them. In fact, all of Howard's friends accepted me.

I suppose I gained their trust because I never told their business to anyone.

So here I am fitting in their territory. They offered me something to drink. I declined. "No thanks. I just came for the company," I said. We talked as they continued to weigh and bag the marijuana. Then someone lit a joint, a marijuana cigarette, and passed it to me. I thought, what the hell, and took it. It was very good dope. I was stoned after only inhaling three hits or puffs.

I sat there for a little while, not moving, I was in a dead trance. It had been so long since I had smoked pot that the first puff took me out of reality. The other two hits put my mind at rest. I found myself thinking about God, but I was quick in forcing myself to stop thinking about God. It had been months since I had smoked marijuana. I had even stopped smoking cigarettes a couple of months before. I could only inhale a little at a time because it choked me. I was so high I could hardly raise my hand to take another hit.

Sitting in a daze, the marijuana was not giving me the high I wanted, which was to forget about Howard, at least temporarily. I sat there like a mummy blocking out their conversation while I was thinking about Howard. I was trying to muster up hate for him. If I hated him, I wouldn't hurt over loving him. His longtime buddy was sitting next to me. I managed, with a lot of effort to turn my head toward him. There was nothing about him that appealed to me. He looked unclean, he was unclean, and his clothes were dirty and wrinkled. But marijuana affects people in different ways. Everything can be funny, and usually is but for me there was dead silence.

Even though I was not attracted to Howard's close friend, I must have stared at him until he became aware of it. He turned his head toward me and I leaned forward until I felt the touch of his lips on mine. For a few moments, I pretended it was Howard's mouth.

The touch of a man desiring me in a way fed my hunger, my need for a man to hold me. I felt no passion, he was not Howard and no pretending was going to make him Howard. Yet I was driven with the need for a man's attention. We kissed for several minutes.

The other men had stopped their bagging marijuana. I'm sure we all looked like cement statues trying to figure out what we were doing.

I'm sure our actions were quite a show for them. I'll have to say one thing. The man knew how to kiss. From too much experience, and many years, I had learned how to pretend, how to make a man think he was the best, at everything! But pretending he was Howard was not possible. He was much smaller in frame, he was too short, and his beard was not anything like Howard's felt on my cheek. His kiss, although very good, was not like Howard's kiss. As we continued to kiss, he drew me close to his chest, and I accepted his passion for another few minutes. Then I came to my senses and I was again aware of where I was and what I was doing.

I stopped kissing him and pulled out of his arms. He looked at me and said, "What was that all about?" With a dull smile I said, "Nothing. I want to hurt Howard. I want to hate him." Just a simple sentence explained it all. He smiled at me and I saw compassion on his face. "Why don't you take him back, as much as you love that bastard? Why don't you go find him? I know where he is," he told me.

"I really love Jesus and I don't want to lose Him. I can't and I don't want to go back to this kind of life." I explained. I hadn't succeeded in pushing Howard out of my heart and I hadn't and didn't want to push Jesus out either. I knew I should leave. But I didn't feel like I had the strength.

After sitting in a daze for a little while longer, I was able to stand up and walk toward the living room. All three men followed me. Somehow we began a conversation about Jesus. I felt like a real hypocrite. Here I was stoned to the gills, telling what God had done for me. I could hardly stand to say His name, I felt so guilty. They listened, and somehow my love for Christ over powered my pain for Howard. It had become my intention to take one of these men to my bed. I was going to shut out God, just for one night, why in the hell couldn't I?

One of the men went back into the kitchen. Shortly afterward, he returned to the living room with five dogs. It was as though Satan himself had entered, in the form of dogs. I sat straight up from the chair I was sitting in and pushed myself to my feet and immediately headed for the door. Scripture raced into my mind. (*Beware of dogs, beware of evil workers, beware of the concision. Philippians 3:2*) (But it is happened unto them according to the true proverb, The dog is turned to his own vomit again; and the sow that was washed to her wallowing in the mire. 2Peter 2:22) I stopped and turned. I know the dogs would have attacked me if told to. I went up to each man and put my arms around him. I told each man that I loved him, and Jesus loved him. Each of us held one another for just a moment. No rejection was shown toward me. Each man held me a few moments like brothers, not enemies. I walked back to the door, turned again, knowing I would never return and smiled. I walked down the street back to my little house wondering why it is so easy for them to accept me yet the Christians for the most part seemed to reject me.

I entered my home feeling very disgusted with myself. I began to ask for forgiveness. Right then, if I had died, I was not sure Jesus would take me into His kingdom. I prayed for the three men just as I prayed for myself. They treated me right. They actually liked me. I did have love for them. I also realized that without Jesus they would go to hell. I still had the drugs in me. It may have been more than marijuana I took into my lungs, but this didn't keep me from praying. I was truly so sorry for going back into my yesterdays trying to gain some kind of joy for my today.

I dressed for bed and crawled into empty arms, no one was there to hold and comfort me. Praying, still praying, crying out to God, "Oh forgive me, forgive me" was my continuous prayer.

The phone rang. "Do you want to see me?" Howard's familiar voice said. "Do you want me to come over?" Howard asked. "No! No!" I screamed into the phone, "Leave me alone! Leave me alone!" I then slammed the phone down. "Please God. Please kill my love for him. Oh God, God, help me!"

I was ashamed, I was sorry, and I hurt. I was very much still in love with Howard, but I wanted to be healed more than I wanted to fall into another trap of Satan. Lying there a few moments, my thoughts going back to my relationship with Jesus Christ, peace over took me and I heard His still, wonderful voice, *"I love you little one, I'm here and remember,"*.....I DO FORGIVE.

Matthew 6:9-14

9   *After this manner therefore pray ye: Our Father which art in heaven, Hallowed be thy name.*

10 *Thy kingdom come. Thy will be done in earth, as it is in heaven.*

11 *Give us this day our daily bread.*

12 *And forgive us our debts, as we forgive our debtors.*

13 *And lead us not into temptation, but deliver us from evil: For thine is the kingdom, and the power, and the glory, for ever. Amen.*

14 *For if ye forgive men their trespasses, your heavenly Father will also forgive you:*

I DO FORGIVE

What are you doing down there under that rock?
What are you doing covered up in heartache and sorrow?
Are you the one who just called My name?
Why for your misery, am I to blame?
It was not I who led you astray.
I did not tell you to look back, the other way!
What are you doing, all bound in sin?
Well, give Me your hand, and I'll lift you out again!
Now listen my child, to what I say.
You are to abide and keep my commandments each and every day.
I'm not the one who causes your tears.
I'm not the one who gives you fear.
Come on and cuddle up to Me, really close.
I'll once again tell you what you need to know.
Stay in the body, which is My word.
Sit still my child, you need not squirm.
*I love you, I will protect you, and my child,......***I DO FORGIVE**.

Chapter 7:
FORGIVE ME

～

Reading the words of God, I hungrily searched for even a greater depth of wisdom and understanding. I didn't pass over the scriptures asking God to search my heart and try my reins (Psalms 26:2 Examine me, O LORD, and prove me; try my reins [essential organ; mind] and my heart.) I wanted to be nothing short of the woman God wanted me to be. I was willing to learn and even suffer to know my Creator to the height of my ability and the height that God would allow me to reach.

But there was much hate stored up inside of me. I had pride as high as a mountain. I was pretty sold on myself. I knew how to get what I wanted. I was not afraid of anyone or anything. My temper was such that I had even backed men up when in a rage.

I was capable of doing anything. Anything was usually wrong. If I set my mind to do something, there was little or no thought of the consequences. I satisfied my ego at the cost of others' sorrow. I was totally and completely rebellious to anyone who got in my way or tried to reason with me. I was the controller, not the controlled. As a whole, I didn't like women or men.

Therefore, I used either one to get what I wanted. The hate inside of me controlled me. I could hate someone to death. For some thirty-five years, I hated hundreds of people. I packed hate down inside of me, always making room for more.

I was beginning to realize as I continued to read the Bible that I had a serious problem. It would be hard for me to release, to give all the hate I carried to God. I didn't know how for one thing. I knew hate would stunt my growth with God. I also knew, as He had *forgiven me of much*, He told me to ***forgive everyone of much***. I was full of hate and it was stopping me from going any further in the relationship I wanted with God. I searched my mind, bringing back the past, my youth.

I went back to when hate was birthed within me. I can't really remember just when it started. It seemed to have always been a part of me. I pulled out all the memories which brought the hate to a bubbling boil within my heart.

I think my first remembering of hate was for my sisters. From then it grew, until it included all my family, then a whole town.

When I married the first time, at the age of seventeen, I remembered well when we moved from our hometown. As I looked back to the town filled with all the years of hurt, hate and sorrow, I said "To hell with all of you." I had made it. I was getting out. I was never coming back. It didn't bother me that I was taking the hate with me. I wanted to keep it. It had been with me all my life and I was going to hold on to it.

I didn't go back home for a long time. The only reason I did go back was to visit my parents. I would duck when going through town. I never wanted to see anyone, or let anyone see me. For years I ducked anyone from Ralls, Texas. For years the hate grew in my heart.

Now that God was the head of my life, I could no longer put on the bottom, hide, overlook, over read what Christ, through His word, kept putting before my eyes. *Love thy neighbor, pray for your enemies, do good to them that persecute you, forgive seventy times seven, don't judge lest you be judged, and how can your Father forgive you, if you don't or won't forgive.

The Bible didn't say anything about who was right or wrong. It said to forgive. For months I had pushed the commandment to love your neighbor as yourself to the bottom of the list of things to do.

God was blessing me more than I could ever put on paper. He was with me daily teaching me about others. I had fought within myself the word, forgive. How do you forgive a whole town, and your family?

I really didn't know how to start to forgive. I spent many hours reading, searching, praying, and seeking God for guidance. He was true to His words. *When you seek, you shall find, when you ask, you shall receive, and when you knock the door is open unto you.

God was Lord of my life and pleasing Him was my goal. I became aware that I wanted to forgive. I really wanted to forgive anyone and everyone I hated. There is no way to be pure in Christ if you are unwilling to forgive.

As I began to really look back into the years, I discovered a lot of the hate was my own doing. I had blamed everyone else for what I had been. It didn't matter to me if a person was right about what they said or did. If they hurt me, then I would hate them. Isn't it amazing how hate comes so easily into a person's heart?

I talked to God about my innermost feelings, although He already knew me and was well aware of my feelings and hurts. I knew I had to confide in Him and trust Him. I had to admit my failings. I had to admit the sin of hate and pray for the death of hate to my soul.

I had taken the first step. I wanted to forgive. It no longer mattered to me who was deserving of my forgiveness, or what had happened to cause such hate in the first place. It was now a priority to obey God. This is what mattered to me.

I asked God to give me His kind of love for people, explaining to God that I didn't know how to forgive, and I didn't know how to love. I also asked God to release the many years of stored up hate rooted in my heart. I put my trust in Him and gave myself up to Christ. I was willing to learn. It was now my desire to love my enemies. He would have to help me; I was not capable on my own to forgive.

The second step I took was to begin praying for people I hated. I prayed for their welfare. Even if I never saw anyone from my hometown again, I prayed that they would forgive me. I called every person by name. People whose names I couldn't remember, I told Jesus where they lived, or where they worked, even going into detail of the day and reason hate was birthed within me.

I was no longer focused on my hate. I was focused on Jesus' love. One by one, day by day, I prayed. I prayed for their salvation, for forgiveness, for their healing and every other thing I could think of.

My prayers grew with more depth of real concern for their lives. I prayed for them as though they were my best friends and each and every one mattered. At first it was very difficult for me. I would cry as the memories would take hold in my mind and the reasons for the hate would come forth. The pain would stab my heart, but I was learning how to let God turn hate to forgiveness and then love.

God didn't make it easy for me. I had to make myself do what I knew He asked of me. I made myself have good thoughts, I made myself forgive, I made myself pray. Why was I doing all of this? I have a simple answer, because God told me to.

At times I would see someone from my family, or hometown, in a store, even at the church I attended. I no longer ran in the opposite direction and the hurt no longer festered in me. I began speaking to them, while asking God to give me the strength to do so.

I no longer cared what anyone talked about, thinking it was probably me and wasn't good. I would talk to them with love and ease as I would make myself hold my head up and smile because it was my Father I wanted to please. It took time for me to release all the hurt, memories, pain, and hate. But, it did come about.

I had to change. I would not be able to grow and become the person I knew God wanted me to be without obeying to the very best of my ability. The Holy Spirit within me guided me through each step. It was my place to obey. It was God's place to rehabilitate or change my heart of hate to a heart of love. I believed the greatest gift we can accept from Christ is His love, His salvation.

Realizing the desire of my heart was to help others, I knew a lot of people who didn't have a clue who Jesus really is. After fasting and many hours of prayer, alone with God, a healing took place.

As time passed, I began to feel the love of Jesus Christ. My heart was sincere. I learned of the sorrows and pain that many of the people from my past were going through. I prayed for God to show His love and power in their lives. I prayed for their salvation. I was actually beginning to love. It was one of the most fulfilling moments of my time with Christ when I realized I no longer hated.

I felt clean inside. The heaviness was gone, and with it went the hurt and pain. I felt like going to the church in my hometown that I vaguely remember, and stand before the crowd and say, "I forgive, please forgive me!"

I no longer hated, blamed, nor wished any harm to come to any of them. I was sure it would have meant very little to most of the people, because they wouldn't have known what I had felt and carried around inside me for years. It had caused me to spend the greater days of my youth in a living hell, Satan's hell on earth.

I just wanted to tell them, "I love you, each and every one of you. I care about your sorrows because Jesus Christ loves and cares. Let me tell you about the peace, the joy. Let me tell you about a living God. He is alive and He is Lord!" This wasn't to be, but the release was so great for me that I wanted to share it with the world.

There were other things I began to realize about myself, other faults that I was now ready to face.

God sure had a lot of cleaning up to do with me. I had a temper, a bad temper, pride, jealousy, stubbornness and an ego. Just to name a few of many problems about me. I also became aware of a lot of things that I hadn't considered sin, the drugs, alcohol, pills, men, lies, cheating and theft had been the real sins, not something as subtle as hate, judgment, gossip and pride.

I had overlooked the subtle sins until I really searched my heart, and then I was willing for God to search my heart. I had to overcome the old self. I had a very long way to go, but I was willing and I had asked God to search my heart, to try me, to test me. I asked Him to remove all that was not of Him. I really didn't understand what I was asking. The one thing I knew for sure was that I wanted Him to be pleased with me. My deepest desire was to know Him, to appreciate His sufferings and His love for me.

The tongue is the vilest weapon we have. Satan uses it more than we are able to realize. We thrive on gossip and so often we throw a person to the wolves by supposedly helping the truth along instead of holding our tongues and stopping it, whether it is truth or lie.

I hate gossip. I hate to hear even the truth, when it is delivered by a Christian person who has forgotten all God has forgiven them. We often justify what we do by thinking we are pure enough to talk about the sins of others.

There is an area that brings sorrow to my heart. I have been a part of a conversation when someone I knew had ugly things still in their closet and would crucify another person. I know I am guilty of the same. Hopefully God will continue to correct me when I am at fault.

Are we to judge another person's sin and sorrow? When we judge, we are judging God's work. We are telling Him He didn't do it right because we can't see the results of the heart. I stay in prayer to God for help with holding my tongue.

God has forgiven me for just about every sin known to man. My daily prayer is that He will bring to my remembrance, as needed, what I was. It helps me today to know who He has made me into. It helps me to keep from judging. It is also a daily reminder that He has.....**FORGIVEN ME**.

*Matthew 18:21-22
Then came Peter to him, and said, Lord, how oft shall my brother sin against me, and I forgive him? till seven times? Jesus saith unto him, *I say not unto thee, Until seven times: but, Until seventy times seven.*

*Matthew 7:7-8
Ask, and it shall be given you; seek, and ye shall find; knock, and it shall be opened unto you: For every one that asketh receiveth; and he that seeketh findeth; and to him that knocketh it shall be opened.

Psalms 139:23-24
Search me, O God, and know my heart: try me, and know my thoughts: And see if there be any wicked way in me, and lead me in the way everlasting.

Matthew 6:14-15
For if ye forgive men their trespasses, your heavenly Father will also forgive you: But if ye forgive not men their trespasses, neither will your Father forgive your trespasses.

Proverbs 11:13
A talebearer revealeth secrets: but he that is of a faithful spirit concealeth the matter.

FORGIVE ME

Father, forgive me when I rebel.
When I refuse You, rebuke You,
When I cast You out.
Forgive me when I strike out on my own.
When I pat myself on the back for the things You have done!
Forgive me when it's self I edify,
When in pride I forget who's by my side.
Forgive me when I think my wisdom is great,
When it's through You, not me, knowledge is made.
Forgive me when I don't take the time,
To humble myself, my own glory I'm trying to find.
Forgive me, my Father, when I'm running ahead.
When it's my own ego, and not Your children that I've fed.
Forgive me Father, when others I judge.
Knowing full well, You pulled me out of the pits of hell.
Forgive me Father when I do not listen,
For all that You do, I seek a reason.
Forgive me when I do not yield,
And to others, 'LOVE' I do not give.
Forgive me for stubbornness.
Forgive me when I kill with words of harshness.
Forgive me, forgive me Father.
When I dwell within not You, but self.
Forgive me Father, when I've stumbled and failed.....**FORGIVE ME.**

Chapter 8:
FATHER

~

It was wonderful waking up this morning. Dressing for work, I chose my clothes with much care. I felt like a new person. I felt like a woman. After so many months of tribulation, God had dried my tears and filled me with His joy. My cup was full and running over.

My world hadn't changed, I still had the same problems, the burdens, the loneliness, the financial stress and the same job that I had the day before and Howard was still making almost nightly visits. Only this morning, I woke up in the protective arms of God. I knew He was giving me a rest in Him. I was going to enjoy every precious minute right down to the last second of it. I didn't let myself start to worry how long it was going to last. I knew my heavenly Father had opened a door. He knew the heartache was more than I could stand. Therefore God, as He said He would, rescued me.

I bathed, washed, dried and curled my hair. I put on just a touch of cologne. I chose to wear an expensive pantsuit with a suede vest, choosing my jewelry with as much care as I had chosen my clothes. I sang as I dressed and laughed at nothing. It was the most wonderful feeling in the world.

I listened to my favorite record with the song, "A Whole Lot of People Goin' Home," sung by John and Ruth Merrell. I played with my little girl, Elizabeth, throwing her on the bed and then smothering her with kisses. I loved the whole world and I wanted to tell everyone how wonderful and mighty God really is. I wanted to share and help someone understand, someone burdened with sorrow. All the months of hurting had been worth this precious time I was now having with God.

After I had finished dressing, I checked once again in the mirror to see that everything was in place. I then knelt beside my bed and talked to my Father. I couldn't stop the tears of joy as they ran down my face. To say thank you wasn't enough for how I felt. I sang Him a song that came to me as I told Him of my love for Him. I don't have a voice for singing, but somehow I felt He enjoyed my praise. Words of peace, joy, love, honor, and understanding came to my mind so easily. I lifted my hands, as I knelt with my eyes opened to the heavens and worshiped Jesus Christ.

I don't know how long I knelt there, but I didn't get up until I knew that God knew how much I loved Him. Of course God knows our hearts, but the love I had for Him was something I don't think I had ever experienced before. It was as though I was before His throne, really worshiping Him. It is a love for Him that I am unable to express.

I let my daughter out at her school with a big hug and kisses. After seeing me with so many tears and a face full of pain, she was indeed happy to see her mother smile, and even laugh. I drove to work singing in my prayer language. I remember so well how the words flowed from my heart with such ease. I had a small taste of what it would be like in heaven, praising our Lord. I sure was looking forward to it.

I was a little late to work that day, something that was rare for me. I'm usually an on-time person, even sometimes as much as thirty minutes to an hour too early!

I bounced into the office with a big smile and even bigger hello to everyone. It wasn't hard to see that the others didn't feel as I did, but I was determined not to let anyone pull me down. It's so true that misery loves company. People can actually hate you because you're happy.

I was not getting use to the dislike and even the hate that was expressed to me. It hurt me. But I was learning to overcome the hurt by releasing it to God. I had learned to put on the whole armor of God, (*Ephesians 6:11-17) and I kept my eyes on Him. Today, I was not concerned how man felt about me.

I knew that more than three fourths of the 10 employees in the office didn't know Christ, and one person denied Him completely.

I got a cup of coffee, gathered the accounts receivable and began my work. I worked with great efficiency and all was good. I felt like a queen and everything I did came out next to perfect. Especially since I usually had to make myself go to work and some of the people never tired of teasing or making fun of me, I was the *Holy Roller*. The atmosphere was full of hate and jealously. While working, I let my mind bring up the past. There had been two events which had taken place within the last months that I allowed myself to think about. They came fresh into my mind.

In obeying God, much sorrow had followed. It seemed that everything that I said I wouldn't do were the things God had me to do. I was going to a church that I really didn't want to go to. I told God I wouldn't go to this church. He didn't pay any attention to me.

In the beginning of my walk with Jesus, I had no idea of where to go to church. After God spoke to me, I went to my parents, and my sister then my friend Kitti. I was lost as where to go. At this time God led me to a church that I, with no one knowing, sat in the little prayer room day after day, reading the Bible, it was dimly lit with such peace.

My parents had listened to me, but they did not believe that God had really come to me in a cloud and spoken to me. I think they thought I had totally lost my mind. I went to my sister's house. Her reaction was to ask me about things in the Bible. I knew nothing, absolutely nothing at the time about the Bible.

Then I had gone to Kitti's house. She was extremely happy for me, and she believed me, yet she didn't tell me what I needed to do from there.

I was running to nowhere, driving for miles wondering what to do. What does a person do when God calls you by your name, and tells you it's time–that you're going to the mountain top with Him. Do I go home and pack a bag? I didn't know where to find a ladder to heaven. It seemed no one else knew either.

There had to be more to God than just reading the Bible and going to church. I felt a tug at my whole being and as of yet, no one had been able to tell me anything. I don't think anyone understood what was going on with me. I didn't know either.

After three days of searching for something, I looked really bad.

I hadn't bathed. I hadn't eaten, nor had I slept. I was fasting and didn't even know there was such a thing as fasting. I looked like I had been on a month's drunk. I was completely worn down, just driving around, lost as to what to do. I had gone to the only places I could think of, searching for answers, no one had helped me.

All that was left for me to do was pray. I didn't even know how to pray. It was the last thing I thought might help, however, I prayed. I don't know how much time passed in just driving. I couldn't remember where even one church was, not even one. It didn't matter to me what kind of church I went to. I thought God was in every church and I'd be able to find Him in one. I continued to drive for what seemed to be hours. I prayed, asking God to help me. "Tell me where to go," I whispered.

I didn't know He was now within me. I only knew I had to find Him somewhere. Then I remembered seeing a big church, a really big church just off the loop that wrapped around the city of Lubbock, Texas. I headed in that direction and parked in their parking lot. It was so big. I didn't want to go in, but I felt like God led me there. I would go in and He would be in some room waiting for me. I looked in the little rear view mirror and I was indeed a sight to see. I knew I didn't smell good either.

I got out of my beat-up old car and looked for the doors into the building. I was determined to find God. I wanted someone to hold me and soothe away the confusion. I needed love and understanding as never before.

Walking up to the large doors, I was talking to God with all my heart. I was crying, and I was very afraid. I pulled back one of the large doors and went into the building. I walked down one of the hallways, not having a clue as to where I was going. I walked past several doors. I opened a door and went in. There were several people standing around talking. A young lady sat behind a desk. I sat down in a chair.

I must have looked like a street person who had stumbled into this church by accident. I was weak, crying silent tears, scared, very tired, and most of all, very alone. Needless to say, all eyes were fixed on me. I told the young girl that I had to talk to someone. I also told her not to put me with someone who didn't have time for me. I didn't want someone who would not stay with me until I knew how to find God.

She got up from her desk and went to a very young man standing on the opposite side of the room. I supposed he was a preacher. I didn't know, and to this day I don't know who he was. He walked up to me and asked me to follow him into a very nice office. There were many things on his wall that looked impressive. There were certificates of some kind. I really wasn't interested in them. His suit was expensive, as was everything on his desk and in his office. I felt very out of place. I wanted to run. His look at me made me feel dirty. It was obvious he was disgusted.

I don't know why I didn't leave. I suppose I was too tired to get up and leave. He waited for me to speak, leaning back in his fancy, leather chair and just looked at me.

I began to tell him everything. He showed little patience. I was talking very fast trying to get in all the things that had taken place from the day I drove away from the farm house to take my life. I told him about God calling my name. I could tell he didn't believe me. He didn't say he didn't believe me, but his grin, or smirk, told me he didn't. I told him about my past, in detail. God had told me to be honest and I was obeying Him.

You would think he would have understood where I was coming from, but he didn't. His attitude and actions showed me his true feelings. However, he did listen to me. For nearly two hours, I poured my heart out and my life out to him. Finally, I finished. I felt like hell. There was no love, no comfort, no compassion, no understanding, no approval, no nothing! I felt like I had just told a stranger a dirty story.

He asked me a few questions about the Bible. I was lost. I had no answers. He then began to explain to me why Jesus was baptized. I didn't understand a thing he was saying. Then he started telling me about a man named Paul. Who was Paul? I thought. I didn't come here to hear about Paul. I came to find out how to find God.

I listened as my insides began to roll with anger. He made absolutely no sense to me. He was so smug. I finally had enough! I was sick inside. I got out of the chair, leaned over his desk and got into his face. "I don't know why God brought me here. You can't help me. You don't understand any more than I do what is going on" were the angry words I spoke.

He had told me he had an appointment and he was going to have to leave. "You keep your appointment, and you don't have to worry about me coming back!" I all but screamed at him.

By now his chair was backed up to the wall as far as he could push it. He had this horrible grin on his face. I don't know if it was hate or fear. But now I didn't care. I walked out of his office. Even the secretary was afraid of me. I stomped down the hall and went through the big doors. Going to my car, I felt totally alone. I got into my car and looked up into the heavens. "I don't know why You sent me here, but I won't be back." I cried to God.

Having nowhere else to go, I went back to the farm house. Howard had believed everything I told him, yet because his wife had accepted Christ either before or during their marriage, and tried to get him to, he wanted nothing to do with God.

A few days later, I was washing dishes, standing in front of the sink, looking at the sky. I realized it was the same kind of day that it had been when God spoke to me in the form of a cloud. My thoughts raced back to that day, it had only been three days before this. In such a short amount of time, I felt totally alone. I began to cry. I had fallen to the floor on my knees and hands. I began pounding the floor with my fist.

Howard was at work. He didn't know what to do with me. He was staying high on drugs all the time. He was in his own world. Talking to him was impossible.

"If you are real, if it really happened, if you are up there, Jesus, please, please, help me. Please come into my life and forgive me for all my sins. I'll do anything you want me to do." This is the first time I can remember crying out to Jesus, and not God. I talked to Jesus for some time, lying there on the floor. I had yielded my all to Jesus Christ.

No one I had run to during these first three days had any idea of what to do with me. No one understood what my problem was.

God had spoken my name and come to me. I was trying to find Him. The moment I cried out the name of Jesus, my destiny in His calling began.

The first reason I didn't want to go to the church God led me to was because of the young minister. He didn't realize that although God had come to me and spoken to me, I had not asked for Christ and I had not asked for forgiveness. I received salvation because I cried out to Jesus. During the years to come, I would realize that God shows Himself to many people, in ways too grand for me to express, yet He is rejected and even denied.

The second reason I didn't want to return to this church was because Howard's ex-wife and their three sons went there. She ended up divorcing him and I thought it was because of me, and I'm sure a lot of women before me. It was hard to believe that now I had a conscience and was aware of another person's pain. I didn't want to cause her any more pain.

Despite all my misgivings, Jesus Christ was telling me to go to this church. I didn't obey Him until after three or four months had passed. Before I went to church for the first time, I called and made an appointment with one of the key pastors. I went to his office, having gone through the same big doors that I told God I would never enter again. God had told me to be honest, so I was.

I told this pastor the truth about my life, all my sins, and now I believed I was supposed to go to church at the same place Howard's ex-wife attended.

We prayed and not once did he judge me. I didn't feel out of place. Thank God, because this man walked with God. He was overjoyed a sinner had found Christ and had yielded her life to Him. The pastor not only prayed for Howard's ex-wife and his boys, he prayed for Howard and his salvation.

I learned from the prayers of this man and have put into practice, to this day, what I had learned. He prayed for God's will. He said he could not tell me what to do. Only God could, but he did understand why I needed help in making my final decision to obey Christ and go where He told me to. After a couple of weeks, I took the hand of my little girl and went to this church.

I thought these two reasons were enough as to why I didn't want to go to this church. But there were more reasons to come.

I went to church telling the truth about myself. I thought people would be so grateful that a sinner had found Christ and was going to church and trying to let go of the past. I wore my wranglers, and my leather jacket with the chains and jewelry which clearly showed that I was a biker's woman.

In 1979, the church people were not ready for this transformation. God had told me to be honest, so I was. When I was asked about something, no matter what it was, I told the truth. This was a mistake. Sometimes, when I had been hurt by ugly words, I rebelled by dressing as a biker as much as possible and sitting in the front, right in front of everyone.

I was still strong enough to fight back at this time of my baby relationship, feeding on the milk of the word, learning about Jesus Christ, (*1Corinthians 3:2) But my desires were changing, and one of the deepest things I wanted to become was a *lady*. I was in my late thirties at that time and had never felt like a *lady*. It was not something I felt to impress others. It was a desire to be a woman in Christ, a *lady* with high integrity.

Before Jesus Christ, I was a rebel. No one and no circumstances were going to stomp me into the ground. Now, Christian people were not going to defeat me either. I would do whatever I learned. I would apply wisdom and knowledge to my way of living.

It became easy for me to know the church goers from the Christians. The pews were full of people who judge, persecute, hate, and cast you out of their approved right for you to be called a Christian. There were cliques.

I believe that women are more extreme in these areas than men. We are continually crying out for approval, acceptance and security. Men seem to have the need to know they are respected, especially by the women who love them. They need sexual contact, women need affection.

At any rate, I was determined to go to church. I didn't want to go to this church, but I did want to obey Christ. So here I was, dealing with it.

Shortly after I began going to this church, I attended a prayer meeting. I'm not sure how it came about, but I gave my testimony. Some of the women, too many, couldn't get past the ugliness. I don't know if I birthed pain back into their memories of something they may have had to go through.

In 1979, women like me were not telling the truth about themselves. I don't believe there were very many street lifestyle people like me in the churches. I told the truth, way too much in detail, I'm sure. Several of the women put no effort into hiding their disgust in me. I was so used to rejection that I returned their disgust with my own judgment of their playing like Christians.

The only thing I knew for sure at this time in my life is that we are supposed to treat people like we want to be treated. The men for the most part listened, showing no expression. I was the kind of woman who had broken up some of their homes. The hate I felt and saw was real.

There were also, in fewer numbers, men and women, whose hearts belonged to Jesus Christ. It was these people who forgave me and encouraged me to continue this journey I was on. Their hugs were real. They were able to get past the person I had been, and in major ways, still was, to the person God was creating. I left that meeting feeling great.

It was the love and compassion shown to me by a few that kept me going. I really didn't care about the eyes of judgment and hate. While sharing my testimony, I had been so controlled by the Holy Spirit that time seemed to stand still. Everything flowed. To have felt such closeness to God meant more to me than anything anyone could say or show in disgust. I drove home feeling very close to God. I was very close to God.

I didn't know why God had chosen me. I was too dumb to realize or understand this new life I was in. I thought maybe because I would obey His directions, He chose me to tell the truth because He wanted to save many others like me. I told my testimony every where I could. I was so amazed to find that God was real, really real!

My name got to the head of the church through word of mouth. I was beginning to be recognized.

The church, which had more than five thousand members, had two services on Sunday. I didn't know anyone, other than a very few people that I had met at prayer meetings, Bible study meetings, or Sunday school classes. No one ever came to my little house. I had only one woman who took me under her wing, Grace. She became my Mother Superior. She was the shoulder I cried on. She was the one who read scripture to me and helped me to know what step to take, step after step.

It was Sunday morning. I looked forward to going to church. I was learning at a high rate of speed, I was knocking, looking and Christ had opened the door for me to find Him. (*Revelation 3:20) It was such a joy to have a time of peace this day.

Time passed, but not enough for people to forget that Sunday morning when I went before the church and apologized to Howard's wife and three sons. I also apologized to the congregation (EAGLE; Chapter 5). It was now another Sunday morning. I awoke knowing as before, something was going to happen. I didn't look forward to it. God knew I would not refuse Him, no matter what He asked of me. God also knew my heart and I wanted no more rejection. Somehow I knew rejection was to come.

Dressing for church I prayed, man did I ever pray! I went to Sunday School then to church as I did every Sunday. Sitting down, I began to pray, "Okay God, I'll do what you want, but please go before me and clear the way." Elizabeth was not sitting with me as she normally would be. She was still in her Sunday School class. I was comforted by knowing that she was not supposed to be next to me.

Becoming aware, quickly, with fast intense pounding around my heart, I knew the Holy Spirit was getting my full attention. The service had just begun, announcements were being made. I didn't hear a word being said. Asking God, "What do You want?" My mind spun back into remembering the day I apologized for adultery to the whole church as well as to the wife and children of the man I had taken from them. I didn't want to obey. I wanted to say, "No!" God knew I wanted to say "No." He also knew that I wouldn't refuse Him. The pounding became more relaxed. I appealed to His gracious heart. "Father, I'm afraid. I don't want to suffer hurt anymore. I love You and if good is going to come out of what You want of me, I will do it. I yield myself to Your will." His Spirit then came forth in full force and once again I heard my own heart beat.

People went to the prayer rail before the service instead of afterward. I walked to the front looking for the pastor who had prayed and stood beside me before. I looked on the platform, and there he was. The Holy Spirit stopped me. It was not this pastor I was to go to. Looking at the people waiting to minister, I approached a man I had not ever noticed before. I knelt in front of him as he was kneeling at the altar rail himself in prayer. I can't explain how I knew it was this man I was to go to, but I knew he was the right person. He smiled at me and looked directly at me. I began to explain to him that God was going to do something. I didn't know what that something was, but it was about to take place. Then I did something I had never done before. I took his hand and placed it upon my heart. The Holy Spirit was still identifying Himself to me with aggressive pounding. The man could feel the pounding inside of me. He knew I was telling him the truth. He prayed for me and with me, his prayers giving God permission to take full control of what He wanted to do. He prayed that I would be led by Him only, also that I would know what He wanted before acting on impulse. He told me not to worry and to let the Holy Spirit guide me, assuring me that God would direct me. I arose and started back to my seat. I couldn't find it. There was not one place for me to sit. I became aware that everyone else was sitting down.

"Oh God, I cried within, don't fail me!" I wanted to simply sit down, anywhere. Walking toward the back of the church, I saw many faces turned toward me and people looking at me. When I reached the back of the church, I leaned on a column feeling weak. I thought I was going to faint. Fear gripped me, I could hear the voice of the man speaking, but didn't have any knowledge what he was saying. I cried out with my mind. "Father, Father, help me!" *"Step out in faith."* was the powerful voice I heard, not audible, quiet, very still, and very peaceful. Taking a deep breath, I took my first step in obedience. All fear left me and in this one step I became aware of nothing else but the direction of God. I no longer heard the voice of the pastor speaking. He was still talking, but I heard nothing. I walked halfway down the aisle when God touched me. Power that I had not ever experienced before fell upon me. I felt the strength of it. Now, God is indeed directing my feet. In a period of less than a second, God revealed to me what He was going to do. He also let me know where to go and who to go to. A great calm came over me. The man who had prayed with me was still standing on the platform. Another man also standing on the platform started toward me. I shook my head no to him. Looking into the eyes of the man who had prayed for me, I motioned him to come to me. By now I am standing directly in front of the pulpit. I wanted someone in authority to stand with me. All was quiet now, a pin drop quiet. The man came to me in front of the prayer rail. "I know what God is doing, and I know what to do," I said to him. "I want an elder to stand with me," I said to him. "I'll go," was his simple reply. Turning back toward the congregation my eyes ran up and down the pews looking for the person I knew God was going to heal. With the man standing by my side, I began walking up the isle slowly. I knew which seating area the person was in, but didn't at this point know who the person was. I walked down the aisle looking directly into the eyes of every person in this seating area. I knew I would know the right person. I had no doubt that God was directing me. About five or six rows from the front, I looked into the face of a man. This is the person who will receive a miracle healing from God. I stepped in front of the people sitting on the same pew. I kept saying "excuse me" until I reached the man who never took his eyes off me. I stopped in front of him. "Stand up, God has healed you," I said in a firm voice. He looked at me in amazement for a moment when I again said in a more stern voice, "stand up, stand up, you're healed." He jumped to his feet, raised his hands and began crying out to God, "Thank you, thank you Jesus." Together, we both came out into the isle. He had crutches in his hands. I had not seen them until now as he had them secured under the pew. I screamed with as loud a voice as I could, from my belly, "Stand, stand and praise God, you have seen Him do a miracle." Everyone jumped to their feet. Their voices ringing in praise like a mighty wind came forth. The man came close to me and told me that the church had been praying for his healing for over a year. I smiled at him and said, "God really loves you." He ran to the man who had stood by me like a body guard all through this, and grabbed him, hugging him with tears streaming down both their faces. I turned looking only toward the floor and walked back to almost the center of the church on the west side, slid to my seat and sat down. I didn't look up for a few minutes. I was praising God. It took several minutes for the church to get still again. I wanted no one to praise me for anything. I just wanted God to tell me He was pleased. A lady sitting next to me reached over and squeezed my hand and smiled. I said, "Thank you." That was all I could think of to say. I appreciated her smile of approval. It was really the smile and squeeze of God's approval. He just used her, as He had done with the young man several weeks back, to comfort me.

Sitting through the sermon, the old familiar loneliness and being separated came over me. Feelings of rejection, fear, of making a fool of myself, questioning if what just happened truly did happen. I was hit by demons. I wanted to run, but where? After the sermon was over, I sat where I was. I did not want to see the ugly looks I had seen when I apologized for adultery. One couple who normally would have spoken to me put out every effort to avoid me. It was obvious they didn't want anyone else to know that they knew me. This was all right by me. I was learning all about people. I didn't feel anything. Not even hurt at their rejection. I walked out of the church, when in my heart I wanted to run. Depression overcame me. I wanted Howard. He was the only person in the world at the time who really knew me. He would know that God had told me what to do. He also would know that no man could keep me from obeying. He would have held me. He would have comforted me. But, I had given him up for God. I couldn't let myself run to him. I had to keep my eyes on God and believe that He would take care of me.

The following Sunday, dressing for church was the hardest thing for me to do. By now I'm getting used to the feelings of doing the hardest things, in obedience, that I ever had to do. Everything at this point in my life was hard, with very little approval.

My little girl, Elizabeth and I sat down in our regular places. I saw many eyes looking at me, including all the preachers. At least those sitting or standing on the platform had their eyes on me. They all looked like Kings Row! No matter how big a church is, the preachers can spot who is there and who is not. They all knew I was there and all of them looked at me. I think there were at least five of them up front. I fought to hold back the tears. A few tears fell before I could stop them, but I gained self control, another tear did not fall. The church was filling up with people. The seats in front and back of my daughter and I were filling up. Elizabeth and I were sitting on a long pew, alone, no one sat on the same pew. Feeling like an outcast is not stating my true feelings. You would have thought that I had committed some horrid sin. I couldn't figure it out. Did I or did I not obey Christ?

I broke. Tears began streaming down my face. No matter how hard I tried, I couldn't stop the tears. I tried to wipe them away without anyone noticing. My daughter and I were still sitting alone, all through the service. All the pews around us were full. My daughter would look up at me at times and smile. I smiled back at her and kept my arm around her. She was all I had. Her love comforted me. I felt sick inside with all emotions of "why Lord, why?" My heart felt like it was tearing apart. Trying to keep eyes off me, I sat looking down only with my head up.

I smelt something. It was so strong that I thought someone had leaned toward me trying to get seated, from behind me. I gently looked, no one was there. Only the people already seated. I took the smell deep within my nostrils. I held onto it. What was it? I wanted all I could get. It was wonderful. It lingered a few more minutes, and then it left. Again, I looked around me trying to figure out where the smell came from. It was like a field of roses, a whole field of beautiful roses. I could smell all of them. "Oh Jesus, if it was You, please let me smell Your presence once again. I have to know if it is You." I said. Peace came over me and again the wonderful fragrance returned stronger than it had been before. It no longer mattered what anyone else thought of me. Jesus was sitting beside me and my little girl. My tears of pain turned to tears of joy. I felt so very blessed and loved. It was as if I had just entered into heaven. I looked up and a family sat down with us, on the same pew. "Thank You Jesus, thank You." I said in silence.

I sat with Elizabeth, my wonderful daughter through the rest of the sermon, only now Jesus was sitting with us. I could feel His presence. It was as though we were being held by the King. Jesus Christ, the King of all Kings was holding us through church. He stayed with us until the sermon was over. I didn't want to get up. I knew when I did He would leave. We were in the arms of God, it was so hard to stand up and leave Him. I knew He would not leave us, and I knew I had to get up and go. I also knew that Jesus Christ had Himself protected my daughter and me, and He was never going to let us go.

Driving home from church, my daughter and I were blessed with peace and a lot of joy. I so loved my little girl. I was just now beginning to know her. I was just now becoming a mother. All the rejection, hate, pain, fears had all been worth it. To have Jesus come right out of heaven and sit through church with you is something no one can explain, you would have to experience such supernatural power for yourself.

To this day I don't know what was wrong with the man God healed. But I heard he was a man of power and influence and his condition was worsening with time. It was slowly crippling him. I never asked any questions about him, but I did listen when someone talked about the miracle. Sometimes, no one knew it was me that God used for His miracle healing. I preferred this.

With my Mother Superior, Grace, we walked into the office of the pastor who had stood with me during the time I had apologized for adultery. We discussed a couple of things I wanted to understand when he said, "You were out of order." "What, what do you mean, how can God be out of order?" I asked. He explained that he was giving the benediction. I was not sure of what the heck he was talking about. I felt my insides turn to the very familiar pain of rejection. I had only been a Christian just about three months. I wasn't strong enough for this correction. I didn't understand why I had to suffer so much pain in following Jesus. No one had ever told me how much pain would follow overcoming, obedience and everything else, and I didn't understand. I left his office broken. Wasn't it important at all that a man had been healed? This didn't seem to be the most wonderful thing in the world. Instead, what was important was that I hadn't waited until he had finished the benediction. I didn't have a clue what this meant. Benediction was a word that I had never heard of before. I was too hurt to ask him what it meant. I sat in silence while he and Grace discussed the matter. Inside I hurt to bad too do anything but close out the voices I heard. I learned later that the man who stood with me was a very important man in the church. I could not have selected a more important man. I still don't know who he was, but I heard that he was heavily corrected for allowing me to be out of order. I didn't know I was out of order, I was trying to obey Jesus. I didn't know or understand what I had done wrong.

Getting drunk, smoking dope was all I wanted to do when I got home. I could not have screamed hard enough to stop the pain. Again, I turned to Jesus for comfort. All this Bible and Church was not anything I expected when I gave my heart to Him.

The following week I attended church. A young man came up to me when I was leaving the sanctuary. He shared with me that he had seen a light all around me during the whole time I was in church. He was sitting just a row or two back from my daughter and I. He also said he complained to Jesus for using a woman instead of a man to do His will. He then told me I was after God's own heart, like King David. I didn't know who King David was at the time, but he was right, I was after my Father's heart. Before I could get out the front door a woman came up to me and shared with me that she started to take my arm and sit me beside her when I was at the front, but God stopped her. She said she heard God say, *"She's obeying me."* The woman told me she knew the voice of God and obeyed Him.

Thank God she did, I still had enough carnal in me that I may have jumped her, trying to take up for myself. I really don't know what I would have done, but Jesus did, and He protected me. Other nice things were said to me. A person told me that God had told them I was His servant. Another person said she knew I was obeying God. Others said they felt that the preacher didn't yield to God. I didn't ever say a word against this man. I really didn't know who was right or wrong, I only knew God had shown over two thousand people just who He was. I do believe the preacher as well as I grew from these experiences. This man is special to me, he will always be.

Following these events, God gave me peace. He let me rest. I must say I needed to rest. During this time, I gained strength in Him. I had learned to enjoy my work and was looking forward to tomorrow. I loved my little girl Elizabeth. I would look at her and swell with love for her. I wanted her not to have to go through the life I had lived. It was good, feeling like a mother.

Howard called. I still loved him and he knew it. He told me he still loved me. I didn't say anything back to him. I would not allow myself to need him! Hanging up the phone I simply said..... **FATHER.**

Mark 16:17-18
And these signs shall follow them that believe; In my name shall they cast out devils; they shall speak with new tongues; They shall take up serpents; and if they drink any deadly thing, it shall not hurt them; they shall lay hands on the sick, and they shall recover.

ARMOR OF GOD
*Ephesians 6:11-17
11 Put on the whole armor of God, that ye may be able to stand against the wiles of the devils.
12 For we wrestle not against flesh and blood, but against principalities, against powers, against the rulers of the darkness of this world, against spiritual wickedness in high places.
13 Wherefore take unto you the whole armor of God, that ye may be able to withstand in the evil day, and having done all, to stand.
14 Stand therefore, having your loins girt about with truth, and having on the breastplate of righteousness;

15 And your feet shod with the preparation of the gospel of peace;

16 Above all, taking the shield of faith, wherewith ye shall be able to quench all the fiery darts of the wicked.

17 And take the helmet of salvation, and the sword of the Spirit, which is the word of God:

BABES IN DUE TIME WILL HUNGER FOR THE PURE MEAT OF THE WORD

*1Corinthians 3:2
I have fed you with milk, and not with meat: for hitherto ye were not able to *bear* it, neither yet now are ye able.

Hebrews 5:12-13

12 For when for the time ye ought to be teachers, ye have need that one teach you again which *be* the first principles of the oracles of God; and are become such as have need of **milk**, and not of strong meat.

13 For every one that useth milk *is* unskillfull in the word of righteousness: for he is a babe.

1Peter 2:2
As newborn babes, desire the sincere milk of the word that ye may grow thereby:

Revelation 3:20
Behold, I stand at the door, and knock: if any man hear my voice, and open the door, I will come in to him, and will sup with him, and he with me.

FATHER

Father, did You know Your work is simply superb.
Did I take the time to tell You, I'm glad You're King of the herd!
As I think of the valleys, where I have been,
I give You praise for the sorrow I felt within.
Did I take the time to tell You, that when You lifted me up,
I saw the smile upon Your face, I felt Your mighty love.
"PRAISE YOU, PRAISE YOU, GLORY TO YOUR NAME!"
I humble myself before You and say, "THANK YOU, THANK YOU
FATHER,
For all Your splendid ways!"
I felt the greatness of Your hand, as You gently lifted up my chin.
I felt the peace You promised, as You dried away my tears.
I heard the rustle of Your wings as You lifted Your mighty arm.
I smelt the presence of Your son, and then I heard You say,
*"COME STAND MY CHILD, THE VALLEYS I LET YOU GO
INTO SO YOU WOULD LEARN MY WAYS, BECAUSE YOU
WERE WILLING, BECAUSE YOU PASSED THE TEST,
YOU, MY DAUGHTER WILL ABIDE WITH ME FOR EVER
AND A DAY!".....FATHER.*

Chapter 9:
MESSAGE FROM GOD

~

It was a Wednesday night and I was going to church. Missing church was something I just didn't do. I needed anyone who would speak to me and be friendly. I had been attending the church long enough to know who was for real and who wasn't or at least some people's actions hurt me inwardly.

I was also part of a prayer group. We prayed for each other that night, we cried together, and we laughed together. The evening was lifting me into a peaceful frame of mind. Nothing but good had just taken place in the prayer group.

Driving home that evening, however, the feeling that had been coming over me for several weeks returned. I had learned to detect fear. The feeling was real. I knew without a mistake what it was – it was fear, and fear without cause.

It seemed that the time I felt fear the most was when I was driving home after dark.

I began to pray. I came against evil. I openly rebuked Satan. I knew to find my strength in Jesus Christ. The fear didn't come from Jesus. I knew He didn't use fear to correct his children, nor did He use fear to get us on the right track. *There is no condemnation in Christ's love for us.

But I didn't understand why Jesus didn't keep Satan from putting fear on me. As His word says in 2Corinthians 2:11, for we are not ignorant of his devices. The fear became more real each time I had to drive home after dark. Instead of Christ releasing me from this fear, the fear seemed to be taking more of a hold on me.

"Jesus, please take the fear away from me. I don't want to be afraid," I prayed. I dreaded getting home, so I began to drive slower. Seeing my little house in the distance should have made me feel safe; instead, I was afraid to go in. I pulled into my driveway and shut off the engine. I looked carefully at the front door. Nothing seemed to be out of place, but I made myself get out of the car. I was not going to let Satan defeat me.

Elizabeth was with me. I talked to her and smiled, protecting her from the fear I felt. She was my little jewel. I reached the front door ahead of her, put the key in the lock and turned it. Suddenly a wave of fear hit me, and I imagined a fist hitting me in my nose, breaking it or sending me backward out the door.

For that reason, I never let my daughter go before me into the house after dark. If a real fist were ever to come out of the dark, it would hit me and not my daughter. The image was that real.

However, once inside our little home, I turned on the light and took a deep breath. "Thank You, Father," I said. It was all right. It had always been all right, but the fear always came.

I don't remember exactly when the fear began. I think it was sometime after Howard had been over, a few weeks earlier. He had come by about three in the morning. He was mad, very mad. I suppose the hurt and hate had built up in him.

When I opened the front door, I could see that Howard was ready for a fight. High on drugs and drunk at the same time, he was furious that I had had him put in jail, a month or so back. He demanded to know why I hadn't gotten him out or why I had not called someone who would get him out.

I tried to explain to him that he would not have left me if I hadn't forced him to leave. I knew he wouldn't leave me alone unless he knew, without doubt that I would put him in jail.

But trying to talk sense or reason with a drugged up, mad drunk was impossible. How do you explain to the man you love that you have chosen God over him? Howard knew I loved him, I didn't tell him that I did, but he knew it. Howard couldn't fathom that I was trying to release him. He couldn't understand how a woman could do such a thing to the man she loved. He had no understanding as to what part he had played in my conversion in asking Jesus Christ into my life. He used drugs and drank so much that he was not rational in any way.

Before I had put the peace bond on Howard, when we were

living together, it was a little like hell. I had stopped drinking, and I didn't use any kind of drug, not even over-the-counter type I could have bought to help me make it through all the emotional pain and stress I was experiencing.

It wasn't watching Howard leave that gave me such pain. It was our continual bedroom fight. He disgusted me with his words and his trying to get me to have sex with him. I didn't want his lovemaking. I knew he was sleeping with any girl who would take drugs, smoke pot or get drunk with him.

I had even slept in my car for almost two weeks when trying to serve him with a peace bond and had stayed in a motel one night. I would go home only if I knew he had left the house.

I would get dressed for work the next morning, go to work and repeat the same routine the following day.

Thankfully, my daughter was safe. She was staying with her grandmother during this time.

After work, I would rush home, get what I needed and leave before Howard came in. I could have stayed with my friend, Kitti, but I didn't want to talk to or be around anyone.

When the day ended, I would usually park in a motel parking lot, where my car would not be spotted. I could sit there without fear until I had prayed prayers that would always be answered. Peace would always come over me at this time, and I would be able to fall asleep. This was the way I lived until Howard was taken to jail.

However, now that I was home again and Howard was out of jail and no longer living with me, he came back night after night. At first, he was not drunk, although he had usually smoked a joint or taken some other drug to calm his nerves before coming to see me.

Over and over again, I tried explaining to him why I did what I had done to him. Why couldn't I just put him in jail again? I had done that twice. Why couldn't I just get all this pain stopped by forcing him to stay away from me? I just couldn't.

I would ask Howard over and over to leave me alone. I was worn out by his in-the-middle-of-the-night visits. But he would come to my back door and knock gently until I opened it.

We would go through it all over again and again. By the time he had left, I would be drained, hurting and very depressed.

It took me a little time to realize that Howard was also going into my house when I was not at home. I had nailed every window shut, but I later found out he would take out two nails from one window and then loosely put them back in, so he could easily pull out the nails and replace them without my knowledge.

I think Howard was looking for evidence of another man in my life. Love to him was proven by sex. He was sure I had a man somewhere taking care of my sexual needs. He could not understand my love for Jesus Christ.

One night about two am, something woke me. I didn't know what it was, but a familiar sense of fear came over me. I lay very still, praying. Suddenly, the door leading outside from my bedroom flew open. Pieces of wood sailed across the room. Startled, I sat up in bed. There stood Howard.

"What's the matter with you," I screamed. "What are you doing? You didn't have to break into my house. I would have opened the door! What's wrong?"

By now, I had regained control of myself and was calm, angry, but calm. I knew enough not to say anything that would make Howard angry.

He had convinced himself that I had another man in bed with me. I don't know how long it had taken him to come to this conclusion.

I could see the drugs were ruling his mind, and I became afraid of him. This was the man I had left, not the man I had fallen in love with. In the beginning, we were so happy. Sin is sure a lot of fun for a season; then it turns into a person's self-destruction.

Howard came close to my bed. He undressed and climbed in beside me. When he was in such a state, there was no arguing with him. Nevertheless, in my mind I began to pray, "God, don't let him. Please don't let this happen."

I tried to stop him from getting on me, but Howard, at over six feet, was a man of strength. There was no stopping him. I then relaxed and began praying aloud. "Though I walk through the valley of the shadow of death, I will fear no evil; for Thou art with me."

(Psalms 23) Howard tried to stop me praying by kissing me. The fear left. I was determined to fight him. I looked right into his eyes and said, "If you do this, I will see to it that you spend a lot of time in prison."

His reply was, "Cute, very cute. I can see it now, Mary Ann Moses raped by Howard ..." At this time, his rage took over. He took a pillow and pressed it over my face. I began fighting him. Howard knew I had an inner fear of choking. Kevin, my ex-husband's tactic was to watch my face because he liked to scare me by putting a knife to my throat or choking me. I hated not being able to breathe.

He only kept the pillow on my face for a short time, a few seconds, less than a minute, but it felt like an hour. He then threw the pillow across the room. I yelled out, "I rebuke you in the name of Jesus Christ!" "What are you talking about? Do you think I'm some kind of devil?" he hollowered back to me.

"Howard, I don't know you anymore," I said. "Look at what you are doing! Why are you doing this? You don't understand. I love Jesus, I don't want to do this. I don't want to have sex. Don't hate me for this. Don't hate me for loving Jesus!"

Howard became calm. I kept talking to him and the more I talked about Jesus, the madder I got at him for doing this to me. This went on the rest of the night.

At daybreak, Howard had to go to work. This is one good thing I can say about him – he did work. He drove a truck, an eighteen wheeler. He would take drugs to keep him awake. I had to go to work also, but I solely trusted on the strength of God to get me through the day. I simply didn't understand why God didn't stop him from coming to me, over and over and over again.

After I got home from work that day, Howard was there again. He was cleaned up and straight, no sign of drugs. The man I had fallen in love with was back. He hated what he had done, and he hated himself. We talked, and he told me he was so tired of being torn between two worlds. He wanted to let go of one of them, but he didn't know how. Nor was he sure just which world he wanted to let go of – the world of drugs or the world of Jesus Christ.

I was also so very tired of it all. What in the world kept me loving and hurting over this man? With all I had, I prayed for hours daily, for God to heal me of my love for Howard. It just hadn't happened. I could have left my lights on when I knew I was going to get home after dark. This would have helped with my times of fear, but I would not do it. First, I couldn't afford it. Secondly, I wasn't going to let Satan win. I would trust Jesus to take care of me. I made myself trust Jesus Christ.

Throughout these months, God had blessed me with the gifts of His Spirit. I had experienced all nine (*1 Corinthians 12:8-10), feeling that faith was the security I stood on during this time of my life. I didn't have every gift, but I had witnessed the flowing of different gifts through the Spirit and won souls when God had used me. He was the King physician, and I had the faith.

I was always fascinated and loved to see God heal, at times right before my eyes. I always felt like a band should start praising Him. It was, and is, always so wonderful.

God had blessed me so greatly, and I was able to share with Howard all the wonderful things God was doing. Although there were times he didn't understand, he knew I was telling the truth. Howard knew me. He knew it was not a game. Jesus Christ was real. God had healed Howard several times for different problems. He knew when I prayed that something was going to happen. He came to me every time he was sick. Not once did God respond to my prayers by saying no. Through this, God was winning Howard little by little, or at least I thought He was. And I knew I was being tested.

It was a Sunday night. The church was not nearly as full as it had been on that Sunday morning. I prayed with all my heart that night as I sat in church. I asked God to overpower Satan and not let him bring fear upon me.

By now, fear had become a real issue. Not really hearing the sermon, I kept praying all through the service. Finally, at the end of the service, I heard the voice of God. My mind clicked, and I was tuned into His words. I grabbed a pen and paper and began writing. *"Listen, listen, my child."* His voice was stern, yet so full of love. I could feel His presence and His great power. It didn't last long, but He didn't have to repeat Himself.

I became unaware of where I was and what was going on around me. I wrote the words God said. He blessed me. I knew why He had allowed the fear. I also knew it would not return.

God had taken a stand for me. He cast the demons of Satan away from me. Fear, like a yoke, lifted from me. I had heard and received a....**MESSAGE FROM GOD.**

*Romans 8:1
There is therefore now no condemnation to them which are in Christ Jesus, who walk not after the flesh, but after the Spirit.

*1Corinthians 12:8-10
8   For to one is given by the Spirit the word of wisdom; to another the word of knowledge by the same Spirit;
9   To another faith by the same Spirit; to another the gifts of healing by the same Spirit;
10 To another the working of miracles; to another prophecy; to another discerning of spirits; to another divers kinds of tongues; to another the interpretation of tongues:

John 10:27
My sheep hear my voice, and I know them, and they follow me:

MESSAGE FROM GOD

LISTEN, LISTEN to Me, My child.
The valley is over; there'll be no more of this kind of trial.
Yield to Me; Listen, Listen, I say.
Obey this message I give you this day.
Be bold, stand firm, don't be afraid.
You are protected by the blood of My Son.
To you from him shall no harm come.
He cannot hurt you with his doubled fist.
My power is within you; he shall fall and resist.
Do not beg, shed no tears, for none of Me, as yet, is his!
Stand, I say, witness to him.
For to you, My child, I have given all my gifts.
To you, My child, is My wisdom, which is not yet his.
To you I have let him come, for through you My child, will
the job be done.
I am the head of this thing and to you will no, not one bit
of harm come.
Witness, witness to him, My child.
For he sees My love in your smile.
LISTEN; LISTEN, for this is a...**MESSAGE FROM GOD.**

Chapter 10:
ENDURE

I was discovering that it was impossible to do and be everything that Jesus says to do and become. I didn't think I would ever get to the point of being perfect. And trying to be perfect wasn't making me happy. It was making me disgusted, and fed up.

But I was not going to quit, nor was I going to give up. It was getting to the point that it seemed like everything was a bunch of hooey. I knew that all that had happened up to this point was very real. I knew God and Jesus Christ had done many miracles and had witnessed Themselves to me in so many ways. Today it all hit me in the face.

I felt there was no way anyone could follow after Jesus, that is, be the person He says to be. I thought I was supposed to be a walking saint, a giant among men, a kind person, and a forgiving person. I was always to have self control, and a person who gives to the poor, and a person able to listen to everyone else's beefs, grief, and never-ending complaints. I was supposed to hold my sorrow, smile and give a loving hug to everyone, the throne sitters, back stabbers and hypocrites of church.

I was supposed to be happy while I became poor, lose my home, furniture, car, diamonds, the man I loved, friends and family, all the things it had taken me thirty five years to accumulate. This was not my idea of heaven.

As I sat on my couch reading the Bible, I wondered if it was all worth it—the moments of peace and joy and the hours of hurt and sorrow. When was it going to be over? When would I begin to live again?

I knew I would not go back to the clubs or the men, yet this in-between *yesterday and tomorrow* was draining me. I wanted to please God so much that I fought to be the woman He would be proud of, so I had to do as He said. I prayed over and over for His strength, for patience, a right Spirit. I prayed for His love that I might love all men as He does. I prayed for His guidance in all that I did, from buying groceries to winning a soul.

I didn't spend thirty or even ten minutes without some thought of God. When you are after God's heart, He is at the head of your life, not the tail end.

I didn't want to turn back. I would not give up. I wasn't angry. I just could not be everything Jesus told me to be. Trying to be perfect is impossible.

I had without really realizing it, let go of God. I was now molding myself, and I wasn't doing too good a job. I was not relaxed in God's work. I was worrying about tomorrow, instead of just getting through today.

I wanted to please God so much that I was not letting Him change me. I was trying to change myself into what I thought He wanted.

Not until I started writing the poem, ENDURE did I realize that God had called my name, that I was pure in Him and that my sins were forgiven on a daily basis, not a yearly one. All I had to do was ask for forgiveness.

I realized that I did have the heart of God. I realized that what I had inside was what He had said He wanted me to be. My failures were of the flesh, and I fought to overcome them. God doesn't make junk. I had yielded myself completely to Him, withholding nothing. I realized the purpose for me was to win souls for Him. I purposed in my heart to learn how to.....**ENDURE.**

2Thessalonians 1:4
So that we ourselves glory in you in the churches of God for your patience and faith in all your persecutions and tribulations that ye endure:

ENDURE

You tell me, you tell me, you tell me to endure.

You tell me to endure the afflictions I feel within.

You tell me to teach, to reprove, rebuke, advise and be ready in and out of seasons.

You tell me to love those, my enemies, when it's I who face their persecution.

You tell me to laugh, when heartache and misery are my only consolation.

You tell me not to judge, nor condemn.

You tell me to clothe, feed, love all those, my fellow men.

You tell me to forsake my all, be willing to give.

You tell me to exalt them, for they to me are not able to recompense.

You tell me to be bold, to pick up my cross, and carry more than my load.

You tell me for the things that I do,

That I must decrease and all the fame and glory are given to You.

You tell me to labor,

That I am the servant and before You, am not greater!

All these things You have told to me.

My Father, I'm willing the commandments to the best of my ability I will keep.

For none is greater than Your comfort within, as the day I first knew You,

And all my sins you forgive, I will.....**ENDURE**.

Chapter 11:
CROWN OF HELL

～

What is there to write about that hasn't been said by so many people that God has forgiven? People He has lifted up off the streets, cleaned, and made whole in Him. I am one of these people. I wasn't as bad as some, and yet much worse than others.

When God came to me, in the form of a cloud, I had reached my depth in sin. I had done everything there was to do in Satan's domain, this earth. I had either done it myself or was a party to it. There were no more thrills for me to experience. Living was a burden without purpose, since I had experienced a little of everything. I had lied, cheated, stolen, fooled, destroyed, and manipulated and bluffed my way through life.

Adultery was just a title or a name pinned on something I did so easily. I had given up three of my four children. I had been in and out of four marriages, a two-year shacked-up living arrangement, on and off the streets, in and out of clubs, in and out of other peoples' marriages, hung up on pills and drugs. I had drunk myself into a stupor each night.

There was nothing left for me to do. Sin no longer excited me. It wasn't fun anymore. I had no problem in destroying anyone or anything that got in my way.

Taking a husband that belonged to someone else was only a challenge for me. There was one wife whom I didn't know until some years later. She was in and out of nervous breakdowns. Her mental state had been broken several times. She and her husband had married young, and she had stayed with him despite his repeated affairs.

His wife was five or six months pregnant with their third child when we started an affair. I was in my twenties when we first met and was with him on the dance floor in a sleazy night club that same night of our meeting.

At the time, I felt no remorse in being with him. Their children didn't matter, and her love for him didn't matter. All that mattered was that he was with me. I never loved this man. He was her life. She always took him back if they separated. He would stop his life style for a short time, and then he would take up with another woman or with me.

For several years he and I saw each other at different times. Somehow we seemed to know where the other one was throughout those years. At one point, we had not seen each other for seven or more years. One day, I was eating breakfast at a café, before going to work. He walked in, and it wasn't long before we started seeing each other again, during our lunch hour and then in the afternoons. We also began meeting on our days off. I was married to Kevin at the time, needless to say very unhappily, but married just the same.

I remember Ken, telling me once when we met on a Sunday afternoon that he was dressing that morning to suit me, putting on clothes he knew I liked. His wife said, "I feel like I've gone through this before." Her words were right. I had her husband, whom I really didn't want. She had all the heartache. It was some kind of obsession with me to hold on to this man, just to prove to myself I could, I guess. It would not be until years later that I realized that she loved Ken in the same sick way I loved Howard.

There were many other lovers who were someone else's husband. Some are divorced now, some separated, some with other lovers, and one out of I don't know how many has found God. The one that I do know about is now a fine person.

I was married part of the time. I had other men and even engaged, but I still had lovers. I was never faithful to any man. At seventeen, I was married for two weeks when I began having an affair with my brother-in-law. My life started and continued this pattern for years.

Not everyone was always married. I went with single guys, but I wasn't faithful to them either. I didn't have a sex problem. I had a love problem. I was trying to find love. I was empty. I wanted to be filled with something that would take away the hurt and loneliness that lived within me every day.

There was one man I remember that I didn't even like, but he was such a challenge for my ego. Once he held me and kissed me, the fun or challenge was over. He was a preacher.

Satan controlled me. He had no problem using me in destroying many lives, homes and children. He didn't have to teach me. He just put the thought in my mind and I obeyed.

Often when I was in a club, just for laughs, I'd approach some man sitting with his wife or date. I'd act as if he had been out with me. I'd ask him why he hadn't called or been back to my apartment. I'd then go back to my table, laugh, dance and drink as I watched them fight for the rest of the evening. Sometime they'd leave arguing. Others who were with me and I thought this was so funny.

I have often wondered how many divorces or separations came about because of my little joy ride with their lives. Even if none occurred, I know that man had hell from that night on because the woman would never forget and she, more than likely, would never let him forget either.

It is no longer funny to me to hurt people. It is a great burden on my heart. If I could go back and find every one of these men and tell them how sorry I am, I would. Even if I had to get on my knees, I would. I hate the destruction I caused.

My children cried their tears without me. I wasn't worried about them. My parents were shamed beyond words, my sisters hated me and my relatives showed their disgust of me as they turned their backs on me.

The more I was rejected, the more I destroyed. If I was hurt, no matter whether the cause was just or not, I set out to pay back by causing as much sorrow as I could. I knew how to hate. I had learned and been taught well. I was a party to causing husbands to stray, especially the ones whose wives had hurt me in my school days. I thought it was great to see their husbands leaving a club with a friend of mine or with me.

Anyone who says sin isn't fun is lying. Satan gives us so many outs from heartaches. Of course the problems are always there, but you can run from them for a short period of time by drinking, taking drugs, or popping pills. You stay on a drunk, a high, or low or you can flat cop out for weeks or even months to years on drugs. Pop a pill to make it through the day then take another two, three, four or however many to make your body go to sleep. Start the same routine the next day to make your body get up. It does not take long to have to take from ten to twenty pills to keep you up. This was my way of life.

While working in a clothing store one time, the owner made me angry. I went to where his pickup was parked and raised the hood and destroyed everything I could get my hands on in broad daylight. I stripped every wire and took or bent or crushed everything I could with a hammer. It took me only a few minutes to cause a lot of damage. I was angry at him because he had caught me stealing and fired me. I showed him, didn't I? I went a lot farther at other times, causing him thousands of dollars of damage.

I never forgot a grudge. Sometimes it took me days, sometimes years to get a person back, but I never forgot until I had caused the person responsible for my shame or hurt to fully experience any kind of destruction I could cause them. Costing them gave me a great deal of fulfillment. Payback dwelt on my mind. I fed on the hate that lived within me.

I survived on the streets, or off, in the money or out, on the top or bottom, no matter, I survived. Others didn't.

I knew at times when a life was taken. A man I considered a friend had given me my first pills in a nightclub. He gave me two uppers, pills to help me party all night. I didn't take them at the time. I actually threw them down when he was not watching. This same young man is still in prison for killing another person, putting his body in the trunk of a car and setting it on fire. This was over a drug deal. He and another man who helped in this killing will be in prison for most of their lives. Now, years later, I have no idea as to the outcome of their lives. This is not the only murder I was aware of. A man walked into the bar owned by the man who gave me cash for my services, and shot him, killing him. His wife never knew about me.

I often engaged in unethical business practices where I was employed. I embezzled a company by putting a non-existing person on payroll in which I forged the signature of the manager. I would do a payroll that was correct. Then take it into his office for his approval and signature. I would then do the same thing on another sheet, adding at the end of the list a made up name and social security number. Then I put the paper up on a glass door and copied the signature which I could clearly trace to the fabricated payroll form. This was mailed to the executive offices which were in another state. This was easy as the company employed a lot of people from another country, it could not be proven if they were in the states legally or not. The payroll money was deposited into a local account. I typed out each check. Computers were not used at this time. I simply signed the check in the same manner with the manager's forged signature. I didn't have a checking account. It was easy to cash the check as I was the secretary for the company. I cashed most of the payroll checks for the workers. How in the world I got this job is somewhat of amazement to me. I had a ninth grade education. The company thought I had gone to college. Papers were easy to forge.

I respected no one. I stole anything and everything I wanted. I taught my children how to steal by stealing in front of them. I drank with them and even smoked dope with them. I took them to bars with me. My youngest daughter, Elizabeth, was not even in school yet when I began taking her into the bar I nearly lived in.

Being a part of the gambling crowd, behind locked doors, I was known and accepted wherever I went. I ran with the rich, who did ugly things. I rode my motorcycle with the outlaw bikers. Street prostitution was never a profession for me, but I did take money for my services. I went to bed with men I wanted to go to bed with. It was not the money, it was feeling wanted and attractive that made it easy for me. These men didn't reject me. They were actually good to me. I never went to bed with a man I didn't want to go to bed with.

Once in a nightclub, the owner, who also paid my rent, rushed me into his office during a high stakes poker game because a fight broke out and a man's eye was cut out by a broken beer bottle.

On another occasion, a girl challenged me when I was entering the same club. I threw her up against the building and attacked her. The girl who was with me ran into the building to get help. The owner ran up to me. He got in front of the girl I was attacking and told her she could never come back to his club. This is the way it was with the club owner who paid my rent for being with him.

The men protected me. I would not understand until years later that it was God who kept me from being killed or in prison for life. I deserved it, but He knew I would be His in time.

There was another time that I offered Howard to another woman, in fact two women. I was doped up and bringing to life the filth that was in my mind. We went to a gay bar to find a third party. Howard ended up mad and slapped me to the floor in the club, in front of everyone. We left the club.

Later I went back to the bar alone, while Howard was gone on a truck run. I talked to the gay crowd. I talked to women who no longer wanted a man in their bed. I talked to women who had never had a man. They fascinated me. I had every intention of finding out everything about this way of life. One of my cousins had introduced this bar to me.

It was something new. I wanted to know about it. It was exciting. I had never really desired another woman, but had during my young years before marriage been introduced to homosexuality through a young girl that lived down the road from us. This only happened once. I didn't like it. But, it happened. I suppose a part of it stayed with me as three more things would take place in the future before I completely turned my back on this way of life.

Under the influence of alcohol and or drugs through the years, I brought to life every vain imagining that came to my mind.

After I met and lived with Howard, I now had a partner who was almost as good as I was at running to filth. None of the men in my life really knew me. None of my husband's had any idea of the things that took place in the dark, before and after marriage. Howard and I brought to life every sexual sin we could think of.

I had nude pictures taken of me by a man I had met on one of my jobs. I was drunk and drugged up when he came to my home and told me what to do. I didn't care. I had no feelings. I never saw the pictures and now I pray that they are never seen on today's Internet.

When I was younger, one of my childhood boyfriends took pictures of me passed out in the back seat of his car after sex. He would not give the pictures back to me, but years later when he came back into my life for a short time, he told me he had destroyed them. He was telling me the truth. I had known him a long time. He had been my boyfriend for three years, I think I was in the second, third and fourth grades. We met every Saturday and sat together at the movies, holding hands. My parents didn't have a clue about this.

I have shared only a very little of all the things I experienced trying to find happiness, love, and acceptance. For over thirty years of my youth, I searched for something to kill the pain I lived with inside of me. I had reached the point of nothing left to do. Nothing left to try. I felt like I not only had hit the bottom, I was wallowing around in pure slime, my own! Money, position, possessions, life, meant nothing to me. It was at this time that God came into my life, in the form of a cloud.

After accepting the forgiveness of Jesus Christ, I could now see the destruction I caused not only to myself but to everyone around me.

Howard was no longer living with me and I was in church a major part of the time. During this time, after many tears, much heartache and countless prayers, I finally released Howard to God.

In a vision, I took Howard's hand and firmly gave it to God. God was sitting before me on the side of a mountain, on a large rock, and His eyes looking straight into mine. I closed my eyes and saw beauty. Peace came over me. I was talking with God and telling Him, as I had for so many months, that Howard's salvation was my prayer. I cannot tell you what God's face looked like. I saw Him, but His face was beyond my seeing. Purity is what I saw.

I looked behind me and there stood Howard. I motioned for him to come to me. With a big smile on his face, he came and stood beside me. *"Father, you know Howard. I give him to You,"* were my simple words. I then took Howard's right hand and God's right hand and made sure God had a good hold on Howard's hand. Then I cut the cord between Howard and me, releasing Howard to God and cutting the tie between us. Tears were streaming down my face. Somehow in this vision I released the hold Howard and I had on one another. When I released him, he was holding the hand of God, not Satan.

It was cold, and snow was falling slowly. I got ready for bed and put Elizabeth to bed, having first listened to her prayers. Then I went to my bed. I was sad, not depressed, but very sad, and extremely lonely. I took the phone off the hook. I couldn't have been any help to anyone that night. Instead, I read the Bible, and lay alone talking to God. He had heard my prayers very often. I knew He was listening now. I could almost see a tear fall from His eye as I cried for Him. I lay very still and tried to think of nothing.

I lay there for I don't know how long. Suddenly I heard a mighty wind. A chill came over me. I pulled the covers high around me. Fear gripped me.

I saw a vast ocean, and I could see the storm pushing the waves higher and higher. There were huge white waves hitting my bed. It was very cold and dark. I was scared, really scared.

My bed was round with a high curved back board. It was covered with a deep blue button material and had a matching bedspread. My bed being a deep blue and round only helped intensify the vision taking place.

I knew in my soul that fear didn't come from God, yet it was very cold in my room and total fear overcame me. It was not the same fear I had felt when after dark I had to go into my little house. This fear was evil. I didn't move. I couldn't move. Then I saw from the depths of the deep a woman began to emerge. Instinctively I knew that she was coming out of hell! She was so close I could have sat up and touched her.

I felt my eyes open as far as they could. I wanted to scream, but could not. As she came closer and closer out of the ocean, I saw her face, her eyes and her hair. She was death! Her eyes were piercing black. Her hair was long, straight and black and the ends were broken and uneven. She emerged halfway from the vast, unending ocean and then she stopped. The waves washed up and followed the round curve of my bed. The wind blew in a fierce anger, causing her hair to blow around her face.

Once she had risen from the ocean, I looked directly into her eyes. Suddenly all fear left me. The wind settled into a cool breeze. Her hair settled, resting on her back. I knew that she was evil. She was death.

Holding her gaze, I knew why she had come. I was not to claim her role again. She was the queen of hell. She came for two reasons. Her title had been challenged by me, and she wanted the soul of Howard.

If I would release him to her by putting his hand into hers, all I wanted would be mine. But I met her glare with no fear. Neither of us spoke a single word, but our minds spoke. We knew what each other was saying, without opening our mouths. I would not claim her position again, but I refused to give her Howard. I felt a power of strength flow through me. I didn't want the title of queen of hell. In my mind, I told her my power was much greater than hers. Jesus Christ was Lord and King, even over hell!

At once, she began to descend back into the ocean. The waves calmed. I felt the mighty hand of God. He reached right out of heaven and picked me up. He put me very close to His breast. I could feel His heart. I could hear His breathing. I could feel His love. I was a child of the King. I had met the challenge of Satan. I had the full armor of God. I could not be broken.

The vision was real. Satan is real, and the queen of hell is real. The fear of the unknown was replaced with the trust I had in Jesus Christ. The reading, obeying, overcoming, talking and going to church had won this battle. *Greater indeed is Jesus Christ that lives within me.

In the days that followed this vision, Satan tempted me over and over again. I was offered two different cars, both Cadillac's, one with blue interior and the other red interior, both for free. Knowing that accepting either of these vehicles would put me into bondage to the man offering a car to me, I refused to accept either car.

I was also offered a three bedroom brick home with fireplace, again for free.

I could have dressed myself and my daughter with name brand clothes. I would have never had to work again. It's amazing how things were dangled before me if only I would release Howard. I refused. I talked to God, expressing my love for Him and I never wanted to be the queen who wears the......**CROWN OF HELL.**

*1John 4:4
Ye are of God, little children, and have overcome them: because greater is he that is in you, than he that is in the world.

Revelation 17:5-6
5   And upon her forehead was a name written, MYSTERY, BABYLON THE GREAT, THE MOTHER OF HARLOTS AND ABOMINATIONS OF THE EARTH.
6   And I saw the woman drunken with the blood of the saints, and with the blood of the martyrs of Jesus: and when I saw her, I wondered with great admiration.

Revelation 17:8
8   The beast that thou sawest was, and is not; and shall ascend out of the bottomless pit, and go into perdition: and they that dwell on the earth shall wonder, whose names were not written in the book of life from the foundation of the world, when they behold the beast that was, and is not, and yet is.

Psalms 139:13-17
13   For thou hast possessed my reins: thou hast covered me in my mother's womb.
14   I will praise thee; for I am fearfully *and* wonderfully made: marvelous are thy works; and that my soul knoweth right well.
15   My substance was not hid from thee, when I was made in secret, and curiously wrought in the lowest parts of the earth.

16 Thine eyes did see my substance, yet being unperfect; <u>and in thy book all my members were written</u>, *which* in continuance were fashioned, when *as yet there was none of them.*
17 How precious also are thy thoughts unto me, O God! how great is the sum of them!

IN THY BOOK ALL MY MEMBERS WERE WRITTEN

It is my belief that all who would be born and all who would be the victims of abortion or miscarriage names are written in the Book of Life even before the earth was formed.

Many women have suffered over their decision to abort a child, but no matter what the state of the fetus, God knew the child and the child is with Him.

I pray that each woman will ask for forgiveness and accept His forgiveness and forgive themselves. The child is in paradise with the Father.

I miscarried when married to my third husband. The fetus looked like an egg with many different colors in it. There was no outward skin but I saw the inward parts. After salvation I have thought of this child many times. I am at peace that the day will come that I will see my child, a boy and I will know my baby.

Revelation 3:5
He that overcometh, the same shall be clothed in white raiment; and I will not blot out his name out of the book of life, but I will confess his name before my Father, and before his angels.

The unsaved, those who do not accept Jesus Christ as Savior who died on the cross for every person and suffered for all our sins, those who do not believe or will not accept the truth, their name's will be removed from the book of life. Just when I'm not sure, but when God chooses, for only He knows when He will no longer strive with man.

Genesis 6:3

And the LORD said, *My spirit shall not always strive with man, for that he also is flesh: yet his days shall be a hundred and twenty years.*

CROWN OF HELL

The vision I had, as I lay in my bed.
My eyes were open, my ears were listening for a message
from above!
When suddenly I realized there was an ocean, and my bed
was the cove.
I was surrounded by the roaring, the violence of the mighty winds.
I was filled with terror, I was filled with fear.
As I remembered the choking, the drawing of my breath in the
past there had been.
And then I saw her, as she raised from the dead.
A queen of VIOLENCE, TERROR, a queen of SIN!
My mind went back to the days when I claimed her roll.
When I claimed the victory of all which come from below!
I had been the one who stood by his side.
I had been the one who wore his crown.
A crown of SHAME, SORROW, to his MISERY I was bound!
Now SHE had come to challenge me.
For now she knows, I work for the KING of all KINGS.
As she glared into my eyes,
I knew she claimed the right hand of Satan's side.
She told me with a voice, from her mind, I heard and understood.
I wear the crown, the crown of DEATH, I am queen of Satan's hell!
I realized, as never before, the crown of hell, I no longer wore.
As she went back into the sea,
I felt the presence, the mighty arms of the KING.
As He put HIS claim of LOVE on me, releasing me from her.....
CROWN OF HELL.

NOTE: At the time of writing this poem I had begun to realize the devastating pain I had caused to others for years. This realization, alongside my memories made me feel like the most disgusting person ever born. I had not up until salvation even considered the pain and rejection I caused to those around me and to my children. I didn't even know there was a queen of hell, but I, because of my actions, felt like I was the most awful person ever born. I didn't understand why God let me be born. He knew all the awful things I would do, yet He created me and formed me in my mother's womb.

    I'm a simple person who has been forgiven for many sins. I know I am not, nor have I ever been evil enough to compare myself to the queen of hell, but my sins, once realized, devastated even me.

Chapter 12:
CONFUSION

~

Several weeks passed and I had been strong. Howard had come by two or three times in the middle of the night. As usual, he was drinking or using drugs regularly. It was taking more and more grams for him to hit his high. I didn't really know what he was taking or smoking. He wasn't just doped up, he was also drugged up. The look on his face would always break my heart. He would look at me with a scream of help!

He was a man and had always been a man to me. He could tell me more through his eyes than he could by trying to explain what he was going through. When he couldn't walk out of reality by taking pills, drinking, or using drugs, then he would come running to me.

He had no idea what he was putting me through. He didn't know how I hurt for him. I couldn't tell him that I was trying to release him that I was not trying to hold on to him. He was trying to let go of me and he had turned to drugs to take the hurt away. It didn't always work. So here he was again at my door at two in the morning.

I had woken up when I heard his bike coming. I knew the sound of it a block away. As I lay there, the tears came. I didn't want to go to the door because I didn't want to go through it again tonight. All I had to do was pick up the phone, call the police and have him put in jail.

I had put him under a peace bond, so I could put him in jail anytime he bothered me. But after the last time I had put him in jail, I knew I could never do it again. Even if he tried to kill me, I felt that I could not do that to him again. I was really not afraid of Howard. Even when fear seemed to come upon me, it wasn't Howard that brought it about, it was evil. I had not seen Howard as evil. He had never really hurt me. He had slapped me a few times, before my salvation, but in all honesty I had asked for it, in fact I think I even wanted it. He had scared me a few times, but he never followed through with causing me pain. My ex-husband, Kevin had physically hurt me. I knew what physical pain was.

I listened as he parked his bike in my front yard. I knew exactly how many steps he'd take to reach my back door. I had spent many lonely days and nights because for me replacing Howard was impossible. I was very lonely and I wanted no man's arms but Howard's around me. I had turned down dates, the opportunity to go out of town, and even marriage.

A man called me on the phone at work. I had never been out on a date with him. I had met him at a cafe and we had talked and that was all. He was a businessman. We didn't talk about our personal lives, just about our jobs. We had each told the other about our desire to climb a little higher on the ladder of success. He was doing pretty good at his job, in fact, very good. He owned his own business.

I hadn't seen him in several months because I had left my job and was now working on the other side of town. I didn't even remember his name. He had to explain who he was when he called me. Then he asked me to marry him. He told me I would never have to worry about money, which sure was a burden on me at the time. I wouldn't have to worry about my daughter being loved and cared for.

I couldn't say yes! I told him I was in love with someone and there was no room for anyone else. He still wanted to marry me. He said he wouldn't push me for my love, that in time he would have my love because he would replace the hurt with his love. It sure sounded good, but that is all it did, sound good.

He wanted us to take a small trip, around the world! I had never been much of anywhere and this sounded even better. I could picture myself on a ship dressed to the hilt in finery. But I could not picture myself in his arms. He was very nice looking, a cowboy. He knew how to dress. I said, "NO, but thank you, I can't." He didn't contact me again after this conversation.

Howard was knocking on my back door. I crawled out of bed, wiped away the tears, put my housecoat on and opened the door.

There he stood, yes there he was, my love. Why, why in the world couldn't I hate him? I don't think I really wanted to hate him. I just didn't want to love him. He looked at me with hurt and pain in his eyes. The drugs hadn't worked. He hadn't been able to stop the hurting so here he was at my door. We just stood there looking at each other. There was no need for words. Just to see me was taking the pain away for him and my seeing him was taking the hurt away for me.

We leaned up against the door screen facing each other. I was on the inside and he was on the outside. "What am I going to do with you? Do you realize that you're driving me crazy?" I asked. He just looked at me and smiled. I opened the screen and I went into the arms of the man I loved with all my heart.

He still hadn't said a word. He held me and it had nothing to do with sex. He just held me. We stood there holding each other and my tears came once again. I looked up toward heaven and saw the glow of millions and millions of stars. I knew that God was watching. Quietly I said, "Why Lord? Why do you let him come?"

I walked into the living room. Howard followed me. I sat down on the couch and he went into the bathroom.

When he came out, he said his first words to me, "Babe, please don't run me off!" He looked awful. His face was aged. He had dark circles under his eyes and a hollow look that hurt me and made my heart bleed for him.

My own hurt was no longer important because I had broken this man. He didn't know how to cope with me. I was his. I had put him into jail twice. I put God before him. All he could think about was his world had gone to pieces, he could not cope, he could not understand.

He sat down beside me, lay his head on my shoulder and soundless tears ran down his face. We didn't talk. We didn't need words. He knew I loved him. I knew he loved me. We had something between us that was a bond, after months of sorrow. This bond had not been broken.

He got up from the couch and looked down at me. He leaned over and took me into his arms. He carried me into the bedroom that we had once shared. I went into his arms with no hesitation. I was happy to once again be in his arms. He knew my heart and he knew me. But he didn't understand what I was going through and why I fought his love and him.

Our time together was spent without words. We loved as lovers love. We touched and held each other. Even with his big hands, he held me so gently. We spent the rest of the night just lying in each other's arms.

As I watched him dress early just before daylight, I felt the pain once again returning. There was no need to ask him where he was going or to whom. I knew someone was always waiting for him. I knew he would return when the pain got to be too much for him.

Just before walking to my back door, he turned and said, "I love you, Babe." Then he walked out of my life again. I lay in my bed asking God, "Why do you let him come?" The hurt took hold of me and I was crushed.

I had failed God, I had failed myself and I had failed Howard. I began praying, asking for forgiveness and for strength. I felt the world once again rest upon my shoulders. I didn't ever want to go through this again. The hell of watching him leave, the confusion and the heartache just weren't worth it. The sin no longer comforted me. I listened to his bike until I could no longer hear the Norton pipes roar.

Getting dressed for work that morning, I realized that I had it all to go through again, the remolding, the melting down, and the pain. No, it was not only the pain of loving Howard. It was also the pain that follows sin. "Please don't let him come back." I prayed trying to let go of all the.....**CONFUSION.**

Romans 6:12-13

12 Let not sin therefore reign in your mortal body, that ye should obey it in the lusts thereof.

13 Neither yield ye your members as instruments of unrighteous-ness unto sin: but yield yourselves unto God, as those that are alive from the dead, and your members as instruments of righteousness unto God.

CONFUSION

It's back again, all the confusion.
I know what it is, I know the reason.
It always comes back, when you come around.
In and out of love, once again I'm bound.
I listen because the words you say are what I want to hear.
Yet with you comes much heartache and fear.
No! I will not yield again.
To hell and back with you, for the last time I've been!
I will stand through Jesus and be bold.
What is not right with authority, I will say NO!
It's not because I don't love you, because I do.
But your kind of hell I no longer am willing to go through!
I know for now you want to change.
But without GOD you'll stay the same.
You find your peace and comfort in me,
You must realize somehow you must see,
GOD is your FATHER, only through HIM, will you find an answer.
The confusion, heartache, the misery you're in,
The only way I can help you is to be your friend.
The help you need, what you're searching to find,
Look up to the HEAVENS and by HIS GRACE,
HE will give you HIS knowledge and teach you all HIS ways,
killing all.....**CONFUSION.**

Chapter 13:
I AM THE WAY, THE TRUTH AND THE LIFE

~

There was a time span of a short season when God lifted me out of sorrow and blessed me with recognition. Coming from a background such as mine and being used by God, I didn't realize until later how much He was teaching me and how fast He was teaching me.

I believed everything I read in the Bible whether it was in the Old Testament or the New Testament. I was teaching people who had searched for years to understand what I had learned in such a short period of time. I wasn't hurting over Howard. He was still coming by my house often but for right now, I had the peace of God. God had either lifted the pain or carried it for me at this time. And He had blessed me with His love to reach out to Howard. I had patience and it wasn't tearing me apart to see Howard walk away from my home. That is for now. Everything in me wanted to help him and to reach out to him, to share with him everything that God was doing in my life. He would listen and ask me questions at times but for the most part he just listened. My phone was ringing night and day. People were turning to me for help in their sorrows. There were many nights I talked all night on the phone teaching others what God had and was teaching me. I was full of faith and knew that what He had done for me He would also do for others. In fact He was doing for others. I would read His words about how He taught His apostles and disciples. Jesus Christ was also teaching me. It was easy for me to believe that what He said to them He was saying to me. I had no problem understanding that I was a disciple and servant unto the Lord. This pleased me. I loved my Savior with all my heart.

I was sought out to pray over the sick. I believed, and God blessed and honored my faith. My prayers for healing weren't long winded nor were they prepared, since I knew God would heal if I asked Him to. I knew, I didn't think, I knew He would heal. I simply gave the problem to Him to take care of.

People came to me with every kind of problem and illness that could be imagined. Broken marriage, broken minds and broken spirits were rampant in the body of Christ. Men as well as women sought my prayers and the wisdom God had given me. I gained some understanding as to the reputation of healing that brought people by numbers for me to lay hands on them and ask Christ for healing.

His Spirit so directed me that at one time or another I had experienced all the spiritual gifts, various kinds of tongues, interpretation of tongues, discerning of spirits, prophecy, gifts of healing, wisdom, knowledge and faith. (1Corinthians 12:8-10) I had also seen God do miracles. All of this was because I had faith, deep inward inner believing faith.

I saw God fix a broken lawn mower right before my eyes. As I stood in a cloud of peace, I saw the King, in just a second, rewire my lawnmower. I had learned that God will fix whatever needs fixing.

But I wasn't running around flaunting the gifts God had blessed me with. When I would witness for Him, one or more of the gifts would come forth. I didn't even know until later about the gifts when I began reading about them in the Bible.

It really surprised me that I had already known about them and they were working in me without my even knowing that the Bible taught on spiritual gifts. I had become a witness for God immediately after my born-again experience.

His Holy Spirit taught me, and it seemed later, I would read about what I already knew. I was winning souls for Christ three months after salvation came to me. (I thought everyone won souls and knew that God heals, that is everyone who went to church.)

Much to my surprise, the church was full of people who were dead to the power of the Holy Spirit. There seemed to be so much emphasis on the gift of tongues. Faith to continue the miracles Jesus Christ had taught the disciples appeared to be of less value. Not making a fool of oneself over-powered the desire of faith for healing miracles or miracles of any kind. The church was full of Christians from all denominations in a non-denominational church.

God had directed me as I fed daily, hourly on His word. I had no problem believing. The problem seemed to be with people submitting.

I wanted to do something for someone, anyone. I wanted to share the love of Jesus Christ. I began going into a nursing home. At first I was a little nervous. I knew how to pray, pray from the heart. This was simple to me. Praying was talking to Christ, sharing everything with Him. I had begun to ask God to show me how to help someone who needed help. It wasn't long before my prayer was answered.

One day while driving around, talking to Jesus about where to go to help someone, I saw a nursing home that was not maintained on the outside as it should have been. I figured the people on the inside were not taken care of, either, as they should have been. I wanted to give love, comfort, hope and even healing to the aged. I prayed for direction from the Lord for a few weeks. I had asked permission from my pastor to go into the nursing home. He told me to go. This first visit was the beginning of months, over a year, of faithfulness in visiting once a week that turned into a daily visit in this facility.

But that first visit was an eye opener for me. The smell was overwhelming. Maybe it was because it was early afternoon and people had not been cleaned. I don't know. The cries of the aged could be heard up and down the halls. "Help me, help me," were the cries I heard.

There were a few people who seemed to be blessed with healthy minds. Some were in well decorated rooms. I walked up to the counter, and a nurse asked me if she could help me. I told her I would like to visit with the residents and simply listen to them and pray with them if they desired.

She merely smiled at me. It was obvious she was extremely busy. She didn't say no, so off I went.

I spent hours holding the crippled bodies of the bedridden. I cleaned their bodies when needed. I listened to stories about their past, when they, with their parents, crossed this vast country in covered wagons. I never tired of hearing their stories, sorrows, and joys. Often I was mistaken for a daughter, niece or sister. I never told them any differently.

On one occasion, which I remember well, I held a woman in her late eighties. I sat down beside her on her bed. She thought I was her daughter. She cried and kissed me several minutes before laying back and resting on her pillow. The tears came easily as I allowed her to see me as her daughter. I later learned she had not had a visitor in a long time. Other Christian people came to minister. She had visitors, but not family, not her daughter.

Family began to recognize me and appreciated my visits. The staff and employees knew me. The facility was understaffed, but the staff I met were doing the best they could to improve the care of the residents. That is for the most part. To a few, it was the only job they could find.

I was allowed to clean the residents, wash the vomit from their faces or bed. It was not easy, but I could not leave a person who needed to be cleaned up. I never changed a diaper, but I would get an aid and stay until I knew the person was cleaned up. I never saw anyone mistreated.

Another resident who really touched me was a man who in his youth had been a cowboy, a real cowboy who either owned a ranch or had worked on them. At any rate, he was still all cowboy. His body was bent with age, and he had some kind of illness that broke out on his feet and legs.

He was sharp in his mind, but broken in his body. I grew to love him. I never saw any family visit him. They could have visited him without me knowing, or they may all have been dead or maybe they didn't know where he was.

In a sense, I became his family as I did to many others, and he got to where he looked for me. God heard my prayers for him and gave him rest from the pain, but my heart would break for him. I wanted to hold him in my arms until God called his name and took him home. Of course this could not be. I don't know why God didn't heal his legs and feet, but I do know he didn't suffer pain from the day I prayed for him until he went home to be with God in a few short weeks.

When I walked into his room one day and it was empty, my heart broke. I had listened to many stories of his adventures. They were true and they held my attention. I think his death made me so aware of heaven. I knew he was with Jesus Christ. We had spent time discussing his salvation and mine. He loved to hear me tell about God coming to me in the form of a cloud. I would read the Bible to him and tell him of his new body he would have and an eternity of life with no tears.

I also received many kisses from these elderly folks. I held many a hand and prayed over everyone I came in contact with. It was of major importance to me to know that their destiny was heaven. I began to see the difference between the peace of the saved and the torment of the unsaved.

God was faithful to my faith. I prayed and He answered. Another circumstance I remember concerned an elderly woman in her nineties. She cried and screamed most all the time she was awake. "Help me, help me!" were her screams. This took place so much that the nurses ignored her cries. There was nothing to do for her. She lived in a cave of fear.

One day when I went into her room, she was sleeping. I stood beside her bed and gently laid my hand on her forehead. I felt the movement of the Holy Spirit within me. This gave me courage to reach out for her healing. With my left hand on her forehead, I raised my right hand and began to pray, "Father, in the name of Jesus Christ, I ask you to heal this woman's burden. Give her your rest. Let her lie in peace." Her murmuring at once became very quiet. Her body was stiff from strain and effort, she lay back in peace. She was still asleep. I stood beside her until she stopped murmuring totally and her body was in rest.

I became overwhelmed with the presence of Jesus Christ. Sitting down beside her bed, I took her hand and spent some time thanking Jesus Christ for delivering her. I didn't know much about evil, but I knew this woman was saved and had been tormented by evil for I don't know how long. I didn't study about Satan. I studied about Jesus Christ.

I visited this woman every time I went into this nursing home. I never heard her hollering or saw her twisting and turning again. I never told anyone about this miracle. No one knew what had happened, but all were aware that something had changed and that she no longer suffered from fear. She knew me when I walked into her room. She didn't talk, but she did smile at me. This miracle was one God allowed me to witness.

Another experience was with a woman also in her nineties. She no longer left her bed. She could no longer hold her head up, she was so weak. She had come to know my face and would smile, raise her little hand as best she could and motion me to come near with her fingers. I would lean over and let her whisper into my ear.

On one particular day, she thought I was her daughter. She asked me if I had done my chores. She needed to go to town. Her mind was in her yesterdays. She held tightly onto my hand. I sat down beside her and began to assure her all was well on the farm that she must at one point in her life have lived on.

I was a farm girl myself, so I began by telling her I had gathered the eggs. Dad had milked the cows, I told her, and on and on until she knew it was alright to go to town. She fell asleep. It was worth the nearly two hours I had spent with her to see the peace and love of this mother.

Salvation was assured to a number of people during my ministry at the nursing home. I prayed with several unsaved elderly people.

I was such a baby Christian myself, yet I knew to ask for forgiveness and to acknowledge Jesus as the Son of God. I continued faithfully to visit this nursing home, often taking Elizabeth, my daughter whom everyone loved to see. We both received a great reward of real happiness together. We were a mother and daughter team.

One day I walked into a room where a woman from my hometown had become a resident. She recognized me immediately, although it took a minute for me to know who she was. We were to spend many hours together. She could no longer walk, but she was clear minded. She knew my family on my dad's side and my mom's. She told me stories about my grandparents and my parents.

This woman never told me anything ugly. She had to have known of my reputation when I was at home there, but she never made me feel uneasy. She always asked me to pray, telling me my prayers blessed her. This was special. It was so easy to love her and just as easy to accept her love for me and my daughter. She always told me how happy she was that I didn't forget to visit her.

I had many experiences at the nursing home. I saw people die. I felt the grief of families. I saw miracles. I saw healing by the power of God. It was indeed an experience of growth. I learned that working in the harvest field of our Lord brought us all together in His body.

By now my name was becoming even more known. Often in church, people would come to me, introduce themselves and shake my hand. I didn't have a clue as to how they had heard about me, but I never asked. I simply responded by being polite.

All of this was easy to accept. It seemed as though God had turned the heart of man toward accepting me, as indeed He had. I wasn't having the problems of rejection I had experienced in the past. The pastors greeted me with smiles of acceptance. I was turning into somebody!

One Wednesday night, I went into the chapel for the sermon. People were greeting me, hugging me, wanting to talk with me. My, my, this was great, I thought. I listened to the sermon, paying more attention to my fame rather than what was said. I felt myself swell with the praise of man.

When the closing prayer was prayed, I slowly stepped into the aisle, heading in the direction of my Wednesday night study class. Of course I wanted to let everyone have the opportunity to speak to me and shake my hand. After all, miracles followed my ministry. I walked down the aisle telling God in my mind what a good job He had done in teaching me how to heal, how to pray, how to have faith, how to go where He sent me. He had taught me everything. I had learned. He didn't have to direct my every step anymore. I understood! I knew what to do!

In less than an instant, less than the blink of an eye, I felt the mighty hand of Jesus Christ swoop down from the heavens. I felt the coolness of the breeze that followed as He with His hand knocked the crown I had on my head off! I fell to my knees. All strength left me. It was hard for me to breathe. I was gasping for air. It took all the strength I had to put my arm down to catch my fall. I was so embarrassed that quickly I pushed myself to my feet. I rocked a little with the weakness of my body. I was not aware of anyone near me. I was struggling to hold myself up. It was the experience a drunken person feels when trying to act sober, when he is totally drunk.

Slowly I was able to stand, but it took a few moments to take a step. Totally weak, humiliated, embarrassed, ashamed, crushed, I took a step and continued toward my class. No longer standing tall, looking to see who might want to shake my hand, I let my shoulders slump, and depression overwhelmed me. It was exceptionally hard for me to sit in class. I fought back tears, no longer holding my head high. I sat there knowing and understanding what had just happened to me.

With my busy days working and my busy days visiting the nursing home, my busy time going to church, I had slacked on my prayers, reading the Bible and listening. I had taken on the pride of self. I had given myself much credit for what God was doing. I had passed His test of approval and graduated. I didn't know when I had put a crown on my head, but during the time of victory and recognition, I began to pat myself on the back for doing such a good job.

With all that I had experienced at church, during this evening, I was extremely grateful that I didn't have to deal with Howard when I got home. Lying in bed that night still feeling very beaten and depressed, I asked for forgiveness for what I knew I had done. I asked Jesus Christ to help me to understand. His way of teaching me was to take me back to the Old Testament. I reread the scriptures of the day Moses was taken into the household of Pharaoh by his daughter.

Exodus 2:5-10

5   And the daughter of Pharaoh came down to wash herself at the river; and her maidens walked along by the river's side; and when she saw the ark among the flags, she sent her maid to fetch it.

6   And when she had opened it, she saw the child: and, behold, the babe wept. And she had compassion on him, and said, This is one of the Hebrews' children.

7   Then said his sister to Pharaoh's daughter, Shall I go and call to thee a nurse of the Hebrew women, that she may nurse the child for thee?

8   And Pharaoh's daughter said to her, Go. And the maid went and called the child's mother.

9   And Pharaoh's daughter said unto her, Take this child away, and nurse it for me, and I will give thee thy wages. And the woman took the child, and nursed it.

10 And the child grew, and she brought him unto Pharaoh's daughter, and he became her son. And she called his name Moses: and she said, Because I drew him out of the water.

I read until I understood. I read Exodus for weeks, reading the same thing over and over until I understood why and what had happened to me. I don't know that I had ever felt a crown on my head, I don't think I had ever felt it before. But I sure felt it knocked off my head. He showed me that He is.....**THE WAY, THE TRUTH AND THE LIFE**.

John 14:6
Jesus saith unto him, *I am the way, the truth, and the life: no man cometh unto the Father, but by me.*

I AM THE WAY, THE TRUTH AND THE LIFE

You gave me a taste of what is yet to come.
How I'd lay hands on the sick and You'd heal in the name
of Your Son.
I remember a day, a few months back,
When my head had swelled, to fit my own made crown!
I remember I thought I was doing so good.
I had no more need, nor time for You!
Oh, I was willing, and very bold.
To have my name spoken in the crowds of your fold.
I was running ahead a mile or two.
I let go of Your hand, I let go of You.
So You pulled back and let me run.
You had to teach me, there was much to learn.
The tears came once again.
The heartache, the burden of misery and sin.
And when the bottom, I had hit.
The bottom of my own made pit.
You reached down with Your mighty hand,
Dusted me off and said,
"Now, let's start over again!"
I AM THE WAY, THE TRUTH AND THE LIFE,
I shall heal the sick, including the blind.
I chose you, because you have the faith.
There's no need to run; I'll win the race.
You just be willing and take time to pray.
Keep your eyes on Me, I'll lead the way.
Take hold of my hand,
Run with patience, for by you, I do stand, knowing that you yield
to me, for.....**I AM THE WAY, THE TRUTH AND THE LIFE.**

Chapter 14:
I WANT TO BE

～

The last nine months had gone by very slowly. The hurt over my love for Howard seemed to be growing instead of being healed. I thought with time, it wouldn't hurt so badly. I was wrong, with time the pain increased. It was living hell for me.

When the pain became too intense, I would cry out to Jesus Christ. He never failed to help me at these times. I didn't cry out with every pain. I cried out when I felt I could no longer stand the pain. It could be a season, a few minutes, an hour or hours, a day or a few days, and then the pain would begin again.

I knew the pain would return. I'm not sure I understood why. When Jesus took the pain for a season, I would think that God had healed my love for Howard. This was not true. The times Christ would take the pain or let me be free of it were very few. I considered myself a strong person, a strong woman. It took a triple load of pain to bring me down.

Jesus would let me rest when I truly felt that I could not stand the pain any longer. When I felt restored, the pain would return. It was during these times of sorrow that I began to learn and really get a grip of what Jesus was teaching me. One time in particular, I had two whole days of pure joy. Nothing hurt within me. I had fallen in love with Jesus Christ and His goodness toward me.

On the third day of peace and joy while kneeling beside my bed, I felt as though I was sitting on a cloud. The peace was superb. "Father I'm ready. I'm strong enough to go on with You. Teach me more. Give me Your wisdom. I'm ready to learn," were my words of trust.

My eyes were closed. I saw a vision of the magnificent face of God. No, I didn't see God. I saw a vision of God. I saw all His power and glory as He smiled at me. With His mighty hand, He reached down and touched my head. Through His touch, I became a tower of strength. I felt the infilling and renewing of His Spirit. He blessed me with Himself.

I sat in silence as He just smiled at me. I felt loved beyond compare and explanation. I saw Jesus in white. He had a glow around Him so grand it opened the heavens. My whole being was in total tranquility as in a sea of peace. Jesus smiled and looked toward His Father and together they looked into my eyes. I saw no interpretation of the way God looks, but I did see the grandeur of His presence. His appearance was not brassy with gold. It was abounding in peace and love. I only saw just the very tip of the power. It was something mightier than I could explain or ever imagine.

I sat for some time, not wanting to move. Tears of peace and not sorrow dropped to the floor. I wanted to remember all over and over again. I tried to relive the vision within my mind but this was not possible. However, the peace was overwhelming. I knew my heavenly Father and His Son were with me and His Spirit lived within me. I began to pray, "How Father? How do I tell others? How do I tell them about all this? How do I tell people that you're real, that You are alive? How do I tell my friends that don't know You? Oh God, I don't want anyone to go to hell. How do I tell the world how You came to me, talked to me, and live within me? How Father, how!"

At this time in my life, I had such a burden for the lost, and even a greater burden for the salvation of the man I loved. My children were next, but God had given me peace that He would fulfill His word and not only save me, but also my household.

Acts 16:30, 31 And brought them out, and said, Sirs, what must I do to be **saved**? And they said, Believe on the Lord Jesus Christ, and thou shalt be **saved**, and thy **house**.

I believed Him. Howard wasn't a part of my house. But he was a part of my world and my life.

God answered my prayer as He always did and still does. I didn't try to learn how to pray. I wasn't hung up on trying to sound good.

I spent more time searching my heart for the truth to talk with my Father about. I wanted to know the truth about God and the truth about me.

In just a split second, the pain returned. But it wasn't sorrow I felt. It was joy. I now knew what it meant to be thankful for all things, even sorrow. There was no other way for me to learn except to seek God in all things. During the time of hurt and pain, I knew God the most. I liked this closeness with God. I knew it was part of my learning and training. I didn't know why God wouldn't heal my love for Howard. I felt I was failing Him by giving in to my own desire or need for Howard's love. I hated failing God.

I also knew that as long as Howard came to me, sooner or later he would come when I was weak. I'd go through the battle of not letting him make love to me. With everything that was within my heart, I most of all didn't want to lose my walk with God. I didn't want to fail Him. It was my desire for Christ to be proud He had chosen me. I wanted Him to be pleased with me. I didn't want Him to look upon me and see me in sin. I knew He did see all and everything that I did or even thought. It hurt me to hurt God, so why wouldn't He keep Howard from coming to me. I was so torn.

Going into my living room, I sat on my couch. I put my Bible down beside me. "Lord, I've come to You daily, hourly, asking You to heal my love for Howard. I've done everything I know to do to fight to stay clean for You. I want to start fasting, but I don't know how to fast for a lengthy time. I want to fast and ask You to let this burden pass. If Howard and I are to be together, put us together, and if we aren't, then separate us," I prayed.

I felt that God heard my request and I put my thoughts on how to fast. I began by eating everything I could get my hands on, preparing for the winter, I supposed, storing up food. The more I ate, the more I wanted. I knew God had to be at the head of my fast. I could in no way do it without Him. I had low blood pressure and anemia.

Needless to say, I was very weak. I didn't have the money for vitamins, so I put my faith in God to get me through each day by giving me His strength. He never failed me. I couldn't miss work or relax on my job. I had to depend on God to give me the strength to do my work.

I began asking people at church how to fast. They sure had a lot of different ideas. The Bible speaks of fasting and what your attitude should be but it doesn't say how to fast. Jesus went right into the wilderness after being baptized and began a forty day fast. He neither ate nor drank the whole time. He didn't prepare for it either, or rather the Bible doesn't state it if He did.

Therefore I had to know whose method of fasting was pure and who gained nothing from their fasting. I listened to everyone and always asked God for discernment. You would be surprised how may fasts aren't of God. A lot of people just starve themselves. I didn't feel that God honored diets. I asked if it was all right to take vitamins or to drink liquids. I didn't ask about food of any kind because I knew that was out. I was more concerned about the vitamins, and liquid and how to start fasting.

God led me to the right person the next Sunday morning as I was leaving church. I saw a young man that I knew walked close to God. I had talked with him several times and he has always been able to help me understand what was troubling me. He was a person that knew how to edify God and not himself. This young man was humble in Christ. Yet he was a tower.

I asked to speak to him. He was very educated and his intelligence was outstanding. We enjoyed each other. How, or why he liked me was something I didn't understand. We were from two different worlds. Still we were friends, good trusting friends. I asked him about fasting, something he had never mentioned in all the times we had previously spoken.

It was a surprise when he began telling me all about fasting. I immediately knew, without doubt that this young man's fasts were pure. He told me the first and most important thing was for God to be the head of my fast. "Okay, how do you put God the head of it?" I asked. "You ask Him!" he replied. He told me to ask God when to begin to prepare me for the fast, how long it should last, and then you tell God the purpose of your fast and pray for an answer.

This made a lot of sense to me. I asked if God would bless my fast if I took vitamins, which I didn't have, and if it was all right if I drank juice. He said **"yes,"** so I bought only bouillon and grape juice.

Now God knew I was without vitamins and couldn't afford them, so He touched my friend to give me some. I was over at Kitti's house one day during my week-long preparation for my fast. I had said nothing to her about the fast. During our conversation, she walked to the bathroom and returned with a full bottle of very expensive vitamins for me. I was overwhelmed that nothing had been said about fasting or my health. It had to be the unction of the Holy Spirit. Kitti gave me the whole, unopened large bottle of vitamins. "My mom brings me this stuff all the time. Here, you take them." She said.

I knew God was helping me to prepare and I knew He was at the head of my fast. I had set a goal for my fast to last fourteen days. I planned to start on Friday, November 9, 1979. The whole week before my fast was to start my training to fast. I drank the bouillon instead of coffee, cokes, tea and water. I ate only one meal a day. I was used to eating all day off and on. I drank one glass of bouillon. I might have allowed myself one or two bites of something in the late afternoon, but that was all. Then I worked myself down to almost nothing two days before my chosen date to begin. I was in constant prayer as to why I wanted to fast, which was Howard.

Thursday morning when I awoke, God spoke, *"Begin today."* That was all He said. So I began my fast. I took two vitamins each day. I drank only a small amount of bouillon or grape juice. I prayed. The first three days were the hardest. I had been told they would be.

However, by the end of the third day, I was in a peaceful fast. I no longer hungered. I realized Jesus also didn't hunger until after He fasted. Everything was beautiful. God blessed me with His continued presence. I talked to God always, either openly or through my mind. He knew all I had to say, yet somehow I knew I was to say it anyway.

I was asking God to break the bond between Howard and me. I wanted to know how to release Howard and keep him released. But this release must come by releasing him only to God. I wanted to make sure I didn't release Howard to Satan to have him for eternity. I also prayed that if by any chance or reason Howard and I were to be together, for God to put us together. I didn't think there was a chance or any reason for us, yet I was willing to accept whatever God wanted. I wanted God's will to be done for both Howard and me. I was ready and willing to live my life with or without Howard.

Howard visited me during my time of fasting, but he never knew what I was doing. He didn't even notice that I was not eating.

About the fifth day of my fast, he came back over to my house late in the day. He was torn. He was hurting. He was in a lot of inner pain. God had him under His conviction. Howard didn't know what was going on.

His tears came freely even though he never made a sound. He just ducked his head as he sat next to me on the couch and let the tears come. This was unusual. Howard didn't cry. He had learned in reform school a long time ago to hold back his tears. I had seen him shed a few tears once or twice before this day, but I had never seen him really cry.

I put my arms around him as I knelt in front of him and silently began to pray. He needed to cry and an ocean of tears flowed from his eyes. Yet not once did a sound flow from his mouth. I held him as a mother holds her child. This man was going through living hell and for the first time, I realized that I wasn't the only person who hurt. He had hid it from everyone and now it was all coming out.

I got my Bible and told him that when two people pray together, God is in the midst of them. I looked up the scripture to prove my words. *Matthew 18:20. Howard agreed to pray with me, but he wanted me to do all the praying.

In my praying, I poured out my heart to God. I told of my love, my confusion, my needs, and my deepest love for Him. I would accept anything He wanted me to do. "Please let it go one way or the other, Lord, please," I said.

At first Howard didn't want to pray. I helped him to realize I had only spoken and it was me God heard. I told him even though God knew his heart. He must speak to God openly himself. We held hands as Howard prayed from his heart. God granted peace to

Howard right then. The hurting stopped.

We didn't know what the outcome would be, but we knew God was going to do something about us. Howard stayed with me for some time. We laughed together and talked of the good old times, leaving out all the bad times. We talked to one another about the people we knew and what was going on in their lives.

I had missed some of Howard's friends that had become my friends also. I couldn't go visit them because they lived in Satan's control and Howard was a part of that world. We enjoyed each other for this moment. He told me how he had tried to change but just couldn't. I knew why he couldn't change. I explained to him that God was down the ladder, probably at the bottom of his heart and not at the top. Until he was willing to bring God up to the very heart of his life, he wouldn't be able to change. Somehow, Howard understood what I was saying. But, as of yet, he wasn't willing to yield to God. At this point God let great sorrow come back into his heart.

Howard finally left. I went into my bedroom and put on a record that had a very beautiful song on it, a song of praise to God. The song was mellow. I then sat on the floor and once again prayed, oh how I prayed. Hope was renewed that God would either put us together or separate us and heal me of so much inner pain.

It was close to Thanksgiving. I had nothing planned. I was still in my fast. Elizabeth's school was having a dinner. The parents were welcome. I had told my daughter that I couldn't go. I didn't tell her why, that I was fasting and I couldn't eat. I didn't realize the hurt in her little heart.

Going on to work, I forgot about the dinner. I was expecting a man from out of town. I didn't know if I wanted him to show up or not. He was another Howard, only he had money. I had gone out with him only once. I had felt the togetherness of communication between us. He wasn't Howard. He could not take his place. I suppose I had some hope in replacing Howard.

I was working at my desk. I looked at the clock. God spoke, *"Go to your daughter!"* I said "What?" He replied, *"Go to your daughter!"*

I got up, picked up my purse, turned and walked out the door. I drove right to her school. There she was sitting all alone. I was the only parent who hadn't shown up. When she saw me, the tears she had been holding back began to flow from her beautiful blue eyes. I walked over to her and held her in my arms. She said, "Oh mom, I didn't think you were coming." She then started introducing me to all the people sitting around her. All the time her little face sparkled. I felt a lot of shame to think that I had put myself first and broken the heart of the person who loved me the most. I got a plate, filled it, and ate with no problem. The food was very rich, but I ate. I was thankful that the man had not shown up.

Fourteen days was the fast I had asked God for. Instead, He gave me seven days and six nights. This was my first fast. I knew God was pleased with my fast. No one but Him knew I was fasting. I had a knowing within me that the answer to my heart's cry for nearly a year was about to take place. I learned a lot during these seven days. It cannot be explained, the closeness to God when a pure fast takes place and knowing that God's decision was about to take place. In His arms is where.....**I WANT TO BE.**

Matthew 7:7-8
Ask, and it shall be given you; seek, and ye shall find; knock, and it shall be opened unto you: For every one that asketh receiveth; and he that seeketh findeth; and to him that knocketh it shall be opened.

Matthew 6:18
That thou appear not unto men to fast, but unto thy Father which is in secret: and thy Father, which seeth in secret, shall reward thee openly.

*Matthew 18:20
For where two or three are gathered together in my name, there am I in the midst of them.

I WANT TO BE

FATHER, what else, what else can I do?
I gave my love, I gave him to You.
With many prayers, and fasting too,
I took his hand, and with a tear, put into Yours.
I was willing to let him go.
As I knew, at stake was the salvation of his soul?
He returns to me over and over again.
YOU tell me I am strong enough, I must witness to him.
Remember my FATHER, my FATHER in heaven,
My love for him, as yet, You have not healed!
When he comes time after time, I falter and fall, my love I yield.
YOU tell me so often in Your words,
YOU witness to me, only YOU am I to serve.
FATHER, FATHER, please understand,
None other has held my love, none other than THIS man.
I do not want to live in fornication.
To yield, to give, I'm not willing, I have deep hesitation!
Yet my flesh, myself, the woman I am,
Only through this man, can release be found!
FATHER, FATHER .....LISTEN, PLEASE!
In the name of Jesus, intercede.
SHIELD me, in YOUR arms is where.....**I WANT TO BE.**

Chapter 15:
I REBEL

~

I shut the door, watching Howard walk away. I wanted to run after him, but I wouldn't allow myself to. He had come just to tell me he loved me. We had talked only a short time. He had said something that had real meaning to me. "Don't you understand? I want what you've got!" he said with eyes that showed his personal pain.

I had told him of the only way I knew how God's love and peace were able and would heal him of the drugs, if only he would yield his life to God. Howard wanted to change, he wanted the peace he at times felt and knew I had. Howard wanted his drugs also. He was not able to face life without them. I understood him. He had caused much sorrow to the people who had loved him.

He had also hidden much of his own heartache within himself. He had received and experienced a lot of hurt during his life of growing up. He was extremely insecure. The pain in his eyes was obvious. His heart was torn. He was afraid to trust God. Life had failed him. He was not going to trust God. How could he trust someone he couldn't see? How do you walk out of a life of living hell and walk into a life of faith?

I listened as Howard drove away. A flood of tears fell, like a raging waterfall. Howard had no idea of how I hurt. He thought I had turned on him. I hadn't. I just couldn't let myself go back into Satan's control through Howard.

I fell to the floor and I hit it with a doubled fist. I raised my eyes toward heaven. "I can't stand this anymore. Do You hear me? Why won't You kill my love for him?" I hit the floor again with my fist with all that was in me. It didn't hurt. I should have had physical pain but I didn't. I continued to pound the floor with all the strength I had. The inner hurt was ripping me apart. It was the hurt of a woman in love with a man she couldn't have.

What should I do? There's got to be something that makes it all stop, I thought. Elizabeth came into the living room. She was crying for me. She sat next to me and put her little arms around me and said, "Mom, God loves you. God loves Howard too."

I took her into my arms and told her that I would hurt all it took to get Howard to give his life to God, that if God wanted to send him to me, I would stand the pain. My little girl wiped the tears from my eyes and together we sat on the floor and prayed. I didn't realize that I was robbing Elizabeth of her childhood.

A couple of nights later, Howard came again. When I heard his car, my heart began pounding. I couldn't wait to see him. Just to see him. Sometimes, was all I needed, but I still would not allow myself to run into his arms. I couldn't yield to my own desire for him. I couldn't let him know how I felt. I was not always this strong.

We talked. I tried to explain more about Christ. Howard was at times like this, really trying to find what I had. We prayed together beside my bed, on our knees. Howard was straight. He hadn't taken any drugs and he wasn't drinking. He was hurting, which gave me no joy. I hurt with him. His prayer was straight from his heart. He was praying to God, he wanted Him to help him and he wanted to know Him. He did believe in God. He had prayed to Him before.

Some months back, Howard had prayed a sinner's prayer asking for his salvation. But he hadn't been willing to give himself. I don't think he knew how to give himself. Now, as we knelt side by side, I heard the man I loved so very much really talk with God. He poured his heart out. Tears came into his eyes. He prayed, "I don't know how to stop being the man I am. I can't do it without You. I don't know why I do the things I do or why I hurt the people I love. Please help me to change. Tell me what to do. Please God, love me and make me a good man." This was not all his prayer, but this was the beginning. It was the real beginning of Howard turning his life over to God. Now God would really start moving in his life. Howard's will was in line with God's will, or so I thought.

Howard left. I still didn't believe he was to be a permanent part of my life. I thought God was only using me to touch Howard. My love for my Maker was very real. My desire to please Him and my will to follow Him were also very real. There was not one part of me that was phony.

I lay in bed with an abundance of peace. Being what God had taught me to be and doing what He told me to do was such a reward of joy within me. I loved God first, Howard came after Him. Seeing Howard in heaven meant more to me than my own life.

Howard called later. I knew he was drinking. It was hard to understand how a person could yield to God one day, and then fall back the same day. The hurt came back. I was torn between my love for God and my love for Howard, and it was killing me. After hanging up the phone, I decided to have some fun. I wasn't going to sit there and hurt all evening. I got dressed and went over to a girlfriend's house. Together we went to a club. It had been a rash quick decision to try to go back to what in the past had been fun for a lot of years in my life.

I sat down at a table and hated everything. I didn't drink. The men who asked me to dance disgusted me. I would not let anyone hold me close. I walked off the dance floor from one man while he stood there not believing that I thought he was sickening. He thought he was God's gift to women. I didn't agree. I sat back down and by now God was letting me know He didn't like where I was. I knew God was convicting me. In other words, God was telling me He wouldn't put up with it. I looked up and said, "Okay, you win." I went home.

Elizabeth was spending the night with a friend, so I was alone and felt very alone. I sure was getting a lot of practice crying. Crying seemed to be the only way I could release the pain. Wouldn't you know it, Howard called. It was about two-thirty. Howard wanted to tell me he was thinking of me. "Leave me alone!" I cried. I slammed the phone down, took it off the receiver and screamed. I pulled the covers over my head and screamed.

Despite all this, Howard was coming by more often, more than he had in the past. One day as I was packing to have my belongings put into storage, I opened the door and there he stood. I was very low at that point. I had to give up my little rented home and move in with Mother Superior, Grace. It seemed I had lost everything because of this man.

I confronted him. "Why won't you leave me alone?" Howard ignored that. "Where are you going? I'll find you wherever you go," he demanded. "Howard, I have to get away from you. Why, why won't you leave me alone?" I pleaded. He was deaf to my pain. "Marry me, why won't you marry me?" He asked. "Because I know you will pull me back into hell. You don't love God," I brutally told him.

"You don't know whether I love God or not!" he said in anger. "Howard, a man that loves God is not able to do the things you do. You can't take drugs one day then go from one woman's bed to another the next. You can't lie, cheat, steal, and say you love God. I will not live my life with a man that is able to destroy me. Please, please get the hell out and leave me alone," I said in frustration.

Howard left. I went walking. It was a very pretty day, a little chilly, but it felt good. I walked down to the park that was at the end of my block. The clouds were beautiful. I walked around the park, and then I stopped and prayed. I was the only person there.

"Please God, please don't let me hurt anymore," I begged. I felt nothing. No peace came. The burden of heartache was very heavy. I walked home. I walked through the house feeling more pain than I had in the past. I wanted to be loved. I wanted to be held and give love. I was hurting so deeply that I couldn't even cry.

The next day was Sunday. I dressed for church, but I was still in deep pain within. I went to church and went through the process of praying, smiling, pretending, holding my sorrow inside.

I drove home and sat in front of my house alone. "God, I can't do it. I can't be a witness to Howard. I love him too much. I just can't," I prayed. *"Yes you can! You are the only one he will listen to,"* God replied. When God speaks, I listen. I knew God's voice. I sat there for several minutes, tears flowing. I didn't pray and I didn't fuss. I knew I had to do what God wanted. There was nothing to fuss about. God had spoken. I had heard.

Then I heard a very familiar sound behind me. It was the deep roar of Howard's car muffler. I got out of my car with renewed strength. This man only came to me when he hurt or felt lost and alone. This walking ball of heartache needed me.

I walked into the arms of a much needed love. I needed his love. His arms were going to have to be enough. I knew this man loved me. Just to be held by him meant so much to me. I allowed myself to absorb his love. I knew I would hurt again when he left, and I knew he would leave. We just stood there for several minutes just holding each other. No words were spoken.

Every time Howard would come over drunk or drugged up, I would lose hope. At least now that I was living with Grace, he no longer came banging on my door. There were no more calls during the night, although I still would hear his motorcycle at times in the night.

He had followed me home from work. He had said that he would find me. Howard often came to my job. He would also come to church, find me in my Sunday School class or sit down beside me in church. I never knew when or where he would show up.

It was now close to a year since my valley with the Lord had begun. Days had turned into weeks of nothingness. I was praying with all that was within me for God to give me purpose, purpose to live, something that would fulfill my life and bring me joy.

I had learned to love people and I wanted to help them so very much. I wanted to share. But I was willing to live alone. I had learned to completely depend on God. He had taught me how to live alone. I'm not saying I liked it, but He had taught me how to overcome loneliness, which was through Him.

There is a lot of difference in living alone, ruling your own roost and living in the same house with another woman, yet still living alone. I had always been a loner. I stayed to myself a lot. My daughter and I stayed in our room most of the time.

Grace, the lady I now rented a bedroom from, encouraged me to become a part of the whole house, to make her home our home. I was welcome to share, but I didn't want to be around anyone more than I had to.

What it all boiled down to was the fact that I was hurting over Howard, my job and our having to move from the privacy of our own little house where my daughter and I had lived. I was not able to find much if anything to be happy about. I knew it was self pity, but my sorrows were very real. I had given up, lost most of all that I had accumulated throughout the years. It was not easy for me to make a one hundred and eighty degree turn. To repent meant a lot of me had to go.

I called my friend Linda Curbo. Linda lived in Euless, Texas (between Dallas & Ft. Worth). I was separated from my third husband, and getting a divorce, when I saw Linda for the first time on top of a table at Rustlers Rest, a western night club. It was January 18, 1969. She had a fancy slip over her pants and was doing the hoc-hie-coo to the rhythm of the music. Everyone was laughing and having a great time. It was her birthday and she was celebrating with a lot of friends. Linda was popular. Linda saw me for the first time the same night. She went into the bathroom and here I was on top of the counter, in front of the mirror, kicking ash trays and breaking them all over the place. Her first impression of me was not too swift. My first impression of her was not too swift either.

A few months after this first encounter, Linda was asked by a person who was going to the Stamford Rodeo with me and a couple of other people. Linda agreed to go with us. Linda and I found out we had been dating the same cowboy, and one of the other girls, we called her Country, that was with us was pregnant with his child. This was July 4, 1969. I met Kevin though this same man and here I am now headed to the rodeo at Stamford. I was now living with Kevin and engaged to him.

There were four women and one man in my car. Linda was in the front seat. There was a console between us. We were in my navy blue and gold Chevy, Super Sport.

I had taken an RJS, speed, black molly. I had also taken a white cross (more speed). I was traveling about eighty-five miles an hour. I came to a curve in the road. I had paid no attention to the warning sign that I'm sure was there.

I tightened my grip on the steering wheel. The curve was sharp and descended quickly headed for the bottom of a hill. I said nothing, Linda said nothing. I did not break. Holding the car in the middle of the highway, we went into a smooth turn. Everyone in the back seat began to scream. My car stayed level on all four tires taking this thirty-five mile an hour curve. Just as I began to go into the straight and narrow part after the curve, a rear tire blew out. Everyone except Linda and I were screaming at the top of their lungs. Linda and I looked at each other and smiled. Man what a trip!

In complete fairness to Linda, I never saw her take a pill, nor did I ever see her smoke a joint, I never saw her drunk. Linda was Linda and for some reason we became fast and lasting friends.

It was not long after the Stamford Rodeo that I decided I didn't want to marry Kevin. I had been out with the bouncer of the Rustlers Rest Club, during the time I was engaged to Kevin. One day I agreed to marry him. Kevin was on a run, he drove an eighteen wheeler. The bouncer and I went downtown Ft. Worth and he bought me a diamond ring. We left for Old Mexico the same evening. We were to be married in Old Mexico. But during the drive, I sobered up a little and was coming down from all the pills I had taken. In the motel room, somewhere in Old Mexico I told Doug that I couldn't marry him. I sat on the bed as he stormed up and down, yelling to me that he was going to leave me there. He went to his car and only by the grace of God he turned and told me to get in. He would take me back to Ft. Worth. Kevin came in late the next evening and never knew about this little trip.

Now, some years later, I'm entangled with Howard. Linda knows Howard and she knows all about everything. When I knew I had to give up our little home, I called Linda. During our conversation, Linda offered to come and get Elizabeth and me. Her love for us had no bounds. Linda was more than just special. She is more precious than the rarest diamond on this earth to me.

After talking with Linda, however, I knew it was not meant for me to go to her. I wanted to go to the safety of Linda's home, but I didn't want to leave Howard. I was running, but I didn't really want to run. I simply knew not to leave Lubbock.

Getting settled at Grace's home didn't take much. The only possessions I had brought with me were my ceramic doves. Other than the necessary clothing we needed, these were all I had.

Elizabeth had taken her little stuffed animal. This was about all she had as well. Not having any of my furniture or possessions around me made me feel just that much more alone. I knew I wasn't alone, but it was still a very hard time for my little girl and me.

However, I woke each morning asking God to renew a right spirit in me and to give me the joy of His salvation. (Create in me a clean heart, O God; and renew a right spirit within me. Psalms 51:10) I had gone through the motions of eating, sleeping, praying, working, praying, crying and praying for weeks now. Living seemed to have no point. Here I was with no home, not knowing what to do, not wanting to go back, hating life and seeing no future. I felt God had given up on me. I felt God had given me back to Satan and God was way off somewhere watching me hurt.

I had by no means turned on God. But I felt like I just existed. I didn't know what I was going through except that each morning meant another day of the routine of nothing!

If this was all there was to living, spending the rest of my days in sorrow, if this was the way it was always going to be to love God, I was beginning to think it wasn't worth it.

I knew God had allowed me to witness miracles of healing in mine and my daughter's lives. God had spoken to me. He had used my testimony to win other lost souls to Him. Yet, I was hurting in a way that I could not explain. I could not pretend to be joyous no matter how hard I tried. I was not able to plaster a false grin on my face or to take the pain from my eyes. I was not able to stop the tears or to stop loving Howard.

I wanted to give up. The strength I had had was no longer there. Living a forced life was horrible. I had to make myself get up, go to work, love my enemies, do my job, drive home, stay home, smile, eat, pray, and most of all to live.

Finally, "Little-Miss-Christian" had had enough. I got mad. I got mad at God. *"I rebel!"* I said to God. It was late one evening. I lay down in bed. I raised my eyes to heaven, and I came up out of my bed full of anger. The tears stopped. I felt like I was broken. I had had enough.

No more, no more was I going to live hating life. No more was I going to be perfect. No more was I going to take everything everyone could dish out to me.

I raised my fist to God. *"If this is Your joy, if this is what comes from giving up my whole life for You, if this pure hell is the reward of living a good life, having to leave my friends, having my family think I'm crazy and part of them turning on me, being blessed by other's hate and jealousy, having to give up my home and the only man I had ever loved, if all these wonderful killing sorrows are all there are to living, then I refuse to live. I quit! I rebel, I rebel, do You hear me God, I rebel."* I cried out. I refused to live like this, striving to keep every commandment, thousands of them, having to live right so others would see all the wonderful blessings of God, pretending to be happy so others would want God in their lives. This was phony. It wasn't worth it, any of it.

I hurt! I was as unhappy as a person could get. I had no desire to live. I had no joy. I felt like a whipped dog. Being a Christian was a living hell. I couldn't go have a drink. I couldn't smoke pot. I couldn't make love. I couldn't laugh. I had even forgotten how to laugh. I was as far from my friends as though we were in two different worlds.

In fact, I no longer had any friends. I was a Christian and Christians live right. They don't love right. Man, this was the pits! I walked around the bedroom until morning building up a lot of fight inside myself. I was not going to whimper anymore. I was not going to just exist anymore. I was on a roll, telling everything to God.

It didn't stop there either. I drove to work prepared for battle. I was angry, mad right down to the bone. I had taken enough. I was the dead duck with the vultures picking at me daily. I walked into that office not with a smile but with fury aimed at months of being ridiculed, joked about and ugly things said to me.

I had enough! My cheeks were not going to turn one more time. I wasn't a puppet, nor was I a weak woman. I had forgiven until now. I was forgiven out. It was past seventy times seven, as the scripture requires.

Despite my anger, I walked into my office and began working. I had no intention of starting any trouble. I wasn't looking for trouble.

I didn't have to. It had a way of finding me. It wasn't just the cruelty of one person. Most all the employees thought I was a real joke. I was a Christian. I had fought to act like one. There was one person at work who was really open with her sarcasm toward me.

That day, I felt the weight of the world on my shoulders. I didn't know myself anymore. I didn't like the new me, broken! But I managed to keep everything hidden. I worked as usual and tried to stay to myself as much as possible. I didn't want anyone to know I was hurting.

I left my desk to get a cup of coffee and as I turned the corner from my office to the adjoining office, the inevitable happened. Fight came into me. I had to make myself have self-control. A woman made an ugly comment about me to another employee. Together they laughed, watching me. They were used to me just letting these remarks pass over me. But this time I turned toward them and yelled, "I'm not Howard's lay! And my name is Mary, not sweetie baby! Other than doing this job, don't you cross me again. I don't give a damn what you think of me, but you better keep your mouth shut. Don't jack with me again. Don't think I won't jump both of you right here! Come on if you think I don't mean it, just move, just say one more word. I'm ready right now!"

Silence, dead silence was everyone's reaction. Two others who had come into the room looked at the two women I had retaliated against. Both of them had a look of pure shock on their faces.

I stood firm looking at both of them. I was ready for battle. I would have knocked one of them out of her chair. Everyone knew I meant business. I wasn't afraid of anyone. Job or no job, Little-Miss-Christian had had enough!

I kept my eyes locked on both women, looking both of them squarely in the eyes. The woman at her desk lowered her head and turned her chair to go back to work. The other one went out of the door back into the warehouse.

I turned and got a cup of coffee. It felt like the whole world had been lifted off me. I was able to stand up again without making myself. I walked back into my office, sat down and knew this battle was over.

I looked at a picture hanging on the wall. Suddenly I could picture Jesus walking on water and I felt remorse. "Forgive me, Father, for the weakness in myself, forgive me for using damn as cussing," I repented.

I had not wanted to have trouble with anyone. In fact, I had spent weeks trying to avoid several office workers, pretending I didn't hear their laughter and remarks about me.

I had prayed for all of them. I had tried to forgive and not let hate take residence in my heart. I really was trying to be a *lady* and live like one. I had shared my testimony, telling the truth, too much of it.

This was when I wrote the poem, "I Rebel." By the time I had composed the last few lines, I realized that God hadn't left me. I realized what I had just gone through was a test. God had tried my reins. He was molding me into a disciple He could use, instead of one struggling to be like others and trying to be accepted by people, a disciple blessed by God.

I don't know exactly what happened that day, but I realized later how much of God had come into that office. It was as though God Himself came right out of heaven and said, ***"Look, this is my kid and I'm the King! It's Me she's been beaten down for. I'll put up with it no more!"*** After completing the poem, I felt like an army of angels were around me. I saw His smile as He went back to His throne.

From that day on, a completely new atmosphere took place. Attitudes changed for the better. We began to work in harmony. The hate and jealousy seemed to die and respect took its place. I was one of the employees instead of the outsider, the Bible banger. Respect that I was a Christian took the place of the rejected.

My love for Christ grew. I felt extremely blessed. I felt the presence of God's Spirit around me every day. His angels did protect me. God, as only He could do, changed the attitude of a whole company of employees for just one of His children, me. Good had come out of the words.....**I Rebel.**

Linda Curbo and Mary
April 21, 1973

Linda Curbo 2008

Matthew 18:21-22

21 Then came Peter to him, and said, Lord, how oft shall my brother sin against me, and I forgive him? till seven times?

22 Jesus saith unto him, *I say not unto thee, Until seven times: but, Until seventy times seven*.

Romans 12:19-21

19 Dearly beloved, avenge not yourselves, but rather give place unto wrath: for it is written, Vengeance is mine; I will repay, saith the Lord.

20 Therefore if thine enemy hunger, feed him; if he thirst, give him drink: for in so doing thou shalt heap coals of fire on his head.

21 Be not overcome of evil, but overcome evil with good.

I REBEL

I want to die, I don't want to live.
I want to live, I don't want to die.
I'm in the domain of Satan's world.
I want to die, NO, not live.
Or is it simply that I have had my gut fill!
I rebel, I rebel, I rebel!
I stand before You with my head held high.
You, are the King, the King of all Kings.
You have all power, glory and strength.
Why do You let me crumble and fall before man?
I rebel, I rebel, You put me into Satan's hand.
When only You have the power to protect me from him!
Why did You put me under your wing,
Only to let him have me again?
I'm not afraid, don't you understand?
How like this can I love my neighbor and friend?
Give me Your power, Your strength within.
And I shall through You, stand up to him.
I will meet him face to face,
I will not falter from this race.
I'm sorry, my Father, I will rebel no more.
For as before You I stand,
I realize with me, You have always been.
Forgive me, You'll not hear me say again.....**I REBEL.**

Chapter 16:
SOUL

~

I was on my way home, but I knew I had to go over to Kitti's apartment. How did I know? I don't know. I just knew.

I walked into Kitti's home still without knowing why I was there. As close as we were, she didn't know why I was there either. I had only been there a few minutes when the phone rang. It was her ex-husband, an alcoholic and the man she still loved who was calling. He was coming over. I knew, yes, I knew, by listening to their conversation that I was there to lead him through a sinner's prayer.

When he arrived a short time later, he was as always, glad to see me. But he was in misery, total misery. He was drunk and wanted to die. To spend most of your life in a stupor had to be a hell I couldn't fully comprehend, yet I could understand the wish to die. He had carried much hurt, abuse, rejection and hate as well as love for many years.

The three of us were in her living room, and Kitti began talking to her ex-husband. She loved him so much. She had always loved him, but as a lot of alcoholic wives do, she chose to live without him rather go through the hell of living with him.

Adultery was also an issue, but it had not always been bad. The couple had a bond between them that only the two of them understood. They had shared and had fed each other's empty space somewhere along their journeys.

Kitti continued talking to him and tried to tell him about Jesus. He would fight it, arguing that it was all a bunch of -----! To say the least. I sat silently praying. "Father, in the name of Jesus Christ lead me with Your Spirit. Let me say the words that will touch his heart. Let me be Your voice and he will yield himself to You and Your salvation."

I began talking to him, when I realized I was not talking but begging him to accept Jesus. I sat back in my chair and said, "Stop, this is not right! You don't have to beg anyone to receive Jesus. He has to want Jesus for himself. I will not beg you or anyone else to ask Jesus to forgive him of his sins. You have to want Jesus to forgive you. You have to want Jesus." I sat back. Kitti and I said nothing. I looked directly into his eyes.

He understood what I said. He knew we were not going to beg him anymore. Then his attitude changed. He began asking us what to do. Somehow Christ had broken the stronghold Satan had on him.

I knelt before the man and took his hand. Kitti put her hand on his shoulder. I said, "You have to talk to Jesus yourself." He answered, "I don't know how."

I replied, "I will help you with the words, but you say them for Jesus, not to me." I then led him through a very simple prayer, asking Jesus for forgiveness, acknowledging Him as Lord and that He died and then was raised.

My friend asked Jesus Christ to come into his heart, to heal him and bless him with His love and peace. He asked for forgiveness for all his sins. Then he opened his eyes and peace had overturned the tears of sorrow to tears of salvation.

I asked Christ to fill him with His joy. We sat still for just a short time when a big smile came upon his face. He leaned back and the tears of joy began running down his face. He laughed, jumped up and down, rolled and we laughed with him. I noticed something else. He was no longer drunk, he was sober!

God in a split second had removed the alcohol from his system before He allowed His Spirit to fill him. Kitti and I hugged each other and enjoyed the joy that the love of her life was experiencing.

I went into her bathroom and prayed, "Christ, why am I not filled with the peace I've always had when I've led a sinner to you?"

I later drove home. On the way, the blessings of joy and peace overcame me.

I still didn't understand everything, but I believed His will had been done that day. I believed my friend had received his salvation, but I had no idea of what was in store for Kitti or my friend.

He had not asked Christ into his heart before this day, and he had much to overcome. The battle for him had just begun. Only Christ knew his heart, and only Christ had paid the price for his.....**Soul.**

Luke 15:10

10 *Likewise, I say unto you, there is joy in the presence of the angels of God over one sinner that repenteth.*

SOUL

One more Soul to the kingdom of heaven.

One SOUL shall enter the gates of glory.

Listen as before the angels there is singing with a shout!

Praise you Lord, for what You have caused to come about.

Praise you Father, Your love and mercy with the angels will sing and shout!

Here was a man lost to darkness.

He was bound to Satan, and all his misery and sin.

You sent him love, You sent him Your Spirit within.

Praise you God, we bow down to Your will.

We'll sing with the angels; his SOUL shall not enter hell!

For You are the way, the truth and the life.

And for Your children, Satan shall You spew and cast out.

Praise You, glory to Your kingdom and name.

As Your words seek and find, I am the KING and always my child, always the same.

I rejoice, I rejoice for even one more.....**SOUL.**

Chapter 17:
DECISION

~

Christmas was so close. It had now been almost a year since God came to me in the form of a cloud. I had spent nearly a year striving to overcome, striving to let go of Howard, striving to go on with Jesus Christ. Howard was still a very live part of me. I still loved him as I had before I had asked Christ into my life and my heart.

Howard was driving a truck again. He had quit or been fired from the company he was driving for when I moved out of the farm house where we were living together. I learned later he worked in a bar somewhere for a period of time.

He had been driving a truck, an eighteen wheeler for nearly sixteen years. He had tried to stop driving, but was always drawn back to it. I didn't try to find out who he was driving for, where he was driving to, where he lived or anything else about him. I didn't talk about him. I kept my feelings to myself.

I simply contemplated quietly the past and the future to myself. When I did see him or talk to him, I knew he was under great conviction from God. He wasn't enjoying the life of the macho man that driving trucks had brought out in him. He had gone from job to job to job. He couldn't hold onto any job for any length of time. He was very limited in job opportunities. He had very little education. He lived the lifestyle of a biker, the outlaw night lifestyle. Howard knew how to lay bricks and set tile, but it was the truck driving that was a part of him and his way of living.

Howard was trying to replace me as hard as I was trying to replace him. It wasn't working for either of us. I was turning to God to heal my pain and he was relying on women and drugs for his joy. It was really something.

He would try to change, and then he would be drawn back. He

would stand, and then he would fall again. I had done everything I knew to do. I had released him to God and cut the cord between us, more than once. But God saw fit for him to return to me over and over. It was hard letting go of him and even harder not to take him back.

I felt that God was using me to reach him. I felt that God was sending Howard to me. I didn't think it was the work of Satan. I didn't go to him. He came to me. God knew my heart. He blessed me at times by lifting the pain from me, but I was not healed of my love for this man, in fact it seemed to be growing deeper.

Howard believed everything about God that I shared with him. He had no struggle with faith. It was commitment that was throwing him. He was afraid to let go of the things that gave him security: his friends, his drugs, and his women. Howard couldn't stand to be alone. At one time neither could I.

I was always married again after a divorce in about a week after it was final. Howard was just like me, only I, through God, could now live without a companion. I wanted God to supply my needs. I really wanted God to be my husband. (For thy Maker is thine husband; the LORD of hosts is his name; and thy Redeemer the Holy One of Israel; The God of the whole earth shall he be called. Isaiah 54:5) I didn't want sex to have a part in what I was learning about love.

Three months after having a peace bond put on Howard and forcing him out of my house, I began to realize just how much God would supply my needs.

There was little money. It took all my pay check to pay the rent and pay the utilities. There was little left even for food. I had gotten just the right change to get a stamp. I had to mail my rent to the owner's home. On my way home from work, I stopped at the post office. I put the change into the machine for one precious stamp. Nothing happened. The change would not come back and a stamp didn't drop. I stood there in the mail station, in total depression. What was I going to do now? I had no more money. Tears filled my eyes. *"Help me Lord."* I cried.

The machine suddenly made a sound like a pin-ball machine. Then a light came on, a bright light. The section next to the one I had put my money in dropped a package of four stamps. I stood in amazement. Tears of depression turned into tears of happiness. God had just performed a miracle for me. There is no explanation as to how this could happen. I simply believed in Jesus. I believed in miracles.

I felt that if anyone on this earth understood Howard, it was me. I now had learned how Satan puts up a real battle for the soul of a person who gives their heart to Jesus. I had read where some seed falls by the wayside. I understood this scripture. Howard had no roots. (*Matthew 13:4-6) He was in a battle and I couldn't fight it for him.

I was sitting in church on a Sunday night, I felt Howard's presence. Even though the church was very large, I sensed that he was looking at me.

The preacher had started the sermon. I sat a few minutes longer and turned and looked toward the back of the church. There Howard stood. It was very quiet.

Others saw me turn and some craned their necks to see what was going on. When I saw Howard, the tears came quickly and plentifully. I couldn't stop them.

Howard came walking down the aisle toward me, his eyes glued to mine. At times, more could be said by the eyes than in words. He sat down beside me. I could tell he was extremely tense. Churches scared him just like they did me most of my life, that is until over a year ago when I began attending the church I was in. I took his hand after he sat down. He relaxed. We sat without words.

At the end of the sermon, the preacher asked for those who wanted special prayer to come forward. I stood beside Howard. Feeling the presence of God I began to pray. "Father, please, please show him the way, witness Your Spirit so powerfully that he can't turn away."

I felt Howard reach for his heart. I looked up into his face. It was red and full of fear. For the first time in his life, he was feeling the Holy Spirit move within him. Yes, inside him. Howard leaned over to me and said, "I think I'm having a heart attack." I couldn't keep from laughing. He didn't think one thing about it was funny.

"It's the Holy Spirit you feel. God is witnessing to you. Please don't tell Him no," I said. Howard relaxed, but he didn't take his hand from his chest. His countenance changed. He didn't want it to stop. He was holding onto the touch of God.

Howard had prayed several times for forgiveness, salvation and peace during this year, but he never really left his way of life. "Praise you Father. Thank You for answering my prayer. I do love You so very much." Howard turned to me and said, "I'll be back in a minute."

He almost ran to the front of the church. It took me a minute for me to realize where he was going. "Father, break him. Don't give him peace until he is willing to make You Lord of his life." I was so excited and my faith in Howard's salvation was renewed.

I saw my Wednesday night teacher, Charles, a man I greatly respected. I considered him a friend. I ran to him and said, "Guess who's here, Charlie! Guess who's here!" I was jumping up and down. He smiled and jumped up and down a couple of times to let me know that he had picked up my excitement and said, "Who, who's here?" I said, "Howard, Howard is here. God's Spirit came alive in him."

I saw Howard coming toward me. I ran to him and threw my arms around him and said, "I love you." He smiled and then I introduced him to Charlie. Poor Charlie didn't have a clue of who Howard was. I hadn't shared my life with Charlie concerning Howard. Later I did share with Charlie who Howard was and the part he played in my life.

A little over a month had passed since that Sunday night. I hadn't seen Howard in a few days. I was hurting, hurting badly. I just wanted to hear his voice, but I wouldn't make any attempt to contact him. I was depressed. It seemed as though my life was somewhere else.

I was alive, but not living. I seldom laughed anymore. My joy was a pretense for those around me. My hurt was only known by God.

I didn't discuss Howard with anyone at this time, except God. I could not lie or hide my feelings from God. It was very seldom that

I would tell Howard that I loved him. In fact during the past year, I don't think I told him this more than once or twice, maybe I had, but at the time I couldn't remember. To tell him that I loved him and then push him out the door was something I was not strong enough to do right now.

I drove home from work and picked up my daughter from the baby sitter. I sat down on my couch with my Bible in hand and began to pray for strength. I seldom watched television. My nose was in my Bible most all my free time. I went to bed early each evening, about eight thirty or nine. I would pray and listen to some religious music. I had long since stopped listening to country and western music. It tore at my heart and the memories made me even more depressed. I lay in bed knowing I had done everything I could to release Howard. The months and months of suffering and the daily burdens made me feel like I had gone through everything to make God Lord of my life, and I had!

But the days seemed to grow longer and longer. The hours seemed so pointless. There seemed to be no purpose to life. Living a clean life of only going to work and to church was getting to me. It was getting to me deep down and everything was becoming so pointless. My joy much of the time depended upon Howard's joy.

The joy of the Lord was seldom felt. From the time Howard felt the Holy Spirit, I saw no change in him. I didn't understand what I was going through. I began to pray. I asked God to give me a purpose to live, a reason to get up in the morning.

Money was a big problem, but so was everything else. It was Christmas. The only person I was concerned about was my little girl, Elizabeth. I wanted to be close to Jesus on His birthday. Santa Claus didn't have anything to do with it. My parents had sent me a check for thirty dollars for my Christmas. It was all the money I had. I was happy to get it. I didn't know what to do with it – buy a tree, buy a gift, and buy food.

The following Sunday I drove to church. My attitude had changed. "This is enough, this is enough God. I want a blessing and I want it today!" I firmly said aloud to God. I expected something from Him. I thought Howard might come in again.

While standing during praise and worship, I felt a tug at my shoulder. I turned, my heart filled with such joy. Standing behind me were Howard's three boys. They had great big smiles on their faces. They hugged me. I hadn't seen them in several weeks. When the service was over, I asked the oldest if he would ask his mother if they could come and eat with me. "Don't lie to her. Tell her the truth." I said.

The boys left and soon returned happy and excited to be going with me. Elizabeth, along with Howard's three sons, Ray, Lee and Neal and I went to Long John Silvers. I spent the whole thirty dollars on this meal. We talked and shared our memories of when Howard and I had been together. It was so much fun to be with them. They had always let me know they loved me.

God hadn't answered my prayers in any way I thought He would. Instead, he gave me something I thought I might not ever have again – these three boys.

I began to grow closer to my daughter. She was becoming my little girl. I began to recognize her needs. For the first time in my life, I was becoming a mother.

Realizing God was with Howard, I didn't know which way he would go. He was going to have to make a.....**DECISION.**

*Matthew 13:4-6
4   *And when he sowed, some seeds fell by the way side, and the fowls came and devoured them up:*
5   *Some fell upon stony places, where they had not much earth: and forthwith they sprung up, because they had no deepness of earth:*
6   *And when the sun was up, they were scorched; and because they had no root, they withered away.*

DECISION

This is a time of decision for you,
And I know what you're going through.
I know of the turmoil, all the confusion.
I know as the memories cross your mind,
I know as Satan gives you his kind of thoughts,
That this time for you, this time of decision,
To turn around, you must know there is a powerful reason!
Remember the healing, He did for you.
Remember His Spirit, He filled within you.
Remember the peace, the comfort, remember He came when He heard your call.
There is nothing more I can do for you.
Except stand back and wait for what you're going to do.
My love, my darling, I stand in the back and say to my Father,
I have done what I had to,
To totally release him to You!
The battle he is feeling, the time for his decision,
Whatever he does, the final step he takes,
I know You have given him, all and every chance!
For now the decision , the decision I wait to see is his.....
DECISION.

Chapter 18:
IT IS BETTER TO GIVE

~

It was a Saturday morning. I sat in my living room ready to read my Bible. Elizabeth was playing outside with her friend, Stormy, who lived just a few houses down the street from ours. Stormy and Elizabeth were about the same age. They had become good friends and were together a lot.

The doorbell rang. It was Stormy's mother, Donna. She had stopped by to pick up her daughter. It was a comfort to me for the girls to be such good friends. Elizabeth got very lonely by herself. It gave me private time to myself when they played together.

I asked Donna to come in. She sat down on my couch and before I knew how it happened, I was telling her about my life. It seemed like I couldn't stop. I couldn't believe that I was telling this woman all this stuff about myself. I told her of my childhood years, followed by the years I spent on the streets, in bars etc.

Donna Ratcliff kept Elizabeth for me at times, but we had not really talked. Our girls were friends and wanted to be together most of the time. This is what brought us together.

I shared with Donna about Howard and then I shared with her about Jesus Christ and God, how God spoke to me in the form of a cloud. Everything came pouring out of me. I couldn't talk fast enough. I was afraid she would leave and the story would be incomplete. But Donna listened for close to two hours. I don't know why I felt so free to tell her everything, but I did. This woman knew nothing about my daughter and me until now.

I was so bound up inside. I needed someone who would listen. I needed someone who didn't know Howard or our past to just listen as I poured out a river of pain. This woman listened the whole time. I didn't lie about anything or try to smooth over the rough edges. I had been a tramp, a whore, a thief, a liar, etc., etc., etc., for many years.

Now I had a changed heart. I hated the things in my past. Many tears had flowed in the privacy of my bedroom when I allowed myself to think about all the horrid things I had done to myself but more importantly to my children, my parents and others.

Many times I had this overwhelming desire to go to some mountain top and shout, "He lives!" He's alive, He is real, Jesus Christ is real and He loves you!" Today I was not on a mountain top but in my little home. As of yet Elizabeth and I had not moved in with Grace, Mother Superior. As I shared with Donna, I became aware of a heaviness being removed from me. I felt clean. I felt pure. I felt free. Jesus Christ loved me. I was learning about love.

Only after Donna knew I had released everything in my heart did she begin to tell me about a portion of her life. God had done a great miracle of healing for the man she loved, her husband and the father of her children. After many tears during several years of faithful prayer, God honored her heart's desire. Then sorrows came due to the rebellion of her children, but she carried this cross and kept it between herself and Jesus Christ.

Our friendship grew, although we didn't visit on a daily basis, and we didn't go places together. Donna became a precious friend. Not once did she talk against, condemn, judge or execute Howard with her tongue. Donna would just listen.

There was another time when she stopped cooking supper, put everything aside, sat down with me in her home and said, "Talk to me Mary Ann. Pour it all out." Donna didn't know it but she kept me from driving off a bridge. I don't know how I may have attempted to do this, but I sure was heading for it.

There was no money for a baby sitter, so Donna kept my daughter for me every day after school until I got home from work. There was no one else, no one to help me, no one. She gave her love to my daughter, her time, her privacy, her energy. I didn't even really know her but she gave me her love and she shared and carried my burdens through her prayers, giving it all to Jesus.

At the time, I was going to all kinds of prayer meetings. I was searching for Christ, a closer walk with Him. I wanted to know Him, to be close to Him. Other people shared their experiences with me.

I fed on every word that would help me to grow and understand.

Christmas was coming up fast. Elizabeth and I were attending a prayer meeting when I looked at her and for the first time realized she had no Christmas. I hadn't decorated at all. My heart was not in it and I had no money. Elizabeth loved to look at the houses we drove by lit up with lights and nice things. I had become so involved with myself that I didn't even see her tears. During prayer time, I silently asked Christ if He would give something to my daughter.

Several days came and went. I drove home from work as I did every day. I pulled into my driveway, got out of my car and opened my front door. Elizabeth started clapping her hands and running all over the living room. Donna and her girls had come while I was at work and put up a Christmas tree. They left out the back door when I arrived. The tree had lights and everything. Underneath it were gifts for Elizabeth and for me. I became overwhelmed with such a miracle. People just don't do this kind of thing. I heaved from within as the tears streamed down my face. I had heard or read of such things happening to people but I never dreamed it could happen for us.

By now Elizabeth and I were both crying with joy. I took my daughter's little hand as she smiled up at me and we both began to thank Jesus for such a blessing. I don't think I expected anything. I had asked for something for Elizabeth, but I didn't really think I could find a way to give Elizabeth a Christmas.

I was lost for the words to express my love and gratitude to Donna and her family for sharing their love for Elizabeth and me. I prayed for several days. I cried and prayed for God to reveal to me how to thank her, how to express the depth of my appreciation and love to her. I wanted to light flashes in the sky for her. I wanted to take her a million dollars. I wanted to give her the world. I had nothing to give in return.

Several days later I tried to express to her my feelings, but I didn't even come close to opening my heart to her. Instead, I began to pray for Donna and her family. I asked God to bless her with His rewarding peace, throughout their lives.

"Thank you," Donna. "To you and your family I send my love.

You helped carry Elizabeth and me through a difficult part of our lives. Your true reward awaits you in heaven. You taught us".....**IT IS BETTER TO GIVE.**

Matthew 25:40

40 ***And the King shall answer and say unto them, Verily I say unto you, Inasmuch as ye have done it unto one of the least of these my brethren, ye have done it unto me.***

Luke 6:38

38 ***Give, and it shall be given unto you; good measure, pressed down, and shaken together, and running over, shall men give into your bosom. For with the same measure that ye mete withal it shall be measured to you again.***

NOTE: This is the last Christmas Elizabeth and I spent in this little house. It was in the days to come that we had to leave and move in with Grace.

Timmi Elizabeth
8 years old
December 1979

IT IS BETTER TO GIVE

When I opened the door, I just stood there in total amazement.
Elizabeth's eyes were full of sparkles as she clapped her hands and
before me she danced.
She told me you had come, while I was at work.
You put up a tree, in celebration of Jesus Christ's birth.
I couldn't cry, I couldn't stand, I knelt and took hold of my
daughter's hand.
Together we prayed and thanked God for this special day.
It's all been worth it, the valley where we have been.
It's all been worth it, to repent of our sins.
You, our neighbors, you, our darling, darling friends,
Have blessed us, you have shown us, IT IS BETTER TO GIVE!
I have no money, I have no gifts.
But to you for the following of all your days, will receive the
promise which comes from GOD, this day.
A band of Angels will He send.
Your home, you and your children shall abide in the middle of
them.
There will no harm come to your door.
You'll see your home prosper as never before.
You'll see your children turn to each other.
God shall bind them and to one there shall come visions.
You have purity, you have kept the ROYAL COMMANDMENT.
The son who is among you now,
Through God you'll see him wear a crown.
God knows what you have done.
This prophecy I give to you,
In the following days, you'll see to come true.....**IT IS BETTER
TO GIVE.**

Chapter 19:
FRIEND

Going back to when I first began this journey with Jesus Christ, I had gone to church at Trinity Fellowship in Lubbock, TX, only two or three times.

It was a Sunday night and I was very confused. I sat in the pew listening to the sermon but my mind was elsewhere. I was thinking of everything that had happened in the last few months. I had put Howard in jail. We were again living together. We shared the same house and the same bed, yet there was a wall between us. The wall was growing deeper and higher as each day passed.

I didn't know what I was going to do. I think I didn't want to face the fact that I was going to have to give Howard up again. This time I couldn't take him back. I was training my thoughts to accept that this time it would be final. I sat quietly in my own little world until the sermon was finished.

The preacher then asked for those seeking prayer or wanting someone to talk to or someone to share with to come forward and pray with a member of the church. I stood there several minutes wondering what I was going to say to someone else. I stepped out into the aisle not really wanting to. But I walked toward the front of the church and a man motioned to me. As I started toward him, I saw a very dignified, poised lady hold her arm out to me.

I froze inside. This woman was one of the well bred, well educated, well accepted, well poised, well everything that I wasn't.

We went into a small room together. I began telling her in all honesty just who I was. The woman, whose name was Grace, sat very quietly and listened to me, her big brown eyes would bat a few extra times as she heard my story. I knew that she was lost as to my background. I was one of those people, not one of them!

I wanted her to tell me that I could stay with Howard. I told her I would share Howard with his children, I would go to church. I would stay out of clubs. I would leave other men alone. I would live right before God with the exception of Howard. I wanted God's permission to keep Howard.

Grace waited until I had completed my heart's plea. "No!" Grace said boldly. She patted her Bible, which was lying in her lap. She looked me right in the eyes and firmly said, "This says you can't."

These were not the understanding comforting words I wanted to hear. She did not compromise what she knew the Bible said. I had not even begun to understand much more than a sentence. I began again to tell her how I would live and what I wanted. She would listen until I finished and again pat her Bible and say, "This says you can't."

What argument did I have? Grace didn't open her Bible one time and read any scripture to me. She simply replied in power to me. I knew this woman was in high authority with God. She didn't have to open her Bible. She knew exactly what she was talking about. It had nothing to do with me, my past, or my living conditions. The Bible was alive for her. It lived within her heart. Grace was patient in listening. She said very few words.

God hadn't directed me to a little old gray-haired lady that would hold my hand, cry with me and tell me everything was all right. God drew Grace to me, and she was a tower of strength. I didn't like her because she wouldn't tell me what I wanted to hear. Instead, she told me the truth.

But I recognized her authority. I couldn't back this woman into a corner. She wasn't afraid of me. I kept trying to explain to her my every good intention. I told the truth about myself. She needed to understand how much pain had been in my life. Then I would clearly explain my love for Howard.

There was no changing Grace's mind, as she continued to pat her Bible and say, "This says you can't if you love God." Love God? Of course I loved God! He had spoken to me, although I was barely learning about Jesus Christ. Surely I loved God, but I longed for Howard also.

Grace wrote her address on a bulletin and we parted after a

prayer. I knew it wouldn't take me long to get rid of her address once I got away from her. I left the church feeling more miserable than when I had arrived. I was in such turmoil that I didn't remember driving home. I was just home. I went into the house and got ready for bed. I lay quietly wondering what was going to happen now.

About three o'clock in the morning, Howard came in, undressed and crawled into bed next to me. I didn't give in to his drunken lust, but I did have an overwhelming desire to blow his head off! What in the world was there about this man that made me love him? Thankfully, he soon fell into a stuporous sleep. I got out of bed and went into my daughter's room and got in bed with her, holding her very close to me.

Several months passed. I was now sleeping in my car a lot. Elizabeth was with her grandmother. I was getting fed up with sleeping in my car in whatever parking lot I felt safe in. I even spent one night in a motel just so I could watch television.

I would leave home in the afternoon before Howard came in. Then I would go back to get ready for work in the morning when I knew he would be gone. There were times he didn't come in.

I didn't care anymore. I still loved him, but I sure was trying to hate him. I stayed away from Howard as much as possible. I felt dead inside. But I was reading the Bible all the time. God was my best friend. He gave me the strength to keep on living. God showed Himself to me on a daily basis. The Holy Spirit manifested Himself within my heart regularly. God said few words, but I recognized His voice.

I knew I was going to have to get Howard out of my little home again! How in the world was I going to be able to go through it? "My God, why don't you kill my love for him?" I pleaded.

I really didn't understand why God wouldn't just speak the words and the pain would be over. My thoughts turned to Grace, the woman who had talked with me in church in the little prayer room.

I had no idea what her last name was and no idea of where she lived. So, on a weekday night, out of desperation, I drove to the church. The parking lot was empty. I only knew I needed this woman right now, "Right Now!"

I didn't know why it was Grace that I needed. I didn't even like her, yet I longed to talk to her. I stopped my car at the side of the church, picked up my Bible on the front seat and opened it toward the back. A piece of paper fell out. I hadn't even remembered that it was there. I reached down and picked it up.

Here was the church bulletin from the meeting with Grace that I thought I had long ago thrown away. Grace's name and address stood out boldly, like lightning. Grace lived just across the street from the church!

I immediately went to her house and knocked on her door. The look of love when she opened the door was what I desperately needed. She held out her arms as I hungrily went into them. I cried and told her what had been going on for the last few months. She said she had prayed for me every night, "Lord, I don't know where she is or what she's doing, but You do. Bring her back into your fold, lead her, and give her the strength to make You Lord of her life." This was the prayer of a woman I didn't even know, but it was a fruitful, faithful prayer.

Grace and I talked for a long time. She told me I wasn't part of her repertoire as she smiled a very pretty smile. I didn't even know what the word meant, but I understood what she was saying. She wasn't in my repertoire either!

Grace showed me verses in the Bible to stand on. The one I needed the most at this time was *Isaiah 54:5-17. Verse five especially stood out to me. God would be my husband. He would lead me through and protect me through all my sorrows.

Grace offered me a bed for the night but I declined. I stayed in my car that night. The next day I again put Howard under a peace bond. He moved out with the help of two officers. I reached out to God with all that was in me.

During this time, Grace was one of the pillars I leaned on. I turned to her daily.

God had brought two people from completely different lives together. God was the foundation and Grace was a pillar stone that helped hold the body of Christ together. Many times I would talk to Grace several times a day.

I didn't share with anyone else what was happening like I did with her. Only Grace was able to quote scripture. And only Grace was able to comfort me. She had a love that surpassed all my understanding. She had God's love. We went to prayer meetings together, and we shared much of our time together.

Grace had faced sorrow, sorrows that made mine seem very minor. She had watched her husband, a successful businessman, turn from a man into a child then into a vegetable. She was in a valley for three years before God took him home.

I believed with all my heart that this woman would have laid down her life for me. Grace bore my burdens, the persecution from my co-workers, the drunken drugged-up visits from Howard, the stabs of hurting words from my family and the rejection from my friends. Not once did she complain. Not once did she not have time for me. Not once did she cast me out and not once did she judge me. I told her about my going to a club once. She didn't condemn me or preach to me. She prayed for me. Only God had the power to control me and she knew who to turn to.

Elizabeth and I later moved into Grace's home. We shared a bedroom together. This was close to the end of the first year of my salvation. But my love for Howard seemed to be growing instead of dying. I was planning on leaving Lubbock very soon. I thought I would go to Linda Curbo, a friend. There was nothing holding me back, except Howard. But I couldn't seem to take the final step of leaving him. Seeing him just a little made it easier, for an hour or two.

Grace was having a hard time watching me hurt. She prayed for me endlessly. She didn't try to tell me God's will for me. No one knew God's will for me, but God. She knew I had done everything in my power to release Howard. She knew I fought with all my heart to please God.

One day, Grace was walking to the church and saw Howard and me driving around together. He had come to my job and forced me to get into the car with him. We had been driving around for some time and talking. Howard stopped the car, and I got out and went to her.

I knew it hurt her to see me with Howard. She had seen me hurt so very much over him. I hugged her and said, "I have to see him. I need him." Grace just smiled and told me she loved me. I got back into the car with Howard. Grace went into the church and prayed as I knew she would. I didn't ever have to ask her to pray.

During this first year, my valley with God, Grace became **MOTHER SUPERIOR** to me. I began calling her this out of much love, enormous respect, and friendship that I had for her. It had nothing to do with my religion, or any religion. I gave her the name because I felt she was superior, in every way.

This woman wore a crown that you might not be able to see, but her recognition of Christ was astounding, and her authority in Christ was bewildering. If I could give to her the love I feel for her it would be to hold her hand before our KING and watch as HE with His son Jesus lifted her to the chosen round table of our Lord. He would smile, knowing she paid a price to be my.....**FRIEND.**

*Isaiah 54:5-17
5   For thy Maker is thine husband; the LORD of hosts is his name; and thy Redeemer the Holy One of Israel; The God of the whole earth shall he be called.
6   For the LORD hath called thee as a woman forsaken and grieved in spirit, and a wife of youth, when thou wast refused, saith thy God.
7   For a small moment have I forsaken thee; but with great mercies will I gather thee.
8   In a little wrath I hid my face from thee for a moment; but with everlasting kindness will I have mercy on thee, saith the LORD thy Redeemer.
9   For this is as the waters of Noah unto me: for as I have sworn that the waters of Noah should no more go over the earth; so have I sworn that I would not be wroth with thee, nor rebuke thee.
10 For the mountains shall depart, and the hills be removed; but my kindness shall not depart from thee, neither shall the covenant of my peace be removed, saith the LORD that hath mercy on thee.

11 O thou afflicted, tossed with tempest, and not comforted, behold, I will lay thy stones with fair colours, and lay thy foundations with sapphires.

12 And I will make thy windows of agates, and thy gates of carbuncles, and all thy borders of pleasant stones.

13 And all thy children shall be taught of the LORD; and great shall be the peace of thy children.

14 In righteousness shalt thou be established: thou shalt be far from oppression; for thou shalt not fear: and from terror; for it shall not come near thee.

15 Behold, they shall surely gather together, but not by me: whosoever shall gather together against thee shall fall for thy sake.

16 Behold, I have created the smith that bloweth the coals in the fire, and that bringeth forth an instrument for his work; and I have created the waster to destroy.

17 No weapon that is formed against thee shall prosper; and every tongue that shall rise against thee in judgment thou shalt condemn. This is the heritage of the servants of the LORD, and their righteousness is of me, saith the LORD.

James 5:16

16 Confess your faults one to another, and pray one for another, that ye may be healed. The effectual fervent prayer of a righteous man availeth much.

The last picture taken of Grace and I was taken several years after our first meeting at Trinity Fellowship Church, Lubbock, Texas. This is the last time I saw Grace. Her last words to me were, "Mary, Jesus trusting me with you is one of my greatest rewards." She patted me on the cheek, and gave me one of her many, many little love kisses on my cheek. I turned from her front porch, and left her home.

Grace Waggoner
MOTHER SUPERIOR

Grace & Mary
(last picture taken)

FRIEND

Come my friend, take hold of my hand.
I'll take you up, I'll take you right before.....HIM.
You in your golden years and I have just begun.
He has blessed me with you,
And I shall bless you, through, and before.....HIM.
Come to me, my eagle, I through GOD command.
Come yea, my angels, take hold of our hands.
Ride with us, as we go to stand before.....HIM.
As we ride through heaven, you shall see, all HIS beauty HE created
for you and me.
Look around you my darling, darling friend.
You are totally, totally away from sin.
Take hold of an angel, step from the side, you with an angel, with an
angel you will fly.
Praise you Jesus, Praise you God.
Give witness unto us, as before you we stand.
I am of the young, in a vision to me you've come.
I bring my friend; I ask you to bless her this day.
Give her witness, as together we pray.
THANK YOU GOD, KING OF KINGS, only through you can
this be done.
THANK YOU JESUS, the SON of OUR KING, for YOU, to your
FATHER, have let us come.
Thank you, thank you for Grace my treasured.....**FRIEND.**

Chapter 20:
KITTI

Kitti and I became friends for the first time after we quit school and had both married. In school we had nothing to do with each other. There were three cliques of friends in school, the upper, middle and lower. Kitti ran with the middle and I was below the lowest. I ran with no one. My reputation was all the way past the bottom of the bottom.

I married at the age of seventeen just a few months before Kitti married. My husband and I lived in his mother's house with her. We lived in town. Kitti and her husband lived in the country. We were the only kids married at such a young age. I don't remember how our relationship began, but we started visiting each other. We would go to the show, play card games and take turns cooking for each other. We didn't drink. Go to clubs, smoke dope or any of the other things we really didn't know about.

Kitti had to fight for our friendship. Her parents didn't want her to run with the kid with such a bad reputation. I was definitely the wrong kind of person. I did what I pleased and when I pleased. I think my parents signed the papers for my marriage because they couldn't do anything with me and they were ashamed of me.

It was a long time after we became friends that Kitti finally asked me if all the things she, her husband, her parents, our past class-mates and the town citizens had heard about me, if the gossip was true. I began to talk, telling her things I had buried deep inside of me. I told her the truth about everything. Most of what she had heard was the truth. Of course there were things added on that didn't happen and things exaggerated. For the most part I had done what I was accused of. Kitti listened. There was much she understood. There was also a lot she didn't understand but she listened anyway. She didn't accuse, judge, blame or show any signs of disgust. Kitti was not ashamed of me or our friendship.

For the first time in my life, at the age of seventeen, I had a friend. Also for the first time in my life, I was accepted just the way I was. I didn't tell Kitti of the hate I felt for being rejected by almost everyone. If there was even one person who had not rejected me, I didn't know who this one person could be. I don't think I knew how to express my hate. This hate made me strong instead of weak. A bond grew between Kitti and me. Our husbands liked each other, and we all enjoyed being together. *"We"* were all I had.

The years passed. I divorced my first husband after a two-and-a-half year marriage. He was a good person. He had rejected the warnings of his friends and family and married me despite all their disapproval of me. My husband couldn't heal the pain and emptiness, the void I felt inside. I had to keep this void filled.

My first affair was with my brother-in-law. The affair began one week after I was married. It began in Ralls. After meeting my brother-in-law he became the reason I made weekly drives and sometimes more to Lubbock, Texas, where he and his wife lived. He would come to Ralls also. We would have sex, laugh and talk for as long as we could, then he went back to his wife and I went home to my husband.

It was at this time that I learned how to get on a high, the high of adultery. I had not been with a married man until my affair with my brother-in-law. Adultery became a way of life for me. Adultery covers a lot of pain. It's exciting. It's dangerous and thrilling in the beginning. The high doesn't last, the thrill dies, the family finds out and many people are hurt, deeply hurt. I had no concern for their hurts at the time. I was busy finding someone else to go with me on this drug and alcohol-free high. Before marriage, I was the only one being hurt, it seemed. The boys put me down as their accomplishment, their trophy, I suppose. The only problem with this is that I would have had sex with anyone, anyone who would hold me and tell me wonderful lies. About how pretty I was, how good I could play basketball or how good it felt to be with me. I was willing to do anything and everything to hear these words. Good things I had never heard as a child.

Not too long after the divorce from my first husband, Kitti and her husband divorced. They had been married for four and a half years. As a result of our divorces, Kitti and I went our separate ways through life. But we ran into each other enough to renew the love we had for one another. The bond between Kitti and me remained unbroken.

One Saturday night, my fourth husband and I went to a western club. There was another couple with us. We lived in Lubbock, TX at the time. A woman from my hometown of Ralls saw me and came to our table to talk to me. I asked her, "Where is Kitti?" Have you seen her?" She smiled and replied, "She's sitting over there across the dance floor." I immediately jumped up and ran to Kitti, leaving her standing there.

I grabbed and hugged Kitti with all my love. For a minute she didn't know who was hugging her. When she saw my face, her joy was as great as mine. We talked, sharing the events of the years we had not seen each other. Kitti told me about spending several months in a mental institution. She had lost her kids after the divorce of her husband at the time. Suddenly, my sorrows seemed so unimportant compared to hers. Our friendship continued, and our love and need for each other grew. Kitti also lived in Lubbock. Our friendship was renewed, we talked on the phone a lot, we visited, we laughed and we cried together. We also started going to clubs together.

One night when Kitti and I went to our regular night club, we ran into a relative, a cousin of mine. He sat with us. I had loved this cousin for a long time. He, during my school years had never rejected me. He always smiled at me when I saw him and he continued to do so even after my reputation sank into the depths of the ocean. I would occasionally run into him in bars. I had two cousins who were a part of the night club life who didn't reject me.

Kitti, my cousin and I were sharing and laughing, having drinks, dancing and doing what night-club people do. I needed another fix, another high, not another husband. I was still living with Kevin, my fourth husband. I knew a divorce was in the making.

We were into ourselves, the three of us. Not really paying attention to our surroundings. My much needed fix boldly sat down in the chair next to me. His name was Howard. The attraction for one another was definitely there. We danced. He was what I considered a good dancer. He bought several drinks for me. It didn't take long for him to ask me to leave with him. I refused. I really don't know why, he had me as soon as our eyes met. He was exciting as well as having a great personality. I rejected his appearance. He was heavy, about six feet two inches, maybe a little taller. He had broad shoulders. He carried himself with pride. He was a shabby dresser with hair that needed grooming and a mustache that made him look like the peg leg sailor Captain Hook, who always had a parrot on his shoulder, that I had seen in the movies. This first impression of dress and grooming didn't matter to me. It was the way he looked at me. The way he held me while dancing and the way he possessed me that made me desire him. After I declined to leave with him, he left our table.

It was getting late, Kitti left with my cousin. I got up from the table, ready to leave also. I looked at Howard, sitting with two girls, at their table. I walked over to their table. He looked up at me. I leaned over and planted my best kiss on his very willing lips. Both girls just watched. I rose up, smiled at him, turned and walked out of the club. But right before walking out the door, I turned and looked into the eyes of Howard, giving him a slight smile of pride. This man, my fix for the night, had stirred something inside of me that was a new experience for me. No sex, but yet I was alive with desire for him.

It took Howard around two months to get my unlisted phone number. I had told him the name of the company my husband was driving a truck for. Howard was able to make contact with other drivers through his CB. Our phone number was given to Howard because he had said he was an old friend of my husband and had been trying to find him.

It was late in the afternoon when the phone rang. I answered. Howard asked, "Do you know who this is?" I didn't recognize his voice. He had to explain to me who he was. After all, it had been a couple of months since our meeting in the night club. I had thought of him only in passing, that is remembering how he made me feel, but I hadn't dwelt on it. I had gone to clubs but had not seen Howard again. Remembering how much he stirred me, I let him become my fix once again. Kevin was gone on a truck, making a run to New Mexico. I talked to Howard for some time. He was the man who made my heart rush.

I can give no reason why I asked Howard and his wife to come to our home when Kevin returned. It was crazy. What was I thinking? When Kevin got home, he could not remember ever meeting Howard. They knew some of the same people, but had not actually met. So here we were sitting together in my living room, visiting. After they left, Kevin said, "Who in the world is that?" I played dumb.

Howard looked like what he was, a druggie. Kevin was a cowboy, a sharp dresser and kept himself looking good all the time. I told him the truth that I met Howard in a club. Since I had been with Kitti and my cousin in the club this didn't make Kevin mad. Howard had said he thought that they had been friends in Ft. Worth while driving for the same company. This was a lie, there is no way Kevin would have been a part of Howard's friendship, but Kevin bought it anyway. Howard's continued calling put me willingly into his arms very quickly.

Kitti met and married a man from our hometown. He was an alcoholic and a few years older than she. It took the arms of a man to soothe away the pain and loneliness from our childhood. Kitti found hers in Thomas. I found mine in Howard.

It didn't take long after my affair with Howard began, to ask my husband for a divorce. I think it was a week or so after Howard and his wife visited in our home. Kevin moved out. I didn't know until years later, that Kevin was having an affair with the Dr.'s secretary who was supplying him all the drugs he wanted. Kevin had taken me to the Dr.'s office only once. I suppose she wanted to see me! They married soon after our divorce was final.

As soon as Kevin moved out, my two oldest children from my second marriage called and asked if they could come and live with me. I could never tell them no. I had left them when they were one and two years old. I could not, now that they were older, tell them they couldn't live with me.

Kevin had come to the house on one occasion to get some more of his things. He had no idea Howard and I were seeing each other. He slapped me down into a chair. He stood over me with his fist tight threatening to kill me. My son went into the bedroom. I begged Kevin to let me go to the bathroom. I went to the closet in our bedroom and got a twenty-two rifle out. I put it into my son's hands. "If he comes near you, shoot him, and shoot to kill, don't let him hurt you or your sister." I said. My son showed no sign of fear. His dad had taught him how to shoot a rifle, just as he had taught me when I was married to him. My son positioned himself, the rifle raised ready to protect his sister and himself. Elizabeth was not there at the time. I really thought Kevin had found out about Howard and was going to kill me. I thought from his words and actions that he might kill us all. But this wasn't the case. He was just drunk, drugged up and mad.

Howard and I began living together. He with his three boys helped move me, Elizabeth and my two oldest children into an apartment. At the same time, Howard moved his clothing into the apartment also. He had left his wife. His three boys stayed with their mother.

Howard, my fix, was needed all the time. Without him, I was empty. I had not shed a tear over four husbands or any man for that fact.

Kitti was going through the pain of being married to an alcoholic. I was going through the pain of Howard moving in and out of my apartment. He would stay with me a while, then remove his clothes and go back to his wife and then move back in with me.

It was a vicious circle for both Kitti and me. Howard and I went deeper into drugs and satisfied our every hidden desire. In time, Kitti divorced Thomas and Howard's wife divorced him. I knew there were countless girls or women in Howard's life, but I assured myself that in time I would be the only one.

The turning point for deep inward pain over divorcing the man she truly loved came for Kitti when she turned to someone totally foreign to me—someone I didn't know and didn't want to know. His name was God.

I turned instead to more and heavier drugs. Kitti would talk to me over the phone and tell me how God loved me and that He would change my life. I listened and put up with her words because I felt I had to, she was my friend. Sometimes I put up with what she said but when I had heard enough, I would tell her I didn't want to hear anymore. She would stop. That is, for the moment. I didn't think her words were getting through to me, but they were.

I began to see a change in Kitti even though she was going through hell with Thomas. He wouldn't let her alone. Her heart hurt. Yet, Kitti had something I didn't.....God.

Kitti was at our home one night when Howard and I were really having it out. Howard and I had moved into a house in the country. His two oldest boys and my youngest daughter Elizabeth were living with us. My two oldest children had gone back to live with their dad, where they were raised, in Brownfield, TX.

I was raving, which I was very good at. I called Howard every name I could think of, plus mean, tearing-down words that I knew would hurt him. My mouth was literally rolling in filth.

Kitti just sat on the couch with her hands folded until I settled down. Then she said, "Mary Ann, you don't want to hear this but I have to say it. If you would get God in your life, He would change your life and Howard's."

"You're right. I don't want to hear it. I don't want to hear it. I don't want to hear anything you have to say about God! 'Who's God'?" I screamed.

Kitti had called on the name of the Lord and He had heard her cry. She started going to church. She had stopped the night life and the clubs. Kitti was building a relationship with God and He was using her to reach me. She was the only person that I would allow to talk to me about God and this was only because I loved her.

In the days that followed I began to wish things could be different. However, my thoughts weren't of God. He was so unreal to me. My thoughts were of the peace my friend had. That peace was what I wanted. I didn't know it was God who was giving her this peace and giving her the strength to go through her valley with Thomas.

Even Howard turned to Kitti when I had left him just before Christmas. It was the same time period when I was driving my car on my way to commit suicide and God came to me in the form of a cloud. I had moved out of the farm house Howard and I had shared and was in hiding from him. He knew no matter what, Kitti would know where I was. She wouldn't lie to Howard or break the trust I had in her. He went to her and pleaded with her to go get me to talk to him.

Kitti came to my house while Howard stayed in her apartment, waiting. "Mary Ann, you have to see him or at least talk to him," she said. It didn't take me long to follow her back to her apartment, because I longed for Howard. I hurt for him with every passing minute.

We fell into each other's arms. I took him to my home, a few blocks from Kitti's apartment. Howard moved in with me and shortly afterward all the pain started all over again.

During all that time Kitti stood by me and never talked against Howard. She always told me she loved him too. She was going through her own tribulation because of her love for Thomas. But she was making God the Lord of her life.

Kitti and I continued to share tears of sorrow as well as tears of joy. We could make each other laugh and we could lift one another up. Kitti was getting it right one time and then failed the next trial, just as I was.

After work one day, I went to Kitti's apartment. She was really hurting. She had been screaming at the kids most of the day. She had shut herself in her bedroom and was sitting by the phone waiting for Thomas to call. She had made him leave and he had not called in about two weeks. She was trying to release him, but just hearing his voice would take the pain away.

I knew just how she felt. I sat while she poured her heart out to me, the hate, the hurt, the abuse, the love, the loneliness, the joy and the sorrow all came out. Praise God that I had His peace and was therefore able to share her burden. We talked of the past and our memories that we shared. Together we held hands and prayed.

About a week later I was in Kitti's shoes. Everything was getting on my nerves. Howard was out of my home again. He was living across town. I had put the second peace bond on him. I hurt like hell for him.

God asked too much. It seemed as if there was such a small amount of peace and always a lot of hurt. I went to see Kitti. She was riding high in peace and controlled the old self she was trying to crucify. She was the good mom to her children at this time. For two or three days, Christ had held her in His peace and love.

I, on the other hand, was restless. I was hurting but I wouldn't go to Howard or call him. Kitti was sitting in her living room. I sat down beside her and spoke my mind. "I'm so damn sick of everything. I don't know what the hell is going on!" I exploded.

Kitti turned toward me with such grace and with her head held high she said, "We don't cuss in my house, this is a house of God." My gut tightened. I felt like knocking her off her throne, pushing her nose back into place since it was about five inches above her head.

Instead I just sat there without saying another word. All I could think of was the week before when her language had been worse than mine. I bit my tongue, got up and said "I need to go. I'll see you later."

I went home and read my Bible for some time. Then I put it down and went to church, to the prayer room. I cried out to the only one who could help me.....God.

Kitti and I have laughed over that day so many times. I'm sure Jesus laughs with us.

There was another time I remember well. I was riding high covered by the wings of God. (Keep me as the apple of the eye, hide me under the shadow of thy wings, Psalms 17:8). I was sitting in my backyard without a care in the world. I was totally enjoying the peace and joy I felt, basking in the presence of God. I heard the back gate open. Opening my eyes I saw Kitti coming through the gate. I knew from the way she looked that she was hurting. She was turning to me more and more for our prayers together. She knew that God was doing something special in my life and He was moving me up His high mountain very swiftly. She came into the backyard, sat down and began pouring out her pain. She wanted to know how I felt about something. I don't remember what it was, but I'm sure it was about Thomas. I listened until she finished. "What do you think?" she asked. We looked at each other for a few seconds. I raised my right arm into the sky and said. "I don't know, let me check!" I then twisted my nose with my left hand and said, "Let me check it out." It surprised her so much, she kinda jumped. Then we both broke out in uncontrollable laughter (copying Bewitch on TV). Her burden was lifted.

We shared so much of the same pain. It seemed that our valleys were so deep that we had to shovel our way out very often. Just about the time we'd see light, we'd fall back into the pain, again and again.

Shortly after this visit, I began to pull away from Kitti. I had become her go-between to Christ. Every time I had prayed for her, God had answered my prayers giving her the peace she was so desperate for. She would call or come to my home just so I would pray for her. Her faith was turning into my walk with God instead of hers.

She wouldn't really get into God's word. She was faithful in going to church and living for Christ, but she was not a reader and had not developed a time set aside for reading the Bible. I felt impressed of the Lord to pull back from her, which I did.

I didn't slowly back off. I stopped calling and visiting her. This hurt her, and she didn't understand why I was putting space between us. I was being blessed, but I was also willing to suffer. I pulled away because God said to. I loved her and I knew she was making me her God. I didn't run from her or refuse to talk with her when she called, but her calls were getting further apart. She was turning to others trying to replace me, instead of going to the only one who could help her, whom of course is God. It's all right to share with others but not if they become a dependency.

A couple of months passed. Kitti had turned her trust back to Christ. Our relationship was renewed. There was once again a peace in our friendship. Kitti had grown in a short period of time. I was now able to share more with her. My knowledge in the word, my faith and my growth had far surpassed many in the church. I was becoming knowledgeable in the word and was applying the wisdom I learned.

Kitti came to me one night very troubled. She had spent time in a mental institution. Satan was telling her that she was going back. She was scared and she needed me and my love for her. I knew God allowed her to turn to me. I also knew why. Kitti was making Satan her focus. She was getting more and more scared that she would have to go back into an institution. I understood what was happening as soon as she began to talk. I listened and prayed silently.

Self pity was something I had just come out of. It took a man, a deacon, to stand up to me. He told me that it made him sick to see self pity in himself as well as others. He opened my eyes to what was wrong. I was swimming in a pool of pity and didn't know how to get out. After this man made it obvious to me, I was able to pull myself out of it and put my trust back into our Lord.

Telling Kitti that she was full of self pity was not easy. I had already hurt her deeply when I had pulled away from her. Now we had been allowed to be close friends again. I knew God's spirit spoke through me because Kitti received my words so very well. They were not harsh, hateful or judging. It was truth in Christ.

We both felt the release for her. Once she understood, God was able to remove the yoke of fear from her. We prayed. We were to share one another's burden's that we might be healed. (Galatians 6:2 Bear ye one another's burdens, and so fulfill the law of Christ).

My prayer was, "Father, in the name of Jesus Christ, intercede and let Kitti have a rest in You. Give her Your strength to overcome. Teach her how to fight against the fiery darts of Satan. Father, as Kitti turns to You, teach her through Your Spirit that she need not fear Satan and through You we are of a strong sound mind." My mind was strong. I had no fear of Satan. I knew he couldn't control my mind unless I let him.

God heard and answered my prayers for Kitti. She obtained His peace. But I went through three weeks of some of the things Kitti had gone through for years. It was awful! I had to fight, to do battle in spiritual warfare.

There were times my mind was in such a battle that I had to make myself stay in control. I would have an overwhelming desire to run through a glass window. At times, I wanted to stab myself with a knife. There were times my mind was so beaten up that I thought about just sitting down and having a nervous breakdown. It was more than just a battle. It was a war. Satan was trying to convince me that by being sick, giving in to a nervous breakdown I wouldn't have to face life. Someone would take care of me. Nothing would matter. But I fought against him. I had on the whole armor of God. (Put on the whole armor of God, that ye may be able to stand against the wiles of the devil. Ephesians 6:11) I spoke the name of Jesus Christ. I refused to weaken. Sometime during that time period, Kitti began to read the Bible, through reading the word and prayer, learned to turn to God instead of me. She learned to overcome. She hasn't been burdened with this fear since then. "PRAISE GOD!"

It was Christmas. I sat on my couch opening the gift Kitti had gotten me. When I opened the box, my heart began beating faster and faster. It was a dove, a single dove. It was the second gift I had received. The first was a music box and on top was a set of doves.

This gift was given to me by Donna and her family. Donna had surprised Elizabeth and me with a Christmas tree and gifts. This made my mind race. Was God telling me I was to walk this path with Him alone? Why had the first doves been a pair and the second gift a single dove?

Birds had never meant much to me until these last few months. God had sent a multitude of sparrows to our home for three days and now it was doves. What was God telling me?

After Elizabeth and I opened our gifts, we went to Kitti's home for the day. We all had a happy day. Elizabeth and I left Kitti's and drove to another friend's home. Elizabeth and I were handed a gift. When I opened mine, I was speechless. It was a pair of doves that was also a music box. I was sitting on the floor in a daze wondering what was going on. Why was God sending me doves? I believed it was God sending them, but why? Now I had two sets of doves and a single dove. God now had my full attention.

I put the doves where I could look at them all the time. I would move them from my bedroom to my living room just so I could look at them. "God, what are You telling me? Am I to be alone without a mate? If it's Your will for me, I'm willing. Why are two mated and one is not? Father what are You doing, are You giving me a choice?"

Kitti and I were in her car on our way to church. I had prayed endlessly for Christ to reveal what He was telling me through the doves. Several days had passed and now it was the beginning of a new year. It had been a year since God first spoke to me in the form of a cloud. Much had happened.

Elizabeth sat quietly in the back seat, while I drove. Kitti was going to church with us. In a split second, God revealed to me why one dove was a single dove. He had a mate for me. This man would knock on my door and hand me a single dove. Excitement grew within me. I laughed and cried at the same time as I revealed this vision to Kitti. Elizabeth was thrilled. We would be a family. I told Kitti and Elizabeth not to share this with anyone. I didn't want anyone to give me a dove that didn't come from God. God was preparing me a knight in shining armor.

It was January 1980. Elizabeth and I were moving in with Grace, whom I called Mother Superior, who was letting me rent a bedroom with kitchen privileges. I could no longer pay rent for the little house that Elizabeth and I called home. My son had picked up our belongings to put into storage. Sad did not adequately express my pain. God had revealed to me to prepare to leave, for now, to go to Grace's home. Other than our clothes, I had kept very few belongings to take with us, our TV, my doves and a few items Elizabeth wanted.

Three days had now passed. Howard had come by and discovered we were moving. I refused to tell him where we were going and he left.

It was then the third day and our last night before packing what little was left into my car and giving up our independence. I wondered if God would require Elizabeth also. "Please don't let me lose my daughter," was my heart's request. We were lying beside each other on our little pallet. I was holding her close to me as she slept.

The doorbell rang. I knew who it was. I pulled myself up from our pallet on the floor, put on my robe and went to the door. "I have something for you Babe." Howard said. He opened the screen door. I simply backed up. He was so happy at bringing me a gift. Looking at him all I could think of is 'Why do I love you so much?' I felt crushed.

At this moment I didn't know if I had lost what seemed to be everything because of Howard or because God was bringing a new thing into my life. I wanted to jump into Howard's arms and ask him to make all the pain go away. I didn't. I just stood there watching him as he pulled something wrapped in a rag out of his pocket. He began to unwrap it. I realized it was a single dove. At this very moment I felt a strong *"NO!"* inside me. It was clear. I had no doubt that the Holy Spirit had given me warning that Howard was not the man for me.

I didn't like the single dove Howard handed me. It was not peaceful. It was mounted on a black surface. Despite the fact that I didn't like it, it was easier to take it than to reject it. My thoughts were, 'Satan heard me when I told Kitti about the single dove she had given me for Christmas.' He had put into Howard's mind to give me the dove. I was sure he had stolen it from someone. But I accepted it anyway. The following day, Elizabeth and I moved into the home of Grace, my Mother Superior.

While living in Grace's home Elizabeth and I stayed in our little bedroom most all of the time. I simply didn't want to talk to anyone. I'm very thankful that for the most part Elizabeth was with someone else, her friends, grandparents, or her dad. She was not confined to our little room as I was.

I hurt more than I ever thought possible. Grace was very good to us, but I had to be alone. I looked at the doves sitting on my little dresser. I didn't believe God had sent Howard to me with the single dove. Every time I looked at it, with the others, I rejected it. I didn't like it yet I couldn't throw it away. Howard was living across town with another woman. He was still taking drugs.

I couldn't make up my mind. Was Howard going to repent? Was I God's instrument? I longed for Howard. The pain seemed to grow with each minute. I was not being healed. I was suffering more. Just to see Howard or to hear his voice stopped the pain for the moment.

Elizabeth and I were sitting in church. She reached over and touched my arm, "Momma, Momma." I shushed her. After all we are in church. She persisted, I leaned over and she whispered in my ear, "I just saw the angels in heaven. They were telling Jesus that they were going to let you marry Howard."

Howard came to my office with a red rose. He would at times be waiting on me after I got off work. He called me at work just to bid me a good day. He was persistent in staying in my every thought. I didn't yield to his attention. I would walk away from him, drive away from him, hang up the phone on him, leave him, yet, I didn't stop longing for him. Besides, the angels told Jesus they were going to let me marry Howard. Surely I was wrong about the dove he gave me.

On a Wednesday evening after work, Howard was waiting for me. He made me get into his car with him. I was fighting within not to want to be with him, but in truth, I fed on his every word of love for me. As we drove and argued, my need for his attention became my focus. Nothing was right, yet being with him brought me peace from the miles and miles of pain. Even though I insisted, he would not take me back to my car. I'm sure his intent was to keep me within his grasp until he was sure I still loved him or that he still had control over me.

It was getting late. We drove to the church to take care of Elizabeth, who was headed to church with Grace. Church was across the street from Grace's home. She had Elizabeth by her little hand. It was a picture to behold. Grace saw me as I got out of the car. "Mary, he will only hurt you," she said. She took Elizabeth on to church and I returned to Howard.

It was at this time that I began to think that maybe I was wrong about Howard and God was indeed sending him to me. I knew without doubt that God had told me *no*, when I accepted the dove he had brought me just a few weeks earlier. Yet I could be misunderstanding what the *no* meant. There was no more fight in me. I submitted to my love and need for Howard. We began seeing each other again. We visited with Kitti often. The three of us would talk and pray. A date was chosen. Our prayer for acceptance and approval for marriage was set for June 7, 1980.

Howard got a job in Amarillo, Texas. We were living in Lubbock, Texas when all this occurred. I stayed with Grace and continued working while Howard found us a home in Amarillo. I spent a lot of time praying. I kept telling God that I would stop this marriage and walk away if He wanted me to. I said the words, but, I don't think I meant any of them. I was going to marry Howard. Howard came to Lubbock on weekends. We were not having sex. Howard called me very often. We talked many hours. I was able to suppress the *NO!* I clearly heard when Howard gave me the dove. I reasoned that at first Jesus said *no*, but He knew Howard's heart and it had truly changed and now the angels were allowing us to marry. The snare of a lie can be made into truth, if you want it to.

I found a note on my windshield early before I left for work. I opened it and read, "Please call me." I went back into the house and dialed the number. "You don't know about me," a woman said. "Would you tell Howard to give me back my key?" she asked. "Yes I do know about you," I replied. She didn't respond. "I will tell him that you called and ask him to return your key." I said and then hung up the phone. Howard had not told me about this young girl, but I knew. I didn't know her name, but I knew he had been living with someone.

Howard called me a little later. He was persistent in asking me what was wrong. I had said nothing about the call. I wanted to wait until he was with me to ask him to return the key.

The call didn't upset me. I felt no anger or pain or hate. I had known he couldn't be by himself. I had accepted the fact that he had someone to live with but now I convinced myself that the relationship was over. I went to Kitti's and shared with her about the note and my call from the girl. I left her home and went to church. Howard called Kitti a little after I had left. She told him about the girl's note and my telephone call to her.

Howard was in Lubbock before I left work the next day. He was desperate to talk to me. He followed me back to Grace's home where I left my car. I got into the car with him and we left to be alone. When Howard began to explain things to me, he was quoting scripture. He had to be going to church like he said he was and he had to be reading the Bible. He didn't have a clue that he was quoting scripture, but I did. He was doing a one hundred and eighty degree turn, just as I had. I had faith, the past didn't matter, all the pain was over, we would be very happy together. He was going to go by the girl's apartment that he had lived with and return her key. Or so he said.

I came to Amarillo, shortly after this. I rode the bus. Howard was waiting for me. When I stepped off the last step of the bus, I was in his arms. He was going around and around in circles telling me how much he loved and missed me. Wonderful joy was between us.

Howard showed me the four bedroom duplex he had rented for us. It was close to his work and large enough for his two oldest sons as well as Elizabeth having her own room. Time was closing in. We now had about two months until we married. That night we stayed in a motel room. We slept in the same bed, but I refused to have sex with him. I wanted to wait until we were married.

Shortly following this trip to Amarillo in April, 1980, two tragedies hit my family. My aunt, my mother's sister whom she was closest to, was shot and killed by her alcoholic husband. He then killed himself. She had her granddaughter with her. The child had the stains of my aunt's blood on her the next morning when my niece came to get her daughter and discovered the bodies. I think it was four days later when I received a phone call from my oldest sister's daughter, "Mom just died. She had a heart attack," she told me. My sister was forty-one. I immediately drove to Ralls to tell my parents. I called Howard. He came to me in Ralls. We drove to Lubbock the next day and got clothes for the funeral.

Howard began talking to me about going ahead and getting married. The idea of having to go back to my bedroom, a job I hated and lonely depression was overwhelming. I didn't want to be left alone anymore, so I agreed. We got our blood test, prayed for God's blessings, and went forward with our plans. It should have taken three days for us to receive the results. It didn't. We got our marriage license and I just knew we had God's approval. Everything was falling into place. Howard and I spent the night in a motel room, in separate beds.

After my sister's death, on April 10, 1980, and her funeral, Howard and I were married the following Saturday afternoon. An Assembly of God pastor agreed to come to the church, the one where I had received the baptism of the Holy Spirit nearly a year earlier. Thomas, invited by Kitti joined us. We prayed together before going to the church, "Lord if this is not of You, please stop us," we all prayed in agreement.

Deep within my knowing, I knew God had said **NO!** Oh well, it will be okay, I thought. I had agreed to go through anything and everything for God to save Howard. I had committed to take on the truth I knew, but rejected the reality of it. The truth was I knew but would not accept the knowing that Howard still had other women in his life. I kept asking for God's approval, knowing His rejection the moment a figurine dove was given to me by Howard. He had already given me His disapproval.

Ironically, the church had a large dove on the roof. Surely this meant His approval. It was easy to let myself believe it was. I knew the church had a carved dove on the top, but it was easy to pretend I didn't know.

I asked the preacher to let Thomas and Kitti hand us the rings instead of him handing them to us. He agreed. Our rings were two of my round earrings bent together. You couldn't tell this unless you looked at them. We said our promises to each other. When Howard was to put the ring on my finger, I put out the wrong hand and was married with the ring on my right finger.

We were riding back to Kitti's home. I looked at the earring on my right finger and said, "I didn't know they changed things and the ring is worn on the right hand." "You nut, you have the ring on the wrong hand," Kitti said. We all laughed at such a stupid mistake. A memory birthed into my mind. Some months back, I had gone to a prayer meeting. A woman and her husband were there from Wichita Falls, Texas. "I see a gold band on your finger. God is preparing a husband for you. You will love him. You will be a comfort to him. God has chosen him. You will stand by him all the days of your life. He will love and protect you like you've never known" were her words of prophecy to me. "But I love Howard." I replied. "Only God knows your heart," she said. I had shared with her before the meeting about Howard. She continued by saying, "I don't know who the man is, but it doesn't sound like Howard is too good if you had to put him in jail twice. I don't know if Howard is the man, but whoever the man is, you will love him because he is chosen by God." The prophecy was over.

This was spoken over me months before I allowed Howard back into my life. A fear gripped me. I had married Howard with the ring on my right hand. Part of the prophecy was right but I knew Howard was not this man she spoke of. I wanted him to be. She said God had chosen him, I knew without doubt that God had not chosen Howard but I kept silent about this. I was now Howard's wife. I could not even share this with you my dearest.....**KITTI.**

John 10:10 *The thief cometh not, but for to steal, and to kill, and to destroy: I am come that they might have life, and that they might have it more abundantly.*

Proverbs 18:7 A fool's mouth is his destruction, and his lips are the snare of his soul.

Ecclesiastes 9:12-13 a)For man also knoweth not his time: as the fishes that are taken in an evil net, and as the birds that are caught in the snare; so are the sons of men snared in an evil time, when it falleth suddenly upon them.

Jeremiah 50:24 I have laid a snare for thee, and thou art also taken, O Babylon, and thou wast not aware: thou art found, and also caught, because thou hast striven against the LORD.

2Timothy 2:26 And that they may recover themselves out of the snare of the devil, who are taken captive by him at his will.

December 1979
Dove given to me by Kitti

KITTI
Feb. 1980

**Kitti & Melvin Lambert
Married; Aug. 28, 1984**

**KITTI
Feb. 2009**

**Mary's 1st real friend a friendship that has
passed the test of time.**

231

KITTI

How long my dear friend, have you waited for God,
To give me the words, I feel in my heart?
I realize why the message for you until now I could not start!
God had a plan, and He chose you, for the most precious part.
In the beginning, when you talked of God,
I REFUSED, I REBELLED.
I would not listen to the words you had to tell.
Yet, in His wisdom God had a plan.
He chose you, to witness for my salvation.
You did not know, you did not realize,
But I saw His love in your life, I saw His love in your smile.
Yes, my dearest, dearest.....friend.
You were the only person I would let talk to me of Him!
Your witness was true.
I trusted and saw that your heart was pure.
And you know what,
This was not the end!
He had a purpose,
He chose you, again!
He put in your heart to give to me a single perfect dove.
I rejoice, I rejoice, as He sent His most powerful precious love.
Then one night when I was full of sorrow and remorse.
The man I so loved, gave to me the mate to your single dove.
Don't you see, my dearest, darling.....friend,
If not for you, this may have never been.
You knew Him first and loved Him so much,
That He chose you, my heart to touch.....**KITTI!**

NOTE: In my heart I knew that Howard was not the man chosen by God, but it was so easy to convince myself that he was because I wanted him to be.

Chapter 21:
REGRET

~

Our wedding night was spent in a cheap motel-room in Lubbock, Texas. Howard went to sleep as soon as he quickly satisfied himself. Looking at him laying next to me, I wondered why I loved this man so much. He was now my fifth husband. The deep overwhelming pain I had experienced during the past year was gone. The longing and loneliness for Howard was gone. In its place was birthed insecure fearful regret.

I relived in memory much of my childhood, the years of divorce and adultery. The years of clubs, and lies, everything it took to survive. Why had I left my children? How could I have walked away from my children? I had no answers other than I had no conscience until I was filled with the Holy Spirit. I believe we are born with a conscience, but years of ignorance, sin and pain sears it, as the Bible says, as with a hot iron. (Speaking lies in hypocrisy; having their conscience seared with a hot iron; 1Timothy 4:2)

Tonight I am married to the only man I felt I have ever loved. I will make it work. I had promised Jesus Christ that I would go through anything and everything for Howard's salvation. In my reasoning, salvation for Howard meant that he would love me as I loved him. Salvation meant that there would be no more adultery, no lies, no stealing, and no drugs. We would fall into a very happy lasting marriage. And then when it was time for our eternity with Christ. Howard and I would be wonderful friends in heaven. I thought that real Christians, the ones who go to church all the time and didn't cuss, drink or hurt each other had wonderful happy marriages. I thought that we would together make it through every storm of life. With each other, we could do so much for Jesus Christ. We could win souls in the street, druggie lifestyle. Together we could really make a difference in people's lives because we understand by having lived this lifestyle ourselves. I had no intentions of quitting. I was going to see this thing through. Lying beside Howard I knew that it was now up to Jesus Christ. I would keep my side of the bargain. I fell to sleep some time during the early dawn.

Driving to Amarillo, we didn't talk much. I was thinking about the prophecy that had been spoken to me before our marriage. "God has a husband for you," the prophet said. Remembering her words, I looked at Howard driving down the highway having his own thoughts. I had wanted the husband to be Howard so bad that I made her prophecy come true by marrying Howard when in my heart I knew it was not him. I knew this because the Holy Spirit had quickened me with a *"NO!"* when Howard handed me the dove. But I accepted it.

At this moment how I wished that I had waited until God brought about the fullness of this prophecy. As much as I loved Howard I was terribly unhappy inside. Only God and I knew this. I had bargained with God for Howard's salvation. I knew, but didn't really know how much adultery, drugs and all the rest would be a part of our lives until he really accepted Christ. I just had to believe and wait and of course be able to put aside what I knew was going to happen. I couldn't let Howard's adultery crush me. After all, it was me that he married. The other women really didn't have a hold on him, I had his love.

Howard was thrilled to show me our new home. He had done the best he could to fix it up. For end tables, he had put cardboard boxes covered with a square piece of material. There were things I knew were from his girl friend's homes sitting on them. Howard didn't buy gifts. He stole them.

Suppressing and hiding my emotions was something I was well trained in. We fell to sleep quickly the second night of our marriage. Howard went to work the next morning. That evening after he got off work, we again lay together. It was the same as our wedding night. I felt nothing.

The following week-end we rented a truck which I drove alone to Brownfield, Texas to get my belongings out of storage. Howard didn't feel the need to take off work to help me. I had spent the week getting our duplex apartment ready for our family. The boys would be moving in soon. We were going to be a family.

I was extremely tired by the drive from Amarillo to Brownfield. I was mad and very hurt that Howard sent me by myself to get my furniture and belongings. He had never let me do this type of work by myself. I didn't understand how he could just go to work and leave it all up to me to get everything loaded and then drive back to Amarillo.

I spent the night in my ex-second husband's house. He owned the old storage building where my things were stored. I slept in my son's room on the mattress that was on the floor. It had fallen from the slats and that's where it stayed. My things were loaded the next morning. I drove back to Amarillo. I cried quietly as I wondered how long it would take for God to change Howard. Surely now that we were married it would be a quick thing. I'll wait I thought, I'll wait. Finally, I parked the truck in the driveway of our first home. Howard was watching for me and came out to question me. The first thing I was asked when I got out of the truck was, "Where did you sleep last night?" "In my son's room," was my reply.

The hidden depression I felt inside grew when my parents showed up as we were unloading my things. This was the first weekend after our marriage. I had to visit with them knowing that Howard was extremely angry with me. In other words, he was mad as hell because I hadn't spent the night in the truck as he thought I would. He knew I had no money for a motel room, and he didn't give me any money, not even for a meal. By late evening Howard and I were totally given out. Regret, work, stress, anger, hurt and depression, for me, was the beginning of our marriage.

We finished unloading, we now had furniture to sit on. I sat down with my parents barely able to hold back my pain. Howard had hid his anger and so had I. We had to talk about something. My last year had been spent focused on Christ. I had tried so hard to change and I had changed. I was sharing with my parents about Jesus walking everywhere He went. How dirty, tired and hungry He must have been. When I said this, my dad responded with total anger at me. "Jesus was not dirty!" I became silent as I had well learned in my youth. "I'm sorry. I didn't mean it that way." I said. He and mom abruptly went to bed. Later, after bathing, I went to sleep making a decision that I would leave my parents completely alone. I had not asked them to come. They would never approve of me. I didn't have to be hurt by them anymore. Howard was silent and turned his back to me. Alone, I'm still alone, and rejected, was my thoughts.

Little was said the next morning. Howard went to work early. My parents drove away shortly afterward, I was so glad. I couldn't understand why they kept showing up in my life when I was convinced they didn't like me, much less love me. I didn't understand them.

Howard had sex with me on our wedding night, the third night afterward and one more time, the night my parents left. I felt like he was marking his territory, which was me! It would be over a year before he sexually touched me again.

The following weekend, after we spent the week arranging furniture and putting up household goods, Howard and I drove to Lubbock to pick up his two oldest boys, Ray and Lee. He had three children. The youngest son, Neal, was to live with his mother. Howard had called and told the two older boys where to meet us and what time to meet us. We would take them to their mother's home to pick up their things. They were two hours late. When the oldest boy crawled out of the car which had five young boys in it, Howard slapped him so hard it threw him backward against the car. The laughing and fun was over. The other son crawled out of the back seat and went directly to Howard's car and got in without saying a word. We went to his ex-wife's house, which used to be their home and waited as the boys carried their things to our car. Howard had gone into the house, a short time passed and he came out the front door. His ex-wife stepped out of the house onto the porch. "Take your whore and leave me alone," She hollered making sure I heard. Instead of anger, I felt compassion, I even understood. I hated to see her pain. During the past year, somehow Christ had changed my cold, black heart. I had taken her husband and now her two oldest sons. I had no doubt that she loved Howard as much or more than I. They had three sons together. She had stayed with him through all her pain that is until I came along. Her words didn't anger me. I understood.

All the way driving back to Amarillo, Howard laid the law down to his boys. No this, no that, no whatever! He told them what it would be like for them if they went to prison. Drugs were a daily part of their lives just as it was Howard's. They were well educated in pornography also, just like their dad. The boys were young yet very street wise. Howard had no problem taking them with him during his nightly lifestyle among his clubs friends, and his riding bros. I'm sure they began smoking pot at a very young age. In the beginning of our relationship, I felt pride in Howard bringing his boys to our home. I had won. I had her husband and her two boys. Someone give me a trophy! They liked me and I liked them. I was that wild thrilling girlfriend that knew how to have fun. I had no feelings for their mother's pain. That is in the beginning. Jesus Christ and time had changed my heart. I now hated the pain that I caused her.

Howard was given custody of Ray and Lee at the time of their divorce. The judge had said that Ann was not strong enough to have control over the boys.

I had a made-up mind in tune with a made-up heart. We were going to become a family. We were going to live for Christ and there would be no divorce. We began going to church the following week-end. Howard had promised me that he and the boys would go to church. He kept his promise for a season. We sure looked good. We attended church activities. We had Christian friends at our home. Even the pastor and his wife came to our house. We were seen as a real family. We were over-comers from a dark past. We had friends. Our kids had friends. This is life, it sure is.

Howard stayed out all night the second week after our first church attendance. We were now married a little less than a month. When he came in the next morning, he took me outside to show me where he said the chain on his motorcycle had broken. He said he had to push the motorcycle most of the night to a friend's house to get his friend to help him fix the chain. He explained that he wanted to call me, but had no money and didn't take the time to call. He just wanted to get the chain fixed and get home. I had not slept all night. I had taken enough over the counter sleeping pills that instead of sleeping, it kept me up. I so wanted to sleep and not feel the pain I had agreed to suffer. When I looked at the chain, I recognized it was the link that connected the chain, I said nothing. Howard thought he had pulled it off. He hadn't. In my mind I knew all of it was a lie, but, oh well a promise to Jesus is a promise.

I found Harley Davidson's biker tee shirts that Howard had hidden. He knew I hated them, along with continued nights out, after a few months had become a way of life. Most of the time, I didn't know where anyone was. The boys were gone during the day. And if their dad was gone at night, so were they. They were skipping school, drugging, fighting along with having sexual activity. Both boys were under the age of eighteen.

The boys would tell Howard anything to get him to react just the way they knew he would. I remember on one of these occasions watching Howard storm through the house taking off his regular clothes and putting on his self-edification and threatening look. They loved for their dad to storm into a situation and take up for them. Howard would dress as a biker outlaw, which he was. He tied a red bandanna around his forehead and bowed-up like a storming bull. This excited his boys, this was dad, and they loved it. He went pounding on the door of another resident, his son was supposed to have started a fight with Howard's oldest son. I knew the boys were probably guilty of what they were accused of, and started the trouble themselves but they were a part of this bargain of mine with Christ. They had lived with us when we lived on the farm. I had learned to love them. They loved me because at first I was that wild crazy woman who could stand up to their dad and would fight just as fast as he would. This sure was a lot more exciting than going to church with their birth-mom, who took them regularly. She didn't put them on a bus and send them. She took them and lived for Christ herself. Before Christ, in the beginning, for me there was some kind of sick satisfaction that I not only had her husband. I had her children. I had won. I had it all. Happiness was sure to come, all this would pass and in time we would really become a family. I told myself daily that in time all would be wonderful.

My oldest son moved in with us some time during this first year. Not too long afterward I began to find needles with syringe in our back yard and in the alley. He knew how to make crank, a homemade drug and was main lining it. He was over eighteen and got a job where Howard worked at a beef plant. I thought, but was not sure if he was the source of these needles. I made him move out and get his own apartment. "You kicked me out because you knew I didn't have any place to go." He told me. "No, this is not the reason. I can't take any more drugs, I can't take needles." I told him. He was able to take care of himself, Howard's boys were not. Dealing with Howard's all-night adventures and his two sons following in his footsteps was burying me alive.

After my son moved out, a couple came to our home very worried about their daughter. They said she had been missing since my son had moved out. I didn't even know he knew the girl. I went to his job and jumped all over him about the girl telling him how worried her parents were. I told him to take her home. He didn't. I then went to his apartment and banged on the door. They were there and I knew it but they would not come to the door. I hollered out, "The police will arrest you, she is under age, you have to give her back to her parents. You'll go to jail if you don't." He then opened the door and I took the girl to her parents. It was a nightmare. We were the druggie people who lived in the community. It was very easy to know that the girl's parents loved her and tried to protect her from people like us.

Our little family was in church every Sunday. No one, and I mean no one, knew what all was going on behind our closed doors.

In the early mornings, I would hear Howard's loud pipes when he left for work and then at the end of the block, his car would idle for a short period of time and then the sound would last until he was out of sight. It didn't take long for me to know about the girlfriend down the street, but I had said nothing. At first Howard was picking her up for work and then bringing her back from work. She was married with one child. He invited her to our church. He was the bus driver for the church. She got to meet me on a one-on-one basis. After all, we had a lot in common. I knew as soon as she got on the bus with her son, she was the girl he was seeing when he married me. When Howard was late getting home after work he always said he had to work overtime. One day they drove past me while I was walking. The look on both of their faces said it all. Howard stopped the car and asked me to ride with them. I wouldn't get into the car with them. I walked back to our duplex where Howard was waiting for me.

I had so lovingly put all my dove collection on the shelves built in the hallway. I slowly walked by them, Howard watching my every move. He was caught, now, what would I do? I slowly pushed each dove or doves off the shelf telling Howard with sure determination, "It better stop, and right now." He knew I was not willing to accept his adultery with this girl, any longer! Standing in front of the shelves, I knocked every deeply-loved treasure off the shelf. I had spent endless hours looking at them. I heard them break when they hit the floor. I was screaming at Howard, "It better stop and don't call me Doll anymore. You never called me that before. I feel like you're calling me someone else's name. You only called me Babe. Don't call me Doll again!" He said nothing. He looked like a little boy who got caught with his hand in the cookie jar. All the doves broke, all except one. I picked it up to break it and stopped. It was the single dove Kitti had given me for Christmas. "Why did you marry me?" I asked. "I don't know. I had to have you." Howard said. "Did you marry me just to raise your kids?" "I don't know." He replied. Reality was trying to show me the truth, but I was not ready to listen, or accept it, not yet!

As time passed, I said nothing about this event. Howard stopped his overnight stay-outs for only a short time then it became a norm again. I supposed I could cope as long as I didn't have to see the girls.

My car was the old clunker car that Howard bought me in Lubbock. He came home from work one day and said, "Get ready, I'm going to buy you a new car." I ran down the hall way jumping and clapping my hands. Howard laughed as he watched me. The car I had was really bad, the seats badly torn, and not much worked. It went down the street, but I never knew when it would take its last breath.

I had my new car only two or three days when Howard came home mad. The boys were in Randall County jail. They were with some of their friends and had tried to steal gas from a gas station. The clerk had watched them and got the license-tag number before they drove off the lot at a high speed to avoid being caught. Howard was called at work and here he was, cussing, hollering and storming through the house demanding that I go with him to get the boys out of jail. This is the first time that I knew of for the boys to be in jail. Howard was driving way past the speed limit. I said nothing. He hit a dip which bounced the front end of the car to hit the pavement with such force that it broke the frame. It was not a new car, but it was beautiful to me. Everything worked and the seats showed no sign of wear. It was about the only real joy I had, when I drove it home from the lot.

The boys were still underage which helped get them released. Just as it had been when we drove from Lubbock after picking up the boys to move in with us, Howard was telling them what-for all the way from Canyon to Amarillo. The boys and I sat quietly as Howard threatened them of what all he would do if this happened again. It didn't take long to realize that the car kinda bounced in the front as well as squeak a little.

In the days that followed, Howard went to town after work. He returned asking me to go to a club with him. He didn't ask me, he begged me. I refused. He stormed out the door leaving his car and taking mine. Early morning he returned, after he went to work in his car, I went to my car and looked inside. There were long blond hairs everywhere in the back seat. I knew, I knew without seeing the hair, but I wanted proof. This is when I decided to leave and show Howard that I was not going to continue to live with drugs and adultery. I packed a few things while Howard was at work and went to the home of a couple who were members of the same church we attended.

The couple made it clear that I could stay a few days. Elizabeth was again with her grandmother, Mary. So I was the only person

I had to worry about at the time. Alone in the bedroom the same evening, I heard Howard's car driving down the small road to the house where I was staying. I heard it turn and leave. My car was hidden. He didn't know I was there. I stayed gone a couple of days and then went to church with the couple on the following Wednesday night. Our pastor asked me if I would talk to Howard. I agreed. After church I went to our duplex, with our pastor. Of course Howard denied everything to our pastor. He tried to explain the girlfriend at the end of the block was not his girlfriend. He also acted really dumb about the hair in my car. He did what he was so good at, look at me with begging eyes of regret and asked me to come home. He was so kind and loving in front of our pastor. I think our pastor knew Howard was lying, but didn't really know what to do. After all, we were married! My pastor drove me back to the church. I went with the couple back to their house and got what little belongings I had taken and got into my car and drove back home. I had shown Howard that I would not continue to live as we had been. If I showed him I would leave then he would stop all the adultery. Surely now he would accept Jesus Christ. If he had any love for me at all he would not want to lose me. At least this was my thinking.

One evening when I was walking through the neighborhood, I heard loud screams, crying, across the street. I stopped and saw three young girls had tried to lift a gutter to get one of the little girl's hair combs. She had dropped the comb and it had fallen into the gutter. It was too heavy for them. Two girls let go before it slammed down on the other little girl's fingers. She was screaming to the top of her lungs. I ran across the street and raised the gutter just enough that she pulled her fingers out. I let it slam back into place. Blood was flowing from her fingers. I felt sure that her fingers were broken, crushed. "Do you believe in Jesus Christ?" I asked her in a firm voice. "Yes, yes!" was her quick reply. "Lord, heal these broken fingers." I said with such assurance that He would and He did. The three girls and I watched as the blood dried up and disappeared. The pain had totally stopped. The girl said, "It doesn't hurt, it doesn't hurt, the blood has stopped." I smiled and told her that Jesus Christ loved her and He didn't want her to hurt so He healed her. I walked back across the street and continued my walk. The next day the little girl with her mother were standing outside of their home when I was walking where I had the day before. The little girl pointed at me. Her mother raised her hand and hollered, "Thank you, thank you so much for helping my daughter." I walked across the street to her and said, "Jesus Christ loves you and your family. He is the one who healed your daughter. I could not have raised the trap without Jesus." "You know we used to go to church, but so much has happened and we haven't gone in a long time. I want to go back." I smiled and walked away. I don't think I ever saw that little girl or her mother again.

On another occasion, I had become friends with a young woman who was living a hard lifestyle. She and her husband were on heavy drugs. They both were addicted. I had shared my salvation with her. On this day she was hurting from all the drugs and the never-ending fear. I brought her to my home and together we prayed. She asked Jesus Christ into her life. As soon as she did, she began bouncing up and down on my couch, almost falling off at times. Her whole body cleared the couch about an inch when she was bouncing. I began to pray loudly for the protection of Christ, from the demotic spirits that I knew were coming out of her. This was my first experience in seeing the reaction when evil spirits are coming out of a person. I called my pastor. He came, looked at her and said, "The evil is leaving her." He began to pray. His love for the woman was flowing from his words as he asked for the protection of the Holy Spirit to guide and keep her safe as she began her overcoming walk. It was now up to her to follow Christ. My husband and children never knew about this happening. By now, Howard was getting fed up of hearing about Jesus Christ.

We lived in this little community east of Amarillo for a short time longer. I was ready to move, I felt like everyone knew the truth about the ugliness behind our closed doors. I was ashamed and hurt. I found a two story house in town. We rented it for three hundred and fifty dollars a month. The house was located close to downtown Amarillo, on Jackson Street. There were a lot of older houses in the area with a lot of druggies living in them.

My oldest son had gone back to Brownfield and married an older woman who had two children. Howard's boys were getting educated in drugs, making crank, selling and taking. With all the pornography from Howard, and the women, parties and clubs they were also being educated in indiscriminate sex acts. I don't know when they began the selling of drugs but I think it began soon after we moved them to Amarillo. My jewelry was stolen, I didn't know if it was being taken from Howard, for his girlfriends or the boys in order to supply their needs.

My oldest daughter B.J. called from Brownfield and wanted to move in with us. She was divorcing her first husband. She had two very young children. Through all this nightmare, I couldn't tell her no. In spite of everything, I was trying to be a mother. I was in my late thirties. I was still fighting to follow Christ. I was also determined that if I kept believing that the day would come when we would truly become a family.

My youngest son, Stoney had come to spend some time with us. I had given him to his dad to raise when I was married to Kevin, an alcoholic. He abused my son. I had custody of Stoney and he lived with me until I discovered black and blue welts on his little bottom. I carried him into the bathroom where Kevin was taking a bath. I looked into the eyes of Kevin showing him what he had done. "If you ever touch him again, I will kill you." I said. I stood there a minute or two looking into the eyes of Kevin. "Do you understand, do you hear me, I will kill you?" I said. Not many months afterwards, I almost did.

My youngest son Stoney was now older and spending time with mom brought nothing but fun, plenty of girls, plenty of dope, plenty of alcohol, plenty of being free and running free. My, my, Mom's home was a blast! On one occasion he had decided to live with us instead of visiting. He didn't tell me about this decision. After spending a few days with us he came in about twenty minutes before his flight back to Ft. Worth where he lived with his dad. I fussed all the way to the airport driving almost a hundred miles an hour to get him there before his plane took off. I loved him, but I didn't want him in our lives. He had a very good dad, who did a great job of raising him. I wouldn't let him come into the mire of our lifestyle and drag him into it with us. We were for sure a blended family. Every child had come from two to three sets of parents.

I kept my relationship with Jesus Christ during the first year, refusing to go to clubs, refusing to smoke pot, refusing to leave, refusing to accept the truth, refusing to give up, refusing to die!

We went to church one time after moving. The fight was gone out of me. I loved everyone, his kids, my kids, all the kids that flowed in and out of our home. It was a constant moving in and moving out with the kids. My oldest daughter, B.J. had moved in with her two children. I was trying to make up for the hurt I had caused by leaving her when she was one year old. I was trying to be a mother to everyone. Inside I was ready to blow. I began to smoke again, not long afterward I started smoking pot again. All the kids stole, ran free, drank, did drugs, and had a ball going to clubs with Howard. Elizabeth was not yet old enough to participate with them. I was left at home most of the time. I didn't want to go back to clubs, I didn't want to smoke pot, but I did. I was turning back into what I had been before I met God. Again, suicide began to take hold of my mind.

Elizabeth suffered the most from my lifestyle. She was just a little girl, always spending the night with some friend. I let her go to her grandmother, on her dad's side and to her dad's all she wanted. It was better for her to be with them than what she was living through in our house. I should have had enough sense to realize with all the drugs and male traffic that she was not safe. She didn't tell me the truth until years later, after she had her first little girl how much she had been molested.

Howard came home in the middle of the day. This was very unusual. I was by myself. He asked me to sit down. "Your dad died last night." He said. I felt nothing. I didn't even know if I wanted to go to the funeral. I had not seen or spoken to him or my mother for over a year. I had shut them out of my life. Going to the funeral meant going back to Ralls. I didn't want to see anyone, especially those related to me. We didn't have a phone yet, it had not been connected. My mother knew where Howard worked and this was the only way for her to reach me. I didn't cry. Howard convinced me that I had to go. I think he thought I would probably get some money. He had gotten the message the day before, but it interfered with his night out so he waited until the following day to tell me.

I was a walking dead person, no feeling. Howard and I had to drive to Lubbock from Ralls, for a place to sleep. There was no room in mom's home for us. My sister had made sure I heard her when she said with hate in her voice, "I don't even know why she's here, she hasn't even called in a year." In fact everyone heard it. Just as I had taught myself in my youth, I showed no emotion. She said it again a little louder. Again I acted as if I heard nothing.

After the funeral, Kay, my middle sister took Dad's pick-up along with everything she could load into it and went back to Oklahoma. Mom gave me Dad's socks, handkerchiefs, his knife and flint. This was my inheritance.

Dad left mom with a nice little house. He also left her with good finances, not a lot of money, but enough. My niece moved in with her, and then later she married. Mom had been driving back and forth to Lubbock where she worked, embroidering for a bowling company. She sold the house and rented a nice little apartment close to her work where she could walk to work. She had bought a new Lincoln Continental, put towels over the seats and kept it well serviced.

"I'm scared," were the words I heard coming into my ears. "Can I come live with you?" Mom said. My heart sank. What do you say? "Mom, I live in a drug infested lifestyle, my husband is gone almost every night. My blended family moving in and out was gone most of the time, except to sleep and eat. I live in a cave, a dark lonely place." I found out later that one of these children called this house "the cave." Everyone was stealing, going to clubs with Howard and keeping quiet about his girlfriends. No one, not one person knew the truth. We had stopped going to church. I had begun to go to clubs with Howard sometimes. There were times that I went with him to parties at other people's houses. We had parties in our home. He even bought me a Honda chopper custom-built motorcycle. Later he bought himself and me Harley-Davidsons. I had not stopped loving him. I wanted him back as it was in the beginning of our relationship. I turned my back on Jesus Christ and for the second time chose Howard over Him.

This didn't last long. I hated the parties and ugly things we did. I pulled a knife in a club one night and was well-ready to stab or kill anyone who got in my way. I put the knife just under my cuff and waited for the fight to begin. It was my dad's knife. Cowboys and bikers were not happy in the same bar. Some of the biker women of these men were just as capable of taking your life as the men were. One of the girls with one of the cowboys saw the knife. We glared at one another. The challenge was on. I know I would have cut her. I didn't want to, but I would have if she attacked me. She turned and walked away from me. Howard had put something in my drink which he often did. I don't remember much of anything after this. I don't remember riding home.

Periods of time would pass. I would sometimes refuse to go to the clubs. I didn't want to live the way we lived anymore. At times Howard would come home and make me dress. He would take me wherever he wanted to go, at times strip bars, which he knew I hated. On our way to a bar one night, he had made me get dressed and go with him, I said, "I don't want to go." He hit me in the face with the back of his hand. He was totally drugged up. My nose poured out blood all over my clothes. I sat silent while he screamed at me all the way back to our house. I stopped the bleeding and changed clothes. I was forced to go to the night club. We sat down with other bikers and their women. I didn't know most of the people. I was not a part of the regular crowd. Howard told them I was his wife. One man looked at me in surprise and said, "She's not who you were with last night!" Howard leaned forward and began to laugh and talk loudly. I said nothing. He thought I didn't hear what the man said. I sat there for about four hours drinking what was put in front of me. It was not usual, but a regular thing for me to be drugged by Howard. He controlled me this way. He always got me home. That's one thing about Howard. He wouldn't let anyone else touch me. We went to a party one night where the motorcycles were pulled into the large old house. It was not pot being passed around, it was a liquid drug.

I watched in a daze as women were all over men and other women. Some were watching. Some were participating in a part of this drug, sexual hell-hole. Howard pulled me next to his bike and got in front of me, to protect me, of course. I got so sick he had to take me home. I nearly fell off the back of the bike several times. When he stopped in front of our house, I did fall off. I couldn't stand. He had to carry me up the stairs. He left me on the bed and he returned to the party. Sometime later when I was in a deep sleep, I was awakened with his weight taking the breath out of me. I was still so drugged up that all I remember is his body weight, his breath and his almost anger at reaching his own satisfaction. The next day after work he came home telling me how sorry he was for what he had done. It was at this time that a little life came back into me. I told him if he ever put anything else in my drink I would go to the police, I would tell the union he worked for the truth about us. It must have been God who kept him from killing me, but he never put anything else into my drink. These were the times when my strong personality would be in control and he knew I would do just what I told him I would do.

Another time when I showed Howard that I meant business was when one afternoon while he was at work after staying out all night. I filed for a divorce, loaded Elizabeth on the back of my little Honda chopper, put an extra can of gas bungeed to the front frame and what little belongs I could get into a saddle bag and left for my mom's. This lasted just a few days when Howard came and loaded my bike, and there we went back to Amarillo. Howard talked me into dropping the divorce. But after a few months and failed attempts to leave, I filed for another divorce. This time I stood my ground and refused to drop it.

How many times did I lay for hours throughout the night smoking dope listening for his motorcycle? I couldn't forget what I had promised Christ, "I'll go through whatever it takes if You'll save him." I had told Jesus on more than one occasion. If I stuck with it, Howard would change. Surely he would.

That's what our life was like but I still answered "Sure Mom, we'll come and get you." Howard didn't put up much of a complaint when I told him when he got home from work that we had to go get Mom. He knew I would be at home all the time if she moved in. He was right. The kids, all the kids, except Elizabeth, our blended family as it's called were gone. B.J. had married some man I didn't even know. The others were living with this one and then that one. I had forced his two boys out of the house more than once. This is the one thing Howard never challenged me on. You have not lived until everyone in your family is doing drugs, stealing, lying, etc. and you are really trying not to. Plus, I didn't want Elizabeth to follow in the path of her brothers and sister and what her mother had been.

We moved Mom into the upstairs bedroom down the hall from Howard and me. She and I began to look for a larger house and soon found one. It was several blocks to the south of where we were living and had fourteen rooms. It was a two story house. Mom and Elizabeth lived downstairs with their own bathrooms. Howard and I lived upstairs. Mom began sewing for a bowling alley company, monogramming shirts. She set up her space in the basement. There were two stair cases in our new, old home. It had been owned by a judge. It had a three car garage. The outside was painted yellow. It was old but had been remodeled on the inside. Mom paid ten thousand down and we began our new, old lifestyle, only now we had more room for friends and drug parties. Howard invited his friends to our house anytime he pleased. Sometimes I smoked dope, other times I pretended to. There was peace when I obeyed Howard.

I didn't know that Elizabeth was now talking with her dad about living with him. When she broke the news to me I was so dead inside that I knew it was best for her. Her grandmother, Nanny was Kevin's mom. Mary loved her and was a wonderful lady. I hoped that she would be with her often. Her dad was mean and an alcoholic, but he would never hurt her, I thought. I really thought that she would be better off with him. She and I put all her boxes outside on the porch. Kevin drove from Lubbock. When he came, I went back into the house and watched as he loaded the boxes into his pickup. I watched my little girl crawl into the seat next to him. They drove off. Elizabeth was 14 years old, it was November 1985. There was no one left. All the children were gone, Howard's two sons had not moved into the house with us. Now here we are, Mom, Howard and me in this fourteen-room house with a three car garage. We were living, just to the outside of hell.

Mom began to see how our lives really were. Howard would come in drugged up and drunk almost nightly. I often took her car and spent the night in it to keep Howard from hurting me. My sister came to see Mom once. She left with a picture Mom had painted for Dad. She took it off my wall not saying anything to me and left with it. Mom probably told her she could have it, yet, even so, it hurt me. I didn't understand why Mom was with me and not her. I knew how much she loved her.

One night Howard came in and slapped me and knocked me against the wall. I was in Mom's room. She began to beg him not to hurt me. "She's my daughter Howard, please don't hurt her." She pleaded with him. He was drugged up and mad at me. Just a few days before, I drank whiskey. When he got home from work, I was ready. I met him at the back door and all fear left me. I picked up a board with nails in it and dared him to come close to me. I walked over to his car and smashed his windshield. I told him I would to this to him while he was sleeping if he messed with me again. He was sober. I was very close to drunk. I knew how to talk street trash, after all that's where I came from.

During the last two years of my marriage, without Mom knowing, I had again chosen to try to take my life. I spent months thinking about it. This was during the time the Tylenol capsules had been tampered with and poison was put into some capsules. Several people died from this action. I thought if I took enough, maybe I would die. I was at a friend's house, again trying to leave Howard when I took a whole bottle of Tylenol. I don't know how many capsules were in the bottle but it was a large bottle. My friend was gone at the time. When she came in I told her what I had done. I didn't really want to die, but I wanted to convince Howard that I meant business. I wanted him to know how much I loved him. I wanted him to change. I wanted him to love me. Of course I wasn't going to die. It just wasn't possible that I would really die. After all God had spared my life on other attempts. The reality of an eternal death or hell just didn't seem possible.

Annette, my friend drove me to the hospital. Suddenly, I was in the emergency room, with a tube down my throat and some kind of white liquid flowing into my stomach. It took hours to get the pills out of me. They were for the most part dissolved by the time I had gotten to the hospital. I lay with my eyes open, watching the clock, a big Coca-Cola clock with a large dial I could clearly see. I broke out in heaves of crying several times. It only made it harder to breath with the tube in my throat. The nurse taking care of me would comfort me to stop my crying. I would control the tears for a little while, and then I would give in to the pain of the hurt I felt inside. As far as I know, the nurse never left my side.

At the end of six hours or so, I began crying almost uncontrollably. My body would heave with the pain in my throat, and gasping for air. I was in complete despair. The nurse jumped out of her chair and put her arms around me as best she could. I looked into her eyes as she leaned over into my face, "Let me tell you, young lady, no man is worth this." She held me and comforted me with her compassion. I calmed down and a peace came over me.

Annette had gone home long before I was put into the ward for people who have serious mental problems. I lay in a bed with sides on it, like those for an infant. A doctor came in and talked to me. He asked me if I realized what I had done. He told me I had chosen one of the most painful deaths a person could go through. Taking Tylenol would have been a very slow, painful death. I had not even thought about this. I told the doctor about my marriage. I told him the truth. I convinced him I would not try to kill myself again. I fell asleep exhausted.

"Mary, Mary," I heard as I was woken by a voice I recognized. Coming out of a deep sleep I smelled the alcohol on his breath. Howard laughed as he told me about the union he worked for, that their lawyer had called a judge in the middle of the night who then contacted the hospital giving Howard permission to come into the restricted area to see me. I don't know how much or if any of it was true, but he was so proud to tell me of his powerful contacts. They weren't his contacts. The union on his job had the contacts, but he did hold a position of authority himself. "You'll never be able to go anywhere where I can't find you. I can get to you no matter where you are." he said with a lot of pride at his accomplishment and his control over me.

Mom was busy working in the basement. I don't think she even realized I was not at home that night. When Howard took me home from the hospital the following day he really didn't say anything to me nor did I to him. My death again, for the third time was a complete failure.

Late one afternoon, I rode my Harley to a bar where no one would know me. I met a younger man who showed interest in me and my motorcycle. He liked to play pool with me. I was pretty good. I ended up in his bed. Up until then, I had not committed adultery during my four-and-a-half year marriage to Howard. We seldom had sex, and when we did, it seemed as though he was controlling or branding his property showing ownership of me. I began to sleep in the extra bedroom. Once he came in and did as he pleased. I called my attorney the following day. She called his attorney and it was made clear to him that we still had a divorce pending and I could file charges on him. He was very mad when he confronted me but he also remembered my putting him in jail two other times. I did have some control over him, he did fear me a little.

This same afternoon when he stormed out the door and getting on his Harley, he drove off with a loud roar following. I went to the young man's house that I had met in the bar and again had sex with him. Within the next week, I lay with him one more time and then I closed all doors to him. I had no desire for sex, didn't need fulfillment in sex, I just needed to be held. I hated what I had done. Howard had been the only man I had ever been faithful to and now my past patterns had come alive once again.

I'm drinking, smoking dope and now I have committed adultery. Would God forgive me?

Soon after the suicide attempt and the adultery, Howard had a wreck on his motorcycle. A girl was riding behind him. The bikers had left one bar heading for another one. Howard chose to see how fast he could exit off the Canyon E-Way. His front tire touched the concrete of the curve and his bike laid over breaking his leg, with the bone sticking out. I had no idea what time it was or how he got to the hospital. Someone took his motorcycle. I don't know who. I was asleep on the couch in the living room when he called from the hospital. I had been awake most of the night listening for his motorcycle. I had fallen to sleep sometime in the early dawn. "I'm in the hospital," Howard said. I don't remember saying anything, but I do remember thinking. Who cares, not me! He told me what happened, leaving out the part about the girl riding with him. He had waited to call after he had been admitted to the hospital and had his own room. At the time, I knew nothing about her being with him. One of my friends told me about the girl later the same day. I went to the hospital but I didn't want to go. I didn't care what happened to him. The bone was clearly sticking out of his leg. Somehow the Dr. or nurse had either forgotten or didn't chart it. So here he was in a lot of pan. I didn't care about his pain either. I went home and slept a few hours when my friend came to my house and told me about the girl. Late afternoon when I went back to the hospital Howard had a Playboy magazine one of the bikers had brought him. He tried to get me to get on top of him in the bed. I drank a few drinks of vodka myself. I lit into him. Everything about him disgusted me. Everything he said disgusted me. I grabbed the large flowers his boss had sent him and all but broke them in pieces. Two nursed entered the room and told me I had to be quiet. I was ashamed, but as soon as they left the room I took up where I had left off. Screaming at him and throwing the book at him. The two nurses came back into the room and told me I had to leave. I left and went to a bar. I drank and played pool. I never did ask anyone about the girl. I don't have any idea if she was in the hospital also or what. I do know it didn't kill her.

One afternoon Howard came home demanding that I go to a club with him. The union he was a part of was having a little get together there. I had no choice but to go, he made it clear that I had no choice. He still had a cast on his leg. I sat disgusted, listening and watching everyone. I finally played pool, won the game and played again with a young man. Howard ended up slapping him to his knees. Howard was used to slapping women. In his anger, he responded by slapping the man instead of hitting him. The young man flirted a little with me. It no longer impressed me when Howard showed off his macho personality.

On the way home after leaving the club I asked him, "Will it ever change?" "I don't want to change. I like who I am," he said. I sat quietly looking out the side window. It was at this point that for the first time before and after marriage, I realized God would never go against Howard's will. He was not going to change Howard as long as Howard didn't want to change. All hope, if I had any left, was gone.

Despite that, all the years of pain had not killed my love for Howard. All the adultery, abuse, lies, heartbreak, physical and mental pain had not made me stop loving him. But his words opened the door of my heart and I was able to reject him. I went home with him silently. I was ready to end my bargain with Christ. It was also at this time that I knew God had not bargained with me, but I had convinced myself that He had.

Somehow I knew God had not thrown me away. It was not easy for me to break my covenant with Jesus. I had stayed with Howard much longer than I wanted to because I was trying to be faithful to my commitment. Howard kept tabs on me day and night. He would call all during the day to make sure I was at home. He had his boys and others watching me. It was hell for me to go anywhere. I had tried to leave him two or three times before Mom moved in, but he always brought me back. At times, especially within the last six months, I went to Faithe's home. She let me stay the night. I smoked my dope and tried to sleep. A couple of times I heard Howard's motorcycle pass the house, but he never found me. During the day there were no problems. He did go to work. It was the nights I couldn't stay at home and wonder if he would kill me after he had taken drugs. He never bothered my mom, only me.

The divorce was still active. Mom knew nothing about it. I told her that I wanted out of my marriage. She had no problem agreeing. We set our plans into action. We began to pack things into boxes. Howard never looked into her closet and bath so she packed everything in her room. We had boxes hid in the attic, under beds, closets, everywhere Howard didn't go or look into. She packed so many dishes that when I opened the cabinet I knew Howard would know a lot of things were gone. We unpacked some things and replace them back into the kitchen cabinet. Mom and I laughed about this. We had a plan: if I got caught, she would go to the police and get me out of the house to keep Howard from hurting me. Things were packed. We were ready for phase two and that was finding a place to live in Lubbock. We had to get out of Amarillo. We both knew that Howard would not leave us alone, that is, he would not leave me alone.

Soon after all the packing was completed, Mom and I got into her car and drove to Lubbock. We rented a two-story house and then drove back to Amarillo. The phone rang just as we got inside the door. "Where have you been, I've called all day, where were you?" Howard demanded. "Mom and I just got out for a while. I took her to buy some things she needed. We went to eat. Can't I go somewhere with my mom without you getting onto me?" I said back to him. He calmed down and all was well. He thought I had told him the truth and he was still in control.

It took a full size moving van and five of their employees to load two motorcycles plus all the possessions I had before we married along with two Doberman dogs and their dog house. We loaded all of Mom's things, also with the help of two friends of mine in five hours to be ready to drive to Lubbock. I took nothing bought after my marriage to Howard, except my motorcycle and the motorcycle he gave to my son, the Norton that I had paid for before marriage. He had bought himself a Harley Davidson.

We were in the last phase of getting the job done when something came over me. It was overpowering. I ran downstairs to the movers. "Let's go, let's go right now, leave it, we have to go right now." I said. Mom and I ran to the car put the dogs in the back seat, slammed the door shut. We literally jumped into the front seats. Somehow I knew Howard was coming home. I pulled into the street and drove south toward Lubbock, Texas. The movers were right behind us. They were to meet us the next day in Lubbock to unload our belongings at our new home. We had done it. We had kept Howard and his boys from knowing what we were doing. I was free. I felt free. We had driven only a few miles when I looked in the rear view mirror and saw black smoke coming out of the car through the closed back window. I had seen this kind of smoke once before. The black smoke as in a furnace came out of me or off of me when Christ healed me of dominates personalities. In my mind I questioned the black smoke going through the window of the back seat. I had thought the smoke came out of me but now I didn't know. I saw it but it was not an issue for me. Seeing the black smoke leave gave me peace, a knowing that Jesus Christ was with us. I said nothing to Mom. She wouldn't understand, but I knew I was free.

After four and a half years of living life in a pig pen, I was going home to Jesus Christ. When I had gotten down on my knees after Howard had his wreck on his motorcycle with some girl on the back, I told Jesus, "If you will get me out of this I will never let anyone or anything come before You again."

Luke 15:10-32

10 *Likewise, I say unto you, there is joy in the presence of the angels of God over one sinner that repenteth.*

11 *And he said, A certain man had two sons:*

12 *And the younger of them said to his father, Father, give me the portion of goods that falleth to me. And he divided unto them his living.*

13 *And not many days after the younger son gathered all together, and took his journey into a far country, and there wasted his substance with riotous living.*

14 *And when he had spent all, there arose a mighty famine in that land; and he began to be in want.*

15 *And he went and joined himself to a citizen of that country; and he sent him into his fields to feed swine.*

16 *And he would fain have filled his belly with the husks that the swine did eat: and no man gave unto him.*

17 *And when he came to himself, he said, How many hired servants of my father's have bread enough and to spare, and I perish with hunger!*

18 *I will arise and go to my father, and will say unto him, Father, I have sinned against heaven, and before thee,*

19 *And am no more worthy to be called thy son: make me as one of thy hired servants.*

20 *And he arose, and came to his father. But when he was yet a great way off, his father saw him, and had compassion, and ran, and fell on his neck, and kissed him.*

21 *And the son said unto him, Father, I have sinned against heaven, and in thy sight, and am no more worthy to be called thy son.*

22 *But the father said to his servants, Bring forth the best robe, and put it on him; and put a ring on his hand, and shoes on his feet:*

23 *And bring hither the fatted calf, and kill it; and let us eat, and be merry:*

24 *For this my son was dead, and is alive again; he was lost, and is found. And they began to be merry.*

25 *Now his elder son was in the field: and as he came and drew nigh to the house, he heard music and dancing.*

26 *And he called one of the servants, and asked what these things meant.*

27 *And he said unto him, Thy brother is come; and thy father hath killed the fatted calf, because he hath received him safe and sound.*

28 *And he was angry, and would not go in: therefore came his father out, and intreated him.*

29 *And he answering said to his father, Lo, these many years do I serve thee, neither transgressed I at any time thy commandment: and yet thou never gavest me a kid, that I might make merry with my friends:*

30 *But as soon as this thy son was come, which hath devoured thy living with harlots, thou hast killed for him the fatted calf.*

31 *And he said unto him, Son, thou art ever with me, and all that I have is thine.*

32 *It was meet that we should make merry, and be glad: for this thy brother was dead, and is alive again; and was lost, and is found.*

OUTLAW

This is the terminology I used to express my biker husband. He was not to my knowledge a member of the organization located in California who go by the colors and name of Outlaws.

Howard belonged to two different biker groups who wore colors, one located in San Antonio, Texas, and the other in another city.

NOTE: After marriage to Howard I no longer wrote poems to express my feelings. Chapters 1 through 20 were written during the first year of my marriage to Howard, 1981. He read every chapter as I completed it. He never asked me to change a word. He never stated that any of it was not true. I had written the first draft of Chapter 21 believing God would save Howard and together with our children would have a good, solid Christian marriage. I had to re-write Chapter 21 when I began to prepare my manuscript for publication. I wrote Chapters 21 through 38 during a time span of over 29 years.

May 6, 1978
Howard's first motorcycle. Mary first bought him a dune buggy, that he pressured her for, he traded it for this Norton. A total biker lifestyle was birthed.

Mary's first Honda chopper. Built by Zeek Henderson at his shop, Classical Metalforming, Amarillo, Texas. Mary won the trophy for this custom bike.

Howard's Harley Davidson
KING KONG

Mary's Harley Davidson
Second Bike bought by Howard

POKER RUN
Mary (center)

SWAP MEET
friend - Mary

FAITHE, KATHY, MARY-PARTY
In fairness to Faithe, I never saw her take
any drugs or smoke any pot. She only
drank a few beers. I never saw her drunk.

MARY - TOYS FOR TOT'S RUN

Howard & Mary

HOWARD & DWAYNE (Mary's oldest son)
June 1978. Picture taken just after we
began to live together.

Howard
Picture taken within last
2 years of marriage.

Howard (anonymous name)

Chapter 22:
CARRY MY CROSS

~

Mom and I felt relieved as we drove from Amarillo to Lubbock. It was to be a new beginning for us. The pressure was gone, the fear as well.

We spent the first night in a motel on the outskirts of Lubbock. Our Dobermans Blackjack and Dutchess were excited to be going somewhere. We had to sneak them into the motel room, but they created no problems. Mom fell asleep quickly. I lay in my bed with my two Dobermans lying beside me. This was the second time I had moved out of the house Howard and I lived in while he had no idea that I had planned it long before I actually did it.

There is no turning back, I thought. I wondered how Howard would feel when he walked into the house with all the emptiness. I remembered how he had explained his feelings to me when he walked into an empty house almost six years ago after I had moved out. Would he feel the same again? I really didn't know. Howard had shown no love for me during our marriage. He had to have me, as he said, but I don't think he ever really loved me, that is, nothing like I had loved him. I didn't understand why he had to have me and probably never will. He owned me. He had told me sometime during our marriage that he believed that married couples should stay together for life, no matter what happened, no matter what anyone did. I responded that it just didn't work that way. Adultery by either person gave the other scriptural grounds for divorce. Adultery is the only divorce that I understand is approved of by Christ. Howard and I both had committed adultery.

Pure exhaustion helped me to get my thoughts intact. I turned to Christ feeling His comfort as I peacefully fell asleep.

Waking early, Mom and I, with our dogs in tow, drove to a restaurant. We ate breakfast and drank coffee in peace, relieved to be out of Amarillo. After eating, we drove to our new home and waited for the delivery, of our belongings. By mid afternoon we were moved in, our furniture set up. We were putting our things in order. I didn't think of Howard too much. I was ready to regain what I had lost during my marriage to Howard. I was hungry, desperate for a renewed relationship with Jesus Christ. My mind was set, my heart was set. I was leaving all that behind. I now wanted Jesus Christ more than Howard. No bargains were made.

Dutchess had chosen to sleep downstairs with Mom. Upstairs, laying in my bed, with Blackjack beside me, I realized that it was over, the months of preparation for the move, the keeping it hidden from Howard and nearly everyone else who knew us. I saw the hand of Christ and realized that He had protected and cleared our path before us. Everything fell into place when I gave my heart back to Him. He had put up with a lot from me. I had gone back to my old ways yet He had not forsaken me. I just didn't realize or understand the depth and the height of His love, and His forgiveness.

The hurt of the last years was now painfully fresh. Once Mom and I had completed the setting up of our new home, I had time to think. It took only a few days for me to long to just see Howard, but I refused to give in to these feelings. Instead of remembering the reality of how horrible my life had been with Howard, my thoughts would settle on how great it was in the beginning when Howard and I first started seeing each other. I would realize that I was in a fantasy, fairytale state of mind of how it could have been and not the way it was. Returning to what I knew to do as written. "Finally, brethren, whatsoever things *are* true, whatsoever things *are* honest, and whatsoever things *are* just, whatsoever things *are* pure, whatsoever things *are* lovely, whatsoever things *are* of good report; if *there* be any virtue, and if *there* be any praise, think on these things." Philippians 4:8. When I would allow myself to think of how it could have been, the pain would manifest. When I made myself think of the way it really was, peace would help to heal me and set me free.

After about a week I again put down the cigarettes and never smoked again. I was putting all my trust in Christ to heal me and

Mom of the never ending stress we had just come out of. I smoked no more marijuana, and I drank no more alcohol.

I didn't want anything but Jesus. I began going to church the first Sunday after our move. I went every Sunday morning and evening. They held revival after revival at the church I attended. I was in church most of the week and weekends. I finally found a part time job working for a lady who was seventy-two at the time. She owned and operated a vitamin shop. I worked only two days a week. My little check paid for the gas to go back and forth to work each week. Mom was paying for everything else. For the first two or three months after the move, I was so exhausted and mentally strained that I just couldn't look for a full time job. On my days off I would leave the house early and go to some park and sleep for hours. Then I would return home and fall into another deep sleep. Mom thought I was looking for a full time job. The battles of the past years left me totally drained of any energy. All I wanted to do was sleep. Mom didn't fuss at me when I didn't get a full time job. She didn't fuss at me for having to use her car either. Mom was becoming a mom, my mom.

Early one afternoon when I was upstairs in my bedroom, I heard Blackjack and Dutchess barking fiercely. I looked out my window and watched them running up and down the back fence line. Then they stopped with their tails wagging in front of the back fence gate. They were putting their paws on the fence, it didn't seem that they were mad but happy to see or smell someone. I passed it off as someone walking down the alley. I thought it was probably some kid stopping and talking to them.

The following day Mom and I left the house without locking the back door. I had noticed it when we walked through the kitchen, but I thought, "Oh well, the dogs won't let anyone in the back yard," and brushed it off. Mom and I went to a small fast-food place to eat. That was something we loved to do together, eating out. Mom could drive that Lincoln sixty in a thirty mile zone with no problem. She drove past the place we were going. We laughed talking about it. Some time earlier, Elizabeth had refused to ride with her. She was afraid of her driving and would not get into the car with her. At the time this was so funny to us. I just about refused myself. You went on a trip when you got in the car with Mom driving.

When we returned home after eating, it was obvious that someone had been in the house. Things had been broken in my bedroom. My Bible had been taken. The dogs were gone. I knew Howard had found me, but how? I called him and threatened to file charges on him. The house was in mom's name. I told him she would put him in jail. The following day he brought the dogs, my Bible and a few other things he had taken back to me. He laughed as he told me who the person was that had given him our address. My heart broke again. I knew the person personally. Howard had no truth in him. He had lied all his life. When he told me who was informing him about me I thought it was another lie. I thought he was telling me this to hurt me. He was not lying as I learned he was telling me the truth as time went on.

God brought the circumstances to pass so that I would meet the owner of several apartment properties. He offered me a job as manager of one. Mom and I gave away most of our furniture and appliances. We moved into our little two bedroom apartment and I began to learn the business of becoming a manager. The apartments had been renovated to draw the middle and upper class. They were just blocks away from Texas Tech College. The owner wanted to fill the apartments with college students. The problem was that they were right in the middle of low income families that lived on the wrong side of town so to speak. It didn't take long for me to realize that two prostitutes lived on the property. Drugs were being sold from the apartment next to Mom's and mine. Because of the way the apartments were built, in a square with a courtyard, you were all but closed in from the surrounding homes. Also, across the street was an adult theater. I was thrilled to get a full time job. I didn't scope the area or background of the property before moving in. I gave all my money to Mom except gas money and twenty dollars spending money. I wanted to pay her back for all the money she had spent on me.

Howard had moved in with a woman who looked a lot like me. Yet he would show up, usually on his motorcycle, at my job when he felt like it. He never stayed long. One time when he came, I hollered and screamed at him so much that he turned and got on his bike and I suppose went back to Amarillo. The same person, who had told him where Mom and I were living, told him where to find me at the apartment properties. The same person also let his girlfriend listen in on phone conversations made to me. I would be asked questions about Howard. It seemed to please the caller and the listener to know I was still suffering. Howard thought all this was so funny when he told me about his girlfriend listening in on my conversations with a family member. Especially when it came through the person who kept him informed about me.

A year had passed and I was carrying my cross. I was given another property to manage a couple of blocks away. My boss wanted me to take a course in property management. He was willing to pay for the extra education. I had no desire to do so. A yearning to leave had taken root in my heart. I hated the area, it was so much like the area Howard and I lived in when we moved to town, from the old air force base in Amarillo. I never told mom about the residents we lived among. I don't really remember telling anyone. It was all beginning to feel like I was dragging balls of iron and the cross of Christ.

I was sitting in church on a Sunday afternoon. I remembered, before we married, when Howard would come into church and find me. Just seeing him had excited me and gave me a little joy. Now here I was sitting in church alone again. It was almost like playing the same scene over again. I had already lived all this. When did things really change and the joy of God's promises takes the place of so much hurt? I thought. I carried my cross during this year totally because that is what I was supposed to do. I did what the Bible said. I knew that there was no going back to Howard. Here I was again, just as before we married, hurting over him most all the time. As before, he kept himself fresh in my mind by calling or coming by. I had not dated anyone, nor did I go to any bars, nor did I smoke, nor did I drink. After all, I was carrying my cross.

I had met several visiting evangelists in our little church. We would go out to eat after services. We were a little body of people who believed whatever the Bible said. We were Bible Banging Fanaticals.

While sitting in church on this one Sunday afternoon, the loneliness had set in. The future did not hold hope for me. After all, I felt that I had done all I could to become a wife, become a mother, and become a Christian family. All had failed. After the service was over I thought, "I don't have a clue what was preached about." This is the way it had been for a little over a year. I did what I was supposed to, but there was no joy in my heart. Leaving the church building I got into the car to drive home. As I was backing the car I heard the voice of Christ. *"I have a husband for you"* was all that was said. I had lost all my hope of happiness. Now, at this time in my life God was giving me new hope. This became the focus of my thoughts. Naturally I paid a lot of attention to every single man. I thought it would only be a matter of days, maybe weeks or just a few months until Jesus Christ would bring Mr. Chosen, Mr. Right, into my life. Happiness was sure to follow. If I waited until I knew without doubt that I had met the very person Jesus had chosen, life on this earth would become full of joy and purpose.

Our pastor decided to have a tent revival. I had only been to one in my life and that was in Brownfield, Texas, years in the past. I was sitting in the tent much to myself. The church I attended had week long revivals almost back to back. The visiting evangelist did the same. It seemed to be a little circle of the same people coming and going. Yet I had the freedom I needed to worship and love Christ openly. Much prophecy came forth in every meeting. As much as I read the Bible and was faithful to church attendance, I still wanted to have some evangelist prophecy over me. Not too many people were there the first night of the revival. "Hurry up and get through with the preaching." I thought to myself as I anxiously waited for the prophecy to begin. It was very seldom that I was not prophesied to. After all, Jesus told me He had a husband for me. Let's get on with it.

Suddenly, I felt a gold band on my left ring finger. I looked down to see it. I saw nothing but I could feel it. I put my thumb on it and could twist it around my finger. It was there, but I could not see the gold band, only feel it. I continued to feel the gold band in the days that followed. I told no one about this. I had wanted prophecy but instead I got a wide gold band on my finger. This had to mean that I was soon to meet my mate.

Later, after a few months had passed I caught a flight from Lubbock, Texas, changing planes at Dallas-Ft. Worth airport to catch a flight to Beaumont, Texas. I was going to Beaumont for another revival. I was running as fast as I could to board my flight. It was a long distance from where my arrival dock was to where I was to board the flight to Beaumont. There was no time for delay. I had to run. I felt the ring drop off my finger. I stopped running and began to look for it when I remembered that to the natural eye there was no ring. I had felt it fall from my finger. I even heard it hit the floor. I had no extra time to look for it. I continued running wondering why Jesus had let it fall off my finger. Why had I heard it fall on the floor? What did it mean? I continued to run and just barely got on my flight. It was a real small plane. We had to be seated according to weight, some on the left and some on the right for the plane to be correctly balanced. The ring was again on my finger. I felt it.

I was going on with life. I was doing everything I knew how to in following Jesus Christ. I was carrying my cross. Yet no matter how I forced myself to forget Howard, no matter how many prayers I prayed, no matter my determination to follow Jesus, Howard was still alive in my heart.

Luke 9:23
And He said to them all, ***If any man will come after me, let him deny himself, and take up his cross daily, and follow me.***

Luke 14:27
And whosoever doth not bear his cross, and come after me, cannot be my disciple.

Chapter 23:
SCARS OF CHRIST

~

Howard and I divorced February 6, 1985. He was still in Amarillo. He was still with the woman who looked a lot like me. But he was no longer working for the union and the big bucks were gone. His car had been repossessed. I had called him and told him to pay for the divorce and get it done. "Are you sure you want to divorce?" he asked. In my heart the answer was no, but in my decision to follow Christ, the answer was yes. I simply said, "Yes." I threatened to expose him if he didn't give me the house. I knew way more than he wanted anyone else to know about him, so he agreed. He paid my lawyer in full.

I drove to Amarillo the day before I was to be in court. I stayed with a family member. The whole evening I was told what an awful person I was. "How could you do it?" The words were flowing from a very angry hurt mouth. The person was talking about me before I accepted Christ. How could I do it? I don't know. I don't know how to tell you how I did it all. I can't tell you what I don't understand myself other than I grew up alone and very lonely. Yet I said nothing. I just listened, thinking I wish I had slept in the car and not come to this house.

Later in the afternoon a person drove me by the house, a few blocks from where I was staying and showed me where Howard was living with his girlfriend, who looked a lot like me. It was a normal little house well groomed on the outside.

I said nothing about the pain I felt when I heard the words, "your divorce is final." Howard was not in the court room. The house was awarded to me. I left the court house and drove back to the neighborhood where Howard lived. There was no one with me. I stopped across the street from the house I knew he lived in. I got out of the car and talked to a man that had been mowing his lawn. "Does Howard live in that house?" I asked. "Yes, but he's gone on a run now, he'll be back in a couple of days," the man said. He asked me if he could tell Howard something for me. "No, but thanks." was my reply. Getting back into the car, I drove back to Lubbock, crying all the way back. Not only about the final divorce but also about the words filled with hate said to me by my family member.

It was my mom's money that had paid the down payment on our home. I could have legally had the money paid by the renters paid to me and maybe kept up with the house payments. Losing the house didn't matter. I didn't want anything else to do with it. But it was very important to me to see that Howard didn't prosper from it. We had lived in it less than two years. After a few months the house was re-posed and the people renting it bought it.

Within the next few days, Howard called when he returned from his trip. The neighbor I had talked to told him about me. He knew who it was. "A woman driving a Lincoln Continental" was all it took. He said his lawyer hadn't even called him to tell him we were divorced. I felt numb for the following weeks and months.

On a Saturday night in late December, 1985, my phone rang. It was the police. "Is this Mary Moses?" the officer asked. I had legally taken back my maiden name. "Yes" I said. "Are you the mother of Timmi Elizabeth?" Again I said "yes." "We have your daughter downtown at the police station. Can you come and get her? She has been picked up for shoplifting," the officer explained. I told him I would be there right away.

I walked into the room where my 15-year-old daughter, Elizabeth, sat. She had a look of fear and bewilderment on her face. She looked up at me and jumped up and ran to me. "Mom, I'm so scared!" she said, tears falling from her eyes. I held her close to me and told her everything was going to be alright. I told her how much I loved her. We sat down next to the officer's desk. He began to ask me question.

In the outer room I recognized a voice I had not heard in some time. It was Kevin, Elizabeth's dad. He was drunk. He had been called first but Elizabeth was afraid to go with him and asked the police to call me. His girlfriend had told the police that she was Elizabeth's mother. She was with Kevin at the police station.

The police told Kevin that if he didn't leave he would be locked up. He stopped arguing with them and the two of then left. I heard one officer say to another, "She's safe with her mother." I continued to hold my daughter and comfort her with my love. There was no reason to scold her. I had done the same thing a few years back. In fact stealing had been a way of life for me.

Early Sunday morning I quietly slipped out of bed. Elizabeth was still sleeping, hugging her pillow. I simply didn't miss church, but today I was not going. I wanted to be alone. I wanted to go into my prayer closet which was the bathtub in my bathroom. I wanted to be alone with just Jesus and me.

The water was warm. I filled the tub as high as I could. I laid back letting the water cover me. I closed my eyes and began praying to Jesus in tongues, my prayer language. I prayed for some time, not really having any thoughts, just crying out for help. There had been too much pain for too long. I continued to pray not really knowing what I was saying but knowing I was being heard.

When I opened my eyes, it was pleasant, peaceful. I was looking at the tiles high above the faucet when I saw a very small little speck beginning to form. I was captivated by it. I watched it grow in size until its color became the color of flesh, tan, a golden tan, a cheek began to form. Peace as I had never known filled the room. The cheek became a face. I watched as if someone were making a perfect drawing, which became a man with hair, brown in color. It rested gently on His shoulders. His eyes were blue, a deep sea blue. He was covered with a white robe.

Our eyes focused on one another. He smiled without moving his lips, yet I saw his smile. He took one step, raising His robe just a little and stepped down from the wall onto the bathroom floor. He then took another step and was standing close to me where I was still lying back in the bath tub. He was beautiful, He was love, and He was everything I had ever dreamed of, thought of, or read about.

Looking into His eyes, He leaned over slightly and held His right hand out to me. His hand was open, His fingers extended. He then said, *"Feel the scar."* I lifted myself just a little and with my finger I touched the middle of His hand where the skin was raised where the large nail or spike had punctured it. I looked at the scar knowing it was real. I slowly ran my finger all around the scar until I had touched ever crevice of it. The skin had been torn severely. The healing had left a large scar taking up most of the middle of His hand. Jesus let me take my time in feeling His wound. He was so patient and gentle with me. When I had finished, I looked back into His eyes as He stood up. He then with His right hand pulled back His white robe where I could see His flesh and another scar on the left side of His body. It was just under his rib cage. The scar was almost identical to the one in his hand. I looked at the scar for a few moments, it was a little larger. I knew what to do without words being spoken. I raised myself almost to a sitting position and with my right hand. I ran my fingers around and all over the scar. There was not a place that I did not touch where the skin had been torn. I looked up again into His eyes, which He had never taken off of me. He said in a voice that comforted me even more, *"I will never leave you."*

At this moment Mom entered her bathroom, which had only a sink and commode. A door separated us. Jesus took a step backwards. "No, no, please don't leave!" I cried out with my eyes and mind. He then stopped. He stood still while my mom was in her bathroom. My mind began to question. 'I will never leave you' was not the whole scripture. There was more. Had Satan deceived me? I was looking into His eyes, crying out with my mind, "Are You real? Are you? Prove it to me that You are Jesus." Mom finished in her bathroom, and I heard the door gently close again.

Jesus had taken only one step backward as if going back into the wall. His face was turned toward me with His back to me. He then turned and was facing me. He took one step and again was next to the tub where I was lying. With both of His hands He raised His white garment just a little above His feet. I raised myself and looked over the top of the bathtub. I looked at the scars in both His feet. They were the same as the scar in His hand and the scar in His side. He let me look until I had seen both of His feet and the scars in both feet. I leaned back letting the water cover me. I looked up into His eyes. *"I will never leave you nor forsake you,"* were the words He said. I knew without doubt that He was indeed Jesus Christ.

He then smiled and I smiled back. The love in His eyes along with the unexplainable peace birthed something within me. No matter what laid ahead for Mom and me, we would be okay. Our Savior would be with us. I knew that He knew what I was thinking. We looked into each other's eyes still smiling at one another. I now could let Him go. He turned, took one step and stepped back in front of the tiles. He was again facing me. I watched until, just as He had come, He went. He became smaller and smaller until all I could see was the small speck. Then even that was gone.

I lay in the tub, realizing for the first time that I was naked. I felt no shame, no embarrassment but abundant peace. Only Jesus Christ mattered. He is awesome above any words known to me to be able to describe Him, He is beautiful, He is love, He is perfect because He is love. I had always thought His eyes were brown, but they are not. They are blue beyond description.

The only things Christ kept, while ascending from this world back to the Father, were His scars. The price He paid for me and for everyone.

John 14:17-18

17 *Even the Spirit of truth, whom the world cannot receive, because it seeth him not, neither knoweth him: but ye know him; for he dwelleth with you, and shall be in you.*

18 *I will not leave you comfortless: I will come to you.*

John 14:21

He that hath my commandments, and keepeth them, he it is that loveth me: and he that loveth me shall be loved of my Father, and I will love him, and will manifest myself to him.

John 20:26-27

26 And after eight days again his disciples were within, and Thomas with them: then came Jesus, the doors being shut, and stood in the midst, and said, *Peace, be unto you.*

27 Then saith he to Thomas, *Reach hither thy finger, and behold my hands; and reach hither thy hand, and thrust it into my side: and be not faithless, but believing*.

Hebrews 13:5
Let your conversation be without covetousness; and be content with such things as ye have: for he hath said, ***I will never leave thee, nor forsake thee***.

FORGIVEN MUCH – LOVES MUCH
SCARS OF JESUS CHRIST

This figurine came in a donation to City Mission. Years had passed since Jesus let me feel His scars and see Him as He is. I asked the Pastor of the mission if I could have the figurine. He agreed.

This likeness of Christ is just as I saw Him when He stood beside me and let me see and feel His scars.

Luke 24:36-47

36 And as they thus spake, Jesus himself stood in the midst of them, and saith unto them, *Peace be unto you.*

37 But they were terrified and affrighted, and supposed that they had seen a spirit.

38 And he said unto them, *Why are ye troubled? and why do thoughts arise in your hearts?*

39 *Behold my hands and my feet, that it is I myself: handle me, and see; for a spirit hath not flesh and bones, as ye see me have.*

40 And when he had thus spoken, he shewed them his hands and his feet.

41 And while they yet believed not for joy, and wondered, he said unto them, *Have ye here any meat?*

42 And they gave him a piece of a broiled fish, and of an honeycomb.

43 And he took it, and did eat before them.

44 And he said unto them, *These are the words which I spake unto you, while I was yet with you, that all things must be fulfilled, which were written in the law of Moses, and in the prophets, and in the psalms, concerning me.*

45 Then opened he their understanding, that they might understand the scriptures,

46 And said unto them, *Thus it is written, and thus it behoved Christ to suffer, and to rise from the dead the third day:*

47 *And that repentance and remission of sins should be preached in his name among all nations, beginning at Jerusalem.*

John 14:21

21 **He that hath my commandments, and keepeth them, he it is that loveth me: and he that loveth me shall be loved of my Father, and *I will love him, and will manifest myself to him.*

277

Revelation 3:20

Behold, I stand at the door, and knock: if any man hear my voice, and open the door, <u>I will come in to him, and will sup with him, and he with me.</u>

Chapter 24:
FASTING

~

I was desperate for some kind of normality in my life as well as Mom's. How does life fall into place with some kind of real peace, happiness, hope, love? It was beyond my understanding why I still had pain for Howard. I knew without doubt that Jesus had a mate for me. I rationalized that it could possibly be Howard since all attempts to stop loving him had failed.

I fasted often. Sometime it was days, and others it was a week or so. Now I was asking Christ for a fast such as His while being tempted by Satan for forty days in the wilderness. I didn't see or talk to Howard for months at a time. I now had a good job with a sod company in Lubbock. Mom was working for the bowling alley she had worked for before. I gave the majority of my earnings to my mom. I really had no needs. My life had fallen into a routine of going to work, going to endless revivals, and cleaning the church on my day off. In fasting as much as possible as Christ's example, I thought He would have compassion on me and kill my pain for Howard and really release him from my thoughts, and heart. This was the foundation of preparing to fast for forty days.

I had prepared for fasting for about two weeks, eating very little, spending much of my off time in the bathtub, which was my place of prayer. This was the only place I had to myself. I was speaking in my prayer-language during this time, my heart crying out to Jesus for a complete healing. I had spent much time in fasting before Howard and now afterward. There had to be a way to get over him.

On November 12, 1986 I began fasting. It was important that no one know I was fasting, not even my mom. The first three to four days were hard, then the first battle passed and I was able to focus my heart and mind on Jesus, the keeper of my soul. I watched no TV. I was willing to give up whatever it took for Jesus to make me complete without Howard. Going to work, to church, being at home I had a smile on my face and my attitude was the way it should have been. I had no gloomy tales to share with anyone. I suppose my mom thought I was over Howard. Peace, a wonderful peace filled my soul. I can't say I was happy, but I was at peace, determined to be successful.

On November 26, 1986 Howard called me at work. I had not heard from him in months. We laughed together. We were both in a good mood. We didn't talk about the past or the future. We just talked. Hearing his voice again birthed the desire to have what we had together when we first met. He didn't have a clue of my pain for him. Somehow at times such as these we both were able to just laugh together. Our conversation ended with, "I still love you." he said. I didn't reply.

I went to a Spanish church in Lubbock, other members from Camp Meeting Tabernacle were there. It was a celebration for the birthday of the pastor. I was still fasting, having only a few days left. After music and testimonies and a short message, it was time to eat. I sat in my seat till the chapel was almost empty. I didn't want to draw attention to myself and not eating. I was going to go home.

Just before I stood to leave, I heard the voice of Jesus, *"Mary do you love me?"* Yes, Father I do," I replied. *"Then feed my sheep."* Jesus said. Again, the same voice, *"Mary, do you love me?"* I replied for the second time, "Yes, Father I do." My mind went to the scripture in *John 21:11-17, where Jesus asked Peter this same question. Again, for the third time I heard the voice of Christ, *"Mary do you love me?"* Again for the third time my answer was the same, "Yes sir I do." *"Feed my sheep,"* was the reply of Jesus for the third time.

My thirty day fast ended December 11, 1986. Jesus brought these scriptures to my knowing in the following days to come.

Ezekiel 34:14-16

14   I will feed them in a good pasture, and upon the high mountains of Israel shall their fold be: there shall they lie in a good fold, and in a fat pasture shall they feed upon the mountains of Israel.

15 I will feed my flock, and I will cause them to lie down saith the Lord God.

16 I will seek that which was lost, and bring again that which was driven away, and will bind up that which was broken and will strengthen that which was sick; but I will destroy the fat and the strong: I will feed them with judgement.

Hebrews 13:5

5 Let your conversation be without covetousness; and be content with such things as ye have: for he hath said, ***I will never leave thee, nor forsake thee.***

Within two or three weeks after my fast, I was sitting at my desk working, thinking about the fast and if I had accomplished my goal. Howard had not called again. Was I healed, set free from him?

I was looking out the window from my desk when I saw a flash, a loud sound as if a rock had hit the window. I stepped outside and saw a little sparrow lying on the ground. I gently picked it up and simply looked at it. A little sparrow, I was sure Jesus had sent the sparrow. He may have had to knock it out for me to hold it, but it was not hurt, it lay still as I gently ran my finger up and down his wings. I then lay him on the ground and walked back into my office. Turning quickly I ran back outside hoping to see the sparrow. He had flown off. "What are you telling me Jesus, what are you telling me?" I asked as tears filled my eyes.

It would be in the years to follow that I would understand the results of my thirty day fast and the answer of the sparrow, one little sparrow I got to hold.

Matthew 6:16

Moreover when ye fast, be not, as the hypocrites, of a sad countenance: for they disfigure their faces, that they may appear unto men to fast. Verily I say unto you, They have their reward.

Matthew 10:29-31

29 *Are not two sparrows sold for a farthing? and one of them shall not fall on the ground without your Father.*

30 *But the very hairs of your head are all numbered.*

31 *Fear ye not therefore, ye are of more value than many sparrows.*

NOTE: I didn't know at the time but learned through a man of God, Exccutive Senior Pastor Bo Williams of Trinity Fellowship Church, Amarillo, Texas that we do not fast to get Christ to do something. We fast to know Him.

Picture captures my holding the sparrow.

Calendar I used to record my 30 day fast.

Ephesians 1:17-19

17 That the God of our Lord Jesus Christ, the Father of glory, may give unto you the spirit of wisdom and revelation in the knowledge of him:

18 The eyes of your understanding being enlightened; that ye may know what is the hope of his calling, and what the riches of the glory of his inheritance in the saints,

19 And what is the exceeding greatness of his power to us-ward who believe, according to the working of his mighty power,

*John 21:11-17

11 Simon Peter went up, and drew the net to land full of great fishes, an hundred and fifty and three: and for all there were so many, yet was not the net broken.

12 Jesus saith unto them, **Come and dine**. And none of the disciples durst ask him, Who art thou? knowing that it was the Lord.

13 Jesus then cometh, and taketh bread, and giveth them, and fish likewise.

14 This is now the third time that Jesus shewed himself to his disciples, after that he was risen from the dead.

15 So when they had dined, Jesus saith to Simon Peter, **Simon, son of Jonas, lovest thou me more than these?** He saith unto him, Yea, Lord; thou knowest that I love thee. He saith unto him, **Feed my lambs**.

16 He saith to him again the second time, **Simon, son of Jonas, lovest thou me?** He saith unto him, Yea, Lord; thou knowest that I love thee. He saith unto him, **Feed my sheep**.

17 He saith unto him the third time, **Simon, son of Jonas, lovest thou me?** Peter was grieved because he said unto him the third time, **Lovest thou me?** And he said unto him, Lord, thou knowest all things; thou knowest that I love thee. Jesus saith unto him, **Feed my sheep**.

Chapter 25:
PREPARATION

~

Mom and I didn't have a clue what the future held for us. Mom was at peace with us living together. There was something missing for me. I longed to be alone.

The ring, a gold band that I couldn't see but could feel was still on my finger. There were times that it manifested and other times I would forget about it. Christ had told me that He had a husband for me. I believed Him, yet the days, months and years passing made it seem impossible. There were times that I questioned if I had heard the words of Christ or even if the ring I felt was real.

My pastor had a brother, who was also a pastor that he wanted me to meet. Through the connection with my pastor, his brother called, and we went out on a date. It was awful. He had been divorced a short period of time. I spent three hours or so listening to him tell me everything about her and their marriage. I couldn't wait to get home. I had no desire to see him again.

Several months passed and through a lady friend at church, I was introduced to a young man living in South Texas, who drove a truck for a living. Come to find out, I knew his wife. She had gone to school in Ralls, my home town. They were close to my age, I didn't really know him, but I had seen him. He called and came to Lubbock, where Mom and I lived in a small three bedroom apartment. Elizabeth, my youngest daughter, lived with us at this time. I went on one date with him. We had talked on the phone before and after our date. It was not long after he went back to South Texas that I stopped all contact with him.

Marty, a young man in his 20's from our church and I had began to run around together. He was a young minister. He was focused on Jesus, this is what made us compatible, and our first desire was to follow Jesus. I was older, but younger in the word. He was younger, but older in the word.

We sometimes went to the airport and sat sharing our dreams with one another. We drove around just talking a lot. He, like me, loved to go shopping at the flea markets. He was really the only friend I had. We were never on a date. His friendship helped with time that seemed to be passing very slowly. I suppose he knew more about me than anyone, most of all about my dreams and hopes. He was also waiting for God's chosen mate. Marty helped me to grow in the Spirit-realm of the power of the Holy Spirit. He had the ability to see in the Spirit. When he would began to talk about Jesus Christ his hands would become very oily to the point of oil dropping off of them. He saw angels. Together we would sit at a park and spend hours talking and sharing what Christ allowed us to see. Through Marty's love and commitment to Christ I learned to also see in the Spirit. He helped me to learn. We could see angels together, describing them to one another.

Because of my friendship with Marty, I was able to release a lot of pain. I was growing in the Lord, beginning to understand that He had some purpose for my life. I wanted to share with others about Christ and my life, what He had done for me. I knew that I was blessed. I also knew that I was free from bondage. My desires had changed. Sin as I knew it, had become a part of my past, not my future. Forgiveness was a key issue. Marty helped me learn how to forgive.

Elizabeth grew older and moved out of our apartment. Howard was still living in Amarillo. He had contact with a person I knew extremely well, who also lived in Amarillo. This person kept him informed about me.

Unexpectedly in December of 1988, Howard called. I had not seen nor talked to him since my thirty day fast in November of 1986. Howard called just in time to birth a renewed desire to see him. I was in no way healed of loving him. I wish I could say I seldom thought about him but this would be a lie. It didn't take much for me to say yes when he asked me to come to Amarillo. We only had Mom's car, she let me take it to go see Howard the following weekend.

Howard had rented a little house close to Thompson Park. When he stepped out of the door, he was the same Howard I had divorced.

I wish I could say that I drove right back to Lubbock but I didn't. Instead, somehow seeing him stopped the pain I had carried for years. I flew into his arms. His words were, "I still love you." I surely didn't understand why we had such feelings for each other, but we did. "I love you too, I don't know if I will ever stop." was my reply.

We spent the evening talking about everything and the people we had known while we were married. I had not been in the biker lifestyle for years. He had never been out of it. Late in the afternoon Ray, Howard's oldest son, came over with one of his friends. Howard asked me to wait in his truck while they did business. I knew the business, drugs. I didn't want to see them taking drugs together so I did as Howard asked. After twenty minutes or so, Ray came out of the house and got into the pickup with me. It was great to see him. I had loved Howard's boys and I still did. "I wish I had gone with you." Ray said to me. We talked a little then he got out of the truck and he and his friend left.

The first night, Howard and I were able to bury our thoughts and be with one another. Our sex was not love, it was sex. I responded to him yet I really didn't want to have sex. Why he could get me to do what I didn't want to do was way beyond my understanding. I knew it was wrong, yet I did it anyway. There was no pleasure in it for me. All I wanted was his arms, this was all I needed. His words of love for me helped me to believe that all things are possible. Could it be that his heart was changing and he longed for a life without drugs?

I woke up in the middle of the night. Howard had slipped out of bed and gone into his living room. He was watching a foursome sex team on the screen. He didn't see or hear me when I stepped into the hall and saw him on the couch. It was the same couch we had bought when we were married. He thought I was a sleep. I knew nothing had changed for the good about him. He came back to bed in the early morning. I had laid in bed awake so very ashamed that I was in bed with him. I didn't feel the pain that I had lived with daily for so many years, yet I felt a deep loneliness. I felt separated from Christ, not that He had left me, but I had left Him.

We dressed and drove to a station to get gas. I waited in his truck. When he went into the station to pay, he was inside way too long. I was sure he had called some woman. I wanted to catch him. I got out of the truck, entered the door of the small convenient store and saw Howard on the pay-phone inside the store. When he saw me he said, "Because I said so," very angrily and slammed the phone down. "I had to make a business call." he told me. Why didn't I confront him? Why did I let him do this to me again? I said nothing, leaving him to believe that I had believed his story. I was sure he had covered his time with me, even having the same excuses, just as he had done to his wife when we first started seeing one another. These excuses had filtered down to me before and after we married. I'm sure the girl he was talking to didn't know about me, or at least she didn't know I was with Howard. I went into the same mode I always had where Howard was concerned. I didn't let myself care.

My time with Howard was nothing like I felt when he and I ran wild when we first met. I suppose I kept dreaming that it could be that way again. I kept waiting for Jesus to do something supernatural, a miracle that would win Howard, and he would change. I kept hoping that Howard's heart would change, that he would want to change.

I drove back to Lubbock determined not to go back to Amarillo. I knew in my heart that having sex with Howard was wrong but it was so easy to justify my actions. He had been my husband. Surely I'd get a couple of good points with Jesus. At least he was not a total stranger!

I had not enjoyed Howard in or out of bed. Nothing about him had changed. I could have stayed longer but as in the past, I made myself leave and drive away from him.

I quit my job in Lubbock and was looking for another one. I had been working for a sod company for three years or longer. The farm had been sold. The owner was going back to his home town and set up farming there. I called one of our landscape customers from Amarillo, Mike Williams, to ask him if he knew of any jobs. His response was, "Mary, there's a job I want you to see about. I have a friend whose secretary has quit." he said. I gave him my phone number. I felt a peace that maybe the stress of looking for a job would soon be over.

A little time passed, perhaps two weeks or more. I was concerned about a job more than anything. I became very depressed. It seemed the more I committed to Christ the more heartache and loss of direction I felt. I saw no future. Hope had dwindled down to very little. It was not only the unknowing that was hard to deal with. It was also my growing desire to live alone.

A day or so more passed. I was sitting on my bed praying, asking God what to do, or where to go. My heart was intense as I cried out to Christ. When I had prayed all I knew to pray, I sat quietly wiping away the tears that flowed down my face. In the silence I heard, *"prepare to leave."* This was all that was said. No explanation, no reason, just Jesus saying, *"Prepare to leave."*

It was impossible for me to leave my mom. There was no way I would leave my mom alone. She was afraid to live alone. I couldn't and I wouldn't hurt her. Where was I going? How was I going to get there? I had no car, no money, no job and no place to go.

With all these questions in my mind, the very next day I began to secretly pack. Somehow I felt like I would be leaving Mom but didn't see any way to do so. I hid boxes under my bed and behind my door. I packed all that I could and kept Mom from finding out. Without having any knowing of my tomorrows, I obeyed and prepared to leave.

It wasn't long after packing all I could that Mom sat with me in our living room. From the look on her face and the tone of her voice I knew I wasn't going to like what she was about to tell me. She told me that a family member was going to move in with us. She was right. I cringed at the thought of all three of us living in a very small three bedroom apartment together.

Soon, my sister, Kay, moved in. I didn't even know they were talking. Mom and I never discussed my sister. She knew we didn't get along and hadn't for years. After she arrived and the unpacking was done, I made the mistake of saying, "Mom has made me take Dad's place, and she wants me with her all the time." The fly back response was full of hate. It was easy to see that nothing had changed between us from our youth. I don't remember saying anything, at all to my sister again.

My things were packed, still ready to leave, with no place to go. I heard the door bell ring. Answering it, there stood Howard, looking real good. How is it he knew just when to call or show up?

"Will you come to Amarillo with me?" Howard asked. "Yes, let me get some clothes." I was so relieved to go somewhere, anywhere but where I was.

The following day, after Howard had gone to work, I was standing in the bathroom of his little two bedroom house, looking in the mirror. ***"I'm going to give you a car today,"*** were the words I heard. A look of surprise on my face was what I saw in the mirror. My mouth opened my mind racing. Then almost at the same time I heard a knock on the front door. I opened it and there stood B.J., my oldest daughter. I was surprised to see her. "Come on, we're going to get you a car today." she said. It didn't take me long to get dressed.

We found just what I wanted, a little two door car with a standard shift, it was a red Yugo. The car was paid for, and then insurance was bought. I was set, ready for anything. I had a car, my car. It had been years since I had a car. It was simply wonderful.

I drove back to Howard's little house knowing Jesus Christ had used B.J. to buy me a car. I had not asked her to help me. Howard was excited when he came in and saw the little red Yugo parked in front of his house. We drove to my daughter's house. Howard took

YUGO; Purchased, December 31, 1988

the car to show his friend. After about two hours, I realized he had taken it to his girlfriend's house. I didn't have to ask, I knew. When he returned, we went back to his house. He left soon afterwards. I packed my things and got into my little red car and drove back to Lubbock.

Marty and I were sharing all these happenings that were going on. He was praying for me just as I was praying for him. We were best of friends. He gave me a couch and chair for when I did get my own apartment.

After a week or so, I called the man I had first spoken to from Amarillo, Mike, a landscaper. "Call and set an appointment, the owner wants to talk to you." he said. Amarillo I thought! The job was in Amarillo. I was sitting on my bed. I stayed in my bedroom. The three of us, Mom, my sister and I didn't live in a happy house together. I was thinking, wondering how I could live in Amarillo and Howard not find out. I felt if he did find out then the never ending drugged up drunks and in the middle of the night visits would begin all over again. It seemed like I was going to move back to Amarillo but it simply seemed so impossible.

"I'm going to give you a job today." Jesus said. I heard Him very clearly. I had been waiting for the business owner to call me but now I did as Mike told me to do and I called Bill Thomas, owner of Thomas & Israel Engineers. An appointment was set. I drove to Amarillo for the interview and was given the job about two weeks later. I knew without doubt that I would get the job because Jesus had told me, *"I'm going to give you a job today."* The job was mine even before we spoke. I told my mom that I was leaving as soon as I returned from the interview. She had no problem with it because my sister was with her. Mom made it clear to me that I couldn't take my bedroom suit with me (she had bought it). She said my sister would need it. I knew and had always known that it was my middle sister who had my mom's heart. I had learned to live with and accept this. I felt she would be happy with her. It would not hurt her to let me go. I began to move my few belongings to Amarillo and stored them in B.J.'s garage. I knew that my new apartment was close to my job and I also knew that it was close to K-Mart. When we

drove past the apartment properties across the street from K-Mart and I first saw them I said with much excitement, "This is it, this is where I am supposed to live!" We went into the manager's office. We were shown the little one bedroom apartment. I paid a month's rent with deposit, it was awesome. It was freshly painted, all very neat, with a new washer and dryer. It was my dream that had come true, just for me. It was my home, my very own home. I was in hog heaven! An expression my dad used.

MARY, THOMAS & ISRAEL ENGINEERS

On February 24, 1989, I spent the first night in my own apartment. Alone, for the first time in years. I was so happy. I had a car, I had an apartment and I had a good job. I began working for Bill Thomas of Thomas & Israel Engineers on March 1, 1989.

It was hard for me to see the familiar surroundings of when Howard and I were married. I learned shortly after my move back to Amarillo that Howard had moved from Amarillo. He had moved to Wichita Falls, TX. He left Amarillo the first week after I had returned. It was safe for me to go anywhere I wanted. I drove to all the places we had lived, including the little house he had lived in. I knew if Howard was gone, his boys were gone also. I cried a lot as I relived so many memories. I believed Jesus had got me back to Amarillo for a complete healing.

During my move, I had seen a church on 10th St. that drew my attention. I attended church the following Sunday March 3, 1989. I quickly became a part of the congregation. It would not be long before I became assistant teacher, under the pastor, to the adult class. I even preached on several occasions. This church was much like the church I had belonged to in Lubbock. I had already begun to grow weary of the never ending revivals I had attended in Lubbock along with the never ending challenges for "Try God and see that He is God!" evangelistic pleas for more and more money. *(Give, and it shall be given unto you, good measure, pressed down, and shaken together, and running over, shall men give into your bosom. For with the same measure that ye mete withal it shall be measured to you again.* Luke 6:38)

I longed for growth. There was such an outward show of the Holy Spirit. I became aware of my own outward appearance, of the moving of the Holy Spirit. I began to question if it was indeed the Holy Spirit or I. I danced, I ran around the pews. I probably would have followed those who jumped over them had I not had a dress on. All this emotion was not satisfying me. It's as if I was building up some kind of performance and God when approved would come through with His end of the bargain. I was waiting for a real break-through. I wanted to minister to the lost, not the saved. A yearning had taken place at some point of this journey with Jesus Christ, a yearning to go into jails and prisons. I had been waiting for such a door to open. From the time I accepted Christ as my Saviour, birthed within me was the desire to win those I walked away from to follow Jesus. I had never forgotten the vision He showed me when I was ascending into heaven and He gave me the choice to go on to Him or stay and try to win the lost. I had chosen to stay. This desire to win the lost was still very much alive within me.

After much prayer and getting the peace I needed, I made a choice to change churches. I stayed in Soul's Harbor church faithfully, giving of my tithe and blessings for close to four years.

I visited several churches but simply didn't have the peace I needed to become a member. Then for a short period of time, three to four weeks I didn't go to any church. On a Saturday morning I went into my kitchen to get a cup of coffee when I cried out to Jesus. "Where do you want me to go to church? I need Your direction. I don't know what to do. I don't know where to go!" Taking a step or two toward my living room I had a vision. I saw in the heavens two large doors. (*I know thy works: behold, I have set before thee an open door, and no man can shut it: for thou hast a little strength, and hast kept my word, and hast not denied my name.* Revelation 3:8) This scripture immediately came into my mind. I then saw the doors open. I had seen these doors before. While searching for a church to attend I had driven by Trinity Fellowship on Hollywood Road. I had driven into the parking lot and when I saw how big the church was, I made a decision that it was too big and I wouldn't go there. This was not Jesus' decision. I didn't ask Him how He felt about it. Big churches were not what I had attended for years. Small congregations had become my comfort zone.

Once I had direction from Christ I simply did as I knew He told me to do. There was no arguing. The following Sunday I walked through the doors I had seen in the vision. I felt like a little ant invading the territory of a lot of ants. This was my first time to see Pastor Jimmy Evans. He led the worship music as well as preached the sermon. I liked him. He had a style of his own. There was no stomping and hollering from the pulpit. If he did raise his voice, it was low key. I was used to loud, very loud. After Pastor Evans completed his message, which I totally enjoyed, I then attended Sunday School. It was just as enjoyable as the sermon was. I had actually learned new meaning of scripture. This had not happened for a long time. These people had a way of simplifying the word.

When the class was over I asked about prison and jail ministry. I was then introduced to Vonna Ossenbeck, the woman in charge of Women's Jail Ministry. The following Saturday, I went with her into Potter County jail located in downtown Amarillo. Vonna had heard my testimony from Ernie Kirkwood, her dad who also worked for

Thomas & Israel Engineers. From this beginning would come years of preparation for a ministry that I would never have even thought of much less dreamed possible.

Mary Moses & Vonna Ossenbeck
July, 1993

After five years and eight months, (Mar.1, 1989 through Nov.18, 1994) of working as secretary for Bill Thomas, owner of Thomas & Israel Engineers, also a Randall County Commissioner, I terminated my position. I had accepted a job opportunity to work for Cathy Barnum. I met Cathy through Prison and Jail Ministry at Trinity Fellowship. She wanted to minister to the women incarcerated in our county jails. She and I became friends with a lot in common. She was in training under my supervision at Randall County Jail. She was my little Barbie doll. Her heart was full of compassion and love for the inmates. Cathy was owner and president of Texas Medical Credentialing. She hired me for the position of Vice President. I began working for Cathy Nov. 21, 1994. The second day of my employment was to be the last time I would see Cathy. Early in the morning on the third day of my employment I received a phone call from her husband. He wanted to know if Cathy had made it to work. "No," was my reply. He continued to ask me several other questions and said, "Wonder why she's not at work?" Tragically, in the days and months that followed, we would all learn that Cathy was murdered by her husband. He had gotten out of a drug treatment facility the day before, my second day of work, and killed Cathy the same afternoon. He strangled her. Cathy's husband eventually received a 35 years sentence for the murder of his wife and the mother of their three boys.

I could possibly have continued to work for the investors of the business. It was discussed with me, but a female lawyer and I bucked horns terribly. She was not an investor but was dating the one I was working with. She came into the business, in my opinion demanding and overpowering. I was single and this was also a problem. I had kept the business going during the investigation when Cathy's disappearance had first occurred. Secretly and privately the key investor hired another woman to take over the business, I was fired. I walked out of the door for the last time with my one week pay check. It was January 13, 1995.

The following Sunday I went to the alter asking for prayer. Pastor Tom Lane, of Trinity Fellowship Church knew me quite well and my involvement in the jail ministry, took my hand. The tears began to flow from my eyes. I shared with him about the situation in my life. He listened and when I had finished he simply said, "Call my office and tell my secretary the bills you have to pay. We'll help you." What, what! I heard my mind say. Needless to say a peace filled my heart and the devastation I was living in ceased.

It was at this time that I remembered while working for Thomas & Israel Engineers of having asked Jesus for a vacation. I asked for three months. I was extremely physically and mentally worn-out. It seemed that I was running at a fast pace and needed rewinding. The problems, pain, fear, learning, doing, obeying, seeking, working and loneliness were the total extent of my life. Well, here I was, on vacation because I had been faithful to God's calling. He touched the heart of Pastor Tom Lane and used him for the approval of my church to pay my rent, put food on my table, pay my utilities and make my car payments. I had traded in my Yugo for a car that Bill Thomas and Linda Curbo helped me to purchase. I now had car payments. This help lasted for the three months that I didn't have full time employment. I was able to work part time for Kelly Services. It's kind of funny to remember, but I had asked for an extra fifty dollars for gas money. Pastor Tom, through his secretary, Sandra Edmond told me I had to trust God for some of my needs. It was at this time that she offered her personal finances to help me. Man, oh man, I was meeting real Christians. I declined because I just didn't have peace about it. But it drew Sandra and me into a friendship relationship.

It was the following evening that Jackie Bolden (Cathy Barnum's mother) came to my apartment to visit with me. I had given her my Bible to go through as I had written the things that mattered to me in my Bible. It was my way of keeping a diary. Jackie wanted me to read my writings to her and explain every detail. She needed to touch her daughter in any way she could. She was broken inside. The despair and pain were at its peak. She listened quietly with tears flowing as I read the prophecies, dates and outcome of Cathy's growth in the Lord. After Jackie left, I picked up my Bible and there was a hundred dollar bill in it. I don't even know when or how she put it there. My gas needs had been met. It was a few days afterwards that I begin working for Kelly Services.

My little vacation turned into something I pray I will never have to go through again. Because of my experience and computer abilities I was getting different assignments continually. I didn't get the easy jobs. I got the jobs which tried my intelligence and my ability. I had to learn what it normally takes months to learn in a very short period of time. I didn't do filing and answering the phone. I sat down in the chairs of professional people, taking over their responsibilities. My responsibilities were doing their jobs while they were on vacation or having been terminated or simply had quit and gone to another position. I never met one of these people where I sat at their desk. I was introduced to an authority figure which told me what to do. I took all the notes I could then I sat down at a desk and did the work. Let me tell you, if it had not been for the Holy Spirit, I would have had a nervous breakdown.

At the end of six months, I went to work for a bank which taught me about financial matters. I was put into the position of working on the computer, entering financial reports, application forms for approval or disapproval of bank loans. What did I know about a bank, about bank loans, mortgages? Absolutely nothing!

One morning I felt like I could not crawl out of bed one more day, but I had no choice. I had to go to work. I received a phone call from Jackie. We had become friends after Cathy's death. Through circumstances she had learned about a position which had not been filled. She told me to apply for the position. The position was not in the newspaper. It was to go in the following morning. She told me to call and set an appointment, which I did. After work I drove by and picked up an application which I returned the following day. Ann Prescott, who held the position was leaving, she had taken another position at Amarillo College. Don Prescott, Ann's husband, was Executive Director. I was hired July 3, 1995 as Financial Secretary for City Mission in Amarillo.

Mary, age 53, Financial Secretary-City Mission

MOSES MOUNTAIN

SHE CLIMBS UP MANY MOUNTAINS,
AND SEES FROM WHENCE SHE CAME
NOT THINKING OF EACH STRUGGLE,
BUT KNOWING HEAVEN IS HER AIM.

THERE MIGHT BE SOME ROCKY CLIFFS,
WITH DARK PITS FAR BELOW
ALONE AT TIMES SHE SEEMS TO CLIMB
BUT JESUS HOLDS HER SOUL.

AND THOUGH HER HANDS GROW WEARY,
AND THOUGH HER HEART GROWS FAINT,
SHE ALWAYS MAKES IT TO THE TOP,
STRENGTH IS WHAT SHE GAINS.

AND THERE UPON EACH MOUNTAIN,
SHE CAN REST AWHILE.
SHE KNOWS THAT IT'S ALL WORTH IT,
JUST TO SEE HER FATHER SMILE.

MARTY E. HAMLIN
6-4-90

Marty E. Hamlin

A True Story of Murder in Texas

JUST ANOTHER MISSING PERSON

NO BODY, NO CASE!

Jackie Mayfield Bolden

Cathy Barnum

A vision was to take place on April 5, 1995 on a Wed: 12:45 am; Cathy was standing in the heavens, an angel on both sides of her, she was smiling, waving her left arm to me. **"Mary, don't give up, God has a wonderful work for you to do."** She said. I lifted my right hand and waved back to her. "Bye little sister till I come and join you." I said to her. Cathy, with the two angels began to ascend upward into the beautiful blue sky, surrounded by huge white clouds. A smile never left her face.

I called Jackie and described this vision to her. I also described what Cathy was wearing. She had on a white blouse with a blue skirt. When her body was found, she had on a white blouse with a blue skirt.

This true story can be purchased by E-Mail to Jackie Mayfield Bolden

Subject Line; JUST ANOTHER MISSING PERSON
j_m_bolden@yahoo.com

Chapter 26:
HARLEY DAVIDSON

~

I had never been to a Life Group which was called Whole Again until going to Trinity Fellowship. Becoming a part of a Life Group, through Trinity Fellowship singles Sunday School Class, gave me the opportunity to meet other Christians. It took pure determination to make myself walk into the homes of these people. I was sure I would be rejected. If I let anyone know my past, I just knew I would be judged, condemned and thrown out. Rejection was something I feared.

I obtained the strength I needed of course through the Holy Spirit and went to my first meeting. Several people were at the Whole Again meeting. It was fun to just listen to others tell of their life's experiences. I heard many testimonies, full of life's challenges. Single women were lonely. Single men were lonely. Loss of families, parents, fired from jobs, business failures, adultery, rejection, fat, skinny, ugly, pretty and on and on. God's children reaching out in the only way we knew how to be set free from our past, healed and living in God's perfect will for our lives. We were all alike, we just had varied backgrounds. There seemed to always be more women than men. It was at these meetings that I learned that some women are not looking for husbands, content with the close relationship they had with Jesus Christ. I was not one of these women.

On one particular meeting I was stretched. I usually listened and did not contribute much to the conversations. We were asked to group in small numbers. We were given many magazines of all kinds, with a piece of white paper and glue. "Look through these things and tell your testimony." Sue said. My, my, what a challenge! I had never done anything like this before. My first reaction was how silly! But I put my pride aside and followed the instructions. Once I got started, there was no stopping me. It's like I came alive, refreshed, renewed. I didn't talk, laugh or discuss the meaning of the pictures I chose. I was too busy telling it the way I had lived it. Through these pictures I was releasing my heart.

November 8, 1991

Billy Graham; Billy Graham became known to me after salvation. If I had heard his name before, or anything about him, I think I would have remembered. I listened to his ministry watching him on TV after salvation. Actually he was the most famous minister, or shall I say the biggest ministry to me at the time. During a course of time it had been prophesied to me that the ministry God had for me was big. I would watch his program and wonder how in the world could a person like me become a big evangelist? I wanted to be like him. I believed that he lived what he preached. He was my ideal of a Man of God during my first years of salvation. I cut the clipping out of the book with the question secretly in my thoughts, how do you get there?

Man praying over son; It grieved me greatly that no one ever prayed over me as a child. I hungered for the approval of my dad and mom. And now being a Christian I grieved that I had never prayed over my own children with the exception of Elizabeth, my youngest daughter that lived with me before and after salvation.

Hurting old woman; This is how I saw myself, a lonely unattractive, overweight, rejected woman.

Waterfalls; This gave me hope, that I could have an overcoming life with rivers of living water flowing from within. I believed Jesus. I believed that He would bring His promises to come about in the days to come. I would learn what real life is and what real love is. I would learn because He would teach me.

Bird with horn; I had made a fool of myself all my life. People didn't know if I was stupid or intelligent. I didn't know for myself. Howard had once said to me, "You are either the smartest woman I've ever met, or you are the dumbest. I can't figure out which one you are." He said these words to me within the last three months of our marriage.

Kathryn Kuhlman; At the end of my fourth marriage which was to Kevin. I was watching TV and came across this woman talking to a young couple. She seemed to be so phony looking, yet I knew she meant just what she said. Her hair and clothes were almost like something out of a story book for children. The way she talked and expressed the greatness of God was almost like she was in a play. With this first impression still I had no doubt that she loved Jesus Christ in a way I didn't understand. I said, "I want to be like her." A simple desire would become an answered prayer in the days to come. I was not saved at the time yet I knew this woman knew love, this woman was love.

Encyclopedias; I wanted to understand and to really know God. He is the Father of all creation. I wanted to understand and know Jesus Christ. I wanted to know and understand the Holy Spirit. I read all the material I could to learn the deep things of the word. I read the Bible faithfully for hours. Now I had branched out in reading Bible Dictionaries, Bible Commentaries and on and on in a hunger to learn. I studied for hours for years and still do.

Computer; It was a deep desire within me to have a computer. I wanted to write my true story. This too would come about in the near future.

Food; Food of all kinds, lots of food. I had been bulimic since I was nineteen years old. I had been healed in the office of a pastor. I saw black smoke as in a furnace come out of me, or off of me. This was the third time since salvation that I saw black smoke leave my body. I was in my first year of being successful in this healing. To go even a day without throwing up was something I had not experienced in years. And now to have control for close to a year was a miracle to me.

Woman; This is how I saw myself in my past. Full of anger, hate, and even power along with street smarts to take from others to feed my own lust. I had spent many years in hate and un-forgiveness.

People sitting together; I was with people. I was trying to have friends, Christian friends. I was pulling myself out of my loner-lifestyle. To become friends with women was something I just didn't do. With the exception of Linda Curbo and Kitti Lambert, women were simply not allowed in some areas of my life.

When we had finished our task of cutting and gluing, we were then called on one by one to share the meaning of our pictures. Oh me, I didn't know I'd have to tell everyone what my pictures meant.

another night in the hospital. The following day he was told that the dehydration was taken care of and the virus was going away.

It took almost six months for Larry to recover from this virus and its after-effects. From what the Doctor had told Larry about the virus lead him to research. The virus fell under the category of Legionnaire and Strophes disease, which can be the effect of working in a cooling tower. Larry's job responsibilities at Amarillo International Airport included taking care of the heating and cooling.

Larry's marriage continued to decline. His way of coping was to ride his motorcycle. He now had a desire to obey Christ and give his testimony. He was reading a motorcycle magazine and in the back he read an advertisement to join Christian Motorcycle Association. He became a member and received a membership card along with a letter stating that a representative would be coming to Amarillo to set up a meeting with potential members interested in ministry. A short time later he read in the Globe News of such a meeting. He attended and it was at this time that he met Ron Sherman and other bikers who were interested in starting a membership charter with Christian Motorcycle Association in Amarillo, TX. Ron and Larry along with other bikers began to organize and talk with other cyclists. In order to become a part of the ministry team or an officer they had to meet the criteria required by the organization in which they did and became charter members.

A meeting was arranged with Herbie Shreve and the district representative in Brady, Texas in the summer of 1994. They were given a charter for ABC (Amarillo Bible Crusaders). Along with John Rodgers and others they began to invite motorcyclists to attend the first meeting. There were ten bikers that attended the first meeting. Larry became very involved. It had taken six months to fulfill criteria required to receive charter membership. When they voted in their first officers Ron Sherman was President and Larry was Vice President of the organization.

Larry had family that attended Kingswood Methodist Church so he began to attend church for the first time in years. He attended Kingswood Methodist Church for a little over three years. Then he

Fear gripped me. Oh well, at the moment I didn't really care what anyone thought of me, me was me, just as I am! I had come a long way in Christ. They could like me or hate me. This was their problem. At least this was the way I looked at it. Lying about the pictures was not an option. God had told me to be honest. I practiced this request in every area of my life.

There was a young man sitting in the group, John Christopher. He was rather quiet. He seemed to really be interested in the testimonies coming forth. When it came my turn to share he listened to my every word. Everyone listened. I was revealing things for the most part they had not experienced. It took me a little more time to even hit the highlights of my life. I had to leave out so much. When I finished talking everyone knew without question that my salvation, my life was a miracle.

John Christopher became my friend. He wanted to understand a life such as mine had been. How do people come to the place of living with no conscience, no integrity? What makes a person leave their children for such a sinful life? How does such sin make one happy? In the beginning of sin, it is fun, real fun until one can no longer see daylight, only the blackness of sin.

John and I would talk on the phone, or at church. We didn't go places together, we didn't run together. John didn't realize that as Marty Hamlin had done, he was helping me in many ways. He knew and believed in my relationship with Jesus Christ. He would ask questions and I would answer him, holding nothing back. In my eyes and heart this man was for real. He didn't ask things so he would be filled in with the dirt, he asked because he had a heart of God, full of compassion. I sure knew a lot of people, men and women who talk the talk, but don't walk the walk; John is not one of these people.

At one of these Whole Again meetings, I met a person who belonged to a Christian organization that rode motorcycles. I was invited to attend a Christmas party held by the Christian Motorcycle Association local group called Amarillo Bible Crusaders. I decided to go. It felt so good to be around people I understood. I had a good time in watching everyone, yet I felt out of place not having a motorcycle.

As I drove home I said aloud, "Jesus if you want me to go to their meetings and be a part of their association, then I want you to give me a motorcycle." Not much of a prayer, but one I meant. There was no begging or trying to justify why I needed a motorcycle. It was a one line prayer. It quickly became a desire to ride a motorcycle again. I found myself turning to look at the person on the bike next to me when I drove to work or home or church or anywhere. It was only a matter of days before I began looking for a motorcycle.

It was all I could do to pay my rent and necessities. There was very little money left for wants. I now had car payments as I had traded in my Yugo for another car. I felt rich in having a car that I didn't have to change gears every time I slowed down or turned a corner. My clothes came from City Mission. Rarely did I actually buy something and if I did it usually came from a vintage store, a used clothing store. You would have thought I had money to burn, and my outward appearance looked like it. In reality, I had learned that buy now and pay later with credit cards was the sure way of buying! It didn't take long for me to get in debt over my head. I didn't realize that monthly payments of the least amount paid would put me into years of debt. It did.

On a regular working day, I got a telephone call from John early one morning. "Can I come and see you?" he asked. "Sure," I replied. John had helped me with some of my debts. He had asked me what I owed or I had told him during one of our conversations. I'm not sure. He had invested in the stock market and had gained a considerable amount of money. I don't know how much but I do remember him telling me that it was more money than he had ever had in his life.

I didn't know why John was coming to see me at work but it had seemed to be important to him. I wondered if I had done or said something wrong and he was going to confront me with it. Of course all kinds of imaginations, possibilities came to my mind.

John walked into my office, standing in front of my desk he asked, "Mary, how do you feel about riding a motorcycle again?" John had asked me this question during one of our phone conversations. I told him I had been looking at Harley's but this was just general conversation. I usually told John the things that were happening in my life, simply sharing with him. When he asked me this question he was leaning over the front of my desk just a little. Somewhat surprised, I looked at him and replied, "I asked Jesus Christ for one. If I am suppose to be a part of Christian Motorcycle Association I won't go without my own motorcycle." "How much does one cost?" John asked. I told him about one I had seen at a motorcycle shop and the cost of it. He took out his checkbook and wrote a check large enough for me to buy a Harley Davidson. I think I just stared at him, dumbfounded. I know I must have thanked him, surely I did. I was so excited that I'm not sure of what was said. By six o'clock the same afternoon I owned my Harley Davidson.

Psalms 37:4-8

4   Delight thyself also in the LORD; and he shall give thee the desires of thine heart.

5   Commit thy way unto the LORD; trust also in him; and he shall bring it to pass.

6   And he shall bring forth thy righteousness as the light, and thy judgment as the noonday.

7   Rest in the LORD, and wait patiently for him: fret not thyself because of him who prospereth in his way, because of the man who bringeth wicked devices to pass.

8   Cease from anger, and forsake wrath: fret not thyself in any wise to do evil.

Luke 6:38

38   *Give, and it shall be given unto you; good measure, pressed down, and shaken together, and running over, shall men give into your bosom. For with the same measure that ye mete withal it shall be measured to you again.*

Mary on 1995 Harley Davidson (Paid for by John Christopher)

John Christopher with daughter Carly

Chapter 27:
HUSBAND

~

Larry was nineteen when he and his first wife married. She had become pregnant. Their marriage lasted about two years. After their divorce Larry was single for almost seven years. It was during these years that he began smoking marijuana and taking various other drugs. His lifestyle became one of promiscuous sex, hard rock clubs and partying. His friends at his workplace were also drug users. From the time they got to work until time to leave the conversation had only been about partying after work. Many times Larry went to work under the influence of marijuana. He and his friends were anxious for breaks as they could get high again. His weekly routine was trying to budget drugs and the necessities of life such as electricity, gas for his car, rent and money for food. Most of the time, the drugs came first. One of his friends told him that they could sell drugs, keep part of the drugs for themselves and pocket the profit.

Because of the extra income life got better, that is financially. He never took into consideration the damage he was doing to his body. Larry had asthma as well as serious allergies. As time went by the effects of the drug use was beginning to wear on his body. Some of the effects were loss of memory, fatigue and more frequent asthma attacks which were becoming more serious. He developed a really bad attitude as well as disrespect for others. He had forgotten what it was like to live a normal life. He had gone to college before marriage. He dreamed of a career. He wanted to be sound man for a band. Larry had the ability to read and learn. But after he chose drugs first, they became his god. His priority from dawn to dusk was drugs.

Larry went to work for Amarillo International Airport, as low man on the totem pole. It was at a Christmas party in 1978 that he met the woman that would become his second wife. She worked for a rental car business at the airport. They began their relationship after the party. They went to her house and had sex. Their relationship continued and they married September 18, 1980. For the first five or six years they were happy. That is Larry was happy and he thought his wife was also. It was at this time that they went to a party. She no longer worked at the airport but the party was where she was working at that time. They had an argument and Larry went home without her. Later when she came home she confessed to him that she had sex with another man before coming home. From this point their marriage grew worse. Larry couldn't get over the continued adultery, he lost any trust in her. He couldn't forgive her.

By 1992 their marriage was just two people living in the same house. Larry purchased a motorcycle. He along with his friend who also rode a bike made a midnight run to the overlook at the South rim of Palo Duro Canyon. The run took about forty-five minutes. They parked their bikes and begin drinking beer. A car pulled up at the rest area and parked next to their bikes. They visited with the people for some time and then decided to leave. Larry got home very late and went directly to bed.

When Larry got up the following morning he felt very ill. He didn't feel like he had drunk too much beer the night before but he knew something was wrong. It was on a Sunday morning. He continued to get worse, to the point that he couldn't stand. It was extremely difficult for him to breath and he was very weak. His wife got a neighbor to help get him into the car. She drove him to the hospital where he was admitted. His wife stayed until the paperwork was finished. When it began to get late she left and went home. After she left he was given an IV. He was told that he was dehydrated and had some type of virus. Respiratory blood work would be done. The next morning they began running test. Hours went by.

In the afternoon while Larry was in bed, all of a sudden, very quickly he realized that his feet and hands were beginning to go numb. Swiftly there was no feeling. This numbness was traveling all the way up his legs and all the way down his arms. His whole body began to grow numb. Everything went dark. He couldn't see.

He began to have feelings of falling. It was extremely dark. Such blackness he had not ever experienced before. Larry began to have visions, remembrances of all the bad things that had ever happened to him. When he had suffered pain, physical pain such as falling on his bike, getting a sting from a wasp, being hit too hard, getting a sticker, all this pain was magnified. Pain that he had felt such as heartache, adultery, past relationships, family issues, relative issues, and all these events made the pain that he was now feeling seem as though he was falling deeper and deeper into a pit of devastating pain. Everything continued to be magnified as he fell deeper into the black darkness. He wanted to scream but he couldn't. He felt things grabbing him. He couldn't see them but he felt them. Fear overwhelmed him. Larry couldn't feel his body yet he was aware of grabbing in the dark trying to find something to stop his falling. In his mind he remembered a song he had sung in Sunday-school class. As a young boy Larry had gone to church, a Lutheran Church. The song he remembered was Jesus Loves Me. He tried to scream again and failed. He tried once more and hollered the name of "Jesus!" He screamed, "Save me Jesus." In an instant he went from the darkness to the light. The feelings in his body instantly returned. He realized his eyes were open and he was back in the hospital room in the bed. He then heard a voice which said, *"Give your testimony."*

At first Larry didn't know what to think but he believes he had died and gone to hell. But the powerful name of Jesus brought him back from death. As he laid in the bed trying to figure out what had happened, a nurse came into the room. He told her that his body had gone numb, completely numb. He told her that his feelings had returned. She looked at his hands and told him that it was a reaction to the dehydration and the virus affecting his body. After several hours the Doctor came into the room and told Larry that he had a virus of undetermined origin and they wanted to give him antibiotics to keep him from having a bacterial infection. They would continue to try and find out what the viral infection was.

His mom, Beverly, his sister and his wife came to visit him. They stayed for about an hour. Larry didn't share his experience with them. But he was thinking about it all the time. Larry spent visited with other riders at Grace Community Church and began to attend on a regular basis with other bikers. Larry's wife never rode his bike with him but she did go to church a couple of times.

Larry's wife had continued to drink very heavily. They had been married nineteen years and she had become an alcoholic. It had gotten to the point that he never knew what would happen when he got home from work. If she was asleep and he woke her, she would be in a drunken stupor. Everything turned into a nightmare, screaming and hollering, cussing and on and on that could last for minutes or up until she fell asleep again. Larry fought back by hollering and trying to control her but it was impossible. Larry had never hit a woman and as hard as it was to control himself he knew he never would. Larry stayed away from home as much as he could. Sometimes he would drive around the block many times trying to get up the courage to go into the house.

Larry and Ron, whose wife had died before they met, began to ride out of town to motorcycle rallies in Federicksburg, Texas and Brady, Texas as well as Joplin, Missouri. They went on several trips, riding across country from the east to the west. Larry loved it and so did Ron. These out of town trips helped Larry to keep his sanity.

Larry had stopped drinking and drugs were no longer a part of his life. He began to pray for his wife on a daily basis. As he learned how to pray he would cry out to Jesus Christ to save her and change her. They had at one time been happy. He believed God could do a miracle and she would be healed of her alcoholism and they could fall in love as before.

After months of prayers and finding out when he would return from a trip that she had gone to night clubs and again committed adultery he was to the point of losing his own mind. They no longer slept in the same bed. His wife had moved into the second bedroom months earlier. Larry knew he could not continue to live in such heartache. He had built a relationship with Jesus Christ. He was on his way to overcoming the sins that had possessed him for so many years. One day when he was totally desperate he got down on his knees by his bed and prayed, "God change her or set me free. I can't take it anymore."

In about two weeks Larry flew to Spokane, Washington for educational purposes for the airport in 1999. When he returned his wife was gone. He had no idea where she was or who she was with. After about five days he got a letter in the mail. She stated that she wanted a divorce and she was coming for her things. Larry was crushed, yet he remembered asking God to save her or take her from him. He had answered Larry's prayer by taking her out of his life. Larry filed for a divorce shortly afterward.

Larry Martin, age 44

Herbie Shreve, Ron Sherman, Larry Martin and District
Representative Amarillo Bible Crusaders Charter 1994

Bo Pearson, Larry Martin, Ron Sherman
July 9, 1995

Larry Martin on his Gold Wing,
Ron & Larry were in California at a rally.

Getting dressed, putting on my Wranglers which I hadn't worn in years. My thoughts were exciting. I was going to ride, with real bikers again. Only now it would be with Christian people. These people loved the Lord and wanted to be used by God to win the lost. This was rich to me. I can be myself again. I loved to ride. I was confident in the way I looked and I felt good. I was ready. Christ had given me a motorcycle. Who would have ever believed it!

Being an on-time person, I sat down by myself about thirty minutes before others started arriving. The group met at a restaurant off of I-40 East. When I began to hear motorcycles, I perked up. Would they accept me? Would I make a complete fool of myself? Did I look like an idiot? What would I do, how do they talk? Street talk or Christian street talk? What is Christian street talk, same as regular talk only without cussing, I guess! I had no confidence in myself. I was very uncomfortable around people, especially women. From what I had learned, bikers owned their ole-ladies! Would these men be any different? I had a ton of questions rush through my mind. Rejection was my biggest fear. When I get real nervous I laugh a lot and talk too much. Could I pull this off?

I had chosen to sit in the middle of a long table and see who might sit down beside me. I spoke as people began to notice me and ask me who I was. This is the part I really dreaded. People want to know everything about you when you're a new face. I didn't want to tell them my past. I didn't want anyone staring at me and focusing on my past. I had been married to an outlaw biker, he was a real biker. He was a real outlaw biker, just like real cowboys are real cowboys! These people rode all kinds of bikes, from Honda, Yamaha, as well as homemade converted things on two wheels!

I was blending in as the members came in and began to sit close to me. I was paying a little more attention to the men. God told me He had a husband for me. This was nearly fifteen years ago. While listening to some woman tell me about something I really wasn't hearing, I looked up as two men were walking in front of my table. The first one wasn't bad. He was nice looking, probably close to my age, but the second one is the one who caught my eye. He was tall, dark and handsome. He had beautiful black hair. He was dressed in a Christian tee shirt, and nice fitting jeans. He looked at me, smiled and spoke as he walked by. I watched the both of them as they walked to the front of the table and sat down. While the woman was still talking, I looked at the one that had really caught my eye and I said, "Lord, I want that one." much to my own amazement.

Minutes were given, the usual comments at a meeting that stands accountable for what they do. I listened as the President, Ron, who was the first man that drew my attention spoke. He told of their rides to churches, ministering to street people, bar people and whoever would listen. Then the second man, Larry, the Vice President spoke. I know I was staring at him. It may have looked like I was just paying attention. This is not true. I thought he was about the most handsome man I had seen in such a long time, and he rides a motorcycle. Wow! What more could a woman want. He is a Christian man, who is tall, dark and handsome, and a biker. This was my dream.

People were curious wondering who I was, plus, I was riding a Harley. After the meeting I talked to several people, laughing a lot, covering the battles I was having thinking about the times Howard and I rode together. This made me really miss him.

We rode a little after the meeting. We stopped, drank a coke and more questions were asked. When they found out about my testimony, my past, all the more questions were asked. I couldn't find a place to stop and I didn't lie. The President, Ron, wanted me to share with the others. I did. I don't know how long it took, but by the time I finished, I felt like a dried out sponge. I rode home thinking about why I had told them so much. I had no intentions of doing so. It just comes out. I don't know how to shorten it. I don't know how to keep the truth a secret. I was sure no man in the group would want a woman who had been married five times and one husband was a gang-related outlaw.

It was at the following meeting that I learned the President was single and the Vice President was married. When I learned this I put a stop on my attraction to him. Married men had not been and would not be a part of my life again. I quickly stayed away from him. I no longer lusted after or found my strength in married men. Adultery had not been a part of my life in many years and it wasn't going to ever be again. This is one commitment I made to Jesus Christ when I left Amarillo and divorced Howard. "When I see You face to face, I will be able to say, I have committed no adultery." Married men were taboo.

The conclusion was drawn that I was just right for Ron. With the influence of others pressing him, he asked me for a date. I dated Ron for a short time. CMA riders thought we would fall in love, get married and the problem of being single would be over. Not so! He just didn't hold my attention. He had lived a life in Christ all his life. He was more interested in hearing about my past. It fascinated him. I didn't like to talk about it just to be talking. I talked about it only when it was useful in helping a lost person to find Christ. My testimony was shared every time I went into a jail or prison. I refused to go into detail about some of the things I could hardly stand to think of myself. I told Ron I just wasn't ready for a relationship. What a joke! I was so ready, but not with Ron. We stayed friends but we stopped dating.

Several of us would ride just to be riding. Some single, some married, and some women, some men. Most of our riding days, we would just show up at someone's home and they would go with us. We picked up other members as the day passed. We didn't pick and choose who to ask to ride with us, if we were in your territory we stopped and invited you to ride. No plans were previously made.

On a Saturday afternoon, about four or five of us were riding down Tenth Street. Someone hollered out, "Let's get Larry." We rode to Larry's (Vice President) house to get him to ride with us. His wife had never ridden with him. I just thought she didn't like to ride. It was no deal with me. Some people just don't like to ride motorcycles.

We stopped in front of his house. We didn't park, we remained in the street. Larry came walking out. He walked up to me because I was the closest to him and with all the noise of our bikes I was the only one who could hear him. He leaned over for me to hear him say, "My wife and I are getting a divorce. We are separating our things." I know the look on my face was pure shock. At first I didn't know what to say. We had ridden with the same crowd for two or three months and no one ever said a word about Larry and his wife having problems. There was no gossip. His friends had been faithful and ethical in their friendship. I didn't have even one thought that they had serious problems. Larry, like me, didn't talk about the pain in his heart. Only Ron and maybe one or two others knew that his wife was an alcoholic.

It took a few seconds for me to respond. The hurt on his face birthed deep compassion within me. With my left hand I reached up to his chest and gently patted him saying, "I'm so sorry, I didn't know. This is very painful for you. We'll leave." When he turned to go back into the house I could see his wife looking at us from the living room. I was sure she saw me pat him on the chest. I wished I hadn't done that, but I did do it. I motioned to the others and we rode off. We went to a place to eat and it was then that Ron told me about the years of problems Larry and his wife had had. His wife being an alcoholic, adultery had taken place more than once.

Larry and I continued to see each other at the meetings, but I didn't go by his house with anyone to get him to ride with us again. I didn't want a man just divorced. They usually talked about all their problems all the time. I didn't want to hear about his marriage. I made no effort to strike up a relationship with him. He was still tall, dark and handsome but he was wounded and his wounds had not healed.

It was time for voting in officers. Ratchet-Jaw (Mike Hamner) was voted in as President of Christian Motorcycle Association. Larry and I continued seeing and riding with everyone. We were friends as everyone, were friends.

I was having a lot of problems with a man that I helped buy a motorcycle for. He had shown such progress at City Mission that I became friends with his family and was helping him to get into CMA to continue on with his walk with Christ. This was after he graduated from City Mission and was living with a Christian man who was also trying to help him. It didn't take but a few months for him to go back to his druggie world riding the motorcycle I bought on two of my credit cards, five thousand on each, with interest. No one knew about this problem.

Mike began to ask me to have coffee with Larry and just talk to him. I was really the only single woman available that could talk with him. At first I declined. Larry didn't ask me, the president did. Mike didn't stop asking me and I didn't stop saying no! Then one night we were riding down 10th St. I was not a happy camper. I was looking for the motorcycle I had bought. I had no idea where it was. I did know that Rick was going deeper and deeper back into his drug lifestyle. I was extremely worried that he would hide the bike or take it to another town for safe keeping, without paying for it. It was time for another payment and he was nowhere to be found. I was fit to be tied. My nerves were shot. I had spent nights looking for Rick. I was going to get the bike away from him. Larry recognized that something was wrong with me.

We stopped on 10th St. and got something to drink, no alcohol. It was at this time that Larry asked me what was wrong with me. I blurted out the truth. He was compassionate. He had a hard time accepting that a man I had helped, even helped get a bike would do this to me. Larry just didn't operate this way. He didn't lie, cheat and steal.

Not long after this the police called me late one evening. Rick had been stopped and arrested for drunk driving. He was on the motorcycle. The police asked me if I would get the motorcycle and take the girl with him back to the bar. I told them I would come for the bike, but not the girl. We hung up and I drove my car to Hollywood Rd. and parked my car off the access road, got on the shovel-head Harley Davidson and rode it home. I hid it in another parking area so Rick could not find it. I went to bed wondering how in the world I was going to pay for it.

A member of CMA wanted the bike and I sold it to him for what was owed on it. Not long afterward he and his wife separated and he couldn't pay for the bike. Instead of bringing it to me, he let another member take it. It was over a week before I learned that another person had it. I went to his work and confronted him. He wanted to buy it. I agreed. (*outcome of this bad mistake)

One day when several members of CMA were riding, Larry asked me to go have coffee with him. By now he was my friend. I told him about the bike because he asked me. He asked me about everything about me. It didn't make me uncomfortable like it had with Ron. Larry had a past, not as bad as mine, but a past of drugs also. We began our relationship by riding some place and just talking. Larry began to call me and make sure I was safe for the night. One of the members said to me when we were all eating together, "You sure picked up on him fast!" He thought it was funny. I didn't. "Let me tell you, I didn't ask Larry out, he asked me. Do you have a problem with this?" I said in a very angry voice. Everyone close heard me. Nothing like this was ever said to me or Larry again. The point was made.

After several rides together and talking in my apartment, I asked Larry if he wanted to come to my house for supper. This made him happy. The man ate out, or opened cans, or TV dinners, or cooked a hamburger on his grill. In other words the man couldn't cook.

Larry knocked on my door and when I opened it I was amazed. There he stood with two red roses in a vase. He had a big grin on his face. It had been years since any flowers were given to me. I was shocked. Larry was just as shocked when he saw the feast on the table, he couldn't believe it. I was a country girl. I could cook. There was roast, gravy, mashed potatoes, carrots, corn, green beans, salad, corn bread and rolls. I put the flowers on the table and Larry said blessing. He ate some of everything. I did most of the talking. After he finished eating we watched a little TV then I turned it off and we just talked. It began to get late and Larry got up to leave. I stood also. He looked at me and very timidly said, "Can I kiss you?"

Larry took me to his mom's. He told her we were just friends. She smiled but she knew it was more and Larry knew she knew there was more to it. Beverly liked me. She had been reading the articles I wrote for publication in the City Mission News Letter. In fact this was the only thing she read. She knew I was a Christian. I was older, ten years older than her son but this didn't matter to her. I also met Becky, Larry's sister. It was a very nice visit.

Larry and I soon afterwards began to talk about marriage. Larry opened his heart to me and told me all about his two marriages. This is when I found out that he had a daughter. They had not seen each other in several years. I understood, there were problems with me and my children also.

This was the beginning of our seeing each other daily. Larry called every morning and every evening to make sure I was okay. He didn't want Rick to hound me about the bike. He was protecting me. My, my, "How good did this feel!"

Larry amazed at such a meal.
He brought Mary 2 red roses.

Larry was riding a 1982 Honda, Gold Wing Aspencade. It weighed about 735 lbs. Our riding together was a trip. By the time the light changed, I was at the next light. Just about the time the light changed again Larry had to stop and wait for it to change again and I was at the next light. I would look back at him and he would be leaning forward as if the bike would go faster. I would get tickled. When we did stop I never missed the opportunity to tell him, my man had to ride a Harley. It was not easy for me to slow down! I had ridden hard and fast for years. I didn't know how to go with the flow. Also, even though I had not told him, my attraction for a man, real attraction was when he rode his bike. Larry was all I wanted in a man, except for that Honda. Larry finally agreed with me and we went shopping. We found a Springer, 1996 Harley Davidson. He sold the Honda (the thang!) a month or so before our marriage. Even his attitude changed on the Harley. He rode tall, as they say, 'walking tall', my man 'rode tall.'

One afternoon we were in my living room talking when the phone rang. It was B.J., my oldest daughter. Her brother, my oldest son and his wife were getting a divorce. There were serious problems. Larry listened as I talked. The conversation opened a book I had closed many years ago. In the beginning of this manuscript I had written that I had done two things that I was deeply ashamed off. One of these things was coming to life again. My X-husband was to learn about the worst of the two. After hanging up the phone I told Larry the truth, all of it. He knew that there were two things in my past that I shared with no one. He never asked me what they were. He didn't even ask now, but I chose to tell him.

Any other man would have walked out the door without a look back, but Larry didn't. The following day we drove to B.J.'s home. I knew she was completely torn up. I was her mother, I wanted to comfort her.

There was more to the reasons for the divorce of my son that just me. It was bad, real bad. B.J. asked me to leave. Larry and I did. On the way back to my apartment I sat quietly. Once we got inside, with a very gentle, comforting voice, Larry said, "That was over thirty years ago. I didn't know you then, but I know you now and you are the best Christian woman I have ever met and that's all that matters to me." This was it. He accepted this truth about me. He also forgave me right then and there. It didn't become a problem for us.

A month or so later Larry and I settled on the man we wanted to marry us, Pastor Gary Burd of Christian Heritage Church. We began moving my things into a storage building. Larry moved in with his mom and sis. I moved into his house with very few belongings. Larry lived with his mom about six months before we married.

It was close to a year from our first having coffee together until

Larry and I married on May 20, 2000. We rode down Sixth Street in Amarillo, Texas with the Bandidos riding lead. Christian Motorcycle Association followed. Dwayne, my oldest son rode my bike. Larry and I rode shotgun (last). People came out of their stores to watch us pass as we rode down 6th St. Outlaws riding with Christians. This was a sight to see. The Bandidos stopped traffic at every light in order for us to stay together. At a four way stop they pulled their bikes in front of the traffic and opened a way for us to continue our ride. Then they would ride back in front of us until we got to Sam Houston Park where Larry and I were married. Time had passed with some healing and B.J. attended our wedding. Stoney, my youngest son was not able to attend.

Larry and I had made a covenant with Jesus Christ, and each other. There would be no separation and there would be no divorce. Larry and I as well as other CMA members had begun to give our business to the Bandidos. Mack owned and operated a cycle shop. The repair on our bikes was the best. I was soon given the name of Mother Mary. We didn't always agree with their way of life, but we do agree that God loves everyone the same. His love is not given by our acts but is given by the crucifixion of his son Jesus Christ and His blood, for redemption of all of us and all of our sins.

MR. & MRS. LARRY & MARY MARTIN
May 20, 2000

B.J., Larry, Mary, Elizabeth, Dwayne
(3 of Mary's 4 children)   **Linda Curbo-lifetime friend**

Elizabeth, Linda, Pastor Gary Burd, Mike, Dale
background; Bandadios

Dwayne walked with his mother Mary, to give in hand to Larry

Dwayne wore a nose ring and other paraphernalia of his choice. I put a removable ear ring in my nose to let him know that I love my son just the way he is. When he first came up to me to escort me to Larry and he saw the ring in my nose, the expression on his face said it all. With a big smile he leaned back a little and his response was "Hey, cool Mom, cool!" He then took his mother's hand and escorted me onto the platform and gave me in hand to Larry.

MARY SHARING A VISION

When Pastor Gary Burd gave the opportunity for anyone to say what they wanted to say, he was little surprised when I said, "I have something to say." Over 15 years had passed since I had a vision and I wanted to share this vision with everyone. There were people who had not been invited standing in the background to see this Biker Wedding that heard about the vision also.

God had given me the opportunity of going on to heaven to be with Him or I could stay on earth longer to win the lost. I chose to stay and because of that decision, the day of unity was accomplished. As I shared the vision I expressed the love of Christ for all. Only God knows who accepted Him just the way he/she was on my wedding day. Only God knows who in the days to follow would remember that love between people is what is important. The lost are won by love only. When Jesus said, *"It is finished."* He opened the way of opportunity for salvation for everyone. It is our choice to choose to obey Him and become a part of His body, the body of Christ.

My heart's desire in a husband. These notes were written in my own hand long before Larry came into my life.

RELATIONSHIP TO JESUS CHRIST
Friday; April 12, 1996

1. Having spent his ordained time in fasting and prayer. Worship the Lord and serve Him with a whole heart.
   a) God is Lord of his life.
   b) He is prepared for ministry.
   c) His heart desire is yielded to Christ.
   d) His time of healing from the past is for the most part completed.
   e) He is baptized in the Holy Spirit.
   f) He has the ability to see beyond the outward appearance and know what God can do.
   g) His eyes shall be clear, his heart shall be clean and his ears shall hear.
   h) He is known by the church body as having a good name.

WISDOM: Shirley Vernon spoke these words to me when I was sharing with her about my past.
"DON'T LOOK AT THE OUTWARD APPERANCE, OR THE WORDS, LOOK AT THE ACTIONS."

The following was written a short time after my first writing of Relationship to Jesus Christ. These notes put the personal desires of my heart in word.

ALL FOR ME
Saturday; May 4, 1996

1. Loves me right after his love for God. Will not put children or prior relationships, friends, family first.
2. Ability to express himself. Willing to communicate.
3. Affectionate, likes to touch, hold hands, etc.
4. Wants me with him, wants to be with me. Having alike or similar taste and desires.
5. Pays attention to my safety and comfort.
6. Knows or able to realize touchy areas such as keeping in touch with me concerning changes, phone call if has to be late, circuitous phone call if can't make it, etc.
7. Protective, yet allows me to minister to others, also knows warning signals if I am ministering to a man or he to another woman.
8. Does not like things loud, music, TV, hearing good.
9. Not real cold natured that our home is kept cold, also riding together in the car is not hot nor cold-just right.
10. Ability to communicate his feelings, willing.
11. Thoughtful, letting me know changes; not letting me wonder.
12. Joy, appreciates laughter, has uplifting personality.
13. Does not repeat things over and over.
14. Taller than me, has hair, large frame, not a hairy body, sweet smile.
15. When he turns to look at me his chest swells with approval, proud of me, sees Jesus in me.
16. Finds me gracious.

Prophecy spoken to Mary by Lou Ella Braddock on Sept.19, 1994. **"He's tall, dark and handsome."** she prophesied.

Larry read my original notes, describing the man I desired on Nov. 11, 1999 before our marriage May 20, 2000.

SOMETIMES FORGIVENESS DOESN'T COME EASY

*I drew up a contract in selling the motorcycle. In the contract I didn't clearly state about the interest amount and that it had to be paid in full also. Larry ended up with the bill.

But we learned a lesson that stays with us to this day. We don't co-sign or loan money or buy things on credit cards.

Proverbs 6:1-2
1   My son, if thou be surety for thy friend, *if* thou hast stricken thy hand with a stranger,
2   **Thou art** snared with the words of thy mouth, **thou art** taken with the words of thy mouth.

Proverbs 24:29
Say **not**, I will do so to him as he hath done to me: I will render to the man according to his work.

The Lord provided the money to pay the credit cards in full. The challenge of forgiveness is greater than the money. We continue to pray that real forgiveness will fill our hearts. We simply pray, "Lord help us to forgive." We rarely discuss this matter anymore.

After all, the motorcycle put Larry into my life and our relationship began by him caring about my feelings, following, he began to protect me. Our relationship began on this solid foundation.

Chapter 28:
HONEYMOON

~

Larry and I spent our first night of marriage in his house, where I had been living. He had been living in the home of his mom until we married. He carried me over the threshold as is customary. We began to pack and prepare our motorcycles for our trip first to Oklahoma City to visit the zoo and then on to Hatfield, Arkansas, where, Christian Motorcycle Association headquarters is located. From there we would go to the Gulf of Mexico and sleep out on the beach. The location was close to Beaumont, TX. We would spend a day riding our motorcycles along the coast line of the gulf, then return to Amarillo.

Early the next morning we were busy getting our motorcycles loaded. The neighbor from across the street who had known Larry and his x-wife for a number of years came over to ask me why I had a housecoat on, with a leer that sickened me! He had been on drugs for years and thought this was funny.

After he left, we continued to load our new van. A car came around the corner and parked in the street. A young man got out and came over and hugged me. He had been a friend of mine from City Mission, where I worked as Financial Secretary. I had become a friend to all his family. I had also helped him get a motorcycle that I thought would help him come out of the drug lifestyle. Larry knew all about him and didn't like his intrusion the first day after our marriage.

The day was not starting out good. We continued to pack our van and load our Harley Davidson motorcycles. Larry and I had not traveled together out of Amarillo but one or two times. It didn't take long for me to realize that he had his own way of doing things. It didn't take Larry long to learn that I had my own way of doing things also!

Deciding where to eat and then what to eat was something that had to be discussed beyond reason. I'm very spontaneous, "Let's stop here," I would say as Larry drove by, saying, "Ugh, I'm not sure. Let's see what else is here." Larry needs to think something over, probably write it down and then have time to decide the outcome. He needs to decide if someone might come in and rob us while we're eating, or the place might not have good food. These things are important. Larry does not like to be rushed.

After eating, when the decision of where to eat had been decided, within the next hour, we continued our travels. Of course it was up to me to help Larry drive correctly. You know, he didn't really say much as I told him how to stop and how far from the other car he should be. These things are extremely important and I was sure I had all the answers. He wasn't asking, but I was sure he wanted to hear all I had to say.

Larry had a hard time deciding where to park. I always knew just the perfect parking area so he wouldn't have to back the trailer. I learned later that he had little or no experience in backing a trailer. I was married to a city boy, a real city boy. I was a country girl who could wire a tire onto a wheel rim if I had to.

When we arrived in Oklahoma City, we went directly to the zoo. We're not having much conversation. We're too busy trying to get to the zoo. I also found out Larry is not good at driving in a big city. He doesn't have time to read the signs. The traffic is going much faster than he's used to. I am watching the signs, telling him everything to do. Many times he had to turn right in the wrong lane. It took me some time to get him to understand that when you know you are going to have to turn, get into the correct lane at least a mile or two before you get to the turn.

Larry's face was set, eyes glued to the road, mouth firm in a determined mindset not to smile. It sure was hot, over a hundred degrees.

We finally arrived at the zoo, parked the van, put on our large brim straw hats and put the day's drive behind us. This is the highlight of the day. We're going to see the large area housing the lions and lionesses. This is the major reason of choosing this zoo above all others. It's the biggest and supposed to be the best. Seeing the lions and their cubs made everything okay.

We walked around looking at the animals on our way to the home of the lions. We were standing in front of their home, with the gates locked and a sign which read, CLOSED DUE TO RENOVATION. SORRY!

Walking back to our van we just couldn't believe that we didn't get to see even one lion. Irritation along with the heat made us forget that we were on our honeymoon. When Larry began to drive back the way we had just come from I asked, "Where are you going?" "Back to the highway to get us on the highway to Hatfield." he replied. "What! You're not going to back track, it's over ten miles to go backwards." I looked at the map. Sure enough, there is a road close to us that we can take and then have to turn back south just a couple of miles to get on the right highway. It took some doing to convince Larry to turn, just turn. He finally did and here we go on a small two-lane road heading east. After two or three miles, I told him to turn back south and we could unite with the right highway. He turned. We drove several blocks to a dead end with no place to turn around. Larry finally lost it. He looked at me with a look of death. Things were really getting serious. It was at this time that I realized that he didn't have the experience needed to back a trailer. Plus he couldn't see the trailer behind our van. I shut up while he told me what for, in a voice and look that showed me a side of him that I had not seen before.

After Larry got us back on the right little road, I looked more closely at the map and found several little roads that would take us to the highway we needed to be on. Larry was driving faster than he had before. I would say, "Slow down so I can read the sign." He would slow down until we got close enough for me to read the sign, then he would speed up and fly by the sign. I would look at him fussing at him. Why wouldn't he slow down? There was no response to my questions. This happened for the next thirty minutes or more until he finally slowed down enough for me to read the sign.

Now we are on the right highway. We were really enjoying the view. Nothing was being said, of course, except my raving at him for not talking, not smiling, not anything, just driving. He said nothing.

We reached Hatfield, found the headquarters for Christians Motorcycle Association, we went inside to meet the people. No one was there except one young girl answering the phone. We asked where we could park our van and trailer for the night. She directed us to their property which had electricity and running water for members. Larry had his choice of parking. Naturally under a tree would be good. He couldn't decide which tree to park under, so helping as best I could, I pointed out the perfect tree and place to park. We were the only people there, this decision was major. Oh yes, the water and lights were off at the time. Larry unloaded our motorcycles. I prepared our bed for the night on the trailer. We were spending the night under the stars. Everything is fixed. We couldn't take a bath, but one night wouldn't matter. I laid down in my summer pj's, burning up. Larry went to the back of the van for something. He returned with a bag of potato chips, munching down hungrily. I looked up at him as he put his foot on the rail to pull himself up and over it to lay beside me. Just about the time he was half way over the rail, I very kindly, but firmly said, **"Not in this bed you're not."** His mouth was full, his eyes blazing as he stepped back on the ground which had grass about three feet high. I just looked at him while he continued to eat the chips. He walked over to a faucet to get some water. He had forgotten that the faucets had not been turned on. He walked back to the trailer, looking as if nothing was wrong, but I knew from the speed he was eating the potato chips that he was aflame inside. I chose to act as nothing was wrong either. Larry was shoveling the chips in his mouth by the hand full. It was very soon that he began to say, "Ouch, ouch, ouch, over and over again. Kinda jumping up and down raising his feet one at a time to scratch the bites and hit the ticks off his legs and feet. He was not a happy camper.

We were learning so much about each other very swiftly. After Larry finally got all the ticks off himself, we settle in for a night of bliss under the stars. The only problem was, there was no bliss.

Turning our backs to each other, we finally went to sleep. It was during this night that Larry learned how loud I snore and I learned he had to relieve himself many times during the night.

Larry had the bikes ready to ride early the next morning. It was beautiful riding up Queen Wilhelmina. It looked like a mountain, but was actually a high hill. Larry was riding to my left and I was hugging the edge of the narrow paved road. We were side by side. We came to a small, very small place we could pull off the road and look at the scenery. We didn't have much chance to do this as I was again helping Larry to understand that if a car came around one of the curves, it would hit him, because they would not be able to see him until it was too late, and this would mean he would hit me. I had searched for death several times, but this was not one of the ways I wanted to go!

Reaching the top, we ate in a nice restaurant, expensive, but nice. We then shopped where I found several small items I wanted, like earrings, a pin, even key rings with a hog on them. I didn't have a clue what the hog stood for, it was cute, I got one for us both. It wasn't until later that Larry told me that the hog was their football mascot. I'm not a football fan so they went into the I-don't-want items of our honeymoon trip. Larry was watching our budget much better than I was. I was in my woman mode and wanted to buy.

We spoke kindly to each other pretending that we were having a wonderful time and so very deeply in love. Underneath, we saw each other in a different view, like we had never met each other!

Reaching Beaumont, TX, we somehow ended up on a little road that took us right through a flea market. Bingo! Wife is happy. Husband on the other hand forced himself to stop the van. Again, I purchased several real cute items that would end up in my treasure box of items that I-don't-want.

We then drove by a Sam's Club store and decided to check it out. Or rather, I decided to check it out. I saw a beautiful diamond heart necklace for the wonderful price of seven hundred dollars. After sufficient begging, I convinced Larry to buy it. Larry's top dollar of fifty dollars spent on a woman was more than enough. He couldn't imagine seven hundred dollars. His face was grim when he handed his credit card to the woman behind the counter. A woman standing at the counter listening to our every word watched us as I kind of demanded, with all the manipulation power I had for him to buy the necklace for me. He did not have a look of love on his face when we left the store. But I was happy!

We then drove to the Gulf Of Mexico to a place on the beach where I had been before and knew how to get there. We were alone. No other people on the beach. This is our night, our honeymoon, tonight we would make up to each other for all the stress up until now. We took our shoes off and began to walk down the beach, having a little silly flirting with each other as we had seen people in the movies do. We were going to be in love, if it killed us.

Looking down at the sand, we realized that there was a lot of stuff on the sand, in the sand and under the sand and a lot of it was alive. We quickly put our shoes on and pretended that we didn't smell the raw aroma. The outdoor toilet had never been cleaned or it had been a long, long, long time since it had been. Trying to hold my breath for way too long, left me running out of it in a fit of fury. I leaned over and tried to spit out all the unknown varmints I had inhaled while coughing and gasping for air, all at the same time. Larry knew better than to laugh. I think I saw a smug grin on his face, but I quickly stopped that by shouting my fit of anger at him. His face quickly became dead!

The wind was beginning to blow, but this helped so much with the heat. We got our fold-out-chairs and sat next to each other with that "Come on, you're mine look." Tonight's the night, for sure, we'll fall in love, and nothing will stop us. You're supposed to have sex on your honeymoon, or at least we thought you were supposed to. We put on our costumes of outward fun and joy. The wind continued to gain strength and began to pick up sand and salt as it filled our faces with stings of pain. Our sitting by the seashore lasted maybe twenty minutes.

We put our sleeping bags close and zipped them up as one. We did the best job we could of removing the salt and sand with a washcloth, but somehow we just didn't get the job done.

Sure enough, tonight was the night. We were talking, looking at the stars. We might love each other after all. It was a little hard to see the stars over the gust of wind blowing. This didn't last long either. We zipped up our sleeping bags, together and went inside to continue our night of bliss on the shifting sand.

It was after dark by now. We were just getting used to the sand and salt scratching our skin when we saw a bright light, from inside our sleeping bags. A pickup stopped right in front of us. We opened the zipper just enough to get our heads out.

"How u'all doing?" He asked. Screaming just enough for us to hear above the roar of the ocean. The man told us he had just left a club and he wanted to talk. Hollering, or rather, I hollered back to him that we wanted to be alone.

He drove a few feet from us and stopped his truck, got out and waded into the water. Larry and I looked at each other in disbelief. Being the aggressive person that I am, I got our best flash light and kept him in the spotlight until he realized that I meant business. Leave us alone. He went back to his pick-up and left. This brought a smug look of triumph on my face.

The wind was blowing forty-five to fifty miles an hour by now. The sand was picking up with the salt, trash, cans and everything else not tied down and blowing it in the wind, as they say. Larry and I separated ourselves from our two sleeping bags, realizing that tonight was not going to be the night.

With our bodies crumpled each inside our own sleeping bag, we pulled it over our heads and zipped it in order to survive the night. Larry found out that having to relieve himself very often was not pleasant. A statement was later made that he thought that he could be watering our grass in Amarillo, TX.

We both were fighting to breathe. Neither one of us had enough sense to get into the van and go to a motel. After all this was our plan, to spend the night on the beach. We were determined to do so.

Early morning we both climbed out of our sleeping bags about the same time. I looked like a rooster head. My hair was standing straight up in the middle of my head. Sand with salt for toner was covering my face as it was also on Larry's face. In fact we looked like we had become the sand people, overnight.

Our bikes were holding the rest of the sand packed on them. The bikes came first. We had to get the salt off of them. We drove to the nearest town, and found a car wash. We first discussed how to wash each other off. It was serious. We were ready to get the sand and salt off us. But we decided to wait until we got a motel room. It probably would make us look even weirder, if this is possible, with the salt, we looked like we were being preserved with sand for a filler, to be buried alive! But somehow we reasoned that this would be better than walking into a motel, soaking wet on a very hot dry day.

Larry went into a motel. Naturally I refused. By the time all that was needed to do was done, we were too tired to even hold hands. Anything else was out of the question. Driving home, there was not much said. I think we were both wondering, what in the world have we gotten ourselves into. Did we tell Jesus, "no divorce" or did He tell us, "no divorce?"

Ephesians 5:33
Nevertheless let every one of you in particular so love his wife even as himself; and the wife see that she reverence her husband.

Ecclesiastes 4:12
And if one prevail against him, two shall withstand him; and a threefold cord is not quickly broken.

Christian Motorcycle
Association, camp
ground. We're getting
ready for the night,
Hatfield, Arkansas.

Larry and Mary's bike
on top of Queen
Wilhelmina, Hatfield,
Arkansas

Mary with bikes loaded,
ready to travel on to
the Gulf Of Mexico,
close to Beaumont, Texas

"Not in this bed, you're not!"

Such joy, such bliss!

Husband, stating his true feelings.
WHERE'S HIS GLASSES! HE CAN'T SEE AN INCH IN FRONT OF HIM!

THE BLUSHING BRIDE
(Wonder if wife has anything to do with husband not having his glasses on!)

Chapter 29:
CHOSEN BY GOD

~

Our married life continued on as our honeymoon had been, really awful! We would soon discover that the only thing we seemed to have in common was our love for Jesus Christ. Our outward appearance showed us to be this striking couple who had the same heart in ministry. We did, but we were totally opposite in how to accomplish this goal of ministering to the lost. Sharing the vision and desire to go into the prisons as a team helped us to want to grow and learn.

When I had moved into Larry's 700 sq. ft. house before marriage I told him I would live in the house for a year after marriage. Therefore, first thing we did was to put the house on the market. We called a Realtor who estimated the property would bring $35,000. Although it was small, Larry and his x-wife had remodeled enough that it was attractive.

Some of the problems that neither Larry nor I had thought of surfaced quickly. I was accustomed to quiet, very quiet, in the mornings. Larry was a talker. Larry also asked a lot of questions. I drank coffee as soon as my feet hit the floor. Larry ate a bowl of cereal. I could hear his spoon hit the side of the bowl with every bite. Larry had developed the habit of continuously scraping the cereal to the center of the bowl. My flesh rocked and rolled on my bones hearing this mound of cereal being created. He would take a big bite and start the whole process over again.

My work-place was extremely stressful. Larry's work-place was extremely stressful. With the exception of Christian programs, we had not watched the same TV programs before marriage. Come to think of it, we very seldom watched TV before marriage. Nothing silly for me, I was into the history programs, true life stories, anything about prisons and jails. Larry was into Chevy Chase and

Steve Martin movies that were completely silly and stupid to me. If I walked into the living room and he was watching some kind of animated comedy, I would look at him and wonder "What's wrong with you?" I suppose I spoke it out loudly several times also. He was quick to change the channel but in my mind I didn't see how any grown man could watch beep, beep, the road runner at the age of forty-eight!

Larry had expressions that were new to me. He would say, "Thank you, thank you very much." all the time. I was not into Elvis Presley. He also laughed like Mr. McGoo! Kinda take a breath between each sound like hoo breath, hoo again and another breath. He has a deep voice which made it sound even more unnatural, weird! When he picked up on something he thought was important he had a way of quickly, and I mean quickly turning his head to one side and doing a side mouth talk. At these times I just stared at him not knowing what to say. I don't ever remember being around a man that could talk and talk about nothing! Larry's clothes consisted of a dozen tee shirts, jeans, one outdated suit, one tie and three good pairs of shoes.

Who is this man and where was I when we dated?

On the other hand I had studied and read the Bible a major amount of time for fifteen years. The TV being on most of the time increased my frustration. And when it was on, the central heat and air system Larry had installed was made for a thousand and up sq. ft. house, not a 700 sq. ft. house. It was a continuing turning up the volume to hear the program and turning it down during commercials. We would almost have to holler at one another if we spoke.

Larry learned quickly not to bother me when I'm dressing. I could turn into a vampire very quickly. He had also learned that when I was in the bathroom it was totally taboo for him to enter. I don't think that I ever sat down on the commode that I didn't picture his x-wife doing the same. He had given me a portion of the storage in the bathroom for my female necessities. I didn't like him knowing what they were, even though he usually did the shopping. When I was asked a question, he learned without doubt not to do it from another room. I learned how to holler back with power! We had brought only a few clothes for me to wear when I first moved in it didn't take long for me to learn they were not enough. We had to convert the extra bedroom into storage to hold the 150 or so outfits I needed, not to say anything about the shoes to match each outfit. And of course the jewelry was extremely important. I was learning very quickly that Larry was gracious and would run to the store for me at any given time in fact he did most everything I asked when I asked. I think I may have been too bold in my asking! After years of cooking, I no longer liked to cook. Now this is the corker, I was used to sleeping alone! It was not long before I discovered that I didn't really like sex. Larry was filled with joy when I told him this! We had been married a very short time. Yet, he was so handsome. I liked looking at him but no touchy, touchy. He never ceased to amaze me. Another Larry would visit every now and then. Like the one who told me after marriage of his addiction to pornography. We were sure learning about each other. His overcoming was not completed when we married and his approach to me was really not what I had expected.

I had a real problem with the difference in our ages. Larry's hair was black. We had found one gray hair when we were dating. My hair was totally gray, colored blond. I was fifty-eight, he was forty-eight. Larry was six feet two inches. I was five feet four inches. He had a nice slim body, mine was not the same.

Larry and I had been married twenty-two days when Larry made a mistake that would cost him mightily. He openly stared at a woman on a Sunday morning at church. She was sitting a few seats down from us. Then he danced with the praise and worship music, turning to see if she was watching. She wasn't but I was. It was after this happened that I spent a lot of time driving to Medi Park and simply sitting for hours and thinking about what I had gotten myself into. I had never understood why people who met in church and gotten married were divorcing in a year. I understood why now. After having been in a marriage where I had accepted adultery to now being in a marriage with a man where I would not put up with adultery. I didn't know what to do or what I could do. He was so very sorry, but I was so very unforgiving!

We went to church faithfully. We didn't stop going and we listened to what Pastor Jimmy was preaching. He often spoke on marriages. Larry and I heard but it was something else for me to forgive. I had absolutely no trust in any man. Could I divorce because of lust? The Bible clearly states that lust with the eyes is the same as a sexual affair. *(But I say unto you, That whosoever looketh on a woman to lust after her hath committed adultery with her already in his heart.* Matthew 5:28)

I believed that God had chosen Larry, but how did it get past Him that Larry would do this to me and so soon after marriage? I decided that the only way I was going to be able to live with it was by doing the same to him. I was going to have to lust after another man. I had to make sure Larry saw me. It wasn't in my heart to lust. I had never been faithful to any man. I had earnestly told God that I would never be unfaithful again. But, of course it was Larry's fault if I did.

Larry and I were headed in the right direction, but not as one and there was an ocean between us, with snarling, disastrous waves. I had decided to stay with Larry. No one, and I do mean no one, knew the reality of our marriage. At least this is what I thought. When I found out that Larry was telling his sister all our problems and our finances I became a wild crazy woman in an instant. When I had finished dragging Larry over the razor blades, I knew this would stop and it did but not before his relatives heard the same stories. I had not told anyone.

My mom called on June 12, 2000 from the hospital in Crosbyton, TX. She had a light stroke or heart attack. I don't know for sure which one. Larry and I drove to Crosbyton at once. We entered her room. She said, "Can I come and live with you? I can't be alone. I'm afraid." I remember looking up at Larry and feeling that there was no way we could pretend to be happy. We were two of the unhappiest people in the world. I told mom not to worry. I didn't say yes or no, I was stunned.

Larry and I sat outside the hospital, under the trees. "I can't leave my mom scared. What can we do?" I asked. "I don't know, but one thing I do know, we have to take care of her." Larry's said as he looked at the ground. We both thought it was more than we could bear. There would have been no problems if we truly loved each other, but we didn't, and I had absolutely no confidence in myself or him. We had been married 24 days.

After assuring Mom she could live with us, Larry and I drove back to Amarillo. The following morning we got my son, Dwayne, and attached our trailer to our van and drove back to Ralls. We loaded our van, and the trailer to the brim with all that we could carry. I called a niece to come and get all she wanted of Mom's things. We had a seven hundred sq. ft. house. It was important to get Mom's bedroom suite and personal items. Larry and I put everything in the little room into storage, mostly my clothes. We set up the room with all of my mom's things. All she had to do when we picked her up was go to bed.

July 1, 2000, Larry and I decided to get a little time to ourselves. Dwayne stayed the night with Mom while Larry and I rode our motorcycles to Lubbock, TX for the night. It was a very unhappy trip. Had my mom not been in his house I'm not sure that I wouldn't have left him right then and there, but I had no choice. We rode our motorcycles back to Amarillo about as depressed as two people could be.

When we reached our little house and before I even closed the door, Mom was in my face, "Don't leave me again," she cried, "Please promise me you will not leave me again."

I had to work, Larry had to work. There was no money to hire someone to help with mom. I called B.J., my daughter and she helped me find a retirement center just blocks away from where we lived. With B.J.'s help we moved Mom into the retirement center. It was hard for her, it was hard for us, but she made the decision to move into her own little apartment. She felt safe with people around her all the time.

Larry and I continued on with our marriage. He didn't forget his big mistake because I made sure he didn't. We kept putting off my mom and his mom meeting. We simply were so unhappy that we couldn't get up enough strength to take care of his mom and mine at the same time.

Larry's mom died on Independence Day, July 4, 2001. He with his sister arranged everything. I was left out, and left at home, other than when Larry told me to come to his mom's house to meet the family. I knew how to look right and act right. I put on a marvelously wonderful wife act. At the funeral Larry sat by his relatives. I was left standing, but I did sit down leaving a chair between myself and Larry.

We continued to look for a house to buy. As unhappy as Larry and I were, we may have wished we hadn't married, but we didn't talk about divorce.

Mark 10:19

19 ***Thou knowest the commandments, Do not commit adultery, Do not kill, Do not steal, Do not bear false witness, Defraud not, Honor thy father and mother.***

Ephesians 6:2-3
2   Honor thy father and mother; (which is the first commandment with promise;)
3   That it may be well with thee, and thou mayest live long on the earth.

Chapter 30:
OUR HOME

Larry was appointed Foreman III at Amarillo International Airport. I was no longer working for City Mission. I was now a housewife. Larry became a member of Trinity Fellowship Church. With all that was happening in our marriage we didn't walk to Jesus Christ, we ran to Him. Neither one of us had any idea of what we needed to do in building a marriage. We read books. We went to Marriage on the Rock seminars held by our Pastor, Jimmy Evans. We tried to put our mate first instead of ourselves. Communication was a priority. We had a new beginning. We just didn't know how to live in it. My past five marriages and Larry's two didn't contribute any knowledge as to what to do now. We both knew all the mistakes we had made in our past relationships but we didn't know how to learn and apply to a committed marriage.

It had been a year, two months and four days since I had told Larry I would live in his house a year. I had totally rejected the east side of Amarillo. Larry had seen an advertisement in the Amarillo Globe Newspaper showing a picture of a house for sale. At first I wouldn't even go see it. After months had passed and we had not found the home we wanted, I agreed to go see the house. When we drove up in front of it, I loved the brick and long windows. I had prayed for windows. It was important to me to have sunlight, lots of sunlight. We walked around the house and into the back yard. The yard was a mess front and back. Small evergreens lined the north front side of the house. These were the only things living. The grass was pasture land with a few spots of grass. The house had been empty for five years. When we looked into the living room area from the back side of the house, the house facing east, we saw a beautiful fireplace. The carpet was new. It had a vaulted ceiling, something we hadn't even prayed for. The kitchen was very small, great with me. I didn't like to cook anymore. The master bedroom bath was small with a shower and not a tub. Larry and I had stopped sleeping in the same bed, a short time after we had moved Mom into the retirement center. We simply couldn't sleep together. I had to have a fan blowing on my face and Christian music playing all night. Larry had to have still, dark, silence. I snored like a man along with holding my breath before gasping for air. Larry went to the bathroom, coughing many times during the night and along with his allergies kept him blowing his nose. It was not out of anger that we slept in separate rooms in separate beds, it was to survive.

After making an offer on the house a contract was drawn up and we spent our first night in our own home July 23, 2001. We felt rich. Christ had given us our heart's desire. We were able to buy new furniture for our living room and other rooms. Larry and I both had offices. We had adopted a red Doberman and he was king of the yard although he slept in the house and slept with me on my bed. He had a great yard. Of course it was full of weeds as we lived on the edge of the city limit where homes were being built on pasture land. The Clements prison and Neal prison were just to the west of us. Larry was ministering every Saturday at the Clements Unit and I was Women's Coordinator Prison/Jail Ministry for Trinity Fellowship. We had a house, our house, which we both considered ours and not a place where he and his previous wife had lived. We had a house but how do you turn a house into a home?

One day I went by Mom's apartment to check on her. B.J. took care of her needs during the day as she didn't work and I went by to see Mom in the afternoons after work. On this day Mom had fallen in the kitchen and was unable to stand back up. She had crawled into the bedroom trying to get to the phone. She had rubbed the skin on her leg completely raw and almost bleeding. I couldn't lift her. I had to call B.J.'s husband to come and help me. Later Larry and I took her to our home. The first few days were killing me. Larry would help me get her into the shower and I would help her bathe and then we would get her back into bed or a wheel chair so she could sit up. Nothing was wrong with her, she simply had no strength. She had gained weight and her weight kept her from being able to get up and down. We put her into my bedroom and I slept on the couch in the living room. I set up a potty chair for her and would empty it and clean it the next morning. By the end of three days I was exhausted. I had taken these three days off to take care of Mom. I was totally lost as what to do now. When we had brought Mom to our house she had said, "Can I come and live with you?" She had moved in with me and out again three times since I was married to Howard. My sister had rejected her and I simply had no one to turn to. It was so easy for family to love her from a distance or simply chose to forget about her. There was no one that even asked me if they could help. Everyone had problems. Mom, my sister and I were all that was left of our little five people family, mom, dad and us three girls. Nieces and nephews and grandchildren all had their marriages and divorces and families to care for.

"Mom, don't worry, I don't know what to do, but Larry and I will take care of you." I knew that she couldn't be left alone and if Sampson (Doberman) were to knock her down she wouldn't be able to get up. I tried to comfort Mom that whatever we needed to do, we would do it. She would be taken care off.

Larry and I discussed what to do. She had been with us for a week. I was totally exhausted. I could hardly raise myself up in the mornings. We were supposed to minister in Gatesville, Texas women's prisons in two weeks. After discussing things with B.J., Larry and I came to the conclusion that Mom had to go to a nursing home. It was killing me to lift her into her wheel chair. It was an all day job to attend to her. Larry and I had put our problems to the side. Our marriage had very little happiness in it as it was. Larry would have to come second if I tried to keep Mom with us.

One afternoon I sat down on the bed beside Mom. I began to tell her of the things we felt were best for her as well as for ourselves. I assured her I would come very often to see her. I would not desert her. She knew I couldn't continue to care for her. My back was giving me a lot of pain. There would be times that I just couldn't be with her. Going anywhere made me run to get back home. Mom was and had always been afraid to be alone. This I'm sure birthed from her childhood. She would be happy to have people help get her dressed. She wouldn't have to worry about a doctor or medication. Her eyes became happy when she thought about these advantages. I called many places and people to help me decide where my mom should live. As hard as it had been, I loved my mom. Forgiveness and understanding had taken place between us. She had asked me questions about how I felt growing up and why I did so many ugly things in my past. I was truthful with her, really honest. She understood me for the first time in our lives. She was now my mom.

We settled on a nursing home close to us. It had been in Amarillo for years and it had the best reputation of good care to the residents. I realized as she did that this would be her last home on this earth. At first I saw her daily and cared for her clothes myself. I never let two days pass without going to see her. Larry went with me every week-end. We took care of Mom. We would bring her to our home and sit with her outside where she loved to look at the cattle in the grazing land across the street from our home. She loved our dog. Mom was an animal person also. I had to change her diaper during these times. Only God knew how hard this was for me. I didn't talk about it even with Larry. I watched my mom have good days to wonderful days. I also watched her sit in her wheel chair at the nursing home and not even realize that I was there. Larry and I would rush to the hospital because her kidneys were not functioning properly. It became a monthly emergency. Only one time I called B.J. to come to the hospital. It was when the Doctor told me she may not make it through the night. We were into our third year of Mom doing well one day and being rushed to the hospital the next. I had begun to feed her at the nursing home. She would look at me with her sparkling baby-blue eyes and smile. She got to where she didn't talk often and when she did she was mostly confused. It was hard for her to finish a sentence. One Wednesday I went to see her and found her asleep. I sat down next to her and said, "Mom, mom I'm here. Do you want to play Bingo?" She sat up and said, "I don't love you as much as you love me." My heart broke into a million pieces. I laughed, pretending that nothing was wrong and replied, "Oh yes you do Mom, you love me." I then continued to tell her I had to leave. She didn't realize that I had just gotten there. I laid her back down and told her to rest I'd be back later. I walked out of that nursing home hurting more than I ever had been hurt even as a little girl. Why had God chosen me to take care of her? She loved my sister and my oldest sister's kids more than she had ever loved me. Yet it was I, with B.J. and Larry that God had given her care to. I went home in a world of heavy depression. I didn't go to see her again the next day or the following day. I just couldn't. The following week I went to town to see her. I stopped in front of the nursing home and just sat there. "God I can't, I just can't. I just can't do this anymore." Tears were streaming down my face, I had been crying for days. I drove back home. The same week I received a call from the nursing home. Larry and I went to the hospital. She was in a room in the emergency room. There was a very young woman and young man standing at the foot of her bed. I went to the side of her bed and sat down in a chair next to her. She was not able to move but the Doctor told me she could hear me. I began telling her how much I loved her and what a wonderful mom she was to me. I assured her that she would go into the arms of Jesus. I praised her and kept saying over and over how beautiful she was and how much I loved her and she was going home to Faye and Dad and her mom and her sister. I wanted so much to help her to want to die, to look forward to seeing her family. I was close to her face, very close and kissed her on the cheek. Her last teardrop fell from her eyes and she was gone. I jumped in pain and lay on top of her, crying "Momma, oh Momma." I cried tears in great heaves. Larry and the two young people in the room said nothing. It didn't matter about the pain of my childhood, it didn't matter about the hurting words she had said just a few days ago. She was my mom and I had forgiven her and she had forgiven me for years of pain. This was all that mattered.

I laid on her crying until I could stop. I then raised myself. The two young people had left the room and now there stood an older woman waiting for me to be able to talk to her. She told me where to go to make the arrangements for her body to be taken back to Ralls where she would be buried beside Dad's. She then left the room. I sat next to Mom for a few minutes. I knew without doubt that she was in heaven and all the pain of this world was over for her. I then got up and before walking out the door I turned and looked at my mom for the last time. A few months before she died she prayed with me for her salvation. I believe she was saved, but when I asked her if she was saved, she said, "I don't know." I discussed with her what she had to look forward to with Jesus Christ. I remember the tears flowed down her cheeks when she said, "Oh that sounds so good." I then prayed as Mom said, "Come into my heart Jesus Christ and save me, forgive me for my sins and help me to learn about You."

It had been very hard during the previous years to become the one Mom depended on. But I walked out of that room knowing I had done my best. I had followed the direction of Christ and Larry had obeyed the Bible that we are to care for our parents when the time comes that they are not able to care for themselves. Larry had put himself behind my mom in his needs of me and our relationship. He helped to care for her just as I had. It was somewhere during these three years that I began to fall in love with a man who was becoming more and more like Jesus as he grew in ministry. He became my trusted friend.

Just a few months later, Sampson, our Doberman had to be put down. He had a large tumor that we didn't know he had until we took him to the veterinarian. It took Larry most of the day to dig a spot in our back yard. He dug a deep hole, close to four foot. We didn't want anyone digging him up. We put all his belongs into his grave. His custom made leather coat. His four beds, his toys and his water bowl. We got everything out of our home and yard the same day. Yet another total heart break for us.

Larry had worked for the airport for twenty-eight years. He retired and together we built a beautiful yard. He had gone to the airport and dug up elm tree roots and replanted them in our back yard. We planted a maple and sycamore tree. He painted the trim on our home with two coats of the best paint. We finished and started painting the inside of the house. I had terminated as Women's Coordinator Prison/Jail Ministry. After a few more months I became very hungry to go back to work for Jesus. I became volunteer secretary for Chaplains Merrell and Doris Gilbert at Randall County

Jail. I worked under their direction for over a year and received a volunteer-of-the-year award.

I had a yearning in my heart. I wanted to go into the prisons. I wanted to minister to the men. I had ministered to women for years. In remembering the vision I had at Thompson Park years ago, it was men and women crying out to me to help them, not just women.

In the course of time I forgave Larry for the flirtation he did right after we married. I was angry and very jealous of him for several years but through his faithfulness to me through much heartache, I made up my mind to forgive him and not bring it up again. I followed through with this commitment. I had watched as young very pretty girls watched him when he ushered in our church or as we were shopping together. Larry had changed. A female member of our church at a Harvest Festival, held for the children of the church literally ran and jumped into his arms when we were helping with a booth. Larry had to catch her. She raised her feet off the floor. He was stunned. After putting her down, he leaned down to arrange gifts in a treasure chest. She leaned down right beside him to his back a little and didn't move. When Larry started to get up they were face to face. I watched to see Larry's way of handling this woman. He ran, he had never had a woman respond to him this way, and a Christian woman at that. I knew Larry was totally shocked. He really didn't know what to do. Lusting, had been my way of life for years, but I was no longer driven by it. I also knew and understood what loneness can do to a woman. I had been single for 15 years before Larry. Preparing me for marriage took a long time.

It took Larry a while to learn how to hug a woman, how to talk to women, how to walk away from women, how to listen to other women. But he learned and our marriage has become a loving one. I no longer distrust Larry. I no longer am jealous. He has run the race and received the prize, which is my trust. I stand at the finish line having ran the same race with him and I have learned to respect him, appreciate him and praise him for all his determination to become a man after God's own heart. On May 20, 2009 we have been married nine years. We have a wonderful beautiful home. We now have two black labs, brother and sister, they are unable to breed. We have a very nice Custom Choo Choo van we travel in, two Harley Davidson motorcycles, his work car, my own car and greatest of all we have Jesus Christ at the helm of our lives. We are a success story, a true story. We have fallen in love. We finally accomplished loving the other more than we loved our self. We have put the past in the past. We have forgiven what needed to be forgiven. We have been long suffering, believing God's word is true. We continue to keep our covenant with Jesus Christ, there will be no divorce.

Matthew 19:8-9

8   He saith unto them, *Moses because of the hardness of your hearts suffered you to put away your wives: but from the beginning it was not so.*

9   *And I say unto you, Whosoever shall put away his wife, except it be for fornication, and shall marry another, committeth adultery: and whoso marrieth her which is put away doth commit adultery.*

Ephesians 4:31-32

31   Let all bitterness, and wrath, and anger, and clamor, and evil speaking, be put away from you, with all malice:

32   And be ye kind one to another, tenderhearted, forgiving one another, even as God for Christ's sake hath forgiven you.

SAMPSON; adopted during our first year of marriage. He helped Larry and I to grow. It was obvious that he got upset if we raised our voices to one another. We were able to love on him when things were not good between us. Through loving him, and being aware of his needs, we learned to do the same for each other. We learned self control. We learned to communicate.

Elizabeth (Liz) and King, our babies (2 yrs. old) same rules apply for them, no hollering!

Larry & I are so thankful for our home.
WE ARE CONTENT

359

Chapter 31:
HIS HIGH CALLING

Before I married Larry Martin, even before I owned my Harley Davidson I was a member of John Curry's Sunday School Class. Dr. Curry and his wife Donna had birthed Trinity Fellowship from its beginning in their home. I was an active member of Prison/Jail Ministry. I had attended Dr. Curry's class about two years when Larry and Becky Miles came and attended the class. This was my first introduction to this new couple. They continued to attend every Sunday.

I was quite a talker. I had an opinion on almost every subject. Sometime Dr. Curry got so tired of listening to me talk about me. My life consisted of church, work and ministry. I didn't really run with anyone and my off time was spent reading and doing what I could for the residents of City Mission. I didn't really let anyone get close to me. I was extremely lonely but growing in ministry and educational growth and knowledge of the Bible was my priority.

An application was put on my desk at City Mission and Larry Miles had become a member of the Board of Directors. He at once became very involved. He would come to eat lunch with the residents. He prayed for them and listened to their stories, their reasons for being at City Mission. He was genuine and I recognized this about him from the start. He would come into my office and spend time talking with me. He had a way of making a person who didn't have a lot of confidence in them-selves have hope and trust in Christ. I was honest with him. It was easy to confide in him. He shared with me that when he and Becky first attended Dr. Curry's Sunday School class that he thought to himself after hearing me talk and by the way I carried myself that there was something about me that he knew set me apart from the norm. I was different. He didn't really know how, but he did recognize that there was an anointing on me that he could relate too.

Time passed and I became confident in sharing my personal life with Larry Miles. We were sitting at the dining room table one day during his visit to the mission when I told Larry how lonely I was. He looked at me and said, "Mary, God has a mate for you. He'll be just what you want and just what you need." There was no doubt in his voice and his strong words settled in my heart. Our friendship continued.

Larry would come into my office and we would have long talks about any and everything. Larry Miles was the first man I truly trusted. He had the ability to reason with me. He had a way of correcting me or guiding me that didn't anger me.

After I bought my Harley Davidson and Larry Martin became a part of my life. Larry Miles would just smile at me whenever we saw one another at church or the mission. Letting me know, I told you so!

Larry Miles became a member of the Elders of Trinity Fellowship Church. His success in his business along with a good marriage and children as well as a very good reputation opened the door for his becoming an Elder.

He and Becky, his wife had come to a church where I gave my testimony. Afterward Larry rode the children on the back of his bike as we all did. He also came to my apartment when I had set up a meeting for a resident of City Mission to meet with his children. There were other times that Larry Miles participated when I needed a covering.

I had been ministering in the jails and prisons for years when Larry Miles first began. He was going to become involved at the Clements Unit, here in Amarillo, TX. He called me at the mission and wanted to know how I felt about a few things he was concerned about in ministering to the men incarcerated in the Clements Unit. It is a high security prison with close to four thousand offenders. I shared with him some of the dos and don'ts in prison ministry. His heart for the lost, outcast, rejected men of society was truly being birthed. He volunteered even more of his time to minister in Clements prison.

Larry Miles rode his Harley Davidson to our marriage on May

20, 2000. He continued to befriend my husband just as he had me. He continued to oversee some decisions as well as keep an eye on the growth of our participation in prison, jail ministry.

On October 22, 2001, I was called into the office of the Executive Director, City Mission, where the Superintendent was also sitting. I was told to sit down in a chair that had been placed there for me. "I hate to tell you this, I didn't want it to happen, I didn't want it this way but the Board of Directors are downsizing and your job is one that we won't have anymore." He looked directly at me with a slight smile. I knew it was all he could do not to jump up laugh and dance at my termination from City Mission. At the very time that these words came out of his mouth, a peace came over me and I felt a crown set upon my head. In my mind I was saying it's fine, it's alright. Jesus is the head of this. I will not cry. I will show no emotion and I didn't. I then said, "When do you want me out?" He replied, "Oh you have a month or so." I got up out of the chair and looked at the Superintendent who had kept his eyes looking out the window all the time. I walked behind him and went back into what had been my office for five and a half years. I picked up the phone and called Larry Miles, who was on the board and had been for some time. "You mean you're still there, get your things and get out of there." He said. The words were not said in a hateful way but a loving way. I did as he said and called Larry, my husband, to bring the van. I went downstairs and got boxes and carried them into the office and began to pack.

I don't remember just when I talked to Larry Miles again but it was shortly afterward. He told me that when it was brought up at the board meeting to fire me that he had said, "This is a lynching party and I won't be a part of it." He left the meeting. He was releasing himself as a board member. He was the only member that stood behind me. The Executive Director and I had not worked together in unity from the time he took the position until now. There had been many problems. I was a very strong woman. He was the same as a man. The board had battled with the divisions between us for months. The person, a member of the board, in charge of finances had called me the morning before the meeting scheduled in late afternoon and asked me about a large figure on the monthly reports. I didn't know how to answer her, but I knew the figure was right. I just didn't know how to explain it. She called the accountant that handled our account and received a bad report about me. That night I was terminated at the board meeting.

I later heard that the owner of the accounting business spoke to the board on my behalf as did the yearly auditors. The decision to terminate me had been made and it would stand.

I spent the first two weeks crying all the time. How or why does Jesus let such pain happen? We had updated the computer and when I printed out payroll the 401K amount was incorrect on the checks. I had been told by the accountant to hand type the figure in before printing the checks. This is one of the things I had a problem with. I didn't want to hand type it, I wanted the problem to be fixed. I could do the work but I could not set up the things needed for the computer to do what was needed. She said she didn't have time to come to the office and solve the problem. At the end of the month I had printed out payroll forgetting about this problem. I had to back up the computer twice to correct the problem. I knew how to correct it, but didn't know how to fix it. This is what caused an outrageous figure to appear on the monthly reports.

Larry Miles kept in touch with me. He called me one morning to tell me that he had been asked to return as President of the Board of Directors, for City Mission. They would not accept his resignation. I told him that I thought it was wonderful that they had such respect for him. He wanted me to hear his decision to return as President of the Board from him and not someone else. He and the Executive Director had their own difficulties in agreeing on how to run the shelter.

I went into a deep depression. You couldn't really see it or detect it unless Jesus told you. Larry, my husband did not share this with anyone. I had told him not to. Sometime after the termination I was standing in church before the service had begun. I looked up and saw employees of City Mission enter the auditorium. I took a deep breath and forced myself not to cry. Larry, my husband was an usher and was not with me. I went to them and hugged then and greeted them, we all let a few tears drop. I was having a real problem holding back the tears of pain so I didn't return to my seat which was close to the front. Instead I went to the last row of the back of the church and sat down, but not before hugging Becky Miles. I told her how much I hurt at seeing the women I had been a part of at City Mission. Up until this time I had not cried at church. I had been able to hide the pain. Larry Miles was overseer of the ushers and sentinels. He hadn't seen me go to the employees of the mission. He touched me on the shoulder and said, "How are you?" The flood doors opened and a flood of tears came rolling down my face. I simply shook my head as if saying, "Not good." I had to turn and bow my head and again force myself to stop crying. It was not easy. I listened to the sermon not hearing it at all. It's as if a scab, not quite healed, was pulled off and I had to go through the pain all over again.

It was well into a year and I could not find a job anywhere. I asked Jesus daily, why? How could He let this happen to me? I loved my job and I loved the people who came from the prisons and streets to get over their drug, alcohol additions or the people who needed a place to stay before going back into society. Some were mothers with children and some were dads with children and it was mom who had left the home. Whatever the reason for a person going to City Mission, they believed they could find help there and they did.

I read my Bible for hours daily. It was all I could hold onto to keep me from losing my mind. It was during one of these times of reading my Bible. It was now into the second year of being terminated, that I read words I had written during the time I was working for the mission. I found four other of my own wittings beside scripture that pertained to my feelings while employed there. Jesus had told me, **"Resign today,"** or **"give notice and resign,"** or **"quit."** When I read my notes beside scripture I began to understand that Jesus had told me what to do but due to pride and arrogant determination to not be defeated, I did not obey. Jesus had no other choice but to let the circumstances needed to take place to get me back on track with Him and that was to leave the mission. I realized this and was able to get over the pain of it all. I no longer questioned

Jesus. I accepted His decision to allow me to be terminated. The pain stopped almost immediately within me when I became aware of Jesus' words to me. I had heard but I had not listened nor had I obeyed. Pride cuddled in arrogance had caused me about one and a half years of unnecessary pain. I will have to say that my car payments, our house payments as well as all other expenses took priority over Jesus simply telling me to *"Resign today."*

Later Larry Miles became Pastor Larry Miles. He had been put on staff at Trinity Fellowship and was called to Pastor's Jimmy and Karen Evans office where he was put in charge of Prison/Jail Ministry. It was Pastor Miles that asked me to take over the position of Coordinator for the women ministering in the jails and prison. He told me that it was me that first came to his mind when he accepted his promotion. I accepted the position and we grew from five members to twenty nine members having thirteen churches involved. When I terminated this position, I became volunteer Secretary for the chaplains of Randall County Jail.

My marriage to Larry was in good standing, we had overcome much. We were now able to minister as a united team. It had not been so the first few years. Larry and I talked about and would never forget a prophecy given to us in the first year of our marriage. On November 8, 2000, Larry and I attended a Life Group meeting at the home of Bill and Cathy Johnson, head of the Prophetic Team Ministry of Trinity Fellowship. I was to teach on this night. Before we began, we, along with the prophetic team, were in a room to ourselves being prayed over. Then Bill began to prophecy to Larry and I, "You're together, going in the same direction, yet you're not together. It's like there's two roads with a row of grass in between. Or it's like railroad tracks run right in the center of the two roads you're on. You're together, one on each road, yet you're separated. God's going to bring you together." Kathy Johnson said "That's right, you're on two roads, but God is going to bring you together, in the middle."

It had taken some doing but this prophecy has come to pass and Larry and I are on the same row of grass headed for the unknown together.

One day after I had prayed for months asking Jesus, "What is it about Pastor Larry that draws me to him? Why do I run to him with so many problems?" *"He's a father image to you. It has nothing to do with age. I chose him to bring you up in the way you should go."* Jesus replied. In the days to come, Jesus would put two other Godly men in my life a trinity of three men would help me and Larry (husband) to develop our ministry in the prison system.

It has not all been easy. I ruffled Pastor Larry's feathers on more than one occasion. And honestly, he has ruffled mine on a few occasions. But God has not severed our relationship. God knew I needed direction and correction in areas that could only be accomplished by someone I respected. Pastor Larry sets the example of what a dad should be. I was drawn to this. He told me during one of our mentoring sessions that his life was purposed to love and obey Jesus Christ first and then to love and honor his wife along with loving and raising his children in the wisdom of Christ. This is his heart that he shared with me.

Pastor Larry had participated in drugs for a season in his youth. But when a divorce was at hand, he talked with Becky at the court house. Neither of them wanted a divorce. They left together. It was at this time that having been raised in church by a Christian dad and mom that he recommitted his life back to Christ and began overcoming. He picked up his cross daily and followed Jesus.

May 31, 1998 Mary sharing her testimony at St. Laurence Cathedral, Amarillo, TX.

Larry Miles & Becky Miles sitting in rear.

Mike Hamner, (silhouette)

Larry Miles riding a youth team member on his Harley Davidson

Larry Miles, attending Mary & Larry's wedding.

Pastor Larry & wife, Becky Miles

Pastor Larry Miles along with all his other responsibilities also became Pastor of Missions and Outreach at Bethesda Outreach Ministries. The Prison/Jail Ministry is under this covering. The outreach is to help with the expenses of daily living as well as medical supplies to other countries along with food and clothing for the needs of people. Generating salvation seasoned with hope and love.

While traveling with friends, on one of their many cross country trips, Pastor Larry and Becky minister to the lost and down trodden no matter if they are dressed in their finest or riding biker style. They work in the harvest field of our Lord, Jesus Christ. Becky Miles is Administrator Assistant to Executive Senior Pastor Bo Williams of Trinity Fellowship Church, Amarillo, Texas.

Proverbs 11:30
The fruit of the righteous is a tree of life; and he that winneth souls is wise.

.

Chapter 32:
YOU ARE FORGIVEN

~

For about a year or so I had begun to really think about the boys, Howard's children. I discussed this with Larry, my husband. I asked him if he cared if I tried to find them. He said, "I know your heart and if you want to find them, its okay with me. But I don't want Howard to call or come to our home." I agreed with his feelings and felt the same way. Howard had become a memory, the major part of it bad. I have had to relive much pain in order to write this autobiography. I loved the boys from the beginning of our affair and through our marriage. My love for them has not died.

I called Faithe. She is the sister to the girl Ray had a daughter with. Nichole was born after I left Amarillo and divorced Howard. Faithe and I had been friends during my marriage to Howard. She dated biker men and was a part of the group. The last time I had seen Ray was in December, 1988. He was living with Howard in a small house across the street from Thompson Park in Amarillo, TX.

"You won't believe this! I got goose bumps all over when I was talking to Nichole. Ray called her at Mom's just a little while ago and he's going to be in Amarillo tomorrow!" Faithe said excitedly.

"Would you call her back and ask her to call Ray and tell him I live in Amarillo and I want to see him?" I asked. She did and called me back to let me know that Ray said he would call me when he got into Amarillo.

Memories flooded my mind. I lay in bed remembering this dark haired boy that had been a part of my life for several years while I was living with and then married to Howard. I had so many questions to ask. Where was Lee, the middle brother that also lived with us? And Neal, what happened to him? He was the youngest of the three boys. I had wondered if Howard was still alive as he had belonged to two different outlaw gangs. Was he in prison? But

Howard was not the focus of my thoughts, the boys were. They had accepted me from the beginning and as far as I know had never rejected me.

The following day my phone rang and Ray asked, "What's up, what's going on?" "Oh Ray, northing's wrong, I just want to see you. I still love you and I always have. How are you? Where do you live?" I asked, wanting to know everything. "I asked my mom if we could visit." "What! You mean you're with your mother?" "Yes," he said. "We're going back to East Texas today. We'll swing by your house on our way back. I'll call you when we get through eating and get directions." "Sure," I replied. We hung up. I was dumbfounded that his mom would come to my home. In my thoughts this simply was not possible. A few minutes later my phone rang again and it was Ray. "Come eat with us, we can visit while we're eating, my daughter, Nichole and her son, my grandson, is with us. Mom said she didn't want to spend the time trying to find your house since we're leaving early to drive back to East Texas." I got directions to where they were eating and we hung up.

I prayed all the way across town that our reunion would go well with no problems. I had only seen Nichole once when she was just learning to walk. It had been after I returned to Amarillo after my divorce from Howard. I had gone to church where my friend Faithe was a member. I remembered a beautiful little girl with big eyes and flowing black hair. I remember thinking, this is my granddaughter also. But because I was no longer a member of Howard's family I chose to keep my feelings within myself. Nichole had run and grabbed her aunt's leg and looked up at me with beautiful innocent eyes.

"Oh Jesus, stop me from saying or doing anything that would hurt Ann." I prayed. I didn't want to hurt Ann, Ray's mom and Howard's first wife. This would be the second time we would really meet. The first time was when Howard and Ann came to my home, when I was married to Kevin, an alcoholic.

I thought about the time when I had gone before the church years earlier and asked from the pulpit before the whole congregation for her and her sons to forgive me for taking her husband and their dad away from them. (Chapter 7; EAGLE) I never knew if she was at church that day or not. I didn't know if someone who may have known her had told her about my apology.

Excitement filled me. I felt like I could park the car and run faster than driving. I was so excited to see Ray. Ray had called me Mary Ann. This is the first time that I could remember that he called me by my name. Both boys, Ray and Lee had called me mom from my meeting them to when I drove away from Amarillo, leaving Howard. I had not asked them to, but had readily accepted their choice to call me mom.

I parked my car in the parking lot of McDonalds. I looked in the mirror and thought, Ray is here and you're going to sit at the same table with Ann. Wait till Howard hears this! I thought.

When I first entered the building I looked around and didn't see them. There were two seating areas with a partition between the two. Ray came around the partition. "Ray, Ray!" I said. He smiled at me with a smile that I recognized. We went into each other's arms and I felt as though one of my sons had come home. I loved him and I had never stopped loving him. We held each other tightly for a few moments. "Come on, I want you to meet Mom and Nichole, my grandson is here too." he said with a big grin on his face. I had pictured Ray as he was when he was younger. But he had changed. I would have walked right past him if I had seen him on the street. He now had gray hair that had taken the place of his black hair. He was taller and was no longer a skinny little boy.

I was extremely nervous. I walked up to the table and said "Hi Ann, it's so nice of you to let me come and visit with Ray." She smiled. Ray then introduced me to Nichole and his grandson. Sitting down, I said, "Let me talk while you finish eating. I'm not hungry." "How long have you been back in Amarillo?" Ray asked. I opened my mouth and didn't stop except to take a breath to talk some more. Ray and I were sharing as fast as we could. I kept looking into his eyes and then I saw Howard. "You look just like your dad." I said. He laughed and replied, "You ought to see Lee. He's the one who looks just like Dad." Ann agreed that the middle of the three boys was the image of Howard. I remembered that Lee was built like Howard but when young I didn't really see Howard in him. Ray and I did most of the talking. He asked me things and I did the same, wanting to know about Lee and his youngest brother, Neal.

I had brought pictures I knew Ray would want of his dad. He looked through them smiling and laughing, he showed them to Ann, Nichole and the grandson. "Dad died about two years ago." Ray said. "What, what did you say, Howard is dead!"

"He had cancer. After chemo he seemed to get better. They thought they had gotten it all but it came back. My family called me and told me I better go see him and I did. In the hospital room he told me he didn't want any more treatments, no more chemo. 'Let me die' were his words to me." I had everything disconnected from him and we took him home. He had bought a little house where he and his third wife lived. He wanted to die at home. "I was holding him in my arms. He knew he was going to die. His wife was sitting on the front porch. Tears came into dad's eyes and he died, he just died." Ray said. "His wife is about two or three years younger than me." Ray said in laughter.

I smiled at him and said, "That sounds just like him, he always liked young girls." Ray smiled and agreed with me.

It was at this time that I began to shake a little. I fought not to let my feelings show. It took all I had to not cry. At first I wanted to stand and scream at the top of my lungs somehow letting the last pain leave me. But I didn't.

Ray laughed and said, "What are you shaking for?" I responded with some kind of excuse.

We continued to share. I think we were enjoying the visit. I looked at Ann and tears began to fill my eyes, "Ann, I'm so sorry," was all I got out when Ray dove in to protect his mom. He told me that through all the pain she had become strong. She had got a job, bought a car and bought her own home and she did it without a man. He was proud of her for doing so good after all the years of pain she had suffered. I had stopped talking and was able to just listen while Ray played with his grandson and daughter, teasing them. They had not seen each other in years. Nichole was about three when Ray last saw her. It wasn't until now that I realized that

Ray had not seen Nichole in years and this was the first time for him to see his grandson. For some reason I thought Ray had seen them before this meeting, he had not.

After a few minutes passed I again said, "Ann, I'm so sorry for all the pain I caused you." Ray let me talk this time. "Please forgive me for the suffering I caused. I'm so sorry." She smiled at me and with a voice that was gentle said, "You are forgiven, I forgive you. You don't have to worry about it anymore, you are forgiven." "Thank you, thank you." I replied. It was done, it was over. For years I had wanted to say these words to her. I was so ashamed of everything I had been and all the pain I had caused. I felt as though Ann had forgiven me long before I had the opportunity to ask for forgiveness. Just as her boys had always told me, Ann is a woman of God.

I showed them pictures of Howard that had been taken when we first met and some on his motorcycle, King Kong. It was time for them to begin their journey back to East Texas. I had brought my camera and pictures were taken. Ray walked me to my car. We held each other tightly. We kissed one another as mom and son then I got into my car and he went back to Ann and her car.

I didn't want it to be over but it had to be. Ray said he was going to talk to Lee, the middle brother, the following day and he would give him my phone number. We had exchanged addresses.

Ann had married a man who was a guard at a local prison. Ray was very proud of his mom. I knew he had always loved her. When he had said something about her, while living with me, he never said anything bad about her. Here a full circle had connected and my husband and I ministered in the Clements Unit prison. Ann and her husband were ministering in the county jails. He is a pastor. It is because of Ann's relationship with God and her husband along with the love she has always had for her children that she could again share her son with me. She had no bitterness. Ray along with his daughter and grandson saw the reality of Jesus Christ being Lord of our lives. The outcome was peace, real peace between Ann and me.

I told Larry everything. My mate allowed me to cry the tears that needed to be cried. I felt totally released, free. Finally free. Larry and I went to a Mike Barber Crusade at the Clements Unit the same evening. As we sat listening to the praise and worship music I remembered asking Ray, "Did Howard turn to Jesus?" "I don't know, I just don't know, he was still an outlaw when he died."

The praise music was being sung. It was a very familiar song, Because He Lives. "Father, did he cry out to you in his last days?" I asked in my mind. Larry sensed my pain and scooted next to me and put his arm around my shoulder drawing me close to him. He smiled at me. A few tears fell as I remembered the evening Howard got on his knees with me beside my bed so many years ago. "I don't know why I hurt the people I love" he prayed as he asked Christ to forgive him of his sins and come into his heart.

No matter how Howard's life had been, maybe it took cancer for him to cry out again. Only God knows his heart but I rest in peace knowing that Howard knew what to do to receive forgiveness and salvation. I am at rest in knowing that Christ loves us. He sometimes allows, to some people a lot of pain, real pain. If Howard said, "Forgive me." and his heart was pure, he was forgiven.

Meeting with Ray; October 9, 2008

Matthew 18:11
For the Son of man is come to save that which was lost.

Luke 15:4
What man of you, having a hundred sheep, if he lose one of them, doth not leave the ninety and nine in the wilderness, and go after that which is lost, until he find it?

Revelation 3:20
Behold, I stand at the door, and knock: if any man hear my voice, and open the door, I will come in to him, and will sup with him, and he with me.

Chapter 33:
IMPERFECT STRANGERS

~

Written by; Neal, the third and youngest son of Howard October, 2008

My earliest memories go back to when I was five years old but clear memories at the age of eight. Life with Howard was the same whether he was at home or whether he was gone. There were family outings, camping trips and trips to visit Grandparents. Overall, if Howard was gone or he was at home. The relationship as father and son pretty much was non-existing.

In the years of the 1977 through the 80s there were CB radios and home base stations a lot like modern day cell-phones without the monthly phone bill. A CB was a small communication radio mainly used in cars and semi-trucks for cross country trucking with a range of 10-12 miles. Base stations were in homes with a much larger communication range. Very tall antennas were connected to the side of the house. The range increased of up to 300 miles or better. In our home we had a base station room where no-one was allowed.

Therefore if Howard was gone or if he was at home he spent his time on the couch asleep or in the base room which for me equaled him not being there!

Not long ago I saw a news report on TV about the high number of divorces in this modern day. The conclusion of the story was that the main factors of the problem were money, youth, and communication. I laughed because in these modern times there are E-mail, cell phones and text messages. We are at the peak of communication be it across town or across the world.

Maybe as in the CB days, modern day or person-to-person is not the quantity of talking but the quality of talking. How did our great grandparents and those before ever survive?

At any rate there was abuse in our home mainly directed at mom. In later years the abuse included sons on mother as well as brother to brother. There was an incident when I came home and interrupted an episode between mom and Howard. I saw something fly through the air and hit the wall landing on the ground. It was a gun. Howard left with Mom crying. This was the last time Howard came to the house except for getting Ray and Lee's belongings after the divorce.

At eleven years old, Mom and I had moved to Northeast Texas. Howard never paid child support and many times I was aware that he was in town and had flat-out avoided me. He had forgotten my birthday, not just no card or gift, he didn't know the date of my birthday. Even at a young age I knew the family would end in divorce. Like a bad tire on a car it's not if it will blow out but where and when. I was mainly concerned with the safety of Mom. I sure didn't want Howard to have custody of me because I knew it wouldn't be good for me. For example my brothers have been in and out of jail since they left with Howard.

We three boys are now in our forty's. Ray just got out of prison for the second time. Lee's been to prison twice and currently has warrants. When he gets caught he will go back to prison. I have been to jail for unpaid traffic tickets but that was twenty years ago. Understand I don't completely blame Howard. I believe at a certain age we all are responsible for our actions, but I hold Howard responsible for an environment of no discipline.

Drugs played a big part in the relationship between Howard, my brothers and I. It was common ground we shared and seemed like a way to relate and deal with each other. Again, I don't hold drugs responsible but the person doing the drugs including myself.

Having moved to Northeast Texas for Mom and me to be closer to relatives, I found myself angry at the religion Mom belongs to because of the church's position on divorce. This caused a strained relationship with some family members. I had been angry with God a lot in my youth and in later years also been angry at religion. Mom has been a God fearing Jesus loving, loyal servant to Christ every since I can remember. She has dealt with a lot of despair and has accomplished so much in her life. It's amazing! She will quickly credit her faith in God and I agree. Mom waited a long time to remarry (24 years). She is married, believe it or not to a God fearing prison guard. In their spare time they minister in local jails.

I am forty-one years old and am still living in Northeast Texas. I have been sober and drug free for close to nine years. There came a time when I knew it was time to stop drinking and doing drugs. I credit God and Mom's answered prayers for seeing me through it. In honesty I should have two dozen DWI (Driving While Intoxicated) arrests and various convictions for dealing drugs and other law violations. I go to AA (Alcohol Anonymous) and NA (Narcotics Anonymous) meetings. They say that you stop maturing if you quit meetings after having been a regular user of drugs, which is something I believe. I'm still apprehensive about religions, but I do work daily on my relationship with God and my faith.

I currently work in transportation and have recently finished college. I plan on doing more college classes. College is the hardest thing I've ever done. If I can do it anybody can.

In my relationship with Howard when we did see each other or talked on the phone, I always ended the conversation by telling him I loved him. A couple of years ago when Howard was on his death bed I again told him that I loved him. I hold Howard responsible for his actions, but for me it was never about hate, I always saw Howard as human.

I have accepted Jesus as my Savior and visit many churches. I enjoy an early morning spiritual program on TV called The Good Shepherd, and work daily on my faith. My favorite book in the Bible is Matthew, especially Chapter 8:5-13, that's what I want my faith to be.

Matthew 8:5-13
5   And when Jesus was entered into Capernaum, there came unto him a centurion, beseeching him,
6   And saying, Lord, my servant lieth at home sick of the palsy, grievously tormented.
7   And Jesus saith unto him, *I will come and heal him*.

8   The centurion answered and said, Lord, I am not worthy that thou shouldest come under my roof: but speak the word only, and my servant shall be healed.

9   For I am a man under authority, having soldiers under me: and I say to this man, Go, and he goeth; and to another, Come, and he cometh; and to my servant, Do this, and he doeth it.

10 When Jesus heard it, he marveled, and said to them that followed, ***Verily I say unto you, I have not found so great faith, no, not in Israel***.

11 ***And I say unto you, That many shall come from the east and west, and shall sit down with Abraham, and Isaac, and Jacob, in the kingdom of heaven.***

12 ***But the children of the kingdom shall be cast out into outer darkness: there shall be weeping and gnashing of teeth.***

13 And Jesus said unto the centurion, ***Go thy way; and as thou hast believed, so be it done unto thee***. And his servant was healed in the selfsame hour.

October 11, 2008
Saturday afternoon 7:10 pm

Larry and I were sitting in the living room watching TV, the phone rang and I answered. "Is this Mary Ann?" "Yes." I replied. "This is Neal." I was overwhelmed to have Neal call me. He had been awarded to his mother's care at the time she divorced Howard.

I thought Neal must really hate me because of the pain I had caused his mother and him. I was totally wrong. His mom had called him telling him about our meeting. She had given him my phone number. We had one of the most pleasant conversations. I would have never dreamed such a thing could be possible. He shared many of his feelings with me. I answered his questions truthfully. I asked him to write a chapter to be a part of this autobiography. He agreed.

Neal calls Howard by his name, this has been his decision.

Note: Neal called me two days after I met with Ray. I still find it somewhat amazing that Ann gave him, her youngest son my phone number. Only God could orchestrate such a time as this. He is putting families together, to be a part of the ushering in of Jesus Christ, coming to take us all home. Forgiven and ready to see Him face to face.

Matthew 6:14-15
14 *For if ye forgive men their trespasses, your heavenly Father will also forgive you:*
15 *But if ye forgive not men their trespasses, neither will your Father forgive your trespasses.*

Matthew 18:21
Then came Peter to him, and said, Lord, how oft shall my brother sin against me, and I forgive him till seven times?

Mark 11:25
And when ye stand praying, forgive, if ye have aught against any: that your Father also which is in heaven may forgive you your trespasses.

Mark 11:26
But if ye do not forgive, neither will your Father which is in heaven forgive your trespasses.

Luke 6:37
Judge not, and ye shall not be judged: condemn not, and ye shall not be condemned: forgive, and ye shall be forgiven:

Luke 17:3
Take heed to yourselves: If thy brother trespass against thee, rebuke him; and if he repent, forgive him.

Luke 17:4
And if he trespass against thee seven times in a day, and seven times in a day turn again to thee, saying, I repent; thou shalt forgive him.

Luke 23:34
Then said Jesus, ***Father, forgive them; for they know not what they do.*** And they parted his raiment, and cast lots.

1John 1:9
If we confess our sins, he is faithful and just to forgive us our sins, and to cleanse us from all unrighteousness.

ETERNITY WITH THE LAMB

Revelation 7:9-17

9 After this I beheld, and, lo, a great multitude, which no man could number, of all nations, and kindreds, and people, and tongues, stood before the throne, and before the Lamb, clothed with white robes, and palms in their hands;

10 And cried with a loud voice, saying, Salvation to our God which sitteth upon the throne, and unto the Lamb.

11 And all the angels stood round about the throne, and *about* the elders and the four beasts, and fell before the throne on their faces, and worshiped God,

12 Saying, Amen: Blessing, and glory, and wisdom, and thanksgiving, and honor, and power, and might, *be* unto our God forever and ever. Amen.

13 And one of the elders answered, saying unto me, What are these which are arrayed in white robes? and whence came they?

14 And I said unto him, Sir, thou knowest. And he said to me, These are they which came out of great tribulation, and have washed their robes, and made them white in the blood of the Lamb.

15 Therefore are they before the throne of God, and serve him day and night in his temple: and he that sitteth on the throne shall dwell among them.

16 They shall hunger no more, neither thirst any more; neither shall the sun light on them, nor any heat.

17 For the Lamb which is in the midst of the throne shall feed them, and shall lead them unto living fountains of waters: and God shall wipe away all tears from their eyes.

Chapter 34:
NEW BEGINNINGS

~

October 27, 2006, I wrote a letter to Chaplain David Schlewitz at the William P. Clements Unit, in Amarillo, TX. The Clements Unit is a high security prison which houses up to 3,700 male offenders. Larry, my husband has been an active Chaplain Volunteer for six years. He ministers every Saturday in Bldg. 4 as well as other pods, housing areas when requested. I have gone with Larry on several occasions and shared my testimony with the men as well as teach.

I met Chaplain Schlewitz when he was Chaplain of the Jordan Unit in Pampa, TX. At the time I was ministering under the leadership of Don and Donna Castleberry of Freedom In Jesus Prison Ministry. The Castleberry ministry gave me the opportunity to minister to men as well as ride my motorcycle into some of the prisons.

Friendship grew between Larry, my husband, and Chaplain Schlewitz and Chaplain Moore. Little did I know in the beginning that God was orchestrating a team, when I had written the letter in October to Chaplain Schlewitz, all that I could envision was secretarial work and office work.

What a challenge. I was taught very swiftly. On the day I began my responsibilities as secretary, Chaplain Schlewitz told me that I had two bosses, Chaplain Moore and himself. The decisions that I made would be backed by the Chaplaincy Department. I was put into a place of leadership from the beginning. Had I not previously volunteered under the supervision of Merrell & Doris Gilbert, Chaplains at Randall County Jail, I know that I would not have had the experience needed to be of assistance to the Chaplains of the Clements prison. Having worked for City Mission was also of great benefit to me.

I walked into a world within a world when the day came that I signed on as Secretary to the Chaplains. It took time for me to learn how to work with the janitors, male offenders assisting in teaching and educating other offenders about venereal diseases, aids, and hepatitis. The Chaplain's office and chapel are located in Building One. Offenders clean as well as help with other beneficial work and education that will help to uphold safety for both the offenders and the officers, workers and leadership of the prison system.

Having had a background such as mine, I began work with the wrong attitude. No-one was going to run over me. It was also a big challenge to learn how to work with chaplains who had given service for years to the prison system. Both Chaplains preach at churches in the surrounding areas. Chaplain Moore also teaches a college class. I'm a little girl from a little town with life experiences being my education.

There is one area I was very happy that I didn't know a lot about. I had read only the King James and New Kings James Bibles for years. I am not challenged by other beliefs. God, from the beginning of my salvation had directed me therefore I didn't judge, condemn, or try to change any volunteer's beliefs or ministry. I don't agree with some other beliefs, but I keep this to myself. The chaplains needed assistance in paper work being done. This is my way of giving back to the Kingdom of God.

Chaplain Rory Murphy, District Chaplain welcomed me and helps me to continue to grow every time he comes on the unit. I am the only woman volunteer currently working on a daily basis in the Chaplain's Office.

Being a bold woman I did as I was told by the chaplains. When they expressed to me what would help make their offices to run smoother, I put it into action to get the job done. Both Chaplains are limited in space. Their offices have to be shared with the volunteers assisting in talking to offenders on a one-on-one basis or to give an offender a telephone call to his family when a person in his immediate family has died. It took time for us to become a team working together to accomplish the goals of the chaplains and assisting them in their heavy work load. The volunteers, no matter what their beliefs or what Bible they read, are there to love and help with the education and growth of a man's faith. There are many different beliefs and many different religions in the prisons. The same is true for the volunteer chaplains, as well as the offenders. There is a small group of men that have beliefs that I don't agree with but they have in my opinion the best team players, love and respect for each other and everyone around them than any other offenders practicing their faith. They don't seem to be bickering with one another and trying to all be leaders. This working together shows me what real faith means. If I am able to assist or show light into my beliefs I do it by the way I treat others and I answer questions according to what Jesus Christ has done for me. I don't try to prove Jesus Christ, I just give my testimony when asked questions.

Both chaplains overheard at times when I was talking to an offender. They put their trust and confidence in me very quickly. As I grew and learned I changed some of my methods in not only working for the chaplains but also being secretary to every volunteer. It is very important for me to listen, hear and do what would help a volunteer in his needs. Some men have years of service in the prison. They are of extreme importance in their knowledge, their love and their service to the offenders. The prison would be extremely limited in every area without volunteers.

Within a matter of a few months I was approved to work on the computer main frame which is controlled by TDCJ in Huntsville, Texas. This gives me access to information about an offender's housing and other needed information to keep the paperwork correct and current. I also record the visits of volunteers, whether it is a single person or a group who ministers on the premises. Through observation, growth and being taught by both chaplains as well as other volunteers, I began to minister to the offenders on a more regular basis. At times an offender just wanted to talk sharing their heart. Emergency phone calls are extremely important to the whole system. The offender's well being on hearing of the death of a loved one can stop problems or increase them. After talking to an immediate family member the offender usually can cope with his pain along with ministering and the sure foundation of prayer.

It is without question that the Holy Spirit gave me wisdom and the ability to learn. Years of ministry taught me the process but I didn't have a clue as to the flow of accountability in every offender's connection with the Chaplain's Office. After a little over a year, the paper work was in good order. I had re-arranged major files in order for the processing and completed files to flow and quickly be obtainable by the Chaplains and the review of audits.

I met Ms. Johnson in the ODR. (Officers Dining Room) She is Supervisor of social workers for Texas Tech who has a contract with TDCJ. I had not worked in the chaplain's office but a month or so when I was sitting in the ODR and several women joined me at the table. Ms. Johnson began to laugh as she shared her attempt of trying to drown a fish in a toilet. My ears were hearing and my mind was trying to understand what was being said. The conversation turned into everyone trying to help in their ways of drowning a fish. I was still puffed up somewhat in self. After all, I'm the chaplain's secretary. It was not until the end of their meal that I finally realized what was going on. No one was trying to drown a fish. It was their way of coping with the stress and putting down for a short time all their responsibilities. They were wonderful together. A connection among these women and me took place. Ms. Johnson had my heart and my respect. What a woman.

Ms. Johnson, Supervisor works in 12 building which is called PAMIO (Program of the Aggressive and Mentally Ill Offender). This building houses the more severe case history, aggressive behavior and some with mental problems. Through Ms. Johnson and under her direction I learned the foundation and goals of the social workers as well as the need to work with the officers who oversee this building. At one time this prison had six chaplains but due to the war and expenses the prison went from six chaplains to two. Ms. Johnson said to me, "If I can make a difference in one man's life, then it's worth it all." She won my trust and my heart. I had learned how to go into restricted areas and give emergency phone calls as well as cell side (going to the door of the offender where he lives in a pod, a pod houses a certain amount of offenders) to take books and Bibles to offenders requesting them. I had learned how to talk to a man on a one-on-one basis at his house, in High Security and Administrative Segregation, special management within TDCJ.

Little did I know, with the help of the Chaplains and others that I would be birthed into a ministry that only God could open such closed doors. My heart is in tune with the men I knew and had become a part of in my past, especially when Howard and I were together. I had felt rejection and had very little or no self esteem for the most part of my life, especially and painfully before Christ. I became accepted by not only outlaws, but most hard core street riders. I felt as though someone loved me, it didn't matter whether I broke the law or not, I was trusted and had men who backed me whatever state I was in. Many times I have relived in memory the day God gave me a choice to go on to heaven or stay and minister to the lost. I chose to minister to the lost, the rejected the down trodden of this world. Never in my wildest dreams did I ever think that it would be in prisons.

Larry my husband and I pray daily. We pray for the chaplains, the volunteers, the officers, the workers, the wardens and the offenders. We have just begun to minister together in these three high security buildings. Larry understands as I do how a person can reject what is good for what is bad. God has allowed us the time to grow together and become beneficial to His kingdom and His glory. We became Certified Volunteer Chaplain's Assistants. This means we have the training needed to be accepted in all prisons in Texas as ministers.

Pastor Larry Miles had told me, "When God opens a door. You need to go through it." Often times when I am walking between buildings I think of the many officers, the employees, the leadership and I am so thankful that good outweighs the bad. I have worked in the Chaplain's office for over two years now. Only a small number of officers or employees hate the offenders and hate their jobs. But we live in this world. There will always be hate to deal with. When I hear a person say such things as, "They don't want to change." I say nothing. There is no argument that can win when a person is not in his/her true calling. The men incarcerated in prison know when a person is for real. They know real love and will yield to it when they feel it. They recognize it. Sometimes I talk face-to-face or cell side with a man I really relate to. It is not difficult at all for me to share with him how much he is loved by Jesus Christ. My heart is tender and compassionate to his pain.

Being Volunteer Chaplains has taken the place of the family who rejected Larry and I, or the school mates that didn't befriend us in our youth, or the people who may have broken our hearts, or leaders who didn't know what to do with us. Larry and I have participated in life groups. We have gone to healing seminars in order to become whole. The blind cannot lead the blind. We have worked at our marriage. We have fallen in love, real love, God's love for one another. We can sit back now and just be ourselves, trying to impress no one. God has healed and set us free from the world. We live in it yet for a season, but we do not take part of the lifestyle of the lost. We have learned through the years of preparation and the years of doing that nothing on this earth takes the place of hearing Jesus Christ say, *"I love you,"* or in the spirit realm set a crown on your head or hold your hand, or call you by your name, or let you feel His scars. There is nothing, nothing that can draw us out of our Father's hand.

Even after having fallen (making mistakes) many, many times, it was Larry or me that turned from Christ. He has never turned from us. We run to Him, no matter what. We never run from Him. Why do some people continue a personal relationship with Christ and others die in their sins? I could write a book on my understanding of the answers to these questions but in reality Jesus didn't give me this assignment. He just told me to go, He told me where to go and I went. (The Spirit of the Lord GOD is upon me; because the LORD hath anointed me to preach good tidings unto the meek; he hath sent me to bind up the brokenhearted, to proclaim liberty to the captives, and the opening of the prison to them that are bound. Isaiah 61:1) In reality this scripture speaks of Jesus Christ, but Jesus Christ told us to follow Him and greater works would we do as He went to the Father. (John 14:12 *Verily, verily, I say unto you, He that believeth on me, the works that I do shall he do also; and greater works than these shall he do; because I go unto my Father.*)

Chaplain David Schlewitz   **Chaplain David Moore**

Pastor Larry Miles, Chaplain Schlewitz and Chaplain Moore make up the trinity of a Father image in my life. These three men have my deepest respect and love as men of God. All three set an example of the character of Jesus Christ. I consider myself blessed beyond words that they are mine and Larry's friends.

Senior Warden Adams, Assistant Warden Sloan and Assistant Warden Baker have allowed Larry and me to minister in all areas of the Clements Unit Prison. We are extremely blessed by the leadership of this prison.

Being in Christ's perfect plan, working with His children and working in His harvest field gives real purpose to life. Christ will give the increase if we will only work together to plant, water and follow His leadership.

**Ms. Johnson, Social Worker, Supervisor-
PAMIO, Bldg.12, W. P. Clements, Jr. Unit**

There are some wonderful people working in our prisons. If Ms. Johnson or her co-workers help with the needs of an offender who is your friend or family member, you are blessed. Pray for Ms. Johnson and her co-workers, they are a team. They labor in love. Their goal is to help an offender in his;
1. Spiritual 2. Emotional 3. Physical and 4. Mental needs.

Mark 2:16, 17 And when the scribes and Pharisees saw him eat with publicans and sinners, they said unto his disciples. How is it that he eateth and drinketh with publicans and sinners? When Jesus heard it, he saith unto them, ***They that are whole have no need of the physician, but they that are sick: I came not to call the righteous, but sinners to repentance.***

Romans 5:19 For as by one man's disobedience many were made sinners, so by the obedience of one shall many be made righteous.

**Ms. McCain, Psychologist, PAMIO,
Bldg.12, W. P. Clements, Jr. Unit**

Ms. McCain was sitting at the same table in the ODR, when I first met Ms. Johnson. She has laughed with me on several occasions about how the conversation of drowning a fish must have appeared to me. She was right, at first I was astonished that such people were working with people who couldn't be as sick as they were.

I learned through a course of time that the people working with the offenders in Building 12 are the same as I, a CVCA. My education is years of study and courses to help me to fully understand the Bible. The Social Workers and Psychologist spent their time in the education required to be able to work with offenders trying to overcome their past and become healthy people whether in prison or living in the free world.

As I approached the ending of this manuscript, I wondered if I am now a healthy woman in my mind, body, Spirit and soul. I asked Ms. McCain to read Chapter 2; NO MORE.

Ms. McCain, after having read the chapter sat in her office with me and patiently taught me the difference between psychological disorders. For years I thought I had been mentally disturbed or had the illness of changing from one person into another. Due to the ability to shut out pain as a child I thought I had really been very sick in mind for many years. I spent many years trying to hide my real self from others.

When I left Ms. McCain's office I no longer had any doubt of me having become a whole healthy person. When Christ healed me as stated in Chapter 2, titled NO MORE, I was healed, yet I had to live out this healing. Once I understood my own personality and the areas I had to work with the hardest, being anger and rejection, I grew into a woman that from her past could now stand before an offender in his living area and share of the wholeness of God. I don't have the Bible down in all its revelations, but one thing I do have and that is a personal relationship with Jesus Christ, and His death on the cross that I am now able to feed to others.

I am free of the lies of Satan that held me in bondage for so many years. He convinced me that I was terribly sick and once people got to know me, they would recognize the faults in my character. I became what I needed to be for what I wanted. Now I am just me, no longer afraid of the judgment of others, no longer living with deep secrets hidden in the closed doors of my mind and heart.

Today, I pray that this, my testimony will help others to understand themselves and know that only God can set us free and only God can cleanse the heart and create a whole new person ready to feed His love to people who suffer the same fears that I did for so many years.

Together working with the Social Workers and the Psychologist, I find that it takes all of us to work together with Christ's approval in the abilities He gave us. I am a Certified Volunteer Chaplains' Assistant, the men call out to me when I go into their pods, "Chaplain, Chaplain. Will you come talk to me?" My, my, who would have ever thought of such a thing!

It is not worth it all, but *He, Jesus Christ* is worth it all.

2Corinthians 5:17-21

17 Therefore if any man be in Christ, he is a new creature: old things are passed away; behold, all things are become new.

18 And all things are of God, who hath reconciled us to himself by Jesus Christ, and hath given to us the ministry of reconciliation;

19 To wit, that God was in Christ, reconciling the world unto himself, not imputing their trespasses unto them; and hath committed unto us the word of reconciliation.

20 Now then we are ambassadors for Christ, as though God did beseech you by us: we pray you in Christ's stead, be ye reconciled to God.

21 For he hath made him to be sin for us, who knew no sin; that we might be made the righteousness of God in him.

James 1:12-27

12 Blessed is the man that endureth temptation: for when he is tried, he shall receive the crown of life, which the Lord hath promised to them that love him.

13 Let no man say when he is tempted, I am tempted of God: for God cannot be tempted with evil, neither tempteth he any man:

14 But every man is tempted, when he is drawn away of his own lust, and enticed.

15 Then when lust hath conceived, it bringeth forth sin: and sin, when it is finished, bringeth forth death.

16 Do not err, my beloved brethren.

17 Every good gift and every perfect gift is from above, and cometh down from the Father of lights, with whom is no variableness, neither shadow of turning.

18 Of his own will begat he us with the word of truth, that we should be a kind of firstfruits of his creatures.

19 Wherefore, my beloved brethren, let every man be swift to hear, slow to speak, slow to wrath:

20 For the wrath of man worketh not the righteousness of God.

21 Wherefore lay apart all filthiness and superfluity of naughtiness, and receive with meekness the engrafted word, which is able to save your souls.

22 But be ye doers of the word, and not hearers only, deceiving your own selves.

23 For if any be a hearer of the word, and not a doer, he is like unto a man beholding his natural face in a glass:

24 For he beholdeth himself, and goeth his way, and straightway forgetteth what manner of man he was.

25 But whoso looketh into the perfect law of liberty, and continueth therein, he being not a forgetful hearer, but a doer of the work, this man shall be blessed in his deed.

26 If any man among you seem to be religious, and bridleth not his tongue, but deceiveth his own heart, this man's religion is vain.

27 Pure religion and undefiled before God and the Father is this, To visit the fatherless and widows in their affliction, and to keep himself unspotted from the world.

This drawing was drawn by an offender at the Clements Unit and mailed to me through my church. It means a great deal to me. I don't have a clue who drew it but this is their story and only they know the true meaning. I have learned a little through research, but very little. It matters more to me that an offender shared their hearts with me.

2Timothy 4:8
Henceforth there is laid up for me a crown of righteousness, which the Lord, the righteous judge, shall give me at that day: and not to me only, but unto all them also that love his appearing.

Chapter 35:
LADY

~

Ireceived a phone call from Jackie Bolden, mother to Cathy Barnum (oldest daughter, who was murdered by her husband).

"Mary, I saw Charlene today (Jackie's youngest daughter and sister to Cathy). There is a girl in Randall County Jail with her that knows you. She met you when you ministered in the women's pod a few years ago. She has read my book, JUST ANOTHER MISSING PERSON, and read your name several times. Barbara asked Charlene if Jackie could get word to me to write to her."

During that time I knew Charlene was destroying her own life and causing much pain to those who loved her beyond reason, had not asked to see me or talk to me. Jackie has asked me on several occasions to talk to her daughter. I refused, "Charlene has to want to see me. Until she is ready and means business with Christ, she will only reject me. Her love for me will turn cold if I force her to see me." "Oh Mary she wants to talk to you. She is asking for you. Will you write her?" "I don't know," was my reply.

After seeking the answer from Jesus Christ, I was overcome with a desire to see Charlene as well as Barbara. I called Jackie and told her that I was going to go into the jail and minister to all the girls who wanted to see me. After leaving Randall County Jail Ministry, I had not desired to return. My time and efforts were at the Bill Clements Unit, working for the chaplains and ministering in PAMIO.

There had to be something to it, more than just a visit. I contacted Sharon Alexander, a member of Trinity Fellowship Prison/Jail Ministry and she made the necessary arrangements. Sharon would go into the facility with me as it was her scheduled time to minister. As I began to search the heart of Christ, I became aware of scripture that had depth and meaning to me. I had spent a lot of time researching the word, heart. In my opinion, the heart, the issues of the heart determine our lives. Therefore, I prepared a teaching on the heart and gave several scripture, with the explanation, to the very hungry women (about 9). Christ changes our hearts as we learn to follow His teachings, but it is us that have to want our heart to be changed. It is a desire that we must realize when giving all the wrong to Christ will help us to work with Him to obey His example, then He will give us the desires of our hearts. When He does this, we become children of a pure heart, desiring God's will and letting go of our own. We in our free will ask Christ to bring to light the deep issues of our heart, that we may understand and work with Him in changing our lives from death to life.

Psalms 26:2
Examine me, O LORD, and prove me; try my reins and my heart.

Psalms 51:10
Create in me a clean heart, O God; and renew a right spirit within me.

Psalms 139:23
Search me, O God, and know my heart: try me, and know my thoughts:

At the end, when time allowed was about over. I stopped teaching and asked Christ for His presence. He honored my heart's desire and set a supernatural crown on every woman's head. We all were in agreement, and knowing that Jesus loves to manifest Himself to those who believe and ask of Him will indeed be blessed with His Abba Father presence.

John 14:21
He that hath my commandments, and keepeth them, he it is that loveth me: and he that loveth me shall be loved of my Father, and I will love him, and will manifest myself to him.

LADY

Lady, you are an angel in my eyes.
Only God in heaven holds your prize.

Walk through this life shining your light.
Eyes upon you beholding a beautiful sight.
Long ago you doubted your own ability.
Come close to drowning in the futility,
Of relying on yourself to make life good.
Instead of relying on God like you should.

Now you know that place where you've been.
Is somewhere you never have to be again.
Now you can save others souls from the hell,
You have lived through and known so well.

Lady, you have endless courage and strength.
Willing, without question, to go to any length,
To serve your Father, to show Him your love.
Your faith is like promises from the dove.

Lady, you are beautiful. I cannot deny.
I am in awe of you and this is why,
Wherever you may travel upon this land,

You truly, belong at my God's right hand.

Charlene Wadley
Sept. 13, 2009

Chapter 8; **FATHER** (8th paragraph)

During the time of my baby relationship with Christ, I was feeding on the milk of the word, learning about Jesus Christ. (*1Corinthians 3:2 I fed you with milk and not with solid food; for until now you were not able to receive it, and even now you are still not able;) My desires were changing, and one of the deepest desires that I held secretly in my heart was I wanted to become a *lady*. I was in my late thirties at the time. I admired women who seemed to have the ability to succeed in their lives as a wife as well as professional standing. Birthing within me was a desire to become a respected woman, a *lady* with high integrity, approved, anointed and useful to the Kingdom of Jesus Christ.

Had I not followed the direction of Christ, I would have missed His personal message to me through the heart of Charlene. I spent three days reading and rereading this poem. Never expecting a reply from Christ, He touched a young girl, whom I love deeply to write her heart and Christ letting me know that I am a *lady*.

Although Jackie (Charlene's mom) helped to edit this book, Charlene chose not to read it at the time. She knew nothing about my heart's desire to become a *lady* approved by Jesus Christ.

Chapter 36:
JOURNEY THROUGH GROWTH
IN MINISTRY

Mary Moses, Pastor's Dale & Rita Maness

First time to minister to congregation. (Mary top right of The Lubbock Christian News, name spelled wrong)

Camp Meeting Tabernacle, Lubbock, Texas - December 19, 1986

Women in Potter County City Jail

Women in Randall County Jail

**Lara Lee,
Randall County Jail**

Dear Trinity Fellowship Jail Ministry,

Hello in the precious name of Jesus. I want to thank all the ladies that go to the Randall County Jail: Audrey, Mary, Eula, Luella and Jackie. I was arrested Dec. 7, 1993. I stayed 13 months at Randall County, and these ladies were faithful to bring the Word and their love every Saturday. I was a broken drug addict and alcoholic. Through the ministry, I became filled with the Holy Spirit and began to speak in tongues. I also learned how to fight against the powers of darkness and win. I am healed of my addiction and alcoholism because of this and the ladies laying hands on me in Jesus' name. Now I am home with my two boys. My mother and father have started going to church regularly because they see how the Lord worked in my life. My mother was healed of arthritis and shoulder pain. She was on your prayer list. A young couple on your prayer list had a baby born blind and deaf. She now can see and hear. Praise the Lord.

I would also like to thank Brenda and Linda. You ladies know who you are, and there's no way you can know the special place you hold in my heart. Keep up the good work. Jesus is Lord.
Love in Christ,
Laura Lee

On a Saturday morning I drove to Canyon, TX. from Amarillo to minister to the women incarcerated in Randall County Jail. When I had completed the service and was about to leave the area an officer approached me and asked if I would visit a young girl who would not leave her cell and had depression issues?

I entered the cell of Starrla who was sitting at her little desk writing. She looked up at me with very little expression. I introduced myself and told her I ministered at the jail every Saturday morning. She was not impressed. Then out of the blue I said, "I have a tattoo of a lion on my back. I use to be married to an outlaw biker." "You have a tattoo?" She asked very excitedly. The cell was very small, barely enough room for two people to stand at one time. Starrla didn't take her eyes off me as I unbuttoned three or four buttons on my blouse and pulled it off my shoulder. I turned and she got up from her concrete stool and ran her fingers over my tattoo. I then turned and buttoned my blouse. She sat back down on her stool and listened as I shared my testimony with her.

"They came to see me but I won't see them. I told the officer to tell them not to come back." Starrla shared with me. She belonged to the same outlaw gang that my ex-husband Howard had belonged too. "They make me do things I don't want to do, ugly things." She said with tears in her eyes. I told her about the day I was going to kill myself and how God stopped me by coming to me in the form of a cloud. I also shared with her of the day I fell to my knees and asked Jesus Christ to come into my life. Starrla listened and freely asked Jesus Christ into her heart and to forgive her of her sins. Joy filled her heart as soon as she spoke the words. Her tears changed to tears of joy and she held me as she put her head on my shoulder and cried saying, "Thank you, thank you for coming."

The following Saturday after I had finished ministering to those who came to the service I asked if Starrla could come into the room so I could visit with her. The officer was so happy that she had received Christ and brought Starrla into the room with me. We sat down at the table and I began to explain to her about the Holy Spirit who now lived inside of her. She has big beautiful eyes and just like a little girl showed her excitement through her eyes. I told her of the day with my friend Kitti and I went to a church and the Evangelist asked those who wanted to be baptized in the Holy Spirit to come forward. I stepped into the isle and went forward. I had not ever heard of the Holy Spirit, yet I was filled with His power and spoke in another tongue or language. Starrla received the baptism of the Holy Spirit with eagerness and excitement. Tears ran down both of our faces.

Through the years I have heard so much said against tattoos and I agree some are not of God's liking but a life was changed because she could see and feel my tattoo. I tried to have it removed when I first came back to Amarillo from Lubbock. The man tattooed over it with lemon juice and salt to pull the ink out with the blood. It hurt extremely. It only made a beautiful tattoo of a lion look smudged.

I'm so thankful that I have a lion tattooed on my back that now for me represents Jesus Christ the Lion of the Tribe of Judah. I'm no longer ashamed of my tattoo. I can't take the liberty in prison to show it but I do share this story about Starrla with some offenders who are tattooed from the top of their head to the bottom of their feet. One in general thought Jesus Christ would not forgive him because of his tattoos. I will have to admit from what I could see the tattoos had nothing to do with good but evil. Yet I knew with all my heart that Jesus Christ loved him. He too without seeing my tattoo but believing me asked Jesus Christ to forgive him, not for his tattoos but his sins, and to come into his heart. The outer appearance is not what our Lord is concerned about it is the inner, the issues of the heart.

Another outlaw, a young man came up to me after I had ministered at a prison in Dalhart, TX. and told me he had just accepted Christ as his Savior. "If my home-boys find out they will kill me." He said. I assured him that Jesus Christ said that no one could pluck one of His children out of His hand. I also assured him that Jesus Christ is head of all things and He would do what was best, if it meant being moved to another prison or another building or another pod, Jesus Christ was in control not his home-boys.

In the old Testament it says not to be tattooed, in the New Testament it says His words will be written on the tables of one's heart. I wonder if that means tattooed, or written with His finger? (Just a thought.)

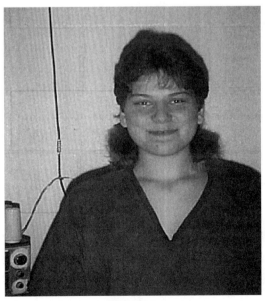

STARRLA
FORGIVEN MUCH-LOVES MUCH

Trinity Jail Testimonies

How challenging is your life?
How bold is your Christian witness?
What are you doing to reach your God-given potential?
Are you being fulfilled or are you staying within your comfort zone?

TRINITY FELLOWSHIP JAIL MINISTRY AT POTTER COUNTY & RANDALL COUNTY NEEDS YOU.

For those needing an extra challenge in their Christian walk and those who have a desire to be a bold witness, we have an exciting, vibrant opportunity for you right now.

Here is a letter from an inmate to a member of our Jail Ministry. Please "catch the blessing" as you read.

"Mary,

I am writing you to say thank you! I was touched mentally and spiritually when you spoke the word of God to me. I am aware that God can save people, but I just wish I could have found Him besides finding Him in jail. Although I have God in my heart and life now, it does not matter where I found Him. I was reading about baptism and wondered if I can be or am ready to be baptized. I know I just received God, but I am wanting the cleanliness, if you can understand what I am saying.

Anyway, I really appreciated you taking that extra time to come and see me. Now I am not thinking of suicide, and my past seems to have faded away. I cannot say I will overcome my shyness, but I feel a lot better about myself. - Smile - You said you were an ex-biker of a gang. You understand where I am coming from! I know I told you that Sunday; I just felt I had to let you know again. I try and live day by day now. Even if I feel that the walls are closing in, I have turned 20 years old (the 18th), I feel I have no other family but them. I would love to be a part of a family who cares and loves, not one that runs my life and makes me do ugly things. I hope you understand what I am saying and where I am coming from.

Well, I must close for now. I hope to receive a letter or some type of word from ya. Take care.

Truly, Starrla

P.S. Thanks again.

Please remember God used ordinary people to do extraordinary things! It is time for us to step up and become a vital part of what God is doing.

We invite you to call Cendy at 355-5652 to let her know if you can be with us Wednesday, May 17, at 7:00 p.m. in room 233-234.

Pastor Phil Mercado of Trinity Fellowship baptizes 6 women
offenders in Randall County Jail July 14, 1994

Don Castleberry & Offender   Mary shared her testimony at Dalhart Unit

Freedom In Jesus Prison Ministry, Dalhart Unit

Team ministered at Jordan Unit, Pampa, TX

407

Lou Ella Braddock, Mary Moses, Jackie Bolden
Neal Unit Women's Prison, Mary held service
under her ministry of Mary Moses Prison/
Jail Ministry.

Lou Ella Braddock & Mary Moses
Opening of Neal Unit in Amarillo, TX
(later converted into a male prison)

Mary ministering at City Mission

Dr. John & Donna Curry, Sue Muir,
Jackie Bolden & Mary

Friends supporting Mary at City Mission.

NOTE: Dr. Curry and his wife Donna birthed Trinity Fellowship
in their home November, 1977.

Mary Moses & team members riding into Neal Unit, Amarillo, TX.

Right-Chaplain Merle Houska

Offenders of the Neal Unit. Only God knows their heart.

Members of Freedom In Jesus Prison Ministry. President; Don Castleberry

**Team members ministering at Neal Unit
Freedom In Jesus Prison Ministry**

**Chaplain Merle Houska & Ron Sherman, President,
Amarillo Bible Crusaders**

BIG DAVE'S FUNERAL

It's easy for me to understand this kind of love.
I was an outcast and Jesus gave me a family.

A biker was stabbed by his ex-girlfriend
in his leg when he started a fight with her
new boyfriend. She dropped the knife in
my pocket before the police arrested her.
Later I gave the knife back to her. She kept
a death from happening that day.

Mary and Patty

THIS T-SHIRT SAYS IT ALL

March 1991

MARCH 1999

Big Dave had played an important part in my life. One night when I was married to Howard, I sat on his couch and told him my testimony. Big Dave was at the time a member of a group of outlaws. He had kept me from harm on several occasions. Because of this, I loved him.

It was after my divorce from Howard and I had returned to Amarillo that I looked up Big Dave and hugged him as my friend. When he was in the last stages of liver disease, I visited him in the hospital. It was shortly afterward that Big Dave died.

Hundreds rode to the point, a part of Palo Duro Canyon. We witnessed Big Dave's ashes as they were poured out into the canyon. There were Christians, who I now rode with as well as outlaws and friends who just rode motorcycles there to show their love for a man who had played a part in their lives.

Afterward, when riding back to a small town, I asked the Lord if I could open up. I rode 110 miles an hour for about 20 miles. I have never ridden this top speed again, but it was a touch of heaven for me at the time. It had been my heart's desire for a long time and He allowed me to do it.

FAREWELL TO BIG DAVE!

Bikers from around the Panhandle and probably beyond, gathered Sunday, February 21st to say "Goodbye" to Big Dave. More than 200 bikes participated in the memorial run that appeared to be a couple of miles long. The Amarillo Bible Crusaders chapter was represented by about 8 members. It started at the Boon Docks and ended at the overlook at the South rim of Palo Duro Canyon. Big Dave's ashes were then scattered over the edge by friends and family.

Big Dave's term on Earth ended last weekend in Dallas where he was waiting for a liver transplant. Rumor had it that he had been waiting for about 4 years for his transplant, and was nearing the top of the list when he lost his battle with liver disease.

Big Dave had been a staple at the Boon Docks Bar & Grill for several years where you were sure to find him behind the Bar B Que grill. Dave had at times donated his cooking expertise to charity bike runs to raise money for fellow bikers or her families in need,

I didn't know Big Dave personally, only by reputation. But by that reputation I knew that he was someone this skinny guy didn't want to tangle with.(honest, I used to be skinny) When I was still living & partying in the world, I had seen Big Dave many times in one bar or another, or at the Boon Docks during the last couple of years.

The memorial run and eulogy were handled in typical Biker style with the

Here If You Need Us...

smell of herbs in the air and Beer flowing freely. Since it has not been that long ago for me, these were things I expected to see and was not surprised nor shocked by them. The only thing that bothered me the most about the whole thing was the fact that I dion't know whether Dave had accepted Christ before he passed away. Don't get me wrong, I am not saying he did not, but I personally never approached him with the Gospel. Did anyone? I can honestly say I would have in the future, and that really bothers me. If not me.....then who?

The purpose of this article is more about what I found out about myself last weekend, and in no way intended to slam, judge or degrade anyone else. Maybe just to get us all thinking of what its all about, The riding season is up us now and it will soon be hard to keep up with all the scheduled runs. I only p[ray that I find boldness, which I have lacked, when it comes to sharing "my" Christ with others, I will undoubtedly be given the opportunity this year as will you.

May we be up to the challenge and may the harvest be plentiful.

In Christ
Walter Randolph

Mary & Kelly,
Better move over,
this woman can ride.

Cindy Randolph and Charlotte Braddock
"Charlotte, let's ride."
I'd holler to her and off we'd go,
riding like the wind.

Bill Duncan and Mary Moses

Bill Duncan, Founder and Director of the CIS Foundation
His mission work was mainly in the former USSR building churches.
May 1999, Historic Route 66 Association, Harley Davidson
Owners Texas State Rally.

415

**CMA riders getting ready for Tri State Fair Parade,
downtown Amarillo, TX
September 1999**

Brothers Of The Third Wheel
Riders Mary met before the parade, Sept. 1999

Farewell to Cindy Randolph (right bottom) on her way to
minister in Belarus – October, 1999

Cindy and Walter Randolph

Mike and Rose Hamner   Moe and Charlotte Braddock

All of the above are friends belonging to CMA.These people as well as many others helped Larry and I in our growth to become ministers in the prison system.

Larry and I drove to Gatesville, Texas and ministered in a female unit.
This was the first time for Larry to be in a female prison.

Larry & Mary ministering at City Mission

PASTOR BOB AND RUTH PARKER
September 1981

This picture was taken when Howard and I were married and living at the old air force base east of Amarillo. Howard with our kids attended this church with Pastor Bob and Ruth Parker of First Baptist Church.

In May 2004, a small team of riders met at Larry's and my home. Together we rode to Pastor Bob and Ruth's church still located in the same area that Howard and I once attended. We shared our testimonies with 75 or more children and adults. We rode members, guest and children on our motorcycles after service. It was my great joy to ride Ruth Parker after all these years. They made such a difference in my life. At one time Pastor Bob was seriously ill in the hospital. Larry and I went to see him and pray with him. "May I pray in my prayer language?" I asked. Pastor Bob smiled at me and gave his permission. They now believe in this wonderful gift of Christ. It was a small reunion time, especially for me. Later Ruth asked us to come to their church and share our testimonies. God has brought me full circle.

MAY 19, 2004

From top left to top right Bynum Morris, Gary Phyonex, Darron Evans, Mary Martin, Mary & Larry Martin, bottom right, Don Phyonex, Darron Evans, Bynum Morris, Tim Clifton (picture taken later).

Six riders shared their personal story of how Jesus uniquely touched and changed their lives from one of strife, pride, hopelessness, selfishness and rebellion to one of hope, humility, peace, joy and gratitude.

JOURNEY TO MANAGUA, NICARAGUA
OCTOBER 2004
TEAM LEADERS; PASTOR'S WAYNE & ELAINE MAGOURIK

It was my great joy to be a part of the ministry team who flew to Nicaragua to be of service, to minister, to distribute food, medication, clothing, eye glasses and much more to the residents of Managua and the surrounding area. Many of the people lived in or close to the dump grounds.

I was able to be a part of this group because of Pastor Wayne MaGourik, he backed me in my Prison/Jail Ministry through Trinity Fellowship Church.

Hosanna Church, where we all attended service.

Building owned by Hosanna Church, where distribution to the
needs of the residents took place.

Small team preparing to enter prison. The van picked up a couple of others along the way.

You don't go into a prison without this woman. She put me under her authority and because of her I was allowed some privileges.

Watch tower of second prison.

Very, very big roaches live here.

Male unit prison, outside wall.

Gatehouse, check in and out for visit.

The smell of filth all but overwhelmed me when we first entered the building. Some family members were visiting with the male offenders between two buildings. Whatever the offender had on at the time of his becoming a part of the prison system is all he had. If no family member brought a change of clothes he would have to wash and wear the same thing as long as he was in prison. He washed them, not the prison system.

Dogs and cats were hungrily begging for food between the buildings. Men were housed for the most part in large rooms or dorms with bars. We walked down the hallway, being sure to stay in the middle so no one could reach between the bars and grab us.

My heart was filled with compassion, these people live worse than the dogs and cats begging for food. I knew very little Spanish and they knew very little English, yet I was allowed to pray for the men coming into the single room for medicine. It was awesome to see their faces light up when I said the name of Jesus. The men would shake their heads in agreement with me, not having a clue what I was saying, we agreed that Jesus is the only way, for sure!

I learned a lot during these visits into the two prisons. The prisons in the United States are five star palaces in comparison. There are so many fights and very few guards that I was told they would have to fight it out until someone could not fight anymore. Fights were not stopped. From the blood stains in the infirmary I realized that there is very little money to keep the much needed supplies. My camera was taken from me when we entered the prison, but was brought to me by the Director. He wanted me to take pictures to bring back with me to America. They were trying to find someone to help them build a larger infirmary, it would take a thousand dollars (in 2004) to build what they wanted and badly needed.

This enlightenment has helped me to appreciate living in the United States. When I minister to the men in the Clements Unit, living in PAMIO, 12 building, I try to help them understand that although the 5'x7' room they live in is blessed in comparison to dirty clothes, which for them in the US prisons are kept clean by the system. When endangerment to the officers, employees, volunteers or offenders takes place, a team of well trained officers hit right in the middle of the situation and gain control. Not so in prison's in very poor countries, where wars that break out can leave you mangled or killed just because the offender is in the same room with many other offenders. They fight until someone stops. They don't have boots made by the system. They are lucky to have shoes on their feet.

One Dr. for hundreds of offenders.
(no nurses)

Injuries and surgery performed here.
This is the room they want to enlarge,
it's about 8'X10' (I was allowed to
take pictures of this room only)

This is the man, the Dr. who
does it all.

Note the light to the left
used for surgery.

Some of the small paved roads we traveled on were worse
than this little road. We had to walk to the prison from here.

Chapel of the second prison we visited, the offenders had not entered the room yet.

All these men and any person housed in our prison's are loved by our Father. He is sending us, all of us to help them. I am blessed to have seen the worst in order to testify of the best. Indeed, no matter the circumstances of our lives, there is someone, some place who has it a lot worse.

Notice the five people standing to the top left of this picture. I boldly asked if I could pray for them. With looks of not really, they allowed me to pray. The anointing of our Lord fell on me and I prayed for everything that came into my mind, I prayed for their families, finances, even the clothes on their backs. (I had an interpreter, and whatever emotions I was having, he had also. If I prayed loud, he prayed loud, if I raised my hands, he raised his, it was awesome, we both were anointed by the Holy Spirit). When I finished and raised my head, all were standing with their hands in the air and tears streaming down their faces.

To this day I sometimes think about what Jesus Christ did for these people. I'm sure of one thing, people don't raise their hands to Christ unless they accept Him or want to accept Him.

The two men on the far end (left), I thought were just officers. They are the El Director & Director, meaning the Warden and Assistant Warden. The others are people who work in the facility. To the right are the people, such as myself who entered the prison to assist in meeting the needs of the offenders. The man in white, sitting at a table is a Dr., we assisted in following his directions. I was honored to put eye salve into the eyes of each offender. Wow, it was an honor to me to look into their faces and smile. The Dr. said afterwards, "I watched you. You really love what you were doing. You wanted to help my people." "Yes sir I do," was my reply.

Also during this time I was allowed to walk amongst the offenders and pray for those who wanted prayer. I asked several of the men sitting in one area if they believed in Jesus. With joy on their faces they shook their heads in a yes manner. Knowing that for the most part they pray to Mary, the mother of Jesus Christ, I then asked, "Have you prayed to Jesus Christ asking Him to come into your heart." "No, no, I have not asked Him to come into my heart and live." I was told by the interpreter. "Would you like to pray to Jesus Christ and ask Him to fill you with His salvation and His Comforter?" "Yes, yes was their reply." I was just as happy and excited as they were. This was something new for them and they were opened to receive the Holy Spirit." I then prayed and through the help of my interpreter, just as happy, the men, about ten to fifteen, accepted Jesus Christ.

I know within my heart that this is the major reason I was in this prison. I was God's instrument in walking among His children and helping them to hunger for more and more of Christ. The joy of my interpreter and my own was as one. What a team. Without him this wonderful miracle would not have happened. It was a very long way from America, traveling over the ocean, to reach NICARAGUA.

I learned through this experience that this little country girl would probably not cross the ocean again. It is not my desire to travel the world, just a small portion of it. I desire to see the United States. All of it. But, the trip to Nicaragua and the people I got to meet as well as work with stays alive in my heart.

WOMEN WHO HAVE MADE A SIGNIFICANT POSITIVE DIFFIRENCE IN MY LIFE

Mary and Larry Martin, married nine years May 20, 2009.

The later days have indeed become the best years of our lives. True purpose, happiness, peace, joy, forgiveness and love comes only from the Father, who gave His Son, who shed His blood on the cross for the redemption of man.

2Corinthians 8:15 As it is written, He that *had gathered* much had nothing over; and he that *had gathered* little had no lack.

Matthew 25:34-40
34 *Then shall the King say unto them on his right hand, Come, ye blessed of my Father, inherit the kingdom prepared for you from the foundation of the world:*
35 *For I was hungry, and ye gave me meat: I was thirsty, and ye gave me drink: I was a stranger, and ye took me in:*

36 *Naked, and ye clothed me: I was sick, and ye visited me: I was in prison, and ye came unto me.*

37 *Then shall the righteous answer him, saying, Lord, when saw we thee hungry, and fed thee? Or thirsty, and gave thee drink?*

38 *When saw we thee a stranger, and took thee in? or naked, and clothed thee?*

39 *Or when saw we thee sick, or in prison, and came unto thee?*

40 *And the King shall answer and say unto them, Verily I say unto you, Inasmuch as ye have done it unto one of the least of these my brethren, ye have done it unto me.*

NOTE: I began to write poems to express my feelings during the time I was not living with Howard during the first year of my salvation (1980). The poems from Chapter 1 through Chapter 20 which are at the end of each of these chapters were written during this time.

After marriage to Howard (1981), I shared my poems with Ruth Parker, wife of Bob Parker, our pastor's at the time, when Ruth returned the poems to me she said, "Mary, you have a book here in these poems. Write their meaning."

I sat down and began to write the meaning of the poems during the first year of my marriage to Howard. It took over 29 years to complete this beginning.

I called my friend Faye on February 20, 2009 at 10:23 am. I had just completed praying asking Jesus to reveal to me that He is pleased with the writing of my testimony? When I was talking with Faye she asked me to get my Bible and read a verse that had meaning. I did as she said and nothing could have touched me more. God told me in the beginning of my salvation, "BE HONEST" and I have practiced to the best of my ability to keep honesty in the things I say and the things I do. My desire is to obtain

integrity and favorable standing with Jesus Christ. I long for the wisdom and knowledge of the Holy Spirit. A pure heart will see the Father, God. I want to see God. I want to say, "THANK YOU" for sending Your Son, JESUS CHRIST and setting me free.

ANSWERED PRAYER

3John 1:3

For I rejoiced greatly, when the brethren came and testified of the truth that is in thee, even as thou walkest in the truth.

Chapter 37:
MOTHER AND DAD

DEAREST MOTHER AND DAD
My love to you, DEAREST MOTHER and DAD,
and I "THANK YOU" for all of your many prayers
I realize at times, because of me, you were deeply sad.
God has answered your heartache, your burden, of my sin.
For without your faith, with HIM I may never have been.
"FORGIVE ME" DEAREST MOTHER AND DAD
for the transgressions I felt within.
Do not talk of others who have tried and failed.
For as Noah, on GOD'S ship will I eternally sail!
Do not look back, and turn to God, through the book of Psalms.
(Ch 141)
Just believe and the sea for you HE will surely calm.
GOD has come to me, in the form of a cloud,
HE has BLESSED me, oh my DEAREST, with me be proud.

Written to my Mom & Dad during my first year of salvation. (1979)

Sarah Juanita Harden Moses & Joshua Benjamin (J.B.) Moses

Kay (middle sister) Mom, Faye (oldest sister),
Dad and Mary (youngest daughter)

When I look back and remember my childhood I find very little to complain about. We never went without clothes, and we were never hungry, we were never left alone in fear. Mom and Dad showed their love for us in many ways. I was never afraid of my parents. Although when my dad said, "Sit down" He meant it and all three of us girls knew it. There was no fussing or arguing with my parents. Dad stood by whatever Mom said. I would learn later in life that Mom was the firm one and Dad had more compassion.

It was not until Mom lived with me that I learned that she and Dad had been divorced. She had moved to Odessa, TX, near her brother who helped care for us. She met a man that she dated. She told me he was good to her and he loved us girls. She also told me that he favored me. When Mom and I were living in Lubbock after my divorce from Howard I tried to find this man. Mom knew his home town and his name and that was all. I was not able to locate him. He made me feel loved. This is all I really remember of him except his hair was red and I liked it.

While living in Odessa, Dad came for Christmas, he gave us three girls an orange apiece. I remember this, but it's all I can remember. Sometime during this time Mom went back to Dad and they remarried. Mom told me when I questioned why she didn't marry the man who loved me, she told me, "I didn't love him. I loved your Dad." I never questioned her again.

Mom also shared with me her memories as a little girl. She told me that when her brothers and sisters got home from school they had a biscuit with a slice of onion in it for a snack. She had a large family as Dad did. Mom told me many things she experienced as a little girl. A lot of them were painful for her. She also asked me to never share these truths with anyone else. I have honored her wishes.

Now that I am sixty-eight January 22, 2010, it gives me much peace to understand that my parents didn't know how to love us. In taking care of our needs, to them, they loved us. I now know in my heart that they did love all three of us girls. I now long for our reunion in heaven.

Mom and Dad didn't know how to express love. They didn't know how to hold us and make us feel beautiful or special. Mom once told me, "My dad never held me and my mom did only when I was sick." Therefore it was, I think, about the same for my Dad. I took this non-nourishing me as non-love. I grew up so very, very alone.

Mom also told me it was Dad who would find me and want to come and see me. Sometimes I let a lot of time pass without calling my parents. I questioned how they found me at these times. They would just show up at my house or apartment.

When I first began living with Howard there was a knock on my apartment door, Howard answered it and jumped behind it. I looked up from setting the table for lunch and he was pointing at the door with big eyes saying in a whisper, "Your mom and dad!" I just laughed and opened the door. My parents really liked Howard. They didn't know a thing about him, but he had a way of making you laugh.

After my salvation when I was talking to my Dad on the phone, before hanging up I said, "I love you Dad." He was quiet for a short time and said, "I love you too." This is the first time I ever heard my Dad say I love you. After salvation I learned to tell my parents that I loved them. When Mom lived with me I learned to serve her as best as I could. During her last two years of life I never said anything but good to her. She, before having problems of forgetting told me many times of her love for me. She had dementia in the last year of her life and this is when she said, "I don't love you like you love me." I now know she didn't mean she loved me any less. I understand now that she knew and saw my love for her. She trusted me and depended on me to keep her safe. I'm so thankful that God chose me, the rejected, and the black sheep of the family to care for mom.

I had the opportunity to be a daughter to my mom. We had many happy times together. We became friends. My mom, my oldest sister and my dad are with Jesus Christ, I have no doubt. The time will come when we will be together and there will be no more tears of the pain of this life. It will be finished.

My parents raised us girls the best they knew how. I am now able to remember the good they did for us. I'm so thankful that Mom and I had the years to understand each other and to learn to love one another and forgive each other. I had been a total disgrace to my parents. I now understand their hurt, their sorrow. I now understand that my Mom and Dad did love me, they just didn't know how to tell me or show me when I was young.

The Harden Family
Right to left, Edgar Ellis Harden (Ed Harden), Chester Harden, Gaskell Odell Harden (Mom's dad), MaryLauna Harden (Mom's mom), Left to right, William Christain Harden (W.C.), Anna Alice Harden, Odell Gaskell Harden, Issac Harold Harden (Bill), Sara Juanita Harden (Mom) held by Odell

"Two other siblings would be born into the family, my aunt, Mildred and the youngest son Author. I think that my grandmother lost one child by miscarriage, but this may not be accurate."

Psalm 141:1-10 A Psalm of David.

1   LORD, I cry unto thee: make haste unto me; give ear unto my voice, when I cry unto thee.

2   Let my prayer be set forth before thee *as* incense; *and* the lifting up of my hands *as* the evening sacrifice.

3   Set a watch, O LORD, before my mouth; keep the door of my lips.

4   Incline not my heart to *any* evil thing, to practice wicked works with men that work iniquity: and let me not eat of their their dainties.

5   Let the righteous smite me; *it shall be* a kindness: and let him reprove me; *it shall be* an excellent oil, *which* shall not break my head: for yet my prayer also *shall be* in their calamities.

6   When their judges are overthrown in stony places, they shall hear my words; for they are sweet.

7   Our bones are scattered at the grave's mouth, as when one cutteth and cleaveth *wood* upon the earth.

8   But mine eyes *are* unto thee, O GOD the Lord: in thee is my trust; leave not my soul destitute.

9   Keep me from the snares *which* they have laid for me, and the gins of the workers of iniquity.

10 Let the wicked fall into their own nets, whilst that I withal escape.

Chapter 38:
LOVE OF A CHILD

~

Overcoming

Looking back on my childhood recalls things I care not to remember. I was born and raised into a more than typically dysfunctional family. I grew up in one house after another that was full of strangers to me.

I lived with my mom but had no clue who she was. I looked at her as this woman who told me where we were going to live, what room was mine and when I was to be seen and when I was to be invisible. I was terrified of and captivated by her all at the same time. I related to my mom through the movie Mommie Dearest. She was not identical to the character, but so close that I felt a strong connection with the story. I wanted so bad to see her look down at me with a spark in her eye just for me. A warm hug or mother-daughter moment, but this was something that was little known to me.

My mom was not like other moms who entered a room quietly and tried to blend in looking like the super mom that all others envied. She was certainly not part of the PTA or any program involving volunteering her time. My mom always made an entrance. She was the one others looked down their nose at, but could not get her off their mind later. Her confidence, looks and outspoken personality drew attention every where she went.

There were times when she would take me on drives with her. I was not sure why because she did not speak to me. I would watch her attentively as she would carry on conversations with herself in the rear view mirror. I felt like a ghost. It was as though the seat next to her was empty. In later years I found out she took me only to avoid getting accused of "screwing around." I did not know how to feel when I was with her. I was terribly scared of making a noise and cause a distraction because I would be sternly scolded verbally. I would imagine her and I as something else loving and happy. I sat there staring at her and visioned her looking over at me to say something that would make my heart smile.

There are no real memories with both my mom and dad. There were no family outings or family functions of any kind other than the occasional fishing trips with friends. Pictures are my only memories of those times. I can mostly recall drinking and fighting between them. On occasions I was taken to bars with them and was thrilled when dad would hold me between them as they danced to a song on the dance floor. I was often left with others so that Mom and Dad could go out, sometimes for days. My mom and dad divorced when I was in elementary, somewhere around the age of six. When my mom knew she was going to leave my dad she had already met and started a relationship with her, later to be, next husband Howard.

Life for me was dark and lonely. I lived in my own little world. When I did go places with my new family I felt as though I did not belong. Actually doing something with them seemed as though it should be a special occasion and I must play the part. I was told children are to be seen and not heard. I did not know life any different. I was like the sad little puppy with eager desperation in its eyes that spends each day chained up with no one showing it love.

My earliest memories, those of which were the start of a troubled adolescence, are of being molested. I learned of, experienced and practiced sexual indecencies going all the way back to the age of five. This was normal behavior for me. I had not been taught anything about sex and did not know the things that were happening to me were wrong. It disturbs me that those that encouraged or were amused by my willingness to entertain, never tried to stop me, even as a child. I was molested by family, babysitters and really anyone that saw they could. This had become the only way I knew how to get attention or affection. As a result I spent many years allowing myself to be taken advantage of and preyed upon by men in hopes that one would love me.

I cannot recall or tell of one Christmas with my mom when she was with my dad or her next husband Howard. I can remember always having to pack up the Christmas tree after Christmas, but cannot recall a single Christmas morning waking up feeling any kind of excitement for what was in store that Christmas day.

I am able to tell of one birthday with my mom while growing up. I played basketball one year and Mom went to one game. It was my birthday and Mom was in a good mood. After my basketball game she allowed me to invite the team over for a slumber party. These were very rare occurrences where my mom felt like doing something just for me.

My favorite story as a child with my mom took place Thanksgiving 1978, I was eight. I relive all of the emotions I experienced that day as I go over it in my mind. Parents were to join their children for a Thanksgiving lunch at school. Mom had already said she wasn't going. I dreaded lunch that day. I wanted to hide and not have to be a part of it all together. As I went through the lunch line trying not to be consumed with the knowing that I was the only student there without a parent to eat with, I found myself filled with feelings of being crushed. I made excuses for my mom's absence. I felt my loneliest in that moment. I went through the line in silence trying my best to be invisible. I took my tray to a table and sat down by myself. I was fighting the tears as I was overwhelmed with complete worthlessness. Then out of nowhere I hear a voice that grabbed my heart. I know this voice and it instantly makes my heart fill with joy as my eyes fill with tears. I look up with sheer excitement trying to locate the familiar voice and then there she is, "Oh Thank You Jesus" there she is. My mom came to be with me. When I looked up and laid my eyes upon her I was the proudest little girl in the world. I felt heaven shining upon me as I looked up at my mom with pride that she truly did love me.

Another rare memorable time was one Christmas when it was just my mom and me. It was during one of her attempts to leave Howard. It was days before Christmas and we had no tree or presents. Mom was at work and some neighbors from down the street knocked on the door before Mom got home from work. They told me they were there to put up a Christmas tree for us. I watched with great excitement. There were some presents as well. My heart was filled with the most overwhelming feeling of joy. I felt as though I wasn't going to be able to hold in all the excitement building and pounding inside my chest. I could not hold back the tears as I hid behind a chair waiting for Mom to enter and be surprised by this wonderful thing. Once Mom got home she too was touched by the love of friends. She later told me she did not think about how not having a tree would hurt me as a child.

My memories of growing up are more sad and lonely than anything else, but all I know. Some of those memories hurt more than others. To me they do not seem so out of the ordinary because it was just the way things were. There is a particular time that I have always been fond of because I'm simply grateful for what made me feel safe. I was about eleven. My mom and Howard had gone out, as they often did. The sitter left soon after them. We lived in an old two story house that was full of scary noises. It was a very stormy night. There was terrible thunder and lightning, and the power went out. We had two Doberman pinschers that were the only things in my world that made me feel safe. Mom had built them a big dog house with a window and heat lamp, which was also out because of the storm. Mom had said not to let them in the house so they do not track mud in. I was very scared and decided to get into the dog house with them. I felt safe there. I loved those dogs and did not feel out of place with them. I do not remember when my mom came home or her sympathy for my fears. All I recall is feeling safest with my keepers, Blackjack and Duchess. I always looked back at this situation and found humor in it because I did not see the sadness. This was how life was for me, but my mom carries a scar from this night.

My mom has turned her life around and carries a tremendous amount of pain for her mistakes as a mother. She has battles with herself having to accept that she can never change the past. I do not hold my mom at fault for the things she did not do right as a mother. How do you teach what you do not know? She is by far a much better person and mother now and I am forever grateful for that. Holding her at fault for my childhood being full of scars is not going to undo what has been done. I look at my childhood as a learning experience and use that knowledge to be the best mother I can be to my children.

I do not allow myself to be a victim to my childhood. We should learn from our yesterdays and use that to make a better tomorrow. What matters are the choices we make today.

There were few joys for me growing up, but the ones I do recall are precious to me. There was a short period of time where my mom had left Howard and was a mother to me. She was still a stranger to me, but I knew I wanted to know her and be loved by her. During this time when she had found peace there was a real connection between us. We went to church and I remember a feeling of belonging. I was not subjected to people that I felt I needed to offer myself to in order to feel any form of connection or love. There were warm greetings and a genuine sense of love and acceptance during this brief time. I felt awkward but liked these new surroundings. This time did not last long before my mom went back to Howard. There were numerous occasions that she would leave Howard and eventually return.

One of the times when Mom left Howard brought encounters with a woman I will remember all the rest of my life, named Grace. Mom and I stayed with Grace for a period of time. I remember this being a *home*. She had taken us into her *home* that was filled with Jesus. I had no awareness of what a *home* was but knew this woman's world that I had presently been welcomed into made me feel safe and was so very heavenly. This too came to pass and I found myself back in turmoil that I was far more familiar with.

During times that Mom would make attempts at walking away from the life that she felt trapped in she would show me love and try very hard to be the best mother she knew how to be. She was not natural at being a mother, but during these times of it just being her and I, her efforts were greater than any I had ever known. She was a different person when she found the strength to stand on her own. She had gotten a taste of the soul's salvation and she longed for more. In her efforts to know Christ and be filled with His blessings, her changes were apparent. She found that she was not a failure despite what she had been told throughout her life thus far.

There are two particular occurrences in my life where I first witnessed the power of a true miracle and God's work. Miracles that some would look at as being improbable. There is no doubt in my mind whatsoever as to the nature of these miracles. They were acts of marvel simplicity that had great impact on my faith and mere belief in the power of Heaven.

I was about to turn fifteen and wanted to live with my dad. After a little over a year with my dad things weren't working out as I had hoped. I decided I wanted to move back in with my mom. Mom had left Howard during the time that I was living with my dad. My mom and Mamaw had not yet decided where to settle and make a new home. In the meantime they were living in Post with one of Mom's friends. I had a few months before school was out and I didn't want to change schools until summer. A friend, Jeri and I talked to our moms about me staying with Jeri's family until school was out. Our mom's agreed and made the necessary arrangements with the school. The parting with my dad was less than desirable. At the time my dad did not know about my staying with a friend to finish out the school year.

Jeri, her brother and I were at the skating rink one Friday night. We went outside to leave and saw my dad asking people about me. I did not know how he had found me or what he wanted. I only felt panic. Jeri and I quickly made our way to her house while her brother stayed behind to keep an eye on my dad. Jeri and I called her mom who was at work. She said she would come home. Jeri's brother then showed up and said my dad was on his way to the house. When Dad arrived, Jeri and I were too scared to open the door. Once Jeri's mom got there she said I had to go outside and talk to my dad. I was scared that he had been drinking and was going to take me away. When I went outside my dad grabbed me by the back of the neck and made me go to the car where his friend waited. He then made me get into the car. My dad told me how he had not known I was staying there and that he would not allow me to stay there. He did not care that I was only staying to finish school. He said I had to live with either him or my mom. I was deeply scared that my dad was going to hurt me. After making it very clear that I had to contact my mom to get me or he would return, he then let me out of the car and left. I went back into the house and told everyone what he said. Jeri's mom said she could not have her children in fear like that and that I had to call my mom. The only phone number I had for my mom was that of the neighbor across the street—a friend Mom and Mamaw were staying with. I tried calling this number numerous times in an effort to contact my mom. There was no answering machine and this was before the use of caller ID's. Unable to reach anyone that could help me contact her, I went to bed thinking I would try again first thing in the morning. I was not able to sleep that night for fear of my dad's return and not knowing how long it would take before I could reach my mom. As soon as I woke up the following morning I tried to contact her—again without any luck. It was around 10:00 am and we heard a car pull up to the back door. I was scared it is my dad. We looked out of the window to see who it was and I realize it was Mom and Mamaw. I go to the door full of amazement and confusion. I open the door and said, "Mom, how did you know to come?" My mom looked at me and said, "When I woke up this morning, Jesus said, *'Go get Elizabeth'.*"

I am still moved every time I relive that story. There is not a single source of reasoning that can convince me that my Mom knowing to come and get me was anything other than the power and love of Jesus Christ.

The second miracle took place when I was 17. I was in a car wreck that I should not have walked away from. It was night and I was headed back into town. I was making a left turn at an intersection and was struck by a truck that was attempting to pass another vehicle and myself. The trucks right front end struck my driver's door. My head hit the hood as it crashed into my door. I had my head down and my eyes closed. We ended up in a field. Neither vehicle rolled but when we went off of the pavement and into the field we went in between two gas meters. There were no tracks in the dirt between the gas meters, only tracks in the dirt before and after the gas meters. I walked away from the wreck completely unharmed. At the time of my wreck my mom and I weren't speaking. I did not know until sometime later that the very night and the very time of my wreck Jesus told Mom to get on her face and pray. She did not know why and she did not question why. She immediately fell on her face and prayed. She continued to pray until she felt peace. My mom did not know what she had prayed for until she found out that was the same night and time of my wreck. I am blessed to be here by the love of Jesus and the prayers of my mom.

My childhood was undoubtedly very lonely, but we adapt to our surroundings. We may not like them, but we learn how to live in them. We cry for change and a better life, but only know how to live in the life we know. During these few times in my childhood that I was able to experience something better I learned of God, Jesus and the Holy Spirit. These were beautiful experiences that I have carried with me throughout my life. I, myself have made many of the same mistakes that my mom made growing up. I went from one relationship to another, each one seeming to have an expiration date. I felt alone and abandoned the better part of my life. I knew only how to survive and wasn't incredibly good at that. I moved away from both my mom and dad at the age of 16. I lived with my Nannie for a school year. I went to school only because I had to, but skipped enough to fail. I had no stability in my life. I was always looking for something to fill the enormous void I felt inside of me. I had no control or ambition. I had no clue what was missing from my life or what I was looking for.

As I went through life trying to conquer my past I became a mother four times throughout the years. That was the turnaround point for me in my life. I still made many mistakes in trying to leave my old ways behind, but as I look back now I know that it was Jesus that helped me overcome the only lifestyle I knew. I wanted my children to have stability and a sense of family. My children know love and they know Jesus. I still have to fight the demons that I grew up with, but every time I look into the faces of my beautiful children I am able to rebuke those demons and encounter the peace that only comes from Jesus.

I know my childhood and life after was full of despair and had a definite impact on me. At times it is very difficult to be reminded of and have to talk about my past. I understand more people can relate to my story and it makes us feel good to know we are not alone in our quest for change. I cannot conceive of my children having to remember their childhood as anything like mine.

My mom and I have come to know each other. We have both had battles overcoming our pasts. We have had our own differences over the years as we have both struggled to find our place and become settled in the glorious graces of God. The life we fought to overcome had made us both hard women and at times we have to remind ourselves that we do not live in that hell anymore. We are now bonded by our pasts, our pains, our triumphs, our knowledge, our love, and in our lives anew. Through Jesus Christ and by the graces of God we have been given the gift of unconditional love. (Written by Timmi; Sept. 2010)

**TIMMI married
JACK OWEN,
May 20, 2007**

**Zayne, Bailey,
Sean, Wade,
Jack, & Timmi,**

December 2009

DUKE DWAYNE EVERETT ZANT

Duke: 1st child-married to 2nd husband

MACHIEL BENJETT (B.J.) ZANT COVEY

Machiel: 2nd child and sister to Duke

STONEY FLEET KERSH
July, 1980

**Stoney: 3rd child,
married to 3rd husband
Picture taken during 1st year
of marriage to Howard**

TIMMI ELIZABETH ALLEN OWEN
Timmi: 4th child,
married to 4th husband, Kevin

Timmi: 2 or 3 years old

MARCH 28, 2010

Top left: Wade, Jack, Duke, Jim, Dillan, Stoney, Stoney, Jr. Bottom left: Bailey, Timmi, (front) Zayne, Mary, Chelsea (center), Larry, Machiel, Stephanie (Dillan's girlfriend) Diana (Stoney's girlfriend). Three grandchildren, Chanel, John & Shane were unable to attend.

OUR CHILDREN HAVE COME HOME

On March 28, 2010 we gathered together for a family reunion in our home for the first time. It had been 22 years since my four children and I had been together at the same time. I was living with my Mom in Lubbock, Texas after divorcing Howard. All four of my children came to see Mom and me.

Throughout the following years there were seasons that we did not see each other and did not talk to one another. Sometimes it was a year and sometime years that pain, misunderstanding and un-forgiveness had kept us separated.

I had not seen one of my grandchildren since he was one or two years old. Another grandson I met for the first time, he is now in his teens. I had been so concerned that because of my many failures as a mom that their pain would still be alive in their hearts and those of my grandchildren also. I was wrong. It took a little time for us to become comfortable with one another. But we all were willing and desired to become a family.

I gave my most treasured items to each of my children. Letters they had written to me when they knew they had a mother but saw or was with me very little. Some pictures they had not seen, as well as other items. I wanted them to know that I loved them. I had always loved them, but I had never given them my love. I didn't know how to. I remember one child asking me a few years back, "How could you do it, how could you leave me?" My reply was, "I don't know." Today I held this child very close to me, really for the first time since she had become an adult. There had been much pain throughout the years between us. "I don't want any more division between us, but I don't know what to do." I said gently in her ear as I clung to her, my arms holding her as tight as I could. She replied, "What you are doing right now is what you need to do."

We went to church at Trinity Fellowship where we were greeted by Pastor Larry Miles and given special seating that we could sit together and also be close to the platform. Stoney is a big fan of the Dallas Cowboys. Jason Witten (82) along with Pastor Robert Morris were guest speakers.

Two of our grandchildren walked to the platform with many others and accepted Jesus Christ as their Saviour. Stoney accompanied his son and Larry and I followed. Man, it was like walking right up face to face with Jesus. Jesus had told me many years earlier what He would do if I would follow Him with a pure heart. He has kept His word, and even done abundantly above what I hoped for.

Years have passed and by faith, prayers and forgiveness, love has birthed into the hearts of us all. We work at staying in touch. We work at listening, we work at being a family, loving one another and continuing to live for today. Today, we have each other, tomorrow, there may be someone gone on to God, our Heavenly Father, greeted at the pearly gate by Jesus Christ. I am now 68 years old and Larry is 58. We feel for the first time in our lives that we are loved and accepted just the way we are by our children, as we love and accept them. All credit is given to our Savior, Jesus Christ who paid the ultimate price of suffering for all our sins, He who knew no sin, that we could be reconciled to God and Himself, united with the Holy Spirit.

Larry and I continue to pray daily for the repentance and salvation of our children and grandchildren. One child of our 5 has not returned yet, but we believe some day she also will come home.

NOTE: When I first began writing my life's story with the idea of having it published, there was hurt feelings, rejection, fear of the truth being told and concern of the public in judging our family.

Now that Forgiven Much–Loves Much is completed, I have the approval and love of my husband and our children to tell it like it was and today, like it is.

We are a *family*, it's only through Jesus Christ and His love and sacrifice on the cross for all of us that I can make this statement.

Jason Witten
Drawn by David Rayes, Inmate at Clements Unit

Jason Witten & Pastor Robert Morris

Jesus Christ orchestrated, as He is in all things, for us to gather and hear the testimony of Jason Witten, and the love of Christ shared by Pastor Robert Morris of Gateway Church, South Lake, TX (suburb of Dallas). His perfect plan united a family and salvation is birthed.

Stoney Kersh has been collecting Dallas Cowboy memorabilia from the age of 10. To view his collections, Google I've Got A Cowboy's House.

Eph 3:9-21

9 And to make all men see what is the fellowship of the mystery, which from the beginning of the world hath been hid in God, who created all things by Jesus Christ:

10 To the intent that now unto the principalities and powers in heavenly places might be known by the church the manifold wisdom of God,

11 According to the eternal purpose which he purposed in Christ Jesus our Lord:

12 In whom we have boldness and access with confidence by the faith of him.

13 Wherefore I desire that ye faint not at my tribulations for you, which is your glory.

14 For this cause I bow my knees unto the Father of our Lord Jesus Christ,

15 Of whom the whole family in heaven and earth is named,

16 That he would grant you, according to the riches of his glory, to be strengthened with might by his Spirit in the inner man;

17 That Christ may dwell in your hearts by faith; that ye, being rooted and grounded in love,

18 May be able to comprehend with all saints what is the breadth, and length, and depth, and height;

19 And to know the love of Christ, which passeth knowledge, that ye might be filled with all the fulness of God.

20 Now unto him that is able to do exceeding abundantly above all that we ask or think, according to the power that worketh in us,

21 Unto him be glory in the church by Christ Jesus throughout all ages, world without end. Amen.

FIRST TIME TO PRAY AS A FAMILY.

Matt 18:20
For where two or three are gathered together in my name, there am I in the midst of them.

John 4:36
And he that reapeth receiveth wages, and gathereth fruit unto life eternal: that both he that soweth and he that reapeth may rejoice together.

IN LOVING MEMORY
Sean Dale Dalton
1992 – 2010

October 15, 2010, two weeks before his 18th birthday, Sean died instantly from a motorcycle accident. He was an accomplished rider. His mom, Timmi Elizabeth and I believe in agreement that from the moment that we are born into this world that Christ knows when He will take us home.

Sometimes we question the love others may have for us. Larry and I saying this in all honesty, never felt anything but that Sean's love for us was alive in his heart, and he never ceased to let us know how much he loved us. We are blessed to have been a part of his life. It was a short season, but one well worth the years of being his grandparents.

This autobiography is also dedicated to Sean Dale Dalton, we are so thankful that we will see and be with him again, for eternity.

Mary & Larry

Available through Trinity Fellowship Press book store
in Amarillo, Texas, 5000 Hollywood Rd 79118
Phone 806/355-8955
or
Mary Moses Martin
Forgiven Much - Loves Much
PO Box 5083
Amarillo, TX 79117

forgivenmuch.lovesmuch@gmail.com

Book: $13.00 (Plus $5.00 shipping)
Check or money order only